Words of Praise fo

I have recorded two of Keith Green's s[...]
I am moved. I am proud to be connected in this small way to his
profound ministry and thankful to God for people like Keith and
Melody Green. Keith's legacy of faith lives on in the lives of people
like myself who also want to be "radical for Jesus"!

—Rebecca St. James,
Recording Artist and Author

Keith's abandonment was unique. His life was one that raised the
standard and called me to go higher in God. His heart for prayer challenged and fueled my own desire for building a lifestyle of prayer. He
handled money in a clean and unquestionable way that spoke volumes
about his integrity. His boldness was unprecedented in our generation
in America. He shattered the mold. This was foundational to the
anointing of his life, which guaranteed his message would be heard.

—Mike Bickle
Founder of the International House of Prayer
Kansas City, MO

After I turned sixteen, I was given some Keith Green music and told,
"You've got to listen to this!" I had never heard of Keith, but I memo-
rized almost every song and was driven to get all of his teachings and
music.

I continued to be inspired by Keith's preaching and music while
at ORU, where I gained a heart for missions. I had heard Keith came
there every year to do a revival. I thought, *finally, I'll get to see him in
concert*. Then I found out he wouldn't be coming back.

The timeless nature of Keith's ministry keeps it relevant for every
generation. I know thousands who love Keith's music, even though
they were born after the plane crash.

In 1996, when our ministry headquarters moved onto the exact
property in Texas where Last Days was for many years, I was humbled.

After being so affected by Keith's ministry, to actually occupy the same grounds seemed like an honor we were certainly not worthy of.

We hope as we continue to reach young people and send them into the nations, Keith would somehow be excited and proud—about all that's happening in the name of the Lord, on the land where he walked and prayed for a harvest.

Keith's impact will forever inspire, challenge, motivate, and disciple young people who want to live on the radical edge of Christianity.

—Ron Luce
President and Founder of Teen Mania Ministries

NO COMPROMISE

the life story of

KEITH GREEN

MELODY GREEN WITH DAVID HAZARD

THOMAS NELSON
Since 1798

NASHVILLE   DALLAS   MEXICO CITY   RIO DE JANEIRO   BEIJING

ISBN : 978-159555-164-1

Printed in the United States of America

11 12 13 QG 7 6 5 4

With all my love to
Rebekah Joy and Rachel Hope

In loving memory of
Keith Green
one of a kind who served One of a kind
and
Josiah David, Bethany Grace, and my mom Helen

CONTENTS

FOREWORD

Once upon a time, in a generation steeped in much emptiness and spiritual darkness, a boy was born who was given a great gift. Deeply talented, trained as a musician, he had a unique ability (some would later say genius) to take spiritual truth and put it in the language and vocabulary of the common people of his time.

His biographical writings (now available for others to see) record the intensity of his struggles, his early odyssey into pathways that promised so much but sadly led nowhere. These records chronicle the search of a young man seemingly out of step with his age—a young man not afraid to risk everything for what he found to be real and right. He was nothing if he was not intense—and in that intensity he questioned everything and everyone that seemed to hold a key to life and reality. Once he found that Answer (as we know now he did), nothing could turn him from it.

That commitment given, he began a lifelong crusade to see his world likewise transformed. No one who knew him would deny that he offended many. He often especially shocked established religious people in his youthful zeal to bring compassion, honesty, and reality back to the church. Perhaps the truest practical test of a real prophet is this: "Does he make me uncomfortable?" If he does, he probably is. If he doesn't, he probably isn't. After all, you never read in the Bible of a popular prophet except the false ones who always went around telling people the things they wanted to hear.

So this young man was blunt. He was funny. He was tactless and sometimes even crude. He steadfastly refused to accept the spiritual status quo. He quietly mocked hypocrisy with laughter while he laid bare his own struggles and fears with tears. Many of his songs are simply sermons set to music—prophetic pieces in harmony that set standards for a generation. He was controversial. He was criticized. He was cut off by some and almost canonized by others—but he was impossible to ignore. His life and work literally affected millions around the world. Although gone from us now, he impacted his generation like a spiritual H-bomb, and the reverberations of his life, courage, and commitment will still be felt for generations to come.

Most people today who have never before had the opportunity to read his writings and journals know him only by his music. (After all, not everyone can write a song that will still be sung five centuries after his death!) We remember him today as the man who launched the Reformation; the musician with the hunger to know God and to make Him known by faith; the man called Martin Luther.

And this, of course, is not his story. But in another century, another culture, and in another country, on a smaller scale, with not as much time to accomplish a task, it might have been. Keith loved Jesus. He did what he could in the few intense years I was privileged to know him. If you have never had the opportunity to share in the life of someone like him who *lived* for Jesus, you will catch a glimpse of that love in this, his story. He was my friend. I miss him.

—Winkie Pratney
May 1989

Winkie Pratney has studied every recorded revival in history, and is a world authority on true revival. He has written over twenty books and speaks to over a half-million young people a year. His background in science and pop culture allows him to interpret current trends for the welfare of youth in our technological and media-dominated society.

"ONE DAY YOU'RE UP . . ."

Anything can happen on the streets of Hollywood. I'd seen some pretty wild things, but never anything so bizarre as what I saw one night on Ventura Boulevard.

As Keith and I walked out of the Bla Bla Cafe, a blast of hot night air hit us in the face. It was after 2:00 A.M., but the street was still awake with activity. Four drag queens swept by us, followed by a couple in disco outfits, all headed inside for a late-night breakfast. Next door the watchdogs at Bruno's Corvette Repairs were pacing inside their chain-linked fence, barking at everything that moved—including us. Keith had played three sets that night, and we were headed for home, exhausted. I was glad to see "Victor von Van," our VW with the hippie-style Indian print curtains I'd sewn, parked at the curb.

Keith had been performing at "the Bla"—as it was affectionately known to its regulars—for almost a year. It was a small showcase nightclub in the San Fernando Valley just a few blocks from Hollywood proper. The Bla spotlighted showbiz hopefuls and was frequented by agents and talent scouts from big record companies. Keith was one of those hopefuls. But tonight he'd given it his all one more time—and now we were leaving, still undiscovered.

As Keith walked around the front of the van, I opened the passenger door. That was when we spotted a figure looming toward us out of the dark. It was Harmony.

Harmony looked like a gruff mountain man with his brown, scraggly hair and beard. Here we were in 1974, but this guy struck us as someone caught in a '60s time warp. He was calm and easy. All he talked about was peace, love, and living off the land. He wasn't a close friend, but he and Keith had gotten stoned together once.

"Hey, how's it goin'?" Keith called. He shut his door and stepped back onto the sidewalk.

Sleepily I leaned my head back, knowing I was in for a wait. Inevitably most of our conversations drifted toward spiritual experiences these days. Keith and I had tried a lot of things—a lot of things. Recently we'd been curious about Jesus. We weren't Christians. Church was a dead institution to us. But Jesus did seem to be a spiritual Master of some sort, and we had a degree of respect for his life and teachings.

Sure enough, Keith and Harmony immediately began talking about the supernatural. It was just a typical conversation—for people who were into drugs and the mystical, which were a lot of the people we knew.

"I've been reading about Jesus lately," Keith was saying. "He was a pretty radical person."

Harmony's eyes seemed to brighten. Then, slowly, a strange look came over his face. His eyes got misty and distant. Very calmly he said, "I am Jesus Christ."

Keith reacted like he'd been stung by a scorpion. Without missing a beat, he shot back, "Beware of the false prophets who come to you in sheep's clothing, but inwardly are ravenous wolves!" I recognized the quote as something Jesus had said. What happened next was really hard to believe.

Harmony's eyes grew wide. Then they narrowed to slits. Furrows creased across his forehead, and his bushy eyebrows knit together. A sneer came over his usually mild face, and his upper lip curled back, exposing yellow, smoke-stained teeth. Leaning toward Keith, his teeth bared, he let out a growl that started in the throat, like that of a wolf, and ended with the horrible hissing sound of a snake.

It happened in only seconds. Harmony's face relaxed. But his eyes looked confused. Embarrassed. The hiss seemed to hang in the still night air.

My skin was still tingling from the shock. Keith had obviously been rocked by it too. He looked from Harmony to me with wide eyes. This was Hollywood, but things like this only happened in the movies. I wondered what Keith was thinking.

It was as if someone or something took control of Harmony momentarily, using him for its own purposes. Then just as quickly it discarded him, leaving him to pick up the pieces in confused embarrassment. Dazed, Harmony mumbled something. But Keith quickly excused himself, jumped into Victor, and shoved the key in the ignition.

As we drove home over the dark streets, we kept looking at each other in disbelief. Keith was more animated than usual. He kept saying, "Did he really do that? I can't believe it!"

We talked about nothing else until we crawled into bed and fell asleep, sometime after 3:30 AM.

The weird experience with Harmony did have one major effect on us. It brought some things into sharp focus. Namely, that there was, indeed, a very real spiritual realm—a realm full of power and possibly even danger. We were just coming to a deeper realization that there must be spiritual forces beyond our knowing. Had we heard a voice from that other side, speaking through Harmony? Or was it just the voice of the age? After all, a lot of musicians, artists, and writers—the "beautiful" people—were saying things like, "You are your own god. Everything's relative. There is no right or wrong." But we wondered: *Is there a dark side and a light side to spiritual energy?*

Keith and I had both been caught up in a search to find our spiritual identities for some time. We were looking for truth—whatever it was—and our search for light had taken us on many strange paths, from Buddhism to stuff like astral projection and, of course, drugs; especially psychedelics. We were convinced the truth was hidden out there somewhere like a pearl in the ocean and that when we found it, it would fill an empty spot in our hearts. It would make life really worth living. Until then every day held the potential of being the day of the great revelation.

At the time of our weird encounter with Harmony, however, we'd been slipping a bit, losing hope, even dabbling with the drugs again that we'd sworn off but kept falling back into. Our spiritual ambitions never kept us out of the fog for long. In fact, the constant lure of those other voices had pretty well convinced us there was a dark and a light side. After Harmony's eruption, Keith, with his usual all-or-nothing manner, was determined to know how to tell the difference. Although we never forgot the incident outside the Bla, there were more pressing matters. Like Keith's all-consuming dream.

In particular, our whole life revolved around Keith's drive to make it big in the music business. Now that he was performing at the Bla, we lived with the constant hunger that the right person would walk in one night and discover Keith Green.

The Bla was just a few blocks down Ventura Boulevard from the infamous nightclub the Queen Mary, and Keith's audience was always seasoned with gays and straights alike. Neither camp seemed to mind the other. To be honest, it was often difficult to tell who belonged where. The biggest standouts were the drag queens, sweeping in after 2:00 AM wearing satin dresses, jangly jewels, and high-styled wigs. Only their exaggerated feminine gestures and five o'clock shadows peeking through heavy layers of makeup betrayed their true gender.

Keith's family and my mom lived here in Southern California. But the Bla was like a second home to us. The people like family. Even though Keith's last set ended at 1:00 AM, we often stayed until Albie, the owner, closed the doors three hours later. Keith and Albie would lift a table onto the empty stage and we'd get a foursome together, shuffling the cards for a lot of laughs and a hot game of Bid-Whist. We hung together away from the Bla too. Keith and I often went over to Albie's house for the evening while Billy, with his tiny white poodle tucked under one arm, fussed over us serving drinks and snacks. Sometimes we'd even meet up with a big gang from the Bla to take a position in their Sunday afternoon softball games. We weren't any good, but it was always fun.

Albie, who was in his forties, took pride in running a successful club and rubbing shoulders with the almost-elite of Hollywood's underside. He doted like a mother hen over his performers and expected the audience to give each act their full attention. The green cards alongside the menus on the tables said so. Albie had become not only a dear friend but a cheerleader and mentor to Keith. That's why his sudden ultimatum threw Keith for such a loop.

It came one Wednesday night after Keith's third set. People-wise, the turnout had been disappointing. Wednesday wasn't the greatest night, of course, but it was a start. Albie's eyes were kind, and his manner fatherly as usual, when he came up to our table. Then he lowered the boom.

"I'm sorry, Keith, but you've got two weeks to pack 'em in or I'll have to replace you with another act."

"You're kidding," Keith said in surprise. I felt a stab of rejection too.

"I'm not," Albie said. "If you want your own night, you gotta draw more people. I've got a club to run. Salaries to pay. I'm sorry, Keith, but I just can't afford to keep losing money on you."

We couldn't believe our ears. Keith went home that night deeply depressed. Even the Quaalude he took to soothe his bruised feelings couldn't touch the real hurt—the whispers of failure. It seemed to me that the worst part about performing was having to sell yourself. Being so vulnerable. When you don't measure up, nothing eases the sickening feeling that maybe it's not just your act that isn't good enough. Maybe it's you.

After Albie's ultimatum Keith sprang into immediate action. He was never one to take a challenge lying down. Starting on Thursday, he spent all week phoning everyone and anyone he knew. He almost begged them to come, telling them about all his new songs, how he wanted to see them, and how he was going to lose his job unless the place was packed. I felt embarrassed for him, and even worse when he insisted I call all my friends as well! But we were in a terrible bind.

Keith had already pitched himself to every major record label in town. That resulted in some nibbles. One company had flown us to New York. Nothing materialized. Keith even tried to sing on a Grand

Funk sound-alike record, but didn't sound enough alike. There were some more nibbles but no bites.

Money was tight and getting tighter. We'd already sold my red Triumph sports car and my prized Martin D-35 guitar. My savings account had breathed its last. So to supplement our small income from the Bla—sometimes less than fifteen dollars a night—Keith clenched his teeth and played proms, parties, and banquets where no one ever listened. It was the bottom of the barrel for any serious artist, but the word for us in 1974 was *survival*. And now the threat of getting fired from the Bla Bla—a small-potatoes club as Hollywood nightspots go—would be the final humiliation.

The following Wednesday, we walked into the Bla about 8:30 PM, feeling quiet apprehension. I looked around and was struck with how empty this place could look. The Bla was dark and narrow inside, with a small stage to the right as you walked in the front door. The bar, which was too small for anyone to sit at, ran across the back, right in front of the tiny, one-man kitchen. The most consistent thing about the decor was its inconsistency. Absolutely nothing matched. Between the stage and the bar was a collection of banged-up wooden tables. On the walls huge dragonflies in vivid yellows and oranges hung beside oversized photos autographed by "sorta knowns." When packed, the Bla could hold about eighty-five people on chrome-and-vinyl chairs, the kind you'd find around a Formica table in someone's kitchen in the 1950s. Right now those chairs were mostly empty.

Only a few patrons sat in quiet conversation as Keith nervously eyed the stage. Albie was getting a check ready at one of the tables. The cook and the two waiters, Eddie and Mr. Sally, were at the back bar, the only others in the whole place. Albie caught Keith's eye. Neither one said anything, but it was a knowing glance. Tonight was it.

Keith and I sat silently in the back of the skinny little club, watching each other watch the door. We certainly looked like West Coast musicians, if nothing else. Married for only eight months, we made quite a pair. Me, in a homemade Indian print skirt, an embroidered gauze blouse, and my long straight hair. And Keith, wearing blue jeans and a new flowered cowboy shirt. His long, curly ponytail had recently been left on the hair stylist's floor. What remained had been layered into a new California style called the shag—short for shaggy. Even freshly cut, his hair still hung well below his shoulders. I silently admired his new professional image. Less hippie, but still very hip.

Slowly, in twos and threes, people started arriving. One cigarette after another was lit, and spirals of blue smoke curled gracefully to the ceiling. As the chairs filled, the noise level began to rise. Chairs scraped against the cement floor. Loud laughter punctuated conversations. Eddie, the headwaiter, clipped his orders to the revolving wheel, and the smell and sizzle of burgers drifted from the tiny kitchen.

Still, there weren't enough people and we knew it. Mr. Sally stepped over to our table to take my order, wearing his usual uniform—a custom-made T-shirt with a sketch of him in a bouffant hairdo and "Mr. Sally" scrawled across the front in fancy white script. In the low light, the black cotton stretching tightly across his ebony skin threatened to cast him into obscurity except for a few well-placed rhinestones striking a pose. I wasn't very hungry so I ordered Guac-and-Papa's— fried potato slices with a bowl of guacamole. Would any of our friends bother to show up? Keith's first hourlong set started at 9:00 P.M. We had only ten minutes to go. Keith's right leg was bouncing nervously. He was all raw energy and ready to start. More tense minutes ticked by.

"Do I look okay?" he asked, poking at his hair.

"You look great, honey," I assured him.

I loved the way Keith looked. His clear blue eyes and fair skin gave him a pure, almost childlike air. Now that he'd shaved off his beard, the fact that he was just twenty years old was much more evident. "It's 8:58," Keith said, breaking into my thoughts. "Where is everybody?" He was all wound up and ready to pop.

I tried to calm him down a bit.

"They'll be here in a few minutes," I responded, trying to conceal my own fears. "We've got a little more time."

"There is no more time. This is it."

Keith shoved back his chair with disappointment written all over him. Yet I sensed his determination. He was a fighter, and even though the odds were against him, I knew Keith would give it his all.

Albie had started to pace in the back as Keith made his way to the stage and sat at the battered upright piano. He squinted into the single spotlight and, leaning toward the microphone, spoke in mock military fashion.

"I'd like the sergeant of arms to call the room to attention! Ladies and gentlemen, and others, I'd like to interrupt your rambling conversation for some music."

Keith started noodling on the piano, but few people in the scant crowd paid attention. Keith fidgeted in his seat while his fingers wandered over the keys for a few moments. I could tell he was trying to figure out what to play. He finally launched into "Life Goes On," a song he'd just written with his new friend Randy Stonehill:

Marvin was a connoisseur of twenty-cent wine.
You could see him bummin' nickels down on Sunset and Vine.
One day his wealthy uncle passed away in Bel Air.
And now he's sippin' from a vintage year.
Marvin's sippin' from a vintage year!

Then the chorus:

Life goes on and the world goes 'round.
One day you're up, the next day you're down.
Don't count on good luck, there's nothing to say except,
"Thank you, Lord, for another day!"

The funny lyrics and funky rhythm grabbed everyone's attention. Keith pounded the keys in a way that sent terror into the heart of every piano teacher he ever had. I often held my breath hoping he wouldn't miss a note, but even when he did it didn't matter. It wasn't perfection that drew you to Keith's music, or to him for that matter. It was heart.

A few more tables were filling up, and to my relief some people were clapping along. Keith paused to do what came naturally—give more directions: "Here's the second verse. But you don't really have to pay attention to the verses. They're just there to keep the choruses coming. Okay, here we go!"

> There was a famous senator that everyone knew.
> One day a sly reporter found a girl in his room.
> The reelection survey said that he'd make a kill.
> But now he's washing dishes down at Joe's Bar and Grill.
> He makes his famous speeches now at Joe's Bar and Grill!

The chorus came around again and people began to sing with enthusiasm, imitating Keith's comical gestures. Keith sang, "One day you're up," pointing to the ceiling. Then he plunged his thumb toward the floor as he shook his head and sang, "Next day you're down—" The night was coming alive.

Eddie danced his orders down the narrow aisles, balancing trays of shish kebabs, burgers, and beer above his head. Mr. Sally ran a fork across the soda fountain grates with the zest of a marimba player, and I kept rhythm by playing my water glass with a spoon. Captured by Keith's enthusiasm, hoots, hollers, and hand claps erupted around the room—and more tables filled while he played his next few songs.

I had yet to see any of our friends. Then a movement at the door caught my eye. It was our friend Michelle Brandes, the youth and family leader at a local Jewish synagogue. I recognized her even in the dim light. Both of her legs were bent in the wrong direction when she was born, which left a noticeable limp. She made her way slowly through the smoky haze and sat beside me. After warm hugs and smiles, she quickly turned to enjoy Keith. Still, I was paying far more attention to the door than I was to Keith. Then he kicked into a Joni Mitchell song, "Free Man in Paris," and I could tell he was starting to relax a little. Since I was wondering where all our friends were, I felt especially tuned-in to the message of the song.

"Free Man in Paris" tells the story of a successful record company executive on vacation in Paris, tired of cranking out hit artists—"stoking the starmaker machinery behind the popular song." Another part of the lyrics lamented his loss of a simpler life without the pressures of his fame and fortune: "I was a free man in Paris, I felt unfettered and alive. Nobody calling me up for favors, nobody's future to decide."

Keith had become all too familiar with the starmaker machinery: the record companies, producers, publishers, and agents—all fighting over "who gets what" of various royalty and performance rights. When an artist becomes a hit, he's a hot property and then everybody "loves him" as they clamor for a piece of the pie. Until then, though, you just look for connections and wait for your big break. The gears of the machinery are oiled with the tears of countless musicians and songwriters who never get their break. Or get used up and spit out along the way. I loved Joni Mitchell's music, and this song was one of my favorites. But it also made me shudder.

Keith's fear of not "making it" was overshadowed only by the fear of blowing it—of getting involved with the wrong people out of desperation.

As I glanced around the smoky room I thought, *Someone could be here right now who could help Keith in a big way.* But then there were some people whose help we definitely did not want.

Like the guy the previous September. He heard Keith at the Bla and just flipped. Keith later met with him in his fancy Hollywood office, and the guy bubbled over with "I can make you a star" noises. Here was a voice promising the success and stardom Keith wanted. But, as Keith confided in his daily journal, a log he kept for years, there was—as usual—a string attached:

> *He's very rich and he has a big name in the business. He's also incredibly gay and I felt him vibing on me. Even though he could do a lot for me—bread and contact wise—I gave a "nay" to working with him.*

And that wasn't the first time a record company executive had tried to hit on Keith.

There had been the movie score with a popular director, but a pretty sleazy movie even by our standards. The more Keith got into it, the more he wanted out. Things soured on the money end, too. Keith had finished the music for two reels when he quit the project. In his journal he said it fell through "due to cheapness and under-handed tactics on their part, and lack of true desire on mine." That was another issue—Keith's high standards.

As Michelle and I watched Keith now, I couldn't help but think that maybe he would have been discovered already if he'd just been a bit more flexible. But for Keith some things were set in concrete. His dad had been his manager for years and had instilled very high standards in him. If something didn't feel right, Keith wasn't going to do it, and that was that. His high principles were admirable, but secretly I was afraid he might be just a little too picky for his own good.

As Keith continued on with the next few songs, he squinted through the glaring stage light, keeping a check on the crowd. A few more people filtered in. Several faithful friends made a two-hour drive from the desert in Lancaster, Keith's parents came to cheer him on—and another friend, Karen Bender, had even brought her daughter Dawn, who had the longest braids I'd ever seen on a little kid. I was disappointed that Todd Fishkind, Keith's best friend, wasn't able to come, but our poker-playing buddies from Marina del Rey showed and so did a few industry friends.

Keith played for another twenty minutes before taking his first break. He finished to an enthusiastic round of applause and joyfully jumped off the stage, his blue eyes sparkling with the victory of the moment.

A full house!

As he walked over to the table, sweat glistening on his face, excitement made his usually springy steps even springier. Not only were we high on the moment, but our friend Harriet had come bearing gifts.

Harriet shoved a shoe box toward Keith.

"Shoes?"

"Open it," she said with a sly smile.

Keith lifted the lid. His eyes brightened. "Brownies!"

"My own special recipe," Harriet said, winking. "Homegrown, if you know what I mean."

"You put grass in them?"

"The best."

"Eddie! Hey, Eddie! Bring me a large milk."

Keith grabbed a handful of the marijuana-laced goodies and passed the box to some select friends in a ritual of sharing the wealth, patterned after Indians passing the peace pipe. We made the rounds, telling everyone we were glad they came.

As the brownies hit bottom, things began to look up even more. The strain left Keith's eyes, and he was obviously soaring with the moment.

Albie walked up, smiling broadly. He slapped Keith on the back and said, "You did it, kid. A great night! I'm happy for you."

Keith's face was one big grin. "Yeah? So when do I get Saturdays?"

Albie chuckled and shook his head. The question didn't demand an answer, not immediately. But Keith already had his eyes on the future, on something far beyond a big night of his own at the Bla Bla Cafe.

When Keith started his second set, the haze, clinking glasses, and melodic piano all merged as my mind started to drift. I stared at the funny dragonflies on the wall—savoring the feeling of success.

Somehow, though, my thoughts were pulled to our future and what might lie ahead. I just knew Keith was supposed to be up in front of a lot of people—people who were being moved by his music and what he had to say. But the problem was that it wasn't clear even to Keith exactly what he had to say. He just felt he had a message to share with the world, something from his spiritual search. An important message.

By the time Keith finished his third set that evening, a decided victory was won. It was one of Keith's best nights yet. Driving home

I was still hyped from the excitement of the evening—and Harriet's tasty brownies. My mind was hung up on a million questions: *Was this the beginning of a big break for Keith? Was he finally on a roll? Why did someone like Keith, who was loaded with talent, need to resort to begging his friends to come hear him play?* It seemed like such a contradiction, but then again there were lots of contradictions in our lives.

In areas like honesty and integrity Keith had the highest standards of anyone I'd ever met. We didn't cheat on our taxes, but sometimes we'd take illegal drugs. Was there a difference?

Even if Keith made it in music, would we make it as a couple? As much as we liked to talk about living in harmony with the universe and each other, we sure had our share of arguments. Big arguments.

It was hard to live with so many unanswered questions, and not just regarding Keith's career. Some of the other battles we were fighting were on an entirely different front—one that was even more vague and elusive. It was as if something were tugging at us, pulling us into uncharted waters—something that would change us forever.

In fact, we had no idea we were on the verge of a breakthrough much bigger than we had ever imagined.

All I knew at the moment was that this man I married sure had a lot of complex facets to his personality. In the days following our victory at the Bla, my mind wandered over the many strands that wove together inside him. I thought about the sensitive inner man who was determined to find spiritual answers. Yet there was another side of him—the little boy who always wanted to be in show business. The little boy side explained so much about who Keith had become. But did it offer any clues about where we were going?

Left: Keith in a silly hat.

Below: Mondays were the worst night of the week!

Above: New Mexico promo shot

Right: High School Concert

Top: Randy Weimer, Keith, and Todd, 1973

Bottom: Todd Fishkind and Keith at the Headband Club

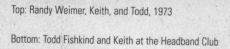

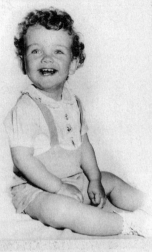

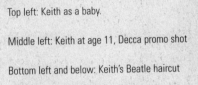

Top left: Keith as a baby.

Middle left: Keith at age 11, Decca promo shot

Bottom left and below: Keith's Beatle haircut

2

"RUN TO THE END OF THE HIGHWAY"

Keith continued playing at the Bla, waiting for "the discovery." In the meantime, we made a discovery of our own. We could write songs together. Keith made room for me inside his "creative bubble," as he called it, and I was thrilled. But sometimes it had its drawbacks.

One day I worked several hours on a song lyric, then I found Keith in the living room and proudly handed him the words all neatly recopied on a fresh piece of paper. Keith read it silently. I knew he would tell me exactly what he thought, so I was holding my breath.

"Mel," Keith said finally, "these rhymes are really trite."

"Trite? What do you mean?"

"They're expected. Like moon, June, spoon—"

"I didn't even use those words."

"I know, but you need to be more creative."

"Well, forget the words I used. What about the message?"

"You're not saying anything new. Anybody could write a song like this."

"Do you realize how long I worked on those? Are you telling me there isn't anything worth saving?" I was starting to get angry now, and hurt too. Blinking back the gathering tears, I took the sheet of paper, wadded it up, and threw it in the trash.

"Don't you want me to tell you the truth?" Keith asked.

"Of course I do," I said, pouting a bit.

"Look. I know you can do better. You just need to keep writing. Keep trying and don't give up."

I calmed down some. It was hard to admit, but I knew he was right. It really wasn't a very good song. I had a musical background of sorts, but nothing like Keith's musical genius. I was glad he wanted me to do my best, but why couldn't he say the same thing in a different way? Walking back to the trash, I retrieved the crumpled lyric. I wished this tension that suddenly rose between us over trivial things would go away—but I knew it sprang from something deeper than petty disagreements.

Keith had been on edge for several months. Sometimes we had great days. Others we'd just as soon forget. Keith had a strong sense of calling on his life, a spiritual destiny, and he knew it wasn't being fulfilled. This was frustrating for him. Coupled with the fact that we were still adjusting to our first year of marriage, it amounted to some anxiety between us.

Married on Christmas Day 1973, we were now only three months away from celebrating our first anniversary. Sometimes I found it hard to believe I was actually married and living in a rented house in the suburbs, with a backyard full of fruit trees. Even Keith's funky upright piano had its own room. We had plenty of time and space to write music. But for Keith it seemed like there was no time. He was always in motion, always searching for something. Where had this drive and energy come from?

It didn't make life any easier that the promise of a recording deal always lingered. We were constantly running all over town to meet with someone in the business. Besides partying and playing poker with a wide assortment of friends, Keith and I kept writing songs together. We usually worked really well as a team and would spend hours transposing concepts and ideas into word pictures and rhymes. Most of the time we worked hard, but when it got too intense, one of us would suggest a stupid rhyme or make a joke to release the tension. Once we wrote a little jingle to help our friends remember our phone number—349-2510. We sang it with a blues feel: "Three-four-nine, a quarter and a dime, let's get together and buy some wine! Oh baby, uh uh huh, oh baby!"

What we really wanted was to write a hit song and get it recorded by a big-name recording artist. A lot of famous singer/songwriters got their big break that way. Keith kept making appointments to play his songs at major publishing companies, hoping they'd "run" the song to a popular artist. Sometimes we'd hear who was looking for new album material, and we'd go home and try to write in their style. So we wrote songs for artists like Cher, Olivia Newton-John, and Helen Reddy. We wrote them, but they never got recorded!

One of the publishers Keith went to all the time was CBS in downtown Hollywood. Never lacking in nerve, Keith always brought our dog Libre up the elevator and right into the executive offices. Before the CBS people knew what was happening, Libre was lying quietly under a desk or a coffee table while Keith assured folks that she was housebroken. In spite of the clumps of hair Libre left on the shag carpeting, CBS really liked hearing Keith's music. In fact, their executives liked his songs so much they asked Keith to go on salary for $250 a week as a staff writer.

As usual, Keith immediately wanted to discuss the proposed contract with his dad. Keith and his family were close, and he was always phoning his parents or running over to their house. So we jumped into Victor and made the twenty-minute drive across the San Fernando Valley to Canoga Park. Keith's folks were glad to see us, and Keith joined his dad at the dining room table where they spread out the bulky contract for close inspection. This was not the first time they'd pored over a contract together, and Keith's father was already eyeing some of the drawbacks of this agreement.

"The normal thing, since you're unknown, would be for them to take 100 percent of your publishing rights," his father began. "But you can't let them have that, Keith. If you do you'll be sorry one day."

"I know, but do you think they'll go along with that?"

"It doesn't hurt to ask."

Keith's mom was in the kitchen, making a pot of her wonderful chicken soup. Overhearing their conversation she poked out her head. "Honey, maybe you ought to go down to CBS with Keith and make sure he gets a fair deal."

"I will if I need to. Now let's take a look at all the fine print . . ."

I wandered out of the kitchen, where I'd made myself a cup of tea, and settled on the couch in the den. I liked visiting Keith's parents. They were always so supportive of Keith. They had recognized his talent long ago, and they did anything they could to help him. Even if Keith and his parents didn't see everything eye-to-eye, they had an obvious love for one another. They had welcomed me into the family with open arms too.

Now that Keith and his dad were deep in discussion of the different points in the CBS contract, I figured they'd be awhile. Looking across the room I spotted one of Keith's baby pictures. He was not only a beautiful little boy, but his genius had appeared early.

Keith once told me he couldn't remember a time when his life was devoid of music or the potential for great success. When you were with him, you had the feeling there were triplets, eighth notes, and drum rolls pumping through his veins. He was definitely not nine-to-five office material. He wanted something more out of life.

Keith was third-generation show business. His grandfather on his mother's side was a successful composer, screenplay writer, and a pioneer in the music industry. He worked for Warner Brothers and wrote for the singer Eddie Cantor. He'd also had the keen eye to put the three Ritz Brothers together as an act, owned Jaguar Records (one of the first rhythm 'n' blues record companies), and had signed the legendary Hank Williams as an artist.

The same love of music was passed on to Keith's mother. From where I sat now, in the den, I could see her as she swept the floor and watered her many plants. She was a pretty woman with short blonde hair and an infectious laugh. Right out of high school she started singing popular music with the big bands. She was even offered a contract to sing with Benny Goodman but turned it down to marry Keith's dad when he was still a handsome baseball rookie on the New York Giants farm team.

After Keith was born, it didn't take long for the distinctive characteristics of this unusual child to emerge. His mom had often told me that as soon as Keith was up off all fours, he walked as if he had springs in his feet. Not the average heel-to-toe lift-off. Keith slapped his whole foot to the ground all at once, then power-launched his body forward from the ball of his foot. Though he was now over six feet tall, Keith never outgrew that springy walk. To his last day he walked fast and with purpose. I always had to rush to keep up with him because Keith was always in a hurry—as if he was rushing to pack every moment with the most it could possibly hold.

Keith's mom, who had studied voice for five years at Carnegie Hall, said that by the time Keith was nine months old he could hum "Rock-a-Bye Baby" on perfect pitch. His grandfather gave him a small record player he could work by himself, so he'd play his gold plastic 78 RPM kiddie records for hours on end, happily singing and bouncing along with the tunes. When he was learning to walk, he'd plop his diapered bottom down right on top of it, leaving his mom to replace many broken needles. But her patience bore lasting fruit. At the age of two and a half, with his Gerber Baby good looks, Keith won a kiddie talent show by singing "Love and Marriage." His young career was underway. By the time Keith was three, he could sing harmony to his mom's alto, and to everyone's amazement he could also strum a ukulele.

It was the Greens' move in 1957 to Canoga Park, a suburb in the San Fernando Valley, that opened new doors of possibility. Keith's talent continued to blossom under the watchful eyes of his parents— and so did his precocious nature. Unlike his older sister, Keith was into everything. On his first day in kindergarten, he was benched by the principal for misbehavior. In fact, wherever Keith went it seemed he found something to cause his mother worry.

The first time he was in a department store he found the control switch for the escalator and pushed it, which brought the escalator to a screaming halt. This caused no small stir. Next he found the Coke machine and shoved his hand up the hole where the bottles came down. Naturally, his hand got stuck and he needed to be rescued, amidst his tearful screams. As he grew, however, his talent for getting attention—and for generating income—carried him far beyond normal limits for a kid his age.

By the time Keith was five, he could play anything he heard on his ukulele; at the age of seven, his parents bought him his first piano. They found Keith a teacher who liked both classical and pop music, and it was at her suggestion that Keith began to take acting lessons too. Keith was seven when he did his first television commercial.

Keith's eighth year, 1962, was an exciting one—the year he began developing a stage presence. He made his live theater debut playing a little Italian street urchin in Arthur Laurents's romantic comedy *The Time of the Cuckoo*. The *Los Angeles Times* reviewed Keith's performance at the outdoor Chatsworth Summer Theater and said, "Roguish-looking, eight-year-old Keith Green gave a winning portrayal . . . alternately amusing and pathetic." Another review said Keith "stole the show."

Keith also wrote his first song that year. His grandfather had taught him three rock 'n' roll chords and that was all it took. Keith quickly became a prolific writer. One day he stayed home from school because he was sick, and he wrote the words and music to three songs.

That year Keith brought the house down at the famous Troubadour nightclub (later called Rocky's) in Hollywood. The Troubadour had one evening they called Hoot Night, when only folk singers—not rock 'n' rollers—were allowed. So Keith learned two folk songs on the guitar, and when he finished his first song on Hoot Night, the audience gave him a standing ovation. He played an encore and people screamed, yelled, and wouldn't let him leave the stage again. Keith told everyone the only other songs he knew were rock 'n' roll. They shouted for him to play one anyway. He launched into the Buddy Holly tune "Peggy Sue" and won a third standing ovation!

Two years later, at ten, Keith moved indoors to legitimate theater. He played Kurt von Trapp opposite Janet Blair's Maria in a 1964 production of *The Sound of Music* in the San Fernando Valley. The local newspaper remarked on Keith's talented performance.

Unfortunately, Keith got a different sort of attention from his sixth-grade classmates. Since Keith's curls had now aged to brown, he needed some help from Lady Clairol to revive his once-golden hair for the part of Kurt von Trapp. Once the production was finished, Keith needed to keep his hair blond for a while to maintain a more youthful appearance. One day as he walked down the school hallway, he noticed a few of his friends standing off to the side snickering. As soon as he passed by, one of them called out behind his back, "Proxy locks! You big sissy!"

Eventually, Keith was able to let his hair grow out, but as the black roots inched their way upward, they were not only a source of embarrassment—they were a painful reminder. They made it evident to everyone, especially Keith, that he was different somehow. As much as he enjoyed being different, he also had the longings of any boy about to hit puberty. He wanted to fit in and be accepted by his classmates as part of the crowd. But that was not going to happen.

In January 1965, upon the release of Keith's first 45 record produced by his grandfather and Jay Colonna, *Teen Scene* magazine called Keith "the youngest new face on the Hollywood scene." This first solo release was called "Cheese and Crackers," backed with "I Want to Hurt You." A photo of Keith with a big smile appeared in *Teen Scene* with an address and the line "We know he'd love to hear from his present and future fans."

It was about this time that Keith's father started to represent him as an artist. After years of exposure to the business of show biz, Keith's dad became quite skilled when it came to dealing with record companies and legal contracts. He also was extremely honest when it came to business—or anything else for that matter. With his dad taking a bigger role in his career, things started to take off. One executive at Capitol Records wanted to sign Keith to a recording contract, but he couldn't get it approved by his superiors because they felt Keith was too young. No one as young as Keith—including the Osmonds or the Jackson Five—was recording yet.

His dad moved on to Decca Records, where Keith was signed to a five-year recording contract. The *Los Angeles Times* watched with interest, and their music reviewer wrote:

Keith's first disc will be released in March, and one of the many songs he's written has been published. The name of the song is "The Way I Used to Be," which at Keith Green's age doesn't leave much leeway. He's only 11. Absolutely nothing else can be heard when, with amazing gusto, the husky blond boy starts slamming away at the piano and singing all out in an alto that promises to become a strong baritone.

He quoted Keith, who said, "I've written about 40 songs and they're still coming. I'll never run out!"

Upon the publishing of Keith's first song, at the age of eleven, he became the youngest member of ASCAP—the American Society of Composers, Authors, and Publishers. The Society flew Keith to New York to honor him along with the songwriter who was the oldest member. Keith's youthful success made him unique in the music world. He was flown to New York to sing on two national network television shows, and from there he landed appearances in a television special with Sammy Davis Jr., was on *The Jack Benny Show, The Joey Bishop Show, I've Got a Secret,* and *Walt Disney's Wonderful World of Color.* He also did a program with Steve Allen, who later asked Keith for his secret of success. Keith replied in all seriousness, "I started when I was very young!"

Around this time, Keith also played his guitar and sang on a local morning television show. When he and his dad got home, there was an important message waiting. They were to phone a certain extension at Metro-Goldwyn-Mayer Studios. They phoned right away, and the mysterious caller turned out to be none other than Colonel Parker, Elvis Presley's long-time manager. Keith's dad listened, astonished, as Colonel Parker said, "Your boy's got a great talent. If I wasn't tied up full-time with Elvis, I'd take Keith on. But you call me if you ever need any help."

In March 1966, *Time* magazine even pointed to Keith as a budding young star in a music article that looked at "harnessing the lucrative potential of the almost untouched pre-teen pocketbook."

The article mentioned new merchandising angles aimed at four- to twelve-year-olds. One of the up-and-coming young talents expected to shake dollars from the preteen piggy banks was Keith, who must have read with growing excitement as *Time* reported, "Decca Records has a pre-pubescent dreamboat named Keith Green. . . . He has already written 50 rock 'n' roll songs, which he croons in a voice trembling with conviction, 'Youuu are the girl / I am the boy / Yes, it seems we're in looove.'"

With such strong support from his family, it's no wonder Keith accomplished so much at such a young age. Keith was not only loaded with performing genius, he had the high energy and stubborn determination it would take to succeed. With everything lining up the way it was, Keith and his family just knew his career was about to take off. Like a rocket on a launching pad, all systems were go. But then, strangely, things didn't quite fall into place.

Keith's record release from Decca made it into the Top 10 in Hawaii. However, the major national breakthrough that was hoped for did not materialize. A short time later, Donny Osmond came on the scene, capturing the preteen and teenage listeners that Decca Records had envisioned for Keith. Suddenly Keith's dreams came crashing down. Success was nearly his, but somehow it had passed him by.

I heard Keith and his father laughing in the other room as they shoved their chairs away from the table noisily. They'd often joke about the outrageous things companies tried to write into their contracts. I wondered if CBS was any different. Looking at my watch, I realized they'd been talking for more than an hour. As they walked into the family room, they were smiling and slapping each other on the back. Whatever questions they had about the CBS contract they must have worked through them.

On the drive home Keith told me more details about what CBS was offering him. It was a great deal. Besides the $250 a week, there were no office hours. He just needed to turn in eighteen acceptable songs in a twelve-month period. Even better, CBS was hiring him mainly to write commercial melodies, not lyrics. His lyrics weren't commercial enough because they had too much "spiritual" content for CBS's taste. That was fine with Keith.

"This is incredibly perfect," he said, beaming. "I don't have to sell out my ideals to commercialism. Music is music."

"That's really great," I replied.

"This new job is really a responsibility and a privilege," he continued. "I need to be careful to stay honest."

"Of course. They're giving you a lot of money."

"Yeah, that's why I'm going to ask CBS to sign you, too."

"What?" I shot back. "Why would you ask them to sign me?"

"Because I don't want to be tempted to cheat."

"What do you mean?"

Keith explained that, since we were starting to write a lot of songs together, if CBS only signed him, they wouldn't own any of my share in a song Keith and I cowrote. This would obviously benefit us financially. It would have been 100 percent legal and ethical for us to get more publishing when we wrote a song together, but Keith didn't want to be tempted by money.

"I don't want you to write with me for the wrong reasons," he said. "I'd rather make less money and have a clear conscience. I don't want to struggle trying to figure out my motives every time we write together."

"But I'm not as good as you are," I protested. "Why would they want to pay me anything?"

"I'm not going to ask them to pay you anything. We'll still get just $250 a week. I only want your name added on to the contract."

When he suggested his idea to CBS a few days later, they were astonished. It was an unusual request, but it meant they were getting two writers for the price of one. It also meant they would own any acceptable songs I might write by myself as part of our yearly eighteen-song quota, which at that point seemed highly unlikely. They accepted Keith's offer and we both became staff writers for CBS.

As much as Keith was caught up in the world of music, there was still another part of him, a side that ran much deeper. Keith was caught up in what seemed to be a lifelong spiritual search. The incident with Harmony a short time before, outside the Bla Bla Cafe, had been a real turning point. Keith had shocked himself when he quoted the words of Jesus into the wolflike face of Harmony. On one hand it felt a little odd to quote a Bible verse since our spiritual life seemed to be so stunted. Yet Harmony's response went a long way toward impressing Keith that some kind of power had forced Harmony out of his weird state the moment Keith had spoken those words.

One night Todd, who was still Keith's best friend and almost a permanent fixture in our house, came over for dinner. He and Keith had known each other for years and they'd even kept a journal together at one time. They were such good friends that sometimes I got a little jealous of their deep relationship. It didn't help matters when Keith, who was so used to talking with his buddy about everything, occasionally forgot who he was talking to and called me Todd. But Todd was a great guy and I usually enjoyed having him around. This night he and Keith were immersed in a debate about some Scripture in the Bible, and I slipped out of the living room to start making the salad. As I listened to them from the kitchen, I was impressed by Keith's unquenchable thirst for the things of the spirit. It was one of the things I loved about him.

Spiritual roots ran deep in Keith's family. His mom's parents were Jewish but had become Christian Scientists sixty years earlier. His mother was raised in Christian Science, and when Keith's parents married, his dad, also Jewish, followed suit. Christian Science followers do not believe in using medicine or going to doctors, so Keith never received vaccinations as a child. He was taught to believe in having divine health by knowing the "perfect truth." As Keith grew up, he witnessed many physical healings, and he often saw his parents study the Bible along with Mary Baker Eddy's teachings in her book *Science and Health*. Eddy's teachings were based on her interpretation of which parts of the Bible were true, and she published those parts in daily readings along with her teachings.

Keith and his father even formed a publishing company together named after one of the names of God, "I Am That I Am," and "I Am Music" became the cradle for all of Keith's early songs.

Keith was raised in a good, moral atmosphere, and he was basically a good kid. What it was exactly that brought on the sudden changes as he entered his teens, no one knew. But when Keith hit puberty, it hit back. Maybe it was the disappointment of having his dream with Decca Records suddenly vanish into thin air, or maybe he was just sucked into the 1960s revolutionary spirit of Southern California. Keith grew dissatisfied with himself and the life he was living. Growing up in an atmosphere of moral purity, free of alcohol and drugs, had a wonderfully preserving effect on Keith during his early years. Not being exposed to those things at home kept him from developing destructive habits—for a while anyway.

When Keith graduated from junior high and entered high school, he came to it from a different universe than most other kids. While most of his friends were trying to figure out what they wanted to be when they grew up, Keith started the tenth grade as an "almost-was." He almost made it, but didn't. Underneath lay the dull pain of failure. Never being a quitter, Keith's bouncy step kept him in a forward momentum, winning talent contests, writing songs, and waiting—it seemed forever—for that magic door to open and lay the world at his feet. There were, however, some dangerous curves ahead.

By the time Keith was fifteen, he was growing more and more restless, and his relationships at home grew stormier. He was becoming more argumentative, more difficult to understand, and less tolerant. Keith felt like his parents didn't understand him at all. From his point of view, they suddenly looked old-fashioned and "totally uncool." The California scene was promising something more to life than Keith was experiencing, and he wasted no time pursuing it. He already had more money in the pockets of his blue jeans than nearly a dozen kids his age and decided to use it to finance every parent's worst fear.

In July 1969, four days after the holiday fireworks, Keith withdrew his bank savings, tucked his coin collection in his backpack, and financed a getaway with two older friends.

On the road, Keith started keeping a record of his daily thoughts and activities in a notebook. This journal would become a lifelong friend, and he confided his innermost feelings to its pages. In fact, it captured so much of Keith's heart and who he was that, once we became serious, Keith sat me down and, with great excitement, read all of his journals to me out loud.

I couldn't believe how he kept track of things in such detail. He'd often stop to fill in details too. I felt honored to have him let me into his private inner world like that. His entries were always interesting and at times even embarrassing because he held nothing back—not even his relationships with other girls or his innermost dreams, fears, and failures. But that was Keith's all-or-nothing nature. He wanted me to know absolutely everything about him—the good and the not-so-good. He needed to know I accepted him for who he was without any illusions.

So I heard them all—from beginning to end—starting with the first entry, written in a car the first time he ran away at fifteen.

The Beginning—July 8, 1969

Sorry about the messy writing. We're driving. Hi there. My name is Keith Green. I'm splitting Canoga Park. Our final goal is Canada! We've been planning to leave for two months. We have luggage, organ and amplifier, $175.39 and my coin collection worth about $100.00. I hope to get some jobs along the coast of California singing and playing. We're going to go as far from L.A. as we can. I feel really sorry about my parents. I love them. They're goin' to feel bad. —Later.

Their "trip to Canada" took them only as far north as San Francisco. There they met a young Eskimo girl and they all rented a cheap hotel room to live in. The guys got backbreaking jobs unloading crates of tires from railroad boxcars. It was a time of first experiments. Keith also wrote:

> *That girl I met in 'Frisco was named Carolyn. . . . She really kind of dug me. She didn't know how old I was. When she found out, she was really surprised. We had it all figured out. We were [all] gonna get an apartment and Carolyn [was] gonna cook and clean. Then we all started getting crabby. I told Carolyn to get lost. I wanted to get rid of her. The rat I was. [One of my friends] started talking about his probation hassles and I started thinking about home. . . . We decided to go back.*

The great runaway lasted a total of four days. Keith called home, and his dad flew up and rented a real limousine from the airport to pick him up. Then they flew back to Los Angeles together. On that trip Keith had his first taste of manual labor, which he hated, and his first taste of life on the road, which he loved.

In the next few years Keith would run away from home two more times. One time, in fact, his parents hoped to teach him a lesson, and they allowed him to be thrown in jail as a runaway. He spent his time there writing songs. Having no paper, he scratched out words on the cell wall with the heel of his shoe.

When Keith entered his junior year in Canoga Park's El Camino Real High School in September 1970, his life had become a blur of friends, parties, music, and trying to stay one step ahead of the principal. Playing the class clown from a back-corner desk, Keith's wild antics and lack of attention in class gave him problems with his teachers, but never with his grades. Keith had a nearly photographic memory. His mind stored facts and figures like a filing cabinet. He could just reach in and pull out the desired information at will. El Camino had two hangouts—the upper lawn and the lower lawn. Between classes everyone who dabbled in drugs and thrived on loud music hung out on the upper lawn. It was there that Todd and Keith first met.

One afternoon Todd saw Keith obviously hitting on a girl he knew. She didn't seem interested but went along with the game of brotherly love and hippie-hugs. Keith pursued girls like someone hunting deer in a game park. He stopped his pursuit that day just long enough to sell Todd a marijuana joint for one dollar. From that day on they became, in their words, "doper brothers."

Besides the dope, Todd and Keith found there were two more important things that bound them together. One was their love of music—the other was their hunger for spiritual things. Todd and Keith both played guitar and would frequently jam on the upper lawn together. Todd was quiet and thoughtful, which complemented Keith's extravagant emotions. Todd's lean good looks, warm green eyes, and long, straight brown hair appealed to the ladies. But his shyness was a handicap. No matter, Keith took care of that. When they were out, instead of just finding a girl for himself, he hunted for pairs, usually giving Todd second choice. But their bond of friendship was ultimately founded on something less tangible than girls, drugs, or music.

Keith was like a magnet. Whatever he was into, he had a way of drawing others into his orbit, like a big planet with a huge gravity field. Keith was like this with his spiritual search. He and Todd would sit and talk for hours on end watching the sunrise and wondering about life, the universe, and God. There had to be more to life than what they were experiencing with their five senses. Everywhere they looked they saw people drowning in mediocrity, traditions, and the boring daily grind. Keith had no intention of winding up like that. There were new things to taste and experience. Why be narrow-minded when the world was full of beautiful things and beautiful people?

Everyone was saying, "If it feels good, do it"—and they did.

Couples everywhere were starting to live together openly. It was the "in" thing to do. It was prehistoric to think a marriage license could hold a relationship together. Who needed a piece of paper if you really loved somebody? And if you really did love someone, you wouldn't want to tie that person down. Stephen Stills's hit song summed it up: "If you can't be with the one you love, love the one you're with!"

Everywhere Keith looked people were basically saying "forget the system." Women had burned their bras and men had burned their draft cards. Someone even burned the American flag.

Nothing was sacred. Everything was up for grabs, and no one over thirty could be trusted. The true power to bring about peace would not, could not, come through brute force, but by embracing the world and each other in brotherly love. What was needed was a Peaceful Revolution. The perfect example was when a demonstrator at an antiwar rally walked up to one of the National Guards and put a flower down his gun barrel. Flower power was born.

It seemed as if seekers everywhere were united in a common theology that dressed itself in bare feet, Indian beads, headbands, wood stoves, incense, Eastern music, and organic gardens that sprouted green beans and homegrown marijuana. Keith joined in the search.

That search led him to Box Canyon, a desolate place in the mountains on the fringe of Los Angeles County. Box Canyon became a popular place to film western movies, and it became equally unpopular when it became known as the hideout of the infamous Charles Manson and his hippie "Manson Family."

Keith started doing Saturday night concerts in Box Canyon at a place called the Fountain of the World, a mansion-like building that resembled a small medieval monastery. A huge white sign out front bore the cryptic letters "F L K W"—standing for Faith, Love, Knowledge, and Wisdom. Over the main entrance was a sign, "He Who Enters Here Walks on Holy Ground." A large stone stairway led down inside the building, which was constructed in dark stonework and stained glass. Inside were lots of tables and chairs and a small stage. This organic-looking church was the perfect place for the sandaled, beaded, and bearded to hang out amid the smoke of incense and pot. Keith and Todd were right at home. What impressed Keith most about the Fountain was its founder. Brother Jeremiah, as he was called, wore sandals, a saffron-colored robe, and frequently performed skits with spiritual significance. He also inspired Keith to uphold some word of truth in the songs he wrote and to be more careful about the content of the ones he chose to play from his Top 40 repertoire. Keith's concerts began to draw quite a crowd.

Keith had been raised as a Christian Scientist, but organized religion started to feel dead to him. What he saw in Brother Jeremiah seemed fresh and alive. It was at the Fountain of the World that Keith's questions about life began to pile up on each other. Behind all the heady spiritual talk, people were still people. Why couldn't everyone live in harmony? Where was the love and the unity? It seemed like people had given up on high ideals and, instead, were looking through the fragmented prism colors of windowpane LSD. Keith's friends were finding their answers over the radio and in the rosy glow of the hash pipe. Maybe the secret of life would be revealed by getting back to Mother Nature—back to life as it was before modern man polluted the world with machines, smog, and greed.

Keith was especially impressed with a guy who called himself Cougar and lived close to the Fountain. Keith frequently went to his house to party and talk. Cougar had rejected materialism and the conventional way of life, and at eighteen he seemed to have all the answers. Keith thought everything about Cougar was cool—where he lived, what he said, and how he said it. Cougar wasn't just preaching brotherhood, he was living it. This, coupled with Brother Jeremiah's influence, seemed to open up a world of mystical truth for Keith.

In the summer of 1970, the second time Keith ran away from home, he felt he made an extraordinary breakthrough into the spiritual realm. Keith got as far north as Seattle this time. While he was there, he tripped on LSD. Parts of the trip were frightening, but Keith felt like he saw things clearly for the first time. In fact, he was so excited that he called Todd from Seattle to tell him, "I found God!"

When Keith returned home, all he wanted to talk about was his spiritual experience.

"Todd, you wouldn't believe it. It was like I was one with everything around me."

"But how do you know you found God? Did you see him?" Todd asked skeptically.

"No, but I felt him. He was warm and pure. It might seem crazy, but I know he was really with me."

"Did you hear his voice?"

Keith hesitated. "Not out loud. But I heard his words clearly in my mind."

That made Todd eager for a similar experience. A short time later, they took their first psychedelic trip together in Keith's backyard. Lying on lounge chairs looking up into the starry night sky, Keith read to Todd out of his "Life Notebook and Journey Guide." Keith's notebook now began to fill up with his philosophy of simplistic naturalism—borrowing from the ideals of the hippie movement, his drug trips, and his understanding of Christian Science.

As Keith and Todd continued sorting through the various things they believed in, they came up with their own philosophy. They gave it the mystical name "New Dawn," borrowed from a line in a David Crosby song—"the darkest hour is just before the dawn." To them New Dawn referred to the time when all mankind would live together in peace and brotherly love. It also included the Eastern idea of karma—that you have to pay for past sins in your next reincarnated life. If you blew it on earth, you always had another chance in your next life to do better.

With this new philosophy and his zealous idealism, it was natural for Keith to evangelize his friends. He was that way with everything. For instance, if Keith fixed his sandwich a certain way in a restaurant, he would tell everyone at his table, "You gotta try this, man. You'll love it!" Imagine his determination when it came to trying to lead others to where he'd been spiritually.

Keith got into the habit of gathering several friends together, usually at someone's house while their parents were gone. Then they'd all drop LSD together and sit in a circle on the floor, holding hands while Keith proceeded to "take them to the light." As they started to come on to the acid, Keith would begin describing the visions he saw. In his mind's eye he could see a great, blue-green sky arching over a vast, empty plain. Moving rapidly across the sky were multicolored clouds, churning and tumbling together. The clouds changed shapes constantly, the last image merging into the next. Keith called out the different images as they came—an eagle, a lion, an Indian doing a rain dance. As the sky filled with shadows, it was like entering a long, dark tunnel. But straight ahead, in the middle, was a pinprick of light. As they raced toward it through the billowing blackness, the light ahead grew bigger and more brilliant. Keith's voice grew louder with excitement as he described the quickly approaching blaze of light, flecked with radiant prisms. Suddenly they'd burst through the blinding light together. Releasing their hands, they fell into a heap on the floor, exhausted but exhilarated.

But even these "spiritual exercises," as Keith called them, raised questions in his mind. *What was this light at the end of the tunnel? Was it God? If it was God, what was he really like?*

Keith and Todd spent lots of time together that fall of 1970 trading their journal back and forth. Their philosophy started to take shape:

Diary of God's Children
October 25, 1970
4:00 P.M.

> *Me and my brother Todd are musicians and songwriters and children of God. (As everyone is.) We feel we have been placed together for a reason—to help the Peaceful Revolutionary movement!*

But for all his ideals, Keith's life was filled with contradictions. He wanted to purify his body in hopes it would lead to spiritual purity, so he became a vegetarian. But on the other hand he bought peyote from friends in Oregon. Keith rationalized taking drugs to trigger his spiritual experiences, even as he teased Todd about taking vitamins to enhance his health.

October 28, 1970
9:30 A.M.

Our dream is to have a big musical family, sort of like a communal living type thing. We'd like to grow our own fruits and vegetables. So I told Todd if he wants to start getting into the commune living type life, to stop taking vitamins, because we can't grow them.

If being careful about what they ate was a step toward purity, they were well on their way. Keith and Todd were not as careful, however, in relating to girls. Keith convinced Todd that the best romances were the ones with no strings attached, which seemed like a pretty good deal to two teenage guys. Keith confided in his journal that "sex is not important to the brotherhood movement." But even though his mind told him it wasn't important, his body was sending different signals.

In the first week of November 1970, Keith ran away from home a third time. To him it was the first step in launching this peaceful brotherhood movement.

Keith hitchhiked up to Seattle to chase down his dream of a musical family. His hopes centered on Timothy, a guy he'd met the first time he ran away. Timothy was the leader of a rock band in Seattle, and Keith hoped they could start a musical group together, one that would bring a message of peace to the world. Keith felt he and Timothy were brothers in the spirit, and that the message of true brotherly love would be spread for the good of mankind through the music they'd make. Keith believed intensely that Timothy was the one who was supposed to start this band with him.

November 10, 1970
9:00 P.M.

We're 30 miles south of Portland. This is my 24th ride and probably my last. I paid this guy $6 for gas. He's tak-

ing me to Tim . . . the time is right for us to come together. I miss Brother Tim . . . the time is right for us to come together. I miss Brother Todd. He's so much a part of it all. Now that me and Tim are coming together, oh, the music!! We will write together, play together, not only be one, but express oneness. . . . A better day has come!

Keith found Timothy playing with his band in a tavern, and became really excited because the new songs Timothy had written reflected the brotherhood philosophy. However, Keith had shown up unannounced and was surprised to learn that the band was about to go to Idaho for three weeks. That didn't throw him. He decided to go to Bellingham until Timothy returned. Still optimistic, Keith felt a strong sense of destiny about this time away from home. Three nights after leaving home he wrote, "I'm up here for a reason and I haven't found out what it is."

While he was waiting for Timothy to return, Keith spent most of his time making new friends, playing his music, and wondering why he was in Seattle. After about a week, Keith decided to take an LSD trip, which was a departure from his latest belief that organic drugs were superior to those made in a test tube. What was striking about this acid trip was that Keith thought he saw God. He was so excited about it, he wrote in his journal while he was tripping, which was in itself quite a feat. As the LSD took effect, the words on the journal pages grew into large, uneven scrawls:

November 20, 1970
11:00 A.M.

It's snowing!!!!!!
I'm tripping!!!!!!!!
It's toooo beautiful for words. . . . It's going to be a long, long, long, cold dark age before the dawn. God walked

with me. Into the sun and out of the snow. He said, "Look at the snow. In it are crystals of brotherhood holding softly but tightly together. For in them you will see the secret to hold through the dark ages ahead. . . ." He left me with a warm, loving, but assured embrace that light is ahead and said "Keep Faith."

Later that day, Keith also wrote:

That trip really was something. I feel different from the guy that took it. I feel like I went to another change. Good feelings. But one thing is for sure. The Dark Age started today. Got to get together with Todd and Tim soon.

Unlike the other times Keith ran away, this time he decided he'd keep in touch with his parents. They started by sending letters back and forth through a friend in Los Angeles so Keith could keep his exact location a secret. His parents were grateful for the contact and didn't call the police.

November 23, 1970
11:30 A.M.

I've been away from home now for two weeks. I hope my people [family] are taking it all pretty well. After a few months they'll have to. Anyway after they get used to me being gone, they will really be better off, for it. They will see. It's right for me to be here.

Keith felt he was learning a lot about himself, and a lot about life. But being out on his own had its ups and downs. He was ecstatic about receiving a three-minute standing ovation at a coffeehouse where he played. But he was also forced to buy boots at the Salvation Army because his shoes had holes in them and his toes were getting "wet, cold, and frozen" in the snow. He didn't have a car and didn't know where he was going to sleep from one night to the next.

As each snowy, rainy day of the Pacific Northwest slowly passed, everywhere Keith turned people were gearing up for the Christmas holidays. Twinkling lights and wreaths were starting to decorate store windows and homes. People all around him were making holiday plans with family and friends. The Christmas season was a difficult time for Keith to be alone. The one thing keeping him going was his hope that when Timothy returned they'd put together a spiritual band with a spiritual message. He hung on to that dream, waiting for the three weeks to pass.

Even beyond wanting to work with Timothy, Keith was on his own personal pilgrimage—watching, listening, hoping. He also was asking many questions. Was there really a way to tell right from wrong? How could he be sure he was going to spend his life doing what he was called to do? He felt as if he was just stumbling in the dark.

At the beginning of December, Keith talked three guys he knew into going to a Sunday morning Christian Science church service. Four nights later he went again. The services underscored what he'd surmised from his own studies—that there's no literal hell, and that only certain parts of the Bible are the inspired Word of God.

Afterward he and his friends somehow ended up at a Christian coffeehouse. The evening exploded into a heated debate.

December 10, 1970
12:45 A.M.

We went to a "Jesus Freak" coffeehouse and they tried the trip on me about believing the whole Bible, word for word, even the part that says God kills my brother and I just don't believe that. Not my wonderful Father! I'm still trusting my bro' Jesus Christ and Father God, who are one together, and one with me, and we're one with everyone. But it's easier to say that the universe and every thing in it is one! Peace through unity.

Keith was irritated when he was confronted with the Christian belief that, although God created us, a redemptive process was needed to enter into a relationship with the Creator. That thought was new to him. He didn't like it. Keith had been taught that if he could only have "perfect thoughts" he would experience God's perfection in body, mind, and spirit.

The other thing that really bothered him was the belief that the whole Bible was the inspired Word of God. Keith believed there were certain inspired parts of the Bible—but everyone knew it was written by men, and men make mistakes. Anyway, didn't the Bible say that God was a loving Father, full of mercy and peace? So how could a loving Father punish any of his children? These "Jesus Freaks," as Keith called them, had challenged his thinking but failed to convince him.

As Timothy's return grew closer, Keith's anticipation ran high.

December 25, 1970
Christmas day

> *I am at Tim's farm. Tim isn't here. He probably won't be here till late today.*
> *I also called home! They are trying very hard, but they still don't understand. Sometimes I don't understand it either! But my Father knows.*
> *Well, it's X-mas day and I feel like giving! I want to play! I am going to crash! Brother Tim; there is a reason! Good night all.*
> *X-mas comes and goes, but feelings last.*

Unfortunately when Tim finally did arrive, after all the waiting the much-hoped-for musical dream did not materialize.

By the end of the first week in January 1971, Keith knew his time in Washington was coming to a close. He made some New Year's resolutions in his journal:

I've decided to put down dope. All phases of it. Grass, psychics, whatever. I'm holding my sex in check, too. I'm really growing but words are useless. I have to prove it with actions.

He returned home January 9 because he missed Todd, and the "settled, stable feeling of home."

Throughout the spring and summer of that year, Keith aggressively pursued a new dream—a record deal. He hung out with Todd, and they became inseparable as they focused on their dream of putting a band together to play music that would lead people to higher levels in their spiritual search.

They wrote songs about all their beliefs, and with guitars in hand sang everywhere to anyone who would listen. They didn't expect, however, to have a chance to sing for their all-time favorite female singer/songwriter—who was also one of the most popular and talented women in music at the time.

On the first day of May, Keith wrote, "Drum roll . . . we played for Joni Mitchell." Joni, a top-selling recording artist, was one of Keith's musical idols. She lived in a rustic area of the Hollywood Hills, and Keith had taken the trouble to find out exactly which house was hers. On this day, Keith and Todd hitchhiked to Jay Leon's house and on the way noticed Joni's gate was open. They got Jay and his guitar and the three of them walked back to Joni's.

Keith, of course, had the nerve to knock on her door. There was no answer, so they decided to serenade her house with a song they'd just written. They put their whole heart into it. As they sang the last note, the door opened and there stood Joni Mitchell. To their amazement, she invited them inside.

Keith made himself right at home. He sat at Joni's piano and sang her all the songs he was writing for his album. He even asked her to write the liner notes, and Todd and Jay nearly died of embarrassment. Keith also wrote, "She gave us organic apple juice. It was all such a beautiful dream . . . I wish it never ended. I left a piece of my soul with her."

Probably one of the most surprising things about the afternoon was that, although Joni was at the peak of success, she had some unanswered spiritual questions too. On one hand, Keith already believed the truth was something much deeper than position or possessions. But he also was disappointed. He had such an immense level of love and respect for Joni he figured if she didn't have the answers, who did? He later wrote:

> She seems troubled with an inner conflict. I love her. God help her and us all. You are our only salvation. I feel so discontented today. I feel unfulfilled. Searching for something to quench my thirst for fulfillment.

In September 1971, the long-sought recording contract finally became a reality. Keith's first album, with Amos Records, would be called *Revelations*. The bulk of the songs centered on his philosophy of peace and hope through the unity of mankind. But even the excitement of an album deal didn't dull the empty ache in Keith's heart.

February 21, 1972

> I have been so confused and off the path. Smoking really kills the pain of being lost. Tests, trials, and tribulations.

When Timothy came down from Seattle to play on the album, it seemed like the dream of a brotherhood band was about to happen. And then, just like Keith's hope of becoming a preteen idol, this dream came crashing in, too.

June 1, 1972

> Lately I've been struggling, purging the blackness from my being. I am spinning around dizzily, and in the process being a very messed person to be around. My brethren are

being very compassionate, which I cannot express enough or any gratitude for. It seems dumb but I am so very withdrawn lately. I am rejecting all and everyone.

God (I cry to God whom I don't know practically anything about—blind faith) help!! Thank you, Lord, your humble son and slave and curious seeker.

There's this force inside me that is so selfish it makes me cringe. It wants all the ladies. And forget all else. It wants all good things and forget everyone else. I see this force and don't want to be near anyone—write any music or be nice—because I am afraid the force will show itself.

I don't care about loneliness anymore. I want to be good. To Shine. I've never prayed with such conviction. Beyond all else, God whatever you are, help us to unite in harmony, without greed and selfishness.

On the same day, Timothy wrote a guest entry in Keith's journal:

[Keith] seems to be dwelling so intensely on all the confusion . . . and personal grief . . . he seems to have too much going on inside to realize why I came here. I pray for what is right. Why are we here? Why are we all here?

Shortly, their dream of working together came to an end. When Keith realized the vision was dead, he laid it to rest, this time with a tinge of sadness, knowing it would never be.

Though the musical family with Timothy did not happen, Keith and Todd continued to hold on a little longer to their dreams. They quit playing for "drunken dances" because no one was paying attention to the message of the music. And they continued their search for a meaningful relationship with God. They were both accepted into the Rosicrucian Order—a mystical occult group espousing ideas like astral projection. After doing some of the studies, they couldn't agree with all of the teachings and dropped out of the order. Keith scratched one more thing off his list of possibilities.

That same summer of 1972, Keith heard about an event in Colorado called the World Family Gathering that was supposed to usher in the New Age. In July, he drove all the way to Rocky Mountain National Park hoping that in such a beautiful setting, with thousands of other seekers, he'd find the answers he was looking for. But there was no sense of family at this "family gathering." Instead people were rowdy, getting high on everything imaginable, and often out of control and violating each other's rights. It ended up being a rather mindless, prolonged party—not the spiritual event Keith had hoped for.

When Keith returned to California, he had one more thing to

Keith in coffeehouse concert

scratch off his list. In fact, it seemed as if he'd been scratching a lot of things off his "list of potential truths" lately. Over the past several months he'd been on a reading marathon examining the works of Hesse, Jung, Heinlein, Castaneda, Gibran, Baba Ram Dass—and the Bible. Keith was finding interesting food for thought, but nothing was totally satisfying. He'd had his tarot cards read, his astrology chart done, and even gone to a lecture on the mystery of the pyramids. The World Family Gathering was a bust, Joni Mitchell didn't have all the answers, the *Revelations* album was not taking off, the musical dream with Timothy died, and he'd burned all his Rosicrucian Order notes to "symbolically and physically cast off the chains of wrong belief."

Even Keith's old friend Cougar ended up letting him down. It was Cougar who first inspired Keith with his brotherhood philosophy, but now Cougar was totally devoid of all brotherhood beliefs. Not only that, he'd become part of "the establishment." Keith wrote, "Cougar got frustrated with me and lost faith in brotherhood, and started acting like a 9:00 to 5:00 freak." Keith couldn't get over the fact that his teacher had sold out to materialism and no longer believed in any of the things he once preached with such passion. Keith felt ripped off. Not only that, but if Cougar had given up, maybe the truth was impossible to find. Maybe there was nothing beyond this life.

Then a startling event shook Keith at a deep level. Keith's nineteenth birthday was near the end of October, and he planned a special way to celebrate the end of a season in his life. He planned to take one final mescaline trip with a close friend named Bill, a record company executive in his late thirties or early forties. Keith, who had been trying to quit drugs, felt this trip would be his very last.

On the evening of October 21, Keith drove to Bill's house in the Hollywood Hills to kick off his "farewell to drugs" trip. Psychedelic drugs are portioned out in small amounts called "hits" or "tabs," and usually taking between a quarter of a tab and a whole tab is plenty to get you where you want to go. But on this night, perhaps because Keith wanted to go out with a bang, he dropped three hits.

He was in for one of the most terrifying experiences of his whole life. When they were in the heaviest part of their trip, Bill started playing with Keith's mind. One of the frightening things about taking psychedelic drugs is that most of the time it's impossible to tell the difference between fantasy and reality. You see and hear things that are not really there, and actual reality is either obscured or terribly distorted. The worst thing that can happen is to have someone you really trust mess with your mind when you're in that vulnerable and confusing state.

As Keith and his friend sat in their car on a high cliff overlooking the Pacific Ocean, Bill told him he'd made an appointment that night to meet with people from another planet. It sounded crazy, but after three hits of mescaline anything could be true. It was a dark night and the moon looked pure white.

"Come off it," Keith said. "You're not serious."

"I am. I've made contact and they should be here soon."

"Come on, don't mess with me."

"It's true. They're meeting us in a few minutes. And they want to take you back with them in their spacecraft."

They talked back and forth like that for quite some time, and Keith started to panic. What if it were true? He'd read stories about people who'd met aliens. His heart was pounding so hard it felt as if it might burst from his chest. The negative energy was real and very frightening. Dark forces were reaching for him. Occult powers seemed to be pushing him close to the edge of a black and empty place. He fought with all his might to keep from falling in.

When the trip was over, Keith did some heavy soul searching. He had a very strong sense that all of the Eastern, mystical, occult paths he'd been walking might actually be leading him in the wrong direction. The spiritual darkness he'd felt that night was an unfriendly presence that he never wanted to experience again. But even as he cut all these things loose, he still had no certainty of where to turn. A few days later he wrote:

October 28, 1972

> *Towers of happiness built on the sand of confusion usually tumble down. I'm digging deep, I'm digging deep, gotta find that solid rock foundation. I'm digging deep, I'm washing with water and cleansing in soil. When I reach a solid self, if there is [one], then I'll build a cabin of home in my heart. And maybe share it with another solid soul.*

As the end of 1972 drew near, Keith had scratched so many things off his spiritual search list he barely had one left. He had narrowed things down quite a bit, and spent a lot of time reading "them two books—the *Bible* and *Science and Health*." For a few weeks he thought he'd get totally into Christian Science. He went to the local reading room and had a deep conversation with his grandfather. Just when he thought he'd take the plunge, he suddenly changed his mind. He wrote, "I dig the teachings, but the organized machine scares me."

Even though Keith was turned off by the idea of an organized group, there did seem to be one common thread running through all the teachings Keith had studied. That thread was the person of Jesus Christ. Everybody seemed to say that, at the very least, Jesus was a "good guy." Some said he was the Son of God. Others said he was a rabbi or a prophet. Yet others said he was an ascended spiritual master—even Buddha thought Jesus was okay. Everyone said something different, but it was all positive. To top it off, Jesus even said good things about himself. He said he was the only way to God.

Keith had been running scared since the mescaline trip he took on his birthday. He doubted everybody and everything. But Jesus seemed like a safe bet. So Keith decided to deal with Jesus directly, not through any man, and not through any organization. He wouldn't even call himself a Christian because he didn't want to be one. He thought they were rejects. Losers. Besides, Christians were so straight it seemed that in order to be one you needed to have a barber in the family and sleep in a suit and tie. Keith was not ready for that, but he was ready to deal with Jesus one-on-one. And that's exactly what he did.

Keith opened his heart to Jesus without really knowing who he was or what it might lead to. Keith only knew he had a deep need and prayed a simple prayer.

December 16, 1972

> *Jesus, you are hereby officially welcomed into me. Now only action will reveal your effect on me.*

Keith had taken a step toward Jesus in a small but definite way. The next day he had a long talk with Todd. Keith wrote, "Todd and I reached an agreement finally today. Christ is the common denominator to all our trips so far." Keith closed out the year with a hopeful heart, feeling he'd stepped onto the right path. But he was still uncertain about where it might lead. On New Year's Eve he wrote:

Gotta Find a Home

> *My roots dangle. Unnourished, I refuse to root here! Gotta find a home and get it settled and peaceful. Gotta find a place inside where I can rest between crises. . . .*
>
> *Please, Jesus! I know you more each day and recognize the signs you show me. The immaculate birth makes you special above all men and strengthens all the links to the Christian trip—keep the signs coming. I'd almost given myself up for lost. Bless you. Beloved clean brother on highest.*

Keith was doing all he knew how to do in trying to get closer to God. He would often fast for one or two days a week—and he was trying to make sure he prayed every day. Still, he was groping. "God is a concept. . . . Everything is getting numb. I am so numb. I need to feel again. I am almost dead." Keith was working on a song called "Manchilde." The second verse was for Timothy:

> Oh, I am a Manchilde
> Lost between the tame and wild
> I'm tired though the journey's just beginning
> A road I traveled led to you
> And we've been through a lot it's true
> For being such close friends it wasn't all that smooth
> I just wanna thank you because you're you
> And there's nothing I wouldn't do for you
> If I could only stop thinking of me. . . .

A short time later, perhaps to show God that he really meant business, Keith decided he wanted to start wearing a cross. He wrote,

"Gotta find a cross to wear. I've already got one to bear." One afternoon he went into a little secondhand shop, and he saw something that caught his eye. The man behind the counter lifted a small cross out of the glass case and handed it to Keith. He held it in the palm of his hand. It wasn't much bigger than a dime and it looked really old.

"Man, this thing looks ancient," Keith said.

"It's over 150 years old," said the shopkeeper.

"Are you kidding me?"

"No. It was worn by a monk in an Ecuadoran monastery."

Keith turned it slowly over in his hand. The man said it was silver, but it looked more like old brass. It obviously was handmade—uneven and rough around the edges. Keith could barely see a faint raised outline of Jesus lying on this beautiful old cross. The shopkeeper explained that was because the monk had rubbed it and rubbed it every time he prayed. It was almost rubbed flat on the front. The cross had a certain mystique to it, a sense of spiritual history. Obviously, somebody who really loved Jesus had worn it. Maybe, Keith hoped, that same intensity of devotion might rub off on him.

"How much is it?"

"Ten dollars."

Keith had fourteen dollars of poker winnings in his pocket from the night before. It was just enough to buy the cross and have a few dollars left over. He paid the man and left the store with a determination to make an even deeper commitment. It seemed as if everybody had someone they were following, a guru or a spiritual teacher of some kind. Keith decided that he would be comfortable making Jesus his spiritual master.

Keith got into his car, slipped the cross around his neck, and started driving. As he drove he found himself praying to a God he didn't know. It wasn't a tidy little religious prayer. Like the cross it was rough and uneven—a prayer of desperation. Keith knew he'd reached the bottom of his list. Everything was scratched off but Jesus. If Jesus didn't come through, he didn't know what he'd do.

But before he could get any words out, gathering tears started spilling down his cheeks and running into his beard. His chest started heaving with deep, uncontrollable sobs. He drove through the blinding tears as an overwhelming urgency filled his heart.

In between broken sobs, he choked out a prayer: "Oh Jesus, Jesus . . . if you're really real . . . if you are who you say you are, please prove it to me. I need you. I need something. . . . Show me the way. Prove that you're real, and I'll serve you forever . . ."

I popped my head out of the kitchen to see if Keith and Todd were winding up their extended spiritual rap yet. It had gone on all evening—through supper, a card game, and now the dishes were done too.

I slipped off to go to bed, figuring they'd be up half the night talking. It seemed to me there was lots of spiritual talk these days, but few real, lasting changes.

Just as I was drifting off to sleep, an old feeling overtook me in a wave. A sense of hopelessness. Of going nowhere. Or was this feeling something else? Was some kind of new dawn experience heading Keith's way after all? Maybe everything in his life before now—the fall of 1974—was only a prelude.

Keith was always so far ahead of me. Would I be ready when it came?

Keith and Todd
playing guitar

3

"YOU'RE ON MY LIST OF THINGS TO DO"

Four days before Christmas in 1974, we had a big going-away party at the Bla Bla Cafe. We were going to Canada for several weeks where Keith would play piano in a band, and we didn't know when we'd return to the Bla. It was a great night. Besides the fact that so many of our friends were there, two industry people came and gave Keith a lot of encouragement. One was Marv Mattis, who had signed Keith to CBS and saw a lot of depth in Keith's new songs. He told him, "Keep writing from that place." The other guy, from Helen Reddy's management team, came to see Keith for the second time and expressed an interest in developing his career. Keith came away from that night excited about what might happen next. This would be our first Christmas in the little house we'd recently rented in the suburbs of Woodland Hills.

Our last house was a few miles away in Northridge, but it actually exploded! Lucky for us we were out that afternoon. As we came home, the moment we turned onto our street we saw emergency vehicles and downed tree branches everywhere. We looked at each other with wide eyes.

"Wow, Mel, something bad happened here," Keith said.

I nodded in agreement. As we drove closer, we realized it was *our* windows being hammered shut with boards. I got the weirdest knot in my stomach and couldn't move. But Keith jumped out of the van without even parking it and ran over to see what happened—and to check on our pets.

Our poor dog, Libre, was cowering in a corner of our neighbor's yard. Her fur was singed, and she smelled like smoke. Our neighbor said he caught her as she ran down the street terrified and rubbed her down with wet towels. We found our cat, Cal, alive and hiding in a closet, and our raccoon, Rocky, was okay too.

There had been a gas leak that collided with the flame from our water heater. The fireman said Rocky was the likely culprit. A small gas valve was in the kitchen in a very tight spot. Rocky was the only one small enough to have squeezed near it, yet heavy enough to budge it. Now we were really sorry we had Rocky. We'd had fun walking her down our street on a dog leash, enjoying the stares of disbelief. But Rocky wasn't a pet you could cuddle with. Anyway we got her by default. Keith originally bought a ferret but didn't even name her because she was no fun at all. But the pet store wouldn't give us our money back. We could only do an exchange. So we got a raccoon, and now Rocky had blown up our house.

That evening we talked about our good luck: the explosion didn't happen when we were home, which I was especially glad of because I was always in the kitchen. But I wondered, *Was it really luck, or some kind of divine protection?*

The next morning we got up early and immediately drove back to the pet store. We bounded in, Keith plopped Rocky down on the counter, cage and all, and then we promptly walked out. We didn't even bother to ask for a refund . . . or an exchange. Keith was a lover of all things breathing, but maybe he'd need to be content with just Cal and Libre. I wondered, *was contentment in the things that really mattered to us even possible?*

We moved into Keith's old bedroom at his parents' house while searching for a new place to live. We were grateful, but it was very difficult to live there. The arguing and lack of peace between his parents was easier for both of us to see this time, in spite of their strong Christian Science beliefs. Would we ever find what we were looking for? Maybe the new home we rented in Woodland Hills would make a difference. Perhaps a change of outside surroundings would bring a change on our insides. At any rate, we were ready for something new and hoped life on Dolorosa Street would be a little less eventful.

Our first anniversary was coming in a few days on Christmas Day—and I wanted to do something special for Keith. I wondered what would make him the happiest and decided to buy him a Bible. When I first met Keith in early 1973, he was just beginning to pray to this man Jesus. He had told me, "Jesus is my master." He was wearing the antique Ecuadoran cross around his neck. It wasn't exactly a bold statement of faith—more like holding up a candle of hope against the darkness. Since Christmas was supposed to be Jesus' birthday, and since all Keith talked about, apart from music, was trying to decide who Jesus was, a Bible seemed like the perfect surprise.

The only Bible I'd ever owned was a Gideon Bible I stole from a hotel room once. I'd never bought one. I wasn't sure where to start. Then I remembered there was a Berean bookstore right next to a vegetarian restaurant Keith and I liked. I made up some excuse to get out of the house and drove there.

As soon as I walked into the bookstore, I felt a twinge of awkwardness. It was really quiet—not at all like the hippie bookstores I was used to. I wondered if I needed to whisper. Then I saw a man behind the counter and thought I'd ask him to show me where the Bibles were. He had very short black hair, perfectly combed, and he was wearing a navy blue suit. I had on my 1940s burgundy velvet thrift store coat and my beat-up leather boots. I didn't know if anyone like me had ever even been in this store before. But the man had kind brown eyes, and I relaxed a little.

"May I help you with something?"

"Uh, yes, I want to buy a Bible," I said.

"What kind of Bible are you interested in?"

"Oh . . ." I started feeling dumb. "Well, what kinds are there?"

He led me to the shelf and I couldn't believe my eyes. There were so many different kinds of Bibles! He started pulling them down one by one and showing them to me. There were several different translations.

Some used common everyday language and others were filled with *thee*'s and *thou*'s. Then there were different grades of covers ranging from genuine leather to paperback, and different grades of paper too. Some had large print, others small. Some even had all the words of Jesus printed in red. As we went through the Bibles, the stack of possibles in my arms grew.

"This one has study notes," he was saying, "and this one has a concordance."

"What's a concordance?"

"You can find a Scripture you want by looking up a single word in it. And this one has colored maps of Paul's missionary journeys."

I didn't know who Paul was, but rather than admit it, I just nodded and said brightly, "Great!" I was beginning to worry about how much one of these Bibles was going to cost.

"Can you tell me the prices of some of these?"

With the clerk's patient help, I finally picked out a small King James red-letter edition with a genuine chocolate-brown leather cover that was waxed to a shine. It had a concordance and maps, and the pages were edged with shiny gold that looked beautiful when it was closed. It was, indeed, a very holy-looking book.

I took it home, where I got out my pen and india ink and inscribed the "presented to" page with: "Keith, my beloved husband, in celebration of the Birth of Christ and our first year of Marriage. With much love, May God always Bless you." Then I wrapped the box and hid it.

On Christmas Eve, I excitedly waited for the right moment to give Keith his Bible. But first we needed to do some more packing for our trip to Canada the next night. Within minutes the peaceful atmosphere changed, and we were having one of our all-too-familiar disagreements. This time it was a "packing fight."

Keith said something I didn't like, and I shot something back. We were both being unreasonable, and we both reacted. Keith picked up one of the shirts I was packing for him and threw it at me. I saw red. I got so angry I grabbed a pair of scissors and threw them all the way across the room. Now we were on a roll. I was even more upset because I'd wanted to bless Keith with the Bible and now the whole evening was being ruined.

We kept arguing and said some really mean things. I got so angry that, without thinking, I pulled off my wedding ring and threw it straight at Keith. Hard. As soon as it hit him, I realized what I'd done. Keith just stared. I felt terrible. Some way to celebrate our first anniversary.

Afterward we were both really sorry—and embarrassed—for everything we'd said and done.

Late that evening I brought out the small, carefully wrapped gift box I'd been hiding and handed it to Keith expectantly. He was sitting on the rug by the antique pine cabinet we'd just nabbed at a garage sale. He unwrapped the box, opened the Bible, and read the inscription. His eyes were shining with happiness. Before we went to bed, we sat there together on the floor because Keith, of course, wanted to read out loud to me from the new Bible. We wished we could somehow learn to practice what that little book preached.

At bedtime Keith made a simple note in his journal:

December 24, 1974

We had the largest fight in months. . . . After the storm died Mel gave me a new beautiful Bible.

That night I wrote in my diary too:

God bless us and keep us growing together, towards you Lord. I am so grateful for my Keith—he is a blessing. I am eternally grateful for You sending him to me.

As we prepared to meet 1975, I found myself wondering why two people who loved each other and wanted to live good lives just couldn't seem to do it. We were more settled down than we'd ever been, but there was a feeling of restlessness we couldn't shake. It just hung in the air.

One day Keith got a wistful look in his eyes while telling me again about one of the times he ran away from home and hitchhiked up to Seattle.

"I wish you would have been with me then . . ." Keith said. "We would have had so much fun together on the road."

Then his eyes lit up, and within an hour Keith had convinced me we should take a road trip together. We did have some free time on our hands. So we grabbed a few things, locked the house, walked to the nearest freeway on-ramp with Libre, and stuck out our thumbs. Soon we were on our way. Even with a big dog, we had no trouble getting rides. All we knew was we were heading north.

We made it all the way up to Carmel staying along the way with people we met on the road. We had endless talks with everyone we met about the spiritual journey we were on. But no one had any answers that rang true to us. Most of them were trying things we'd already left behind. At the time we were kind of slaphappy because we had actually run away from home. We'd had a great time and gathered lots of fun road stories to tell our friends, but nothing had really changed. Our questions had not been answered. We were gone several days but came back none the wiser, and our problems were not solved.

Within a few days after returning, everything was back to normal on Dolorosa Street. We were busy but bored, tired but still restless. Libre was the most contented member of our family. She simply fell asleep every time Keith and I had an argument.

Sometimes I got so upset with Keith. He sparked those feelings in a lot of people. You either loved him or got mad at him. Sometimes both. There weren't many "grays" in Keith's world. There was black or white, good or bad. My approach was much more to go with the flow. In many ways Keith was exactly what I needed. But I also was finding that some of the things I really liked about him—especially his intensity—could be difficult to live with. Like right after he'd first moved in with me. When Keith moved into my apartment, I began to lose some of my things as he started moving some of my stuff out.

Because he'd made Jesus his master, some of the books on my shelf made him really uneasy. Especially the ones having to do with astrology and the occult. He wanted me to get rid of them, and I wasn't exactly happy or willing. Some of them were very expensive hardcover books. I thought Keith had a lot of nerve moving into my apartment, and then insisting that I throw away my books. Even though I hadn't found the answers I had been looking for after all my years of reading these books, I wasn't convinced they were totally wrong either. But Keith was so persistent that I reluctantly gave in. Deep in my heart I knew he meant it for my good.

It seemed as if Keith was always challenging me about something. Mostly he challenged me to know who I was.

Even though Keith could drive me to the brink, there was something about being with him that made me face tough questions and comb back through my life to figure out what I believed and why. He seemed to have a compass, but I was more unsure of my direction. At the time I met Keith, even though I was twenty-six years old, I really wasn't sure who I was. Unlike Keith's close-knit family that always pulled together to help him build a career, whenever I thought of my family I was left with kind of a hollow feeling. It was Keith's influence on me—after a difficult and painful past—that was pushing me further away from the dangerous places where I'd been wandering.

I was born in a place many people would die to live—Hollywood, California. Actually, I lived just off the boardwalk at Venice Beach, but the hospital I was born in was in Hollywood, and it was a nice name to drop when anyone asked where I was born.

Cedars of Lebanon Hospital on Fountain Avenue was past capacity with women in labor the morning I was born. The post–World War II baby boom was in its early stages and hospital beds were scarce everywhere. My mom landed on a hallway cot along with many other women having babies. So in that hectic hallway she labored alone, without a nurse or even my dad by her side.

"I fought my own battle that night," my mom said. "I prayed nonstop that I would survive and you'd be born healthy and safe." Near dawn that August 25 I made my quiet entrance into the world. I guess God must have heard my mother's prayers. But had he ever heard mine?

As a young woman, I wondered what was to come of all of us baby boomers. Were we a gift of peace to a war-torn world, or would my generation one day have to fight even bigger battles of our own? At least I was given a harmonious name, inspired by a character in the movie *Gone with the Wind.* But more importantly, I was named through the Jewish tradition of giving your children the first name, or first initial, of a loved one who had passed away. In my case my mom honored her father by starting my name with an *M*—for my grandfather Mautle Sosnovsky.

Sometimes I felt marked by strange and symbolic signposts during my life. Maybe I read too much into simple coincidences, but I left no stone unturned to find a spiritual identity. Since our family was poor, how was it I was born at such a highly acclaimed hospital—and the only Jewish hospital in California? It was named after the famous cedar trees that grew in Lebanon. The wood was so highly valued for its aroma and strength, it was used to build the Jewish temple in Jerusalem. Cedar also prevented decay and symbolized eternity and was used to preserve Egyptian mummies. Jewish priests used its bark to treat lepers. It was even used during the ceremony of circumcision—and it doesn't get more personal than that! But I felt no personal oneness with this ancient God.

My life seemed like a puzzle without all the pieces. Maybe some of these things were mystical signs pointing me in the right direction. Was there an eternal truth somewhere? Even my mother's life held some mysteries to unravel.

While I was an only child, my mother was one of seven children. Her parents were Jewish immigrants from the Ukraine area of Russia. They lived in the bustling "Jewish City" of Odessa where the Czarist persecution was beginning to intensify. Even so, it was hard for people there to believe the terrors that were rumored about in the marketplace and quietly spoken of at night within the safety of four walls. But somehow my grandparents must have received answers to their questioning prayers and heard their God correctly. They made brave plans to escape by ship and sail across the waters to America, leaving behind all their possessions and loved ones who couldn't or wouldn't join them.

On the train ride to the port city, my whole family had to lie between the seats on the floor, covered with pillows to protect them from the bullets being shot through the windows. Shattered glass fell on their backs as bullets whizzed overhead, but they made it to the port safely. There they boarded the very last ship to leave with fleeing Jews before the worst of the coming devastation.

My mom was the first Sosnovsky child born in America. Her legal given name, Udil, was Yiddish, but her called name was Helen. In Greek the meaning was "reed" or "basket." Perhaps she was called Helen to honor God for their safe escape from Odessa—in memory of the baby Moses who escaped slavery and death by being placed on the waters in his own tiny ship, a basket made of reeds that floated him across the waters to safety. I'll never know for sure, but I like to think that's the way it happened.

My mom and her little sister, my aunt Minnie, were both born in San Francisco where the family settled. My grandfather Mautel opened a kosher poultry store and taught Hebrew at their synagogue. In Odessa he had been a rabbi, just like his father before him. My grandmother Brona also came from a religious family. Her father had been a Grand Rabbi in Russia, one who was an overseer of many other rabbis. She was also very devoted to God. That, and the fact that she was very beautiful and generous, won Mautel's heart. My mom told me even with seven children to feed, she always had extra for any hungry stranger who came to their door looking for a meal.

When my mom was about seven, her family moved south to an area in East Los Angeles called Boyle Heights, which was its own little melting pot of colors and cultures. Asians, Mexicans, and Eastern

European Jews all lived side-by-side peacefully. My mom had lots of friends but lived a very sheltered life. Since she was raised in a strictly kosher home, she had never eaten in a restaurant until she graduated high school, got a job, and moved in with one of her older sisters. Grandma and Grandpa Sosnovsky died before I was born, and I always felt a sadness that I never got to meet them and learn from their rich heritage. As a young girl I would go to temple with my mother. This was usually on Yom Kippur, the Day of Atonement—the highest of all Jewish holidays. Each year my mom would fast for twenty-four hours so God would cleanse her from the sins of the past year. When I got older, I fasted with her. As was customary we walked to the synagogue, even though we lived a few miles away.

I remember sitting on the wooden pews for hours. The room was mostly filled with elderly people. Even the rabbi, with his long gray beard, seemed very old and extremely holy. I loved it when the rabbi sang in Hebrew and blew the ram's horn, the shofar. But my favorite part was when the Torah, the scrolls of God's Word, was taken from its case. The Torah was wrapped in fine velvet that was covered with beautiful intricate embroidery—the Star of David, golden fringed cords, and brilliant scattered sparkles that made it look like a king's royal treasure.

At one point the Torah would be carried down the aisle, and when it passed by me, I'd catch myself holding my breath. Then I'd breathe in deeply, hoping to absorb the very presence of God into my soul. It was the closest I ever felt to God, and I longed to touch it, to be even closer. Of course I knew someone like me could only look. I didn't understand much of what was going on, but I did feel a powerful sense of awe and wonder about being in the house of God. It was always very special to me. Even when I grew up and moved away from home, my mom's devotion left a mark on me. I always tried to fast on Yom Kippur. My mother had been the most spiritually devoted of all her brothers and sisters. With her strong convictions, I often wondered why she consented to marry my father because it was forbidden to wed a man who wasn't Jewish.

My dad, Charles Steiner, was of German descent and his parents were devout Methodists. His father was a doctor and his mother visited the sick and needy in their church. Even so, my father never went to church.

What I do remember about my dad was seeing him sit at his workbench in our tiny living room, winding pure silk thread around the bamboo fishing rods he made by hand. He also tied beautiful fishing flies. I would quietly walk up and look at all the brightly colored feathers, spools of silk, sinkers, and barbed hooks. One look from my dad kept me from touching anything, but I loved to watch. My dad loved working with his hands, even if he had a hard time making a go of it financially.

Because money was tight, we lived in a tiny one-bedroom apartment on Brooks Avenue and Speedway, which was a narrow alley that ran parallel to the beach some one hundred feet behind the buildings sitting on the boardwalk. With no front yard but this little alley, the long stretch of sand between the boardwalk and the ocean was my only place to play. Maybe that's why I loved going to visit my grandmother. She lived alone in a little house in Redondo Beach—but she had a yard, with a flower garden and a large fig tree. I guess it made such an impression on me because my world was one of cement sidewalks and alleyways. I grew up with dreams of living in a nicer house, in a nicer place.

My parents managed to save up a little nest egg while my dad was in the navy. When he got home, my mom wanted to use the money for a down payment on a house. But Dad wanted to start a business. While they were deciding, we went to look at a small duplex. I was so excited, especially because the duplex was carpeted! Hungry for the stability it represented, I wanted to move there more than anything. Dad won out, however, and the savings was used to open a small bait and tackle shop. I can still remember the stinging disappointment I felt when I heard we weren't moving.

When I was three, my mom had a miscarriage. A short time later she started having severe pains in her side. I had been sleeping in a crib in my parents' room, and I remember seeing my mom lying in bed, crying in pain. One day the doctor told my father, "If you want your wife to live, get her to the hospital immediately!" Mom wouldn't go because we had no money and no insurance. Dad said he wouldn't force her to go. But my grandmother was there and firmly told the doctor, "Call the ambulance—now!" My mom got to the county hospital and into surgery just in time. Her life was spared, but she could not have any more children.

My grandmother ended up in a nursing home because she started getting very frail and confused. She rode a bus to see us a few times, but kept getting lost and they stopped letting her come. I only saw her once after that. She just quietly disappeared from my life.

Dad, it turned out, was not really a very good businessman. At his shop he gave away as much as he sold, and money problems got worse. It resulted in some loud "discussions" between him and my mom and even more strain when the business folded. Mom wanted nothing more than to stay home and raise me in a loving environment, but after I started school she reluctantly took a secretarial job to pay the bills.

When I was six, I would go off to kindergarten wearing the key to our front door on a string around my neck so I could let myself in after school. That same year we moved one block farther east on Brooks Avenue. It wasn't the house of my dreams, but it was a nicer and larger upstairs duplex. Two great things happened then. I got a bedroom to myelf with a brand-new "grown up" bed, and I met Mrs. Hilliard.

Mrs. Hilliard lived two houses down, and it was like having my very own grandmother right next door. Mrs. Hilliard had one of the only front yards on the block. It was very small, but filled with flowers. My favorites were the red and yellow snapdragons. I spent hours at her house, and I was especially interested in Mrs. Hilliard's birds—several beautiful blue-and-white parakeets and a yellow canary. My mom wasn't big on pets, but she let Mrs. Hilliard give me a parakeet that I trained to sit on my finger.

Mostly I loved just being with Mrs. Hilliard inside her house. Everything was tidy and spotless; even the knickknacks always stayed in the same place. She had pretty carpets, and her dining room chairs had upholstered seats. But I never sat on those chairs because we spent all our time together in her kitchen. After school I'd rush over and sit on a tall stool and watch her cook dinner. I'd make up songs and sing them to her. We talked a lot and I knew that she loved me. I really loved her too. That's why I couldn't understand why she did what she did.

One day when I knocked on her door, it took her longer than usual to answer. I fidgeted with the buckle of my sandal while I waited. When she didn't come, I figured she was at the store or something and skipped back home.

But the next day, the same thing happened. Mrs. Hilliard didn't answer my knock. For days, in fact, I felt an unexplained sadness every time I looked at her silent house.

Finally I asked my mom if she knew where Mrs. Hilliard was. She hesitated. "Mrs. Hilliard moved away, honey. She won't be coming back."

I noticed that Mom wouldn't look at me, and I stood there, confused. Mrs. Hilliard was my friend. She wouldn't just leave without saying good-bye.

Tears came to my eyes, and a crushing pain filled my chest. Why didn't she tell me? I thought she loved me, but maybe I was wrong. Maybe I wasn't as important to her as I thought. Mrs. Hilliard never answered her door again.

Years later I found out that Mrs. Hilliard had actually died, but my parents had wanted to spare me the pain of knowing the truth. Of course they meant well, but knowing what really happened would have explained her leaving me so suddenly. Then maybe I wouldn't have been left with such a lingering sense of loss and abandonment.

Even that young, I started to hunger for something I couldn't define.

There was a little Jewish Center right next door to us. I played handball on their wall almost every day after dinner until it got dark outside. But one day when I was about seven years old, I had a desire to go inside, and I asked my mom to sign me up for their Sabbath school. The classroom space was long and narrow and a little dim. It had concrete walls and very high ceilings. But my heart was comfortable there. I felt happy because I knew I was doing something to get closer to God. They taught us out of the same book I'd seen in the Synagogue on the High Holidays, the Old Testament. I learned about baby Moses and how God performed a miracle through him when he grew up and parted the Red Sea. We drew pictures of Noah's Ark and the rainbow promise and taped them onto the wall. Although I didn't go to the school for very long, I really enjoyed it. I always had a warm feeling when we talked about God, but he was still somehow just out of reach. I don't remember why I stopped going.

Next I set my sights on the church across the street from us—the Twenty-First Church of Christian Science. I found myself wondering what kind of things they believed in there. From my second-story window I had watched everyone come and go from the church. The crowds were extra big on holidays like Christmas, and everyone got really dressed up on Easter. The little girls wore frilly, pastel-colored dresses and white, patent-leather shoes with matching pocketbooks. It seemed as if those little girls were always holding hands with two happy parents, and everyone was smiling and laughing.

To me Easter was the Easter Bunny, colored-egg hunts, yellow marshmallow chickens, and chocolate rabbits. Why people wanted to go to church on Easter was a mystery to me.

One Saturday my curiosity got the best of me. I announced to my parents that I'd be getting up the next morning and going to church. All by myself I got dressed and bravely walked across the street. I went alone since my mom was Jewish and, I guess, my dad wasn't interested. The church had really high ceilings and it wasn't very crowded. I sat toward the back and just listened. Someone was up front talking for a while and then some people in the congregation stood up and talked a little. Their words seemed as empty as the building itself. At the end of the service, I walked slowly back across the street disappointed. I was hoping to feel different. Instead I didn't feel anything.

Meanwhile one of the biggest questions at school seemed to be

"What are you?" Everyone had an answer: "I'm Catholic," "I'm Jewish," or "I'm Baptist." Everyone, that is, but me. At first it was fun to be two things. I'd say, "I'm Jewish and Protestant. I'm both!" But after a while it seemed like being two things was the same as being nothing. I wanted to be something, so I made a choice. I decided to be Jewish. My mom had told me that by Jewish law, the children of a Jewish mother are always considered Jewish anyway. But this wasn't a legal issue for me. It was a choice of the heart. Still, I had no sense of having a real connection with God.

The upside was I could stay home on the Jewish holidays. The downside was when I got called names at school like "you dirty Jew" or "you kike." I also heard some jokes about Jewish people being cheap or just wanting to get rich. To mask my hurt, I'd just laugh along. But the biggest shock was being told that "the Jews killed Jesus!" I didn't know much about Jesus, or why we killed him, or even if we really did. It was confusing. And it all made me feel really ashamed and guilty, but I wasn't exactly sure why.

Even though I decided to be Jewish, we always celebrated Christmas at my house. We'd get a big tree, and I'd leave cookies and milk out for Santa Claus. One year was extra special to me because I'd saved up my money to buy my dad a really nice wallet for a present. The only problem was, someone else had the same idea.

There was a boy in the neighborhood whom my dad had taken under his wing. The very Christmas I bought my dad the expensive wallet, this boy gave him a wallet he'd made for my dad. I couldn't believe it. Then my father told me he didn't want to hurt this boy's feelings, so the boy's wallet went into Dad's pocket and mine went into his dresser drawer. He never used it.

My relationship with Dad continued to be strained—especially with this boy still in the picture. My dad was an avid fisherman, and for years I begged him to take me with him. His reply was always the same: "When you get older, Melody." But my dad never took me fishing when I got older. Instead, he started taking this boy, who was the same age I was.

For the next few years I was caught in a tension between two worlds. There was the shaky adult world at home, and my young-girl's world of singing and tap-dancing lessons. Those lessons were the brightest spot of my life. Every year I'd get a new pair of shiny black patent-leather shoes with big silver taps on the soles—all held together with a pretty black ribbon bow. Tap dancing was all about rhythm, timing, and coordination. I felt as if I could fly while "playing drums" with my feet. My class would learn songs, skits, and dance routines and then we'd go out to put on shows for war veterans and other lonely people. I was often chosen by the teacher to do a "specialty number" during a performance, usually singing a song all by myself. Singing and dancing seemed as natural as breathing to me. I always felt like I was being "the me" I was created to be.

But one day something happened in class. I had gotten as thin as a rail after almost dying from pneumonia. So when the doctor told my mother to fatten me up, she took it seriously. Soon I'd gained a ravenous appetite, eating everything in sight—including triple-decker peanut butter and jelly sandwiches as bedtime snacks. The pounds had crept on without me noticing, and dancing became more and more difficult. I would find myself out of breath and sweating like crazy. One afternoon my teacher stopped the whole class, and looking at me sternly he said, "Melody, you're just getting too fat to dance!" Everyone stared at me silently . . . as streams of sweat ran down my face. I couldn't say anything, so I just acted like I needed to go to the bathroom, went to the lobby area, and cried.

That day my mom was surprised to find me waiting outside early. I gave her some lame excuse why, while in my heart I vowed I'd never go back. I never told my mom what happened, and I never did go back. The door to my young girl's world of singing and dancing had slammed shut in my face, but at the same time there was a whole new world opening up.

I put myself on a very strict diet and began liking my reflection in the mirror. I also started experimenting with my hair and makeup. As I got more and more interested in boys, I hoped I'd have better luck than my parents. My mom still worked hard at a full-time job, and my dad worked on and off. When my dad was home, he spent most of his time secluded in the basement. His craftsmanship now expanded to making rifles. He hand-carved the stock, tooled and blued the barrels, and engraved the metal part above the trigger. It seemed just as well that he spent so much time downstairs because whenever he was upstairs the arguments grew louder. I started shutting out that world. Once I felt so overwhelmed by their loud yelling that I got dizzy and fainted alone on the hard bathroom floor.

The year I turned twelve, my parents decided to get a divorce. However painful it was for them, for me it was a relief. I was glad it was over. My mother and I moved to a one-bedroom apartment in Santa Monica, where I started a new life at a new school with new friends I'd met at the bus stop. My new friends weren't as innocent as the ones I'd left behind in Venice—and I immediately decided to keep pace to fit in.

Almost overnight I was a different kid. I was already taller than my petite five-foot-one-inch mom, and I decided I was too big to give in to her tearful pleas. I wanted to do my own thing and so I did. Before my mom knew what hit her, I was smoking, drinking, and had a sixteen-year-old boyfriend with a car. Eddie was Bolivian and had beautiful olive skin and dark brown eyes. His family came to America when the Communists moved into the government where his father had been an official. I was in love, and at the age of twelve I started a steady relationship with Eddie that lasted four years before we broke up.

One experience with Eddie would later linger in my mind. It was a Sunday when we drove up the coast toward Malibu, and it started to rain really hard. So much for walking on the beach. Then Eddie noticed a church, and wanted us to go in together. It was pouring as we walked into a huge cathedral. I'd never been in a Catholic church before so I didn't know how to cross myself or when to kneel. The priest spoke in Latin during the Mass so I couldn't understand anything. But as I looked around at the high arched ceilings, the statues, the candles, and the big cross in front with Jesus hanging on it, I had an overwhelming sense that I was in the presence of God. The air was charged with a beautiful energy that settled over me. I'd never felt this way before, and I soaked up every minute like a dry sponge. I thought, *It must be wonderful to really know God.*

About a year after my parents' divorce, my dad had a stroke. He was only forty-nine. A World War II vet, he ended up in the Veterans Hospital in West Los Angeles, paralyzed on the left side. My mom and I went to visit him once a week. I don't know what was worse about that hospital—the awful green walls or the sickening unclean smell that hit you in the face as soon as you walked in. And there was my dad slumped slightly to one side in his wheelchair, his light brown hair turning gray, a two-day stubble of beard, and a bit of saliva trickling down the weak corner of his mouth. He could talk fairly well, but his words were slurred. We'd bring him spending money, a bag of assorted candy bars, and several packs of Chesterfield unfiltered cigarettes. With his good right hand he'd reach out and take the brown paper bag and set it on his lap.

We'd make small talk on those visits, but there really wasn't much to say. Dad would always pay a lot of attention to his paralyzed leg, adjusting his foot on the little wheelchair platform so it wouldn't drag on the floor. But mostly he would cry. The tears would well up in his eyes and he'd just hang his head over his chest and weep uncontrollably. When he could talk again, he'd beg my mom to take him home and take care of him even though they were divorced. Tears still streaming down his face, he'd say, "You can have my Social Security checks. Please take me home with you." But our dream of having a home together had been paralyzed years ago.

My years in high school were one big blur of parties and skipping school. My mother was less and less able to keep me in line. I totally resisted all of her "suggestions," which is what I considered her guidance to be. My mom eventually remarried and, after a while, stopped visiting my dad. From then on I went to see him alone or with a boyfriend.

When I graduated from high school in 1964, I got an office job and moved into my own apartment. Moving out of my mom's and being on my own was exciting. But my job was just that—a job. Boring but necessary. I also did something else at the same time, however, that gave my life the boost it needed. I had no idea then that it would also help shape my destiny. I simply went out and bought myself a graduation gift: my first guitar, a small steel-string Guild. I bought it at McCabe's in Santa Monica, and they were so helpful that I decided to take my guitar lessons there too. I learned chording and different fingerpicking styles and loved it so much I signed up for a songwriting class too. It was a group class, and students were paired up to write a song together as a homework assignment. The next week we'd all come back and play our songs for the class and critique each other.

It was in that class that I made one of the biggest discoveries of my life. A passion was ignited that I didn't know I had. I had the gift of writing real songs that other people liked. The magical thing about it was that I felt as if I could actually hear the melodies and words forming in my mind. I also realized it was something I'd always done without thinking much about it. These were the songs I sang to Mrs. Hilliard or to myself when I was alone. But now I learned how to capture the words and music so I could remember the songs I liked and sing them again. It was like a deep fountain opened up inside my heart that gave my life new meaning, a new identity.

From that point on, wherever I went, my six-string Guild went with me. I began playing and singing my own songs at small clubs on open mic nights, and I was always jamming with friends at the beach or at parties. I had finally found a piece of the mysterious puzzle I called my life: music.

But my music remained only a hobby. It gave my heart some wings, but it wasn't going to pay my rent or buy me dinner. I knew I wasn't cut out for office work, and after a few years of it I couldn't see myself spending my life at a job I didn't like just to survive. If I wanted to enjoy my life, I knew I had to make some big changes. So I did something I never thought I'd do. I moved back into my old bedroom at my mom's house to take some time to figure things out.

One morning in my mom's kitchen an odd thing happened. Out of nowhere a random comment made by my high school art teacher suddenly popped into my mind. She mentioned that Los Angeles has a huge downtown fashion district, so some of us might want to study fashion design. I had quickly dismissed that idea back then, but now it seemed kind of glamorous and exciting. So even though I couldn't sew a stitch, I decided to enroll at Los Angeles Trade Technical College to study fashion design and get into the fashion industry. If I couldn't find a deeper spiritual meaning to life, at least I wanted to do something that had some color and some creative flair.

One day at LA Trade Tech a film producer from Hollywood came in to talk about wardrobe design for movies. As he was leaving, he casually invited our whole class to a party at his house that weekend. His address was in a very posh neighborhood in the Hollywood Hills.

When my friend and I arrived at this gorgeous home, we were surprised to see a huge pile of shoes at the front door. We just shrugged, took off our shoes, and went in. Instead of the wild Hollywood party I expected, there was a room full of people sitting around calmly with all the lights on. At one end of the living room a man was standing up, talking, and behind him was some type of oriental shrine with a scroll hanging in it. I wanted to leave, but there was no way to slip out gracefully. Just then, a nicely dressed man across the room stood up and was given a moment to speak.

"When I came here last month, I thought all the chanting stuff they talked about was crazy. But my company was failing and I had nothing to lose, so I gave it a try. Now we're miraculously back in the black. Chanting has saved my business!"

Immediately a really pretty lady right in front of me jumped to her feet. She was almost in tears. "I'd given up on my marriage. My husband had already left and was going to file for divorce. But I started chanting, and within weeks he totally changed his mind. Now we're back together."

With that, everyone burst into spontaneous applause and cheers.

I couldn't help but join in. It was a touching story, even though I didn't understand what was going on.

The evening went on like that, with more interesting testimonies, and even some rousing, pep-rally-type songs, which we stood up and sang together. When the man at the front dismissed the meeting, I went to get some punch at the dining room table. A young girl introduced herself to me there.

"Hi. I'm Morgana. Did you enjoy the meeting?"

"Well," I hesitated, "it was interesting. But what's it all about?"

"Oh, this is Nichiren Sho Shu. It's Buddhist and it's really cool. I've been doing it for five months."

"What do you do? I mean, what's this chanting they were talking about?"

She smiled. "It's really simple. Here, let me show you." She led me over to the shrine at the front of the living room. It was made out of shiny black lacquered wood about three feet tall and maybe a foot-and-a-half wide. It looked kind of like a deep-set TV cabinet, but instead of having a TV in it, there was an open scroll hanging on its back wall. The scroll was made out of white paper, about six inches across and eight inches long. On it were Japanese characters in elegant, black brush strokes. There were also small drawers in the front of the shrine.

"What are the drawers for?" I asked.

"That's where you keep your incense, your prayer book, and your Gongyo beads."

"Gongyo beads?"

"That's what the chanting's called. You do Gongyo at least once a day and rub the beads in your hand. They're made out of sandalwood. Smell them," she said as she picked up the beads lying on the shrine and handed them to me.

They did smell good. But the rest of this smelled a little fishy to me. I knew I needed something, only I wasn't sure this was what I wanted.

Morgana explained, "You just chant a simple prayer to this scroll, called a Gohonzon, and you can get anything you want—physical, material, or spiritual. That's all there is to it, and it really works."

"Are you serious?"

"Yeah. And besides that, chanting is going to usher in world peace."

"How's it going to do that?"

"Easy. As soon as one-third of the world is chanting we'll have peace."

"Why just a third?"

"One-third will be against it, and the other third will be neutral. But when you add up those who are neutral and those who are chanting, you'll have more good energy than bad."

Who wasn't for world peace? I knew I was. And it sure sounded good, this idea of releasing as much good energy into the universe as possible. I thought for a moment and asked, "How many people in the world are chanting?"

"I'm not sure, but one-third of Japan is already chanting. It's really a cool thing, they're already experiencing peace over there," she said wistfully.

Morgana looked at me and smiled. "You should try chanting for a few weeks. If it doesn't work, you haven't lost anything, right?"

She opened up the small Gongyo prayer book and showed me how to do it. It was all in Japanese, but under each character was the phonetic pronunciation of the words. It looked easy enough, and Morgana said it took only about twenty minutes a day. All I had to do was chant out loud while concentrating on something I wanted. The same chant worked for everything—whatever you desired.

Well, I had at least one desire just then. His name was Mark. I'd met him the previous summer, and we connected big time. At the moment, he was in the army, and I hadn't heard from him in a while. I'd been hoping for a letter from him. Maybe I could chant for one. It seemed a little strange, but I decided I'd give it a try. All the folks I'd met at the Hollywood Hills party seemed very nice, so why not?

I went out and bought everything I needed: a scroll, beads, incense, a prayer book, and an inexpensive version of the shrine. I set it all up in my bedroom so I could have my own place to chant like everyone else. From the people I met at the party, I soon learned that Nichiren Sho Shu was a national organization with a leadership structure that went all the way from home group leaders to Mr. Sadanaga, the director for the United States. President Ikeda, the international director, lived in Japan. Very quickly I was drawn into it all.

The organization was putting together a singing group to represent all the American women who were chanting. This group would be featured at some concerts in the States, but they would also perform in Japan. I'd been taking guitar lessons for some time and going to a songwriting class, and I loved to sing. So I decided to audition. If nothing else, it seemed like a great chance to travel.

Much to my surprise I passed the audition, was approved by Mr. Sadanaga, and got a spot with six other girls. We were called, of all things, the "Sweetie Seven." We started learning some Beatles and Simon and Garfunkel songs in preparation for a program at the Santa Monica Civic Auditorium. We also were going to travel to Japan for what was called Tozon. Going "on Tozon" was to this group what going to Israel was for Christians and Jews. Although I was chanting regularly, I realized right away that I was not as serious in my faith as the other girls in the group. They'd been involved for several years and were known for their strong commitment. But the exciting idea of a trip to Asia, along with the opportunity to sing, kept me rehearsing half the night for weeks and driving almost an hour each way to do it. Even if I was a novice I could go along for the ride. I was open, even hoping I might find some spiritual reality along the way.

As the trip to Japan got closer, the excitement grew. Most of the talk centered around the possibility of meeting President Ikeda. One night, as we took a short break from rehearsal, one of the girls said, "I've heard that President Ikeda is enlightened."

Another girl added, "I was told that if I was lucky enough to just see him drive by in a car, I could be instantly enlightened—just by catching a glimpse of him."

I sat there wondering what it might feel like to be enlightened. It sounded like pretty wild stuff, but then again I'd been chanting and things were starting to happen. To my complete amazement, I'd already received that letter I wanted from Mark. Now there was the Sweetie Seven and hope of enlightenment.

With all the potential good about to come my way, I didn't want to make a big deal about their request for me to cut my hair. I'd been growing it out for a long time and loved the feel of it on my back. Since I didn't really want to cut it, I just put it off. But soon before leaving for Tokyo, my rehearsal coach led me to a mirror and cupped my hair in her hands and said, "Melody, look how nice it would look short. Then you could all have the uniform look of a true group—the Sweetie Seven!" Well, I was the only one with long hair. I was the only blonde too, but no matter what they said I wasn't going to change that.

As soon as the plane touched down in Tokyo, I was riveted to my window, amazed that I was on the other side of the world. Outside I was hit by the dense August humidity of Asia, the sounds of a language I didn't know, and crowds of people with jet black hair and dark eyes. I tucked my short hair behind my ears and decided it was definitely worth a haircut to be in this amazing place. We were all so excited that as soon as we got into our chartered bus we opened the windows and burst into a song. Immediately, though, one of the leaders shushed us. "Oh, no . . . don't sing that song now." I wondered why, but didn't think too much about it at the time.

An hour later we were driving through downtown Tokyo and someone started to chant. We all joined in loudly, half expecting the people on the sidewalks to chime in too. After all, this was our holy land! But right away our leader said, "Maybe you should wait until we get to the countryside. You know, some people might not like what you're doing." I was curious. I thought, *What do you mean? I thought these people were all into this.*

I had expected to feel an immediate oneness of spirit with the Japanese people—that our arrival as the American counterpart of this world peace movement would somehow be a big event to them. As I watched from the window of the bus, I saw skyscrapers, rickshaws, blue-jeaned teenagers, and old ladies in kimonos—but nobody was chanting, and there wasn't a welcoming committee in sight.

For the next few days, everywhere I went, I hoped to get a glimpse of this President Ikeda, never imagining what would happen next.

The Sweetie Seven sang for a gathering of about 20,000 Nichiren Sho Shu devotees in a large arena in Tokyo. We sang three songs in English and two in Japanese. The thunderous applause at the end was absolutely electrifying. Buzzing with energy, plus the No-Doz I took to fight jet lag, I ran back to the dressing room with the others. We quickly changed from our all-the-same singing dresses into our marching band uniforms to join the drill team in their floor exercises. There were 150 of us marching together, and once again 20,000 cheering people honored us when we were finished. We all filed off the arena floor in perfect order and headed for the exit door. I happened to be one of the last ones about to go out.

Then I heard a commotion behind me in the auditorium. As I turned, I saw a Japanese man standing at the railing all the way across the arena. He had on a suit and was waving. The crowd was going wild and some people were screaming. The girl next to me said, "It's President Ikeda!" She took off running toward him and I followed.

I was one of the first ones to get to President Ikeda, and I pressed myself against the stadium wall, stretching my arm as far up as it would go, trying to touch him. He put his hand over the railing to make a speech, and the palm of his hand closed over my little finger! For the next few minutes he addressed the crowd in Japanese—and the whole time his hand still rested on top of my pinkie. All around me people were pressing against me to get closer, to try and touch him. But there I was, the luckiest one of all.

Strong emotions rose in me and my tears started flowing. I cried through the whole speech. There were tear-stained faces everywhere I looked. But something inside of me was almost standing back watching the whole scene—the hysteria, the tears. Why? What was I caught up in anyway?

President Ikeda finished his message and his escorts whisked him out of the arena. People all around me were still sobbing. I just stood there thinking, *I not only saw him—he touched me. But nothing happened. I don't think I got enlightened.*

Before I left Japan, two more incidents slowly dampened my enthusiasm. First we traveled to a Buddhist temple called Taisegigi, near the foot of Mount Fuji. The holy of holies was there—the original Gohonzon Scroll, over ten feet high and carved in stone. We all got a turn to see it briefly. Then we were told to make a list of everything we wanted to take into the shrine when our turn came. My group leader said, "Anything you ask for in front of this Gohonzon will be granted to you. Just read your list when you go in." After waiting in the sun for hours, my group was finally let inside. As we settled onto floor mats for our twenty-minute stay, many around me started crying and chanting as they read their lists. I felt a little mercenary for bringing my list of wants here. Like a child asking Santa for every toy I could recite fast enough. Something just didn't feel right. All I knew was that I felt as cold as the stone I was staring at.

Shortly before we were to leave Japan, my group leader woke me in the middle of the night. "Be quiet. Come with me." I got up off my straw sleeping mat and was led down a winding path by strangers with flashlights.

President Ikeda had summoned the Sweetie Seven. When we arrived at his house, we stood there in a sleepy daze as he spoke to us through an interpreter. He gave us gifts—silk purses and sandalwood beads. We were only there about ten minutes, but it was enough. I kept thinking, *If he's so enlightened, why can't he even speak English? And why did we have to sneak out?* It was then and there that I decided to drop out of this group as soon as I got home.

At the Tokyo airport waiting for my flight back, I picked up an American newspaper. It was August 9, and the headline was shocking. Sharon Tate, a beautiful Hollywood actress who was eight and a half months pregnant, had been brutally murdered in her Beverly Hills home along with six of her friends. Her husband, Roman Polanski, had been traveling, but his name rang a bell. A creepy feeling washed over me as I read further.

Roman Polanski was the writer and director of the movie *Rosemary's Baby*. I had seen it the previous summer when it first came out. It was chilling. I went alone to the Elmiro Theater on 3rd Street in Santa Monica and sat in their sweeping balcony—my usual spot. The tag line in all the movie promos had been "Pray for Rosemary's baby." I thought this movie might hold some spiritual nuggets for me.

It was about a young couple, Guy and Rosemary. They became friends with an older couple who took almost a parental interest in their lives. They were kind and caring and seemed totally normal. But it turned out that in reality they were part of their city's coven of witches who were networked together by dark satanic secrets. And they only wanted one thing from Guy and Rosemary—besides their souls. They wanted Rosemary's baby.

I had always wondered if pure on-purpose evil really existed. But that day in the theater I felt something I didn't want to experience again. It felt like a thick unwelcoming cloud had filled the Elmiro and—even worse—settled into my chest with a dark heaviness. It was hard to breathe. It was as if an actual presence was gripping my heart and squeezing out the air. At the same time my chest was being filled with an uneasy, creepy feeling. I'd never felt anything like it before. Deep inside an alarm sounded. I had a "knowing"—a gut feeling that Satan and his worshipers were very real. I knew they were neatly tucked away into the everyday fabric of society everywhere. I felt a little crazy, but I swear I kept hearing the words "it's all true" ringing inside my heart.

As the credits rolled, I promised myself that in all my searching, I would never have anything to do with witches or satanic practices. That movie convinced me I wanted nothing from the dark side.

Now only a year after Roman Polanski's movie was released, pure evil made a visit to his very own home. It came in and murdered everyone in the house, including his pregnant wife and their about-to-be-born baby.

Reading the story, I felt shaken just as I did when I saw the movie. I thought about it a lot on my flight home and felt more urgency than ever to find light at the end of my spiritual tunnel. If such pure evil really existed, then wouldn't there also be pure goodness somewhere to balance out the universe? But where was it? I sure didn't find it on this trip. But was it in a place? Would I find it back in America? And if pure goodness did exist, why would it allow such evil in the world?

After I got settled back home, I immediately followed through with my decision to quit being a Buddhist. Several members continued to phone me for about a year, encouraging me to keep chanting and not give up. I had been in a high-profile position representing the faith. They wanted me back so badly that they came knocking on my mom's door, but I acted like no one was home and didn't answer. Then the United States director, Mr. Sadanaga, wanted to talk to me in person. I caved in and actually let some members drive me to their headquarters. But they left me sitting alone for a few minutes before the big meeting and, with a pounding heart, I decided to ditch them all. I slipped out and called an old boyfriend for a ride home. I couldn't go back. I knew this group didn't have the answers I was looking for.

Leaving, though, left a big hole in my life because I'd invested so much time and energy. As I started to think about adjusting to a more normal lifestyle, I remembered friends I hadn't seen in quite a while. I also thought of my father.

Earlier in the year my dad had started begging me to get him out of the West Los Angeles Veterans Hospital and take care of him myself. Every time he asked, I'd feel a battle raging in my heart. I'd always say, "No, Dad, I can't." The truth was I *wouldn't*, and I felt so guilty. Maybe he wasn't the best dad in the world, but he was still my father and I loved him. On the other hand, I didn't know him, and he didn't know me. We'd shared the same house for twelve years, but he was like a total stranger.

I was so torn by my dad's tearful pleas and the tug to live my own life that my visits had become more sporadic. I felt too guilty and too hurt to keep telling him no. I'd also gotten so busy with the Buddhists. It had been about six months since I'd made one of my routine visits to see my dad. Even though I didn't see any way I could take care of him, I hoped there was still a chance for us to build a deeper relationship. So one Sunday after returning from Japan, I decided to go visit him.

On the way to the hospital, I stopped and bought him the candy and cigarettes he liked. When I got to the hospital and went to his room, he wasn't there. Figuring he'd been moved, I went to the nursing station. I gave the nurse his name, but she gave me a blank stare and asked, "Who is it you want?"

"Charles Steiner," I repeated.

"We don't have anyone by that name here."

I insisted I was in the right place.

"When was the last time you saw your father?" she asked me.

My eyes avoided hers. "About six months . . . uh, I've been traveling."

"Six months? I haven't been here that long. Let me get someone else for you."

When a second nurse walked up, she looked right at me and asked, "Who are you?"

"I came to see Charles Steiner. I'm Melody, his daughter."

Without much hesitation she said, "Honey, he's dead. He died several months ago. Didn't you know?"

I was stunned. Grabbing the bag of candy and cigarettes, I ran to my car in disbelief. I was angry, sad, and feeling like the stone I'd seen in the Japanese temple. I slammed my car into gear and raced to my mom's place. Why had she kept this from me? Why didn't she tell me and spare me this painful, humiliating moment?

I burst through the living room door and cornered my mom. "Why didn't you tell me Daddy was dead?" I cried.

She just stared at me. Now she was the one who was stunned. "Dead? Charlie's dead? I didn't know . . . I didn't know."

Now my mother was upset. Could I blame her after my bold accusation?

As we started to inquire about my father, the hospital told us he died from pneumonia, but a friend who worked there pulled his records and told us the details surrounding his death. It seems the nurses had been taking my father's cigarettes away from him because he was coughing so badly. Also, since he could only use one hand, he constantly was burning himself. He must have gone into the bathroom with some cigarettes to sneak a smoke. He evidently caught himself on fire and was burned seriously before anyone could come to his rescue. During his recovery, pneumonia set in as a complication, and he died. We were never notified when he was burned or when his life was threatened by pneumonia. My dad died pretty much as he lived. Alone.

I knew we hadn't had the greatest relationship, but at least I'd had a father or somebody I could call my father. Now there was no chance for a relationship. I was told he had been buried somewhere under a simple white cross in the Veterans Cemetery near the hospital. It was by the 405, so I drove by it often but never stopped. All I could do was stare at the straight rows of perfectly sized white crosses, acres and acres of them. My dad was somewhere out there beneath one of them, but I never did visit his grave.

I was left to wonder why so much of what I really wanted in life had been taken away from me. I never had the family or the home I wanted, Mrs. Hilliard had slipped from my life, the Buddhist experience was a flop, and now my father was dead.

For the next few years I bounced around like a rubber ball. I graduated from design college with an AA in fashion design after winning the prestigious Gold Thimble Award. I landed several jobs in the fashion industry, working my way up from cutting patterns to selecting fabrics and designing lines of clothing.

One day the top designer where I worked invited me to her home in Beverly Hills for the evening. I felt honored and excited. She seemed really nice. If we became friends, I'd have a cooler group of people to hang out with at better parties, and maybe even get a promotion. I arrived hungry, thinking I was invited to dinner. But once inside her lovely home, there was no food in sight, not even appetizers. As we stood in her formal dining room making small talk, she didn't offer me a drink either. Finally she did offer me something that shocked me as she made an overt pass at me. I acted like I didn't know what she meant and just kept backing away from her, nervously talking the whole time. After all she was my boss, but it got tense quickly, and she was not offering me an easy exit plan. So I just muttered something about needing to leave and excused myself as gracefully as I could. Within a week I got laid off, and I knew exactly why.

The fashion industry was seasonal anyway, and there were always layoffs unless you were really important. This wasn't my first time, so I had my routine down. Between jobs I'd just party and do what I wanted until I ran my unemployment benefits totally dry, which only reflected how I was feeling inside. Dry.

I continued my spiritual search, going from astrology to yoga to getting a mantra and meditating to studying an obscure occult science to my last escapade with the Buddhists. I was still writing songs and singing, but even music didn't fill the empty place inside that just wouldn't go away.

The only thing left that held out any promise of happiness and a hopeful future were the letters from Mark. I found I was able to pour out my heart to him, but he was still in the army. The loneliness I felt left me open to all kinds of influences.

A girl I'd gone to design college with came to my apartment one spring evening. We decided to drop some acid. I was playing the Beatles's *Abbey Road* album on my stereo, but as we came on to the LSD, the music started sounding all jumbled together. The acid hit us hard. As I stared at the lit candle on the coffee table, it was like watching time-lapse photography. I saw it melt down then grow back to its original size and melt down again. The walls seemed to be closing in on us too. Everything was spinning and moving so fast I thought I might flip out. We needed more space, so we decided to get outside for some fresh air even though it was after midnight.

Walking down the side streets of Santa Monica, I was wishing I could come down, but the acid had just hit—and it was stronger than I expected. I felt like I was being turned inside out.

Then the strangest thing happened. We were standing at the bottom of a hill, and as I looked up into the black midnight sky, I saw a huge glowing cross hanging in the heavens. I blinked, but it didn't go away. It was a fiery, radiant gold. And it was beautiful. I stared at it in awe, and felt a peace wash into my heart. Everything around me became calm and still. Hoping to hold on to the moment, I was afraid to even move. Something deep inside me was responding, saying, *I need this peace so bad. I don't ever want to lose it.*

I glanced at my friend and noticed that she now had a long, flowing shawl draped over her head. To my surprise, so did I. We had on long dresses too, gently blowing in the evening breeze. As I stared up at the cross, all the turmoil stopped. It was as if I was in another place, at another time, standing at the foot of this cross—a place I never wanted to leave.

Of course, my friend wasn't seeing the same thing, and in a moment she started talking about something. I tried to stop her, but it was too late. The scene of us at the cross dissolved before my eyes. I caught my breath in disappointment, but try as I might I couldn't get back the image. Gone were the shawls, the long dresses, and the beautiful glowing cross. My peace was gone as well. I felt as if something precious had just been torn from my hands. Again I was caught up in the agitation of the trip. We wandered the streets for a few more hours before we returned to my apartment.

It was after 3:00 AM when I finally crawled into bed. I was still thinking about what I'd seen in the night sky, when my phone rang. A late phone call even for me. It was a good friend I often went to parties with, but tonight he was sobbing uncontrollably. His boyfriend had just broken up with him and abruptly moved out. He needed to talk. I consoled him for more than an hour until he finally calmed down. I also told him all about my vision in the sky and found out he was looking for answers just as I was. It was daylight before I could get some sleep, but I didn't forget the cross or the peace. Later on I went back to the spot where it all happened. In the place of the cross, there was only a tall telephone pole with a crossbeam. That must have been what my hallucination hung itself upon.

But the peace that came with it puzzled me. I knew Jesus died on a cross, but I'd never thought of looking to him for any answers. Jews didn't believe in Jesus. Anyway, could you really have a valid spiritual experience on drugs? I didn't think these questions had answers, so I hid that experience in my heart and tried to move forward with life.

Eventually Mark got discharged from the army, and we made plans to move in together. After four years of being apart we were like total strangers, but our excitement about each other overshadowed everything else. For me it was a dream come true. I finally had somebody I could call my own. Mark soon enrolled in college, and a songwriting buddy helped me land a job at his brother's company, Matrix Image, a videotape production studio in Canoga Park. Now I had every reason to be happy. I had a good relationship with Mark and another creative job. Yet I found myself deeply dissatisfied with everything around me. I looked for ways to forget the growing emptiness I felt. Even Mark couldn't fill the void.

I was at a real low point in my life, and getting numb was more attractive than ever. Almost every day at lunch, I'd go out with the receptionist next door and drink margaritas. Only in her midtwenties, she already had a drinking problem, and I wasn't doing much better. During work I'd also go into the ladies' room frequently and smoke some marijuana or hash just to get through the afternoon.

But getting drugs was becoming a problem. I always got them for free at parties from the guys. But now I was using more, and I didn't like buying my own. So I made a plan. I would buy a pound of hash, sell off the excess, and basically be getting mine for free. I'd always said I'd never be a dope dealer. But now I thought, *I could be doing worse.* I was proud of turning down a recent offer for a totally free hit of heroin just to test it out. A friend tried to convince me it wasn't habit forming if I only used it on weekends. The trip he described sounded like something I'd really like. But I was never going to be a junkie.

Still, inch by inch I knew I was getting into a dangerous place. Even worse, it didn't seem to bother me all that much.

Inwardly I was giving up. For all my lofty ideals and all my endless searching for purity and truth, I was coming up empty.

Then the bottom dropped out.

One evening after dinner, Mark and I were having a casual conversation, when he suddenly got quiet. Then he said, "Babe, I want to tell you about something really beautiful that just happened to me."

"What?" I asked, smiling.

"Well, Marie and I got together."

"Got together? What do you mean?"

"You know, we made love. It was inevitable. I believe it was meant to be."

I felt like someone had just kicked me in the stomach. Marie was married to Mark's best friend, Nate. Was I really supposed to be happy?

"Where was Nate? Does he know?"

"He was right there, babe. He saw it coming and just left the room—left us alone. He came in and woke us up in the morning. He's such a beautiful brother."

I didn't want to get upset and be uncool. But even though I'd read the book *Open Marriage,* it was hard to get my mind open that far. I didn't know how to compute this in my emotions. As much as I tried to deny it, I felt betrayed. I sure wasn't perfect, but at least I'd been faithful. I let it go and we didn't talk about it again, but something inside of me was broken and dying.

A short time later I walked into our living room and saw Mark kissing one of my best friends. This time I was so upset I took a few Quaaludes and went to bed pretending I didn't see anything. What was wrong with me anyway? Why was I comfortable dealing dope and uncomfortable dealing with real life? The next morning I realized Mark had been with my friend all night. I phoned in sick while he walked her to her car and kissed her good-bye. For breakfast I had something to smoke, acting like nothing happened, while Mark and I made plans for the day.

So nothing was sacred after all. Reality was getting too hard to deal with. I didn't want to feel pain again. Mark and I didn't break up, but that bond of loyalty was shattered. Somehow I always knew I was living out of a sense of loss, a sense of wanting something that would last. This only highlighted that feeling. It just seemed a lot better to be numb—and I was getting more numb all the time.

The day I met Keith Green, the last thing I wanted was a serious relationship. In fact, all I could think of was getting out of the relationship with Mark.

Near the end of January 1973, Keith showed up at Matrix Image along with his dad, his grandfather, and his friend Jay Leon. Rumor had it that video would be the next big thing. They were looking into the possibility of combining Keith's music with some of the new video effects we were producing.

As I gave them a tour, Keith seemed to stay right on my heels, asking questions and telling me more about himself than I really cared to know. But I soon found out you couldn't ignore Keith for long, especially if he wanted to get your attention.

About a week after the tour, I was sitting at my desk when the phone rang.

"Matrix Image. May I help you?"

When I answered, a voice on the other end of the line said cheerfully, "Hi, I miss you."

"Who is this?" I said coolly.

"It's me—Keith. You know, I was in last week."

"Oh yes, I remember," I said as I thought, *How can he say he misses me? He barely knows me.*

"I was calling to see if your boss listened to the music tape I left him."

"I don't know, but I can check on it."

"Okay. Great. Have you listened to it yet?"

"No . . . not yet," I said, feeling a bit on the spot. "But I will soon."

"Great. Hey, do you wanna meet me for lunch today?"

I stalled him, my mind racing for an excuse. My excuse worked—

that day. But Keith was cheerfully persistent. Over the next few weeks, he kept calling, and I finally gave in. When I hung up, I was a bit surprised at myself for saying I'd go. Although I was hurt about Mark's betrayal, I still really cared about him, and I definitely didn't feel ready to jump into another relationship. I needed some space.

But this Keith Green—his directness threw me a bit. Most guys played it extremely cool. Keith was aggressive and up front, not a game player at all. His openness was very refreshing, and it was flattering to be so blatantly pursued.

I changed my mind several times before lunchtime arrived, but met Keith as planned. He'd made sandwiches, and we went to Chatsworth Park for a picnic. He brought along his guitar. As we sat cross-legged on the grass, he played me a song he'd just finished. It was a really beautiful tune, but more than the music struck me. I immediately heard Keith's heart—or maybe I should say his heart cry. As he sang for me there in the park, he voiced some of the same questions I'd been struggling with, but said them in a way I never would have thought of saying them, like, "Is death the answer, or just a door? Does anyone know?"

I already had told Keith I wrote songs too, but after I heard how good he was I felt a twinge of regret as he passed me his guitar and asked me to play him one. I sang a few of my songs and, to my relief, he seemed to really like them. Then he said, "I've got some other songs I want to play for you, but I need a piano."

We drove to Pierce College, where Keith was taking some classes, and found an empty practice room with a piano. As he started playing, it was obvious he was in his element. He played easily and powerfully. He threw himself into each song with energy and emotion, and sweat started to show on his forehead. And his voice . . . his voice was soul-stirring. I stood there speechless. To say I was impressed would be an understatement.

I had never heard anyone, anywhere, like Keith Green. As I listened to him, I thought, *This guy is incredible. I can't believe he's not making records.* But it wasn't just his music. It was all of him. The energy. The sincerity. The sheer power of his performance.

I was already going to be late getting back from lunch. Keith walked me to my car and gave me a small hug. I drove back to work thinking that this lunch had turned out to be very interesting.

It also hit me that I had just gone out with someone else while I was still in a relationship with Mark. That was really out of character for me—no matter that Mark had been with other girls.

Keith kept calling me at work, so I decided to listen to the tape of songs he'd left for my boss. I was especially taken up by one beautiful love song. It had a soaring, haunting melody line. But the words haunted me even more. Most love songs out then were about revolving-door relationships—here today, gone tomorrow. This song was different. And it was clear that this Keith Green was different as well.

About three weeks later, during another lunchtime get-together, Keith walked me to my car as I got ready to head back to work. We stood there for a moment and Keith looked at me intently. My car door was open, and I was just about to get in when he stepped closer and warmly kissed me. I didn't resist. I liked the way he kissed, and I kissed him back.

As I drove back to work, I wondered what I was getting myself into. Keith immediately wrote some free verse about our first kiss in his journal and later gave me a copy, which read:

February 22, 1973
Poem 30
Potential Energy (In five movements)
Inspired by Melody

There are two kinds of lightning
But it takes two poles
Cloud to cloud
Or cloud to ground

I am a cloud
So you can be a cloud or the ground

You have the choice
We are lightning either way.

You kiss so good—
We kiss so good!
It takes two poles
Never stop this kiss—
Oh oh oh oh but, I've got to get to a class.

We are a switch for potential energy
The energy is quiet, mellow, undemanding
(and surprisingly well hidden)

Until you conduct it between us and complete the circuit
(Love is forming) Then a spark—And if we're patient we can conduct
    many sparks
And if we build on to the switch
(Maybe add a battery—to store energy for low fueling times)
We can have a constant current.

But let's not talk nor even think of such long-term things now
There are little tingling pulses of love–electric
You–and–me to send out and receive

With our electricity, and music–through–me
We can amplify the beautiful song of us.
After all, you are a Melody and I am a minstrel
And we are becoming a fact—US.

   Inspired by Keith, I sent some free verse back to him:

As so fair man
Of twilight blue eyes
Your gift of soul, your song

My soul feels free
You inspire me
You inspire me

The next few months were filled with long phone calls from Keith as he juggled his travels and his girlfriends. One girl Keith especially liked was getting married and she invited him to play at her wedding in Bellingham, Washington. Keith immediately wrote her a song called "Your Wedding's on My Mind," where he lamented her marriage. He had the nerve to play it in front of the groom and get a lingering kiss from the bride.

Keith came to see me as soon as he returned. He told me he felt as if a chapter of his life was closing before his eyes, that old friends and old places had lost their magic. He said he realized that his happiness could not be found in a relationship, even with me.

In the meantime, things were shifting around in my little world too. Mark had decided to go to New York and finish the last semester of a college career he had left dangling to go into the army. He was planning to come back to California six months later. I was keeping my mouth shut about Keith.

True to form, Keith wrote a rather humorous song about the situation. He called it "You're on My List of Things to Do!" No one had ever written a song for me before, and I was really touched when Keith sang it for me. The first verse said:

Well I met you at the office
Then you know it grew
And then there was your boyfriend
But then he never knew
That you liked me
And you hate it
'Cause you don't know what to do
But honey, you're on my list of things to do!

And Keith kept writing in his poetry book, too.

April 9, 1973
Poem 49
"Melody"

She's coming up fast
No expectations
She's almost in reach
Shelter my heart
She's smiling right at me
Balance it out
She's full of potential
It's happening quickly (let it happen)!!!

Keith was anxiously counting the days until Mark left. A few weeks later in mid-April, I waved good-bye to Mark as he drove out of the Matrix Image parking lot on his way back east. Telling people things they might not want to hear was difficult for me, so I let him leave without saying anything about my growing feelings for Keith.

Keith wanted to see me right away, but I needed some breathing room. I told him I wanted to take things slowly. I'd just regained my freedom and my heart didn't feel ready to make another commitment. So I actually managed to hold him off—for a week.

On Easter Sunday, Keith and I had plans to go to the Renaissance Fair in Ventura County. When Easter arrived, so did Keith—at 7:00 AM, a few hours before the time we'd agreed on! His early knock woke me up and I stumbled to the door in a daze. I couldn't believe it when I found him standing there with a big grin on his face. He looked so good in his woven Indian-print shirt and sandals.

"I was so excited I just couldn't wait any longer," he said sheepishly. I sighed and let him come in while I went off to get ready. What girl in her right mind could stay mad after an explanation like that?

I dressed quickly, putting on my prettiest embroidered gauze blouse and a long, flowered skirt. We were dressed for the fair, but we looked pretty much like we usually did. As we drove through the Ventura Mountains in Keith's VW van, I had a warm glow in my heart. The fair was a big event, and I had always wanted to go. It felt extra special to be going with Keith.

At the fair, Keith and I walked around for hours, buying organic food and looking at everyone in their medieval outfits. There were wandering minstrels, jugglers, palm readers, and artisans selling every kind of homemade item you could imagine. The smell of burning incense and food cooking mingled together in a pleasant way; the smell of perfumed oils floated on the breeze—strawberry, sandalwood, patchouli. A lot of people had taken psychedelic drugs, and some of them looked very wiped out. Keith told me his last drug trip was on his nineteenth birthday last October when he took mescaline. It had been such an intense experience, he said, that he hadn't taken any drugs since. I was a bit more involved in the drug scene, but I hadn't done any tripping for a while.

We sat on the grass in the warm sun and talked. Just talked—all afternoon. There was something about Keith that was different from anyone I'd ever known. He was a true seeker. A deep thinker. And even though he was quite serious about life, he had a crazy sense of humor that I really liked.

The difference in our ages did bother me a bit, but at least Keith's life experience and perspective on things helped close the seven-and-a-half-year gap between us. He was young and full of potential and hope for the future, but at the same time he said he often felt "old and senile" at nineteen. At just twenty-six, I knew what he meant about feeling old. Yet I felt like I had barely begun to live.

Within a week, Mark phoned me long-distance. Keith was there, and I took the phone into the bathroom to talk privately. I half expected Keith to get mad and leave, acting like he didn't care, but not Keith. He refused to play games.

Afraid I might get back together with Mark, Keith stayed right there in the living room—fuming and pacing the floor. I was on the spot.

Keith opened the bathroom door, motioning for me to come out to talk with him. I told Mark to hold on while I grabbed some water, and then I went out to see what Keith wanted.

"You need to tell him about us right now," Keith said. "Tell him it's over, and that's that. You have to be firm. I'll wait out here for you."

Talk about being between a rock and a hard place. It was killing me to think I was going to hurt Mark, but I knew I needed to face Keith when I got off the phone. I had to make a choice between them.

When I told Mark about Keith, Mark started crying. He wanted to turn around and drive right back to California, saying he was willing to make our relationship more permanent. A few months earlier, I would have jumped at his marriage proposal. But now it was too late. I told him firmly to not come back for me. We spent more than an hour on the phone and I cried too. I felt so torn and like I was the most terrible person in the world at that moment. I thought the phone call ended my relationship with Mark forever.

A week later I came home from work only to find Keith sitting on my couch holding a small, unopened package. "It's from Mark," he said, while holding it out to me. Inside was a cassette tape and note from Mark asking me to listen while I was alone. I figured Keith wouldn't want me to listen to anything Mark might say. But he was full of surprises. Keith grabbed my cassette player and popped in the tape.

"Let's listen now."

"I don't really want to—"

"No, we need to do this."

It was like our talk on the phone, the crying and begging. I guess I should have felt flattered, but I was choking back my tears. It was embarrassing too, with Keith sitting like a rock, not saying a word. When it was over, Keith jumped up, grabbed the tape, and soundly tossed it into the trash. It was as if he was saying, "Okay, we're done with that!"

Within a month, Keith moved into my apartment—and into my life.

Top row L to R: Melody at age 2; young Melody with Mom

Middle row L to R: Melody's mom at 14; Melody and Dad; Melody and Mom, 1955.

Bottom row L to R: Melody and the Sweetie Seven; Melody as a teenager

Officially engaged

Birthday and Engagement party

Above: Keith with long hair

Left: Keith and Melody

4

"LOVE WITH ME"

When Keith moved into my apartment, it was the biggest moving in I'd ever experienced. When God made Keith, he threw away the mold. Keith's whole approach to life was unique. Actually, he was a ball of contradictions. On the outside he looked like everyone else our age—but underneath it all he seemed out of step with the times. His ideas, even his whole character, seemed to oppose the values that were so popular. Sometimes I'd jokingly think that he'd been airlifted in from some other time and place.

One thing I particularly liked was the spark of freshness Keith brought into my life. His crazy and wonderful ways kept me interested and laughing. I loved the feeling of security I had when we were together. He knew how to take care of himself, and he liked taking care of me too.

Sometimes I thought Keith might be a bona fide genius. His mind held facts and figures like a magnet. There was rarely a subject he didn't know at least something about. He questioned everything about everything, which challenged me to stretch my thinking too. And when Keith was into something, he wanted everybody he knew to get into it too.

One really beautiful morning in May we woke up and Keith convinced me to play hooky from Matrix Image. It wasn't hard. It was a beautiful day, and Keith wanted to take a long drive. He picked the route—the back roads of Simi Valley that eventually led up the coast to Santa Barbara. The lazy rambling hills were beautiful and refreshing.

We found a little fruit stand and Keith bought some fresh dates and apple juice for our journey. We kept talking and laughing nonstop.

We were almost to Santa Barbara when we came upon a little resale shop. We stopped and went inside. I started looking at some old jewelry, and immediately Keith spotted something and called me over. I wasn't sure what it was, a broach or necklace, but it was cool looking. The silver was tarnished, and it had a turquoise stone in the center. He picked it up.

"Wow, look at this great Jerusalem Cross, Mel! Let's get it for you."

For the first time all day I was at a loss for words.

"A cross? It's really pretty but . . . well, I've never worn a cross in my life."

"Oh come on, Mel, we have been looking into Jesus."

"I know but I'm . . . I'm Jewish. I'll always be Jewish."

I had only been open to Jesus because of Keith's enthusiasm about him and because I liked what I saw in Keith. But wearing a cross? That was a different story. What would my mother think? Something inside me totally rejected that idea. Keith came from a Jewish background too. I wondered, *Why doesn't this Jesus stuff bother him like it does me?*

Instantly my mind flashed back to one of our first conversations. Keith had said rather smugly, "I was almost twelve when I realized I was Jewish. My parents kept it hidden. I just figured it out by myself."

"How?" I asked.

"One day it just dawned on me that all my relatives in New York were Jewish. I would have figured it out a lot sooner if they didn't live so far away."

I said, "Well, you're in good company. Moses didn't find out he was Jewish until he was a grown man."

Right there in the thrift store I finally connected the dots. I realized that even though Keith was Jewish, it had never become his spiritual identity. Instead he was raised in Christian Science and taught to follow "the enlightened" teachings of Jesus and the woman who began the group. She was also the one who decided which teachings were enlightened. It seemed weird, but it helped me understand this spiritual paradox in Keith's life: being Jewish and being into Jesus too.

"Mel—" Keith broke into my thoughts. He was holding the Jerusalem Cross, and his eyes were bright and expectant. I was beginning to realize just how hard it was to say no to him. Besides, in a strange way, I was starting to feel some kind of a connection to this Jesus, whoever he was.

"Well, maybe—" I said as I took the cross from Keith's hand.

At least it didn't look like a real cross. It was about the size of a silver dollar, with several crossbars at different angles. Best of all, nobody was hanging on it.

"Honey, it's beautiful. Come on, please let me get it for you," Keith insisted.

I felt that Keith really wanted me to have a cross so I could be wearing one like he was. I knew it would be a tangible symbol of the togetherness of our hearts in our spiritual search.

"Well, all right. I guess it would be okay."

A big grin spread across Keith's face. He quickly pulled out his wallet and plunked down the money. The cross didn't have a chain on it so I slipped it into my pocket. I knew Keith really wanted to share his budding faith with me, and after all, I was hungry for something too. If Jesus held the answers, I was open, even though the whole idea was a bit alien to me.

Later as we drove, I quietly took the cross out of my pocket and turned it over. Something was stamped on the back. I held it closer and read "Jerusalem." At least it was from Israel, which was a point of great comfort for my Jewish heart.

It was quickly becoming clear that if I was going to be involved with this guy, I was going to be carried along with him on his spiritual journey too. But for now I was just falling in love.

We connected deeply on wanting to find answers for our lives. But I also thrived on his whacky and fearless sense of humor. He drew out my crazy side with a kick of newfound boldness. We had a lot of fun together, even if it was sometimes at the expense of others. We were an unpredictable combination and easily fell into silly situations and pranks together.

Keith loved hamburgers, so we always went to his favorite spots. We'd usually sit at the counter or in a central location. Then we'd start talking loudly in absurd accents, discussing imaginary dilemmas or pretending to argue. People couldn't help but hear us, and we loved to watch them react or, better, get annoyed. We'd crack ourselves up on the way home just talking about the crazy stories we made up on the spot.

One time we went to the Brown Derby, a famous upscale restaurant in Beverly Hills, and ordered a light lunch. After we finished eating, I excused myself and left a small purse on the table to indicate I was coming back. I asked a waiter where the ladies' room was, then slipped outside instead. A few minutes later, Keith got up and left. We met up down the block laughing hysterically, wondering how long it would take them to realize we'd walked out on the bill.

"It's a good thing we aren't really interested in a life of crime," Keith said.

"Yeah, we're pretty good. We could become the next Bonnie and Clyde," I joked back.

We knew it was wrong, but it seemed harmless. We just wanted to see if we could get away with it.

There were lots of quirky things between us that just seemed to click. But the very best thing I discovered about Keith during the next few months was that he was capable of making deep commitments. I thought this was interesting, considering everyone around us had such a "hang-loose, whatever will be, will be" attitude. Keith wasn't that way. When he cared about a person, it was more than just pretty words. He wanted to show it. For instance, Keith liked to spend a lot of time with Dawn, the ten-year-old daughter of his friend Karen Bender.

Dawn was a beautiful child with long, thick hair and freckles sprinkled lightly across her turned-up nose. She seemed a bit more withdrawn than a kid her age should have been. She didn't smile a lot, but when she did it was like a burst of sunshine. Keith really loved her, and as I got to know her, she won my heart as well. Her mom was divorced and worked long hours, so one weekend Keith decided to bring Dawn home with us so we could have extra time together. We took her swimming, to an amusement park, and to the movies. We had a great time, but by the end of the weekend we realized being parents, even for a day, was a bigger job than we thought. Still we tried to get together with Dawn and Karen as often as we could.

In fact, it was at a rather wild party at Karen's house one night late in the summer that Keith and I wandered off to talk about where we were in our relationship. We ended up in Dawn's bedroom, sitting on her bed. As we talked, Keith totally surprised me.

"Mel, I've been wondering if it's really right for us to be living together."

I couldn't believe it. No one else we knew would even be raising this question.

"What do you mean 'really right'? We love each other, don't we?"

"Yeah, but that's just the point. If we really love each other, maybe we should have a deeper commitment."

I found myself staring at the frayed squares of the granny quilt on Dawn's bed, wondering where this conversation was going to lead. I'd never heard anyone talk like this before, and I was getting a little nervous.

"What I'm trying to say," Keith continued, "is maybe we should be thinking about getting married. I'm not sure we should be living together without being married."

"Married?"

"Of course we'd need to get engaged first. So maybe we could get 'engaged to be engaged.'"

"Keith, what does that mean?"

"It would be kind of a trial period. That way if things don't work out we won't have to break our engagement."

I'd never heard of anything like it. This was crazy—and a little wonderful. I was learning that Keith never did things the way everyone else did.

"I don't know, Keith—"

"It'll be great. Who else do you know who ever got 'engaged to be engaged'?"

I thought about it for a moment. The idea had its merits. Since my disastrous relationship with Mark I still wasn't ready for a real commitment, even after several months of living with Keith.

"Well, you might have a good idea. That way we'd have time to decide what we really want to do."

"Mel, I want you to know that if we do end up getting married, I believe it's a lifetime commitment. I don't believe in divorce."

As Keith continued talking, my mind started to reel. To me divorce seemed like too big a possibility to ever rule out. I really didn't know any happily married couples and wasn't even sure about the whole idea of marriage. Part of me was overwhelmed that someone as wonderful and talented as Keith wanted to marry me. But what if things didn't work out? It seemed much safer to leave a door open somewhere.

"Some of the things you're saying really scare me," I finally replied.

But Keith was insistent. "Melody, I love you, and I believe you love me. Let's not be afraid of this. If we get married, I always want to be there for you, and I want to know you'll be there for me too."

He continued to press his point. Finally, we did decide to be "engaged to be engaged." We also made plans to get officially engaged on Keith's twentieth birthday in October. It seemed like a safe enough position since it gave us a few months to weigh everything. True to form, I was most comfortable keeping my options open.

On October 21, we had a birthday party for Keith and, as planned, became officially engaged. Our house was full of friends and little Dawn was among them. She gave Keith a piece of driftwood for a present, and we all clowned around, taking pictures and eating the cake I'd baked.

Keith wanted to set our wedding date for December 25, Christmas Day, in honor of Jesus, at the Little Brown Church on Coldwater Canyon Boulevard. It was a funky little dark brown wooden chapel that stayed open twenty-four hours a day. We'd sometimes stop there really late at night on our way home from Hollywood. It was always empty, which was a plus for our favorite activity.

On the church altar sat what we called the prayer can—a rusty tin can with a large hole on top. People wrote their prayers on odd bits of paper and stuffed them into the can. We never put a prayer into the can ourselves, but we did like to read other people's prayers. It was Keith's idea.

I protested the first time.

"Keith, don't! You might be messing with something sacred and private."

Keith said, "Mel, I'll put them back. I just want to see what people are praying for."

He was so sincere I got off my soapbox, and after that we always read a bunch of them together. Some were folded neatly into tiny squares; others were just kind of jammed inside. Most of the prayers were like ours. People searching for answers, help, healing, just a touch from someone, somewhere, who cared. On the way out, we'd always jiggle the padlock on the piano, but unlike the prayer can, it was always locked. The Little Brown Church was the perfect place to get married. Almost.

I still had my doubts about the Jesus thing, but Keith was making sure I learned more about this Jesus he liked so much.

One of our nightly rituals had become reading together. Keith picked out several books, and we'd sit up in bed and take turns reading a chapter out loud to each other until we couldn't stay awake any longer. We mostly read novels, including *The Robe* and *The Great Fisherman*. We also read the words written in red from a Bible I'd stolen from the Palm Springs hotel room so many years earlier. We both liked to read, so it was fun and drew us closer together in our search. On the night we got engaged, we not only had our wedding place picked out, but we also started trying to live with another major decision we'd made. Several months before, Keith had come to the conclusion that if he didn't truly love someone, then having a sexual relationship with them was wrong. A few days before we'd even met, Keith confided this decision in his journal:

I've been questioning the righteousness of sex in my heart. I know for a fact that sex without love is dead wrong. Now my use of the word "love" has a changeable definition. I know it has changed extremely the past four years. (Or has it? Have I become more cynical and does it take "love" longer to break through and reach me?) At any rate, love has been a different, deeper thing for me. Anyway, sex with love rings true in me. If it is wrong out of marriage . . . let it be shown to me.

The big question we'd been recently talking about centered on the last sentence of Keith's entry. What if you really did love someone but weren't married to them? Most of our friends were barreling down the road in the opposite direction—trying to figure out how many people they could sleep with and how fast. Here we were, wondering how to make right choices. But this question was really important to Keith, and before we got officially engaged on Keith's twentieth birthday, we talked about it a lot.

"I'm thinking that maybe we should go celibate until we get married," Keith said one day, to my shock. "I've read some things in the Bible, and I'm beginning to think that sex outside of marriage is wrong."

"But we're living in the same house, sleeping in the same bed," I protested.

"Yeah, but we can do it."

"Keith, this is even crazier than getting 'engaged to be engaged.'"

"Well, it worked didn't it?"

"And how long would you want to do this?"

"Until we get married."

"Keith, I'm not that much against the idea of it, but how in the world do you expect it to work?"

"Well, I really think it's the right thing to do. Let's give it a try. Please . . ."

Of course, I gave in and we made a decision to go celibate on Keith's birthday. But, as I suspected, it was easier said than done. In early

December, Keith came to me with a mysterious look on his face. He took me by the hand and said, "Come here, I want you to listen to something." Then he led me over to the piano. "Stand there where I can see you."

He sat down and just started singing.

You wanna love with me
Love with me, then.
I only ask
That you still be my friend.
For there are many
Where friendship's unknown.
They live together
But really alone.
And the days
Go their ways
In silence, tense hours of woe.
We do not mean to have it so . . .

As I listened to him sing, I got so caught up in the soaring melody that it took me a minute to realize the song was a surprise. It was for me! My throat tightened up and I found myself starting to blink back a few tears. As Keith sang he closed his eyes, then peeked at me to see how I was reacting. I couldn't say a word.

The song was all about commitment. About a love that wouldn't change its mind, even during the hard times. It was Keith's way of saying that he knew he wasn't perfect, but he would give me a love that would keep growing and never give up . . .

I know that sometimes
I'm harder to love.
I thrash out blindly,
Like nothing's thought of.
But I will love you,

And love you, I do!
It's not complete yet,
But you know we're not through.
And the days
Go their ways
In blessings, moments of truth.
We truly dare not waste our youth.
You wanna love with me,
Love with me then.

It was a bit overwhelming to have a song written for me, especially one as beautiful as "Love with Me."

The beauty of that moment helped offset the terrible arguments we were having, stemming mostly from what I was beginning to think was a silly and annoying rule—Keith's idea about staying celibate until we got married. Since Keith made the rule, I figured he should make more of an effort to keep it. But when I reminded him of that fact, he would get mad at me. That fall was a very difficult time for us. We thought we had the right idea, but it wasn't easy to live up to our own convictions.

Fortunately our wedding day arrived quickly. We woke up early on Christmas morning and dressed in our favorite Goodwill finds. I wore a green turtleneck sweater and a long yellow cotton skirt, and Keith wore his Levi's and a nubby beige sweater. I'd never pictured myself walking down the aisle in a white dress, but it felt odd to climb out of bed, help each other pick out clothes, and drive off to get married.

Keith and I were both nervously quiet as we drove down to the Little Brown Church. When we arrived, the dim lighting made the old wooden pews look warm and inviting as we stood in front and said our vows before the minister. It was a quick and simple ceremony, and within minutes we were married. And Keith made sure it was "in the name of Jesus." Todd was our only witness as we hammered another tiny stake of faith into the ground.

Afterward we drove off to visit Keith's folks. Keith's parents were surprised to see us so early in the day. With our crazy late-night sched-ule, we never showed up anywhere before noon. We hung around with silly grins, waiting for them to guess what we'd done.

Besides Todd, only my mom knew ahead of time, but we wouldn't let her come to the wedding since Keith's family didn't know about it. Keith kept waving his left hand around, hoping they'd notice his wed-ding ring. But they didn't. So we kept smiling and dropping hints. After a few hours, his mom finally ventured a smiling guess. "Did you two get married?" They were surprised, but it wasn't totally unexpected. Keith and I had become inseparable.

As word got out, their house filled with friends and relatives, including my mom. Some goodies were pulled together, and the day turned into a real party with Mr. and Mrs. Keith Green at the center of attention. We were on the receiving end of lots of hugs and kisses. As I looked across the room at Keith, he seemed really happy, as if he was sure we'd made the right decision. I hoped he was right.

Since we were already living together, going off to some romantic spot for a honeymoon didn't seem really important. We were pretty broke. We'd even had to sleep in Victor for two nights as we drove home from a recent trip to Seattle because we couldn't afford a motel. But Keith, never lacking for good ideas when it came to making money, got us a new job.

Three days after our wedding, we started working at the local Pizza Man. We spent our honeymoon racing pizzas around the San Fernando Valley—and I do mean racing. We got paid for each deliv-ery, so speed was of the utmost importance—and speed was right up Keith's alley. He knew all the shortcuts and drove like crazy. My job was to walk the pizza to the door, flash my prettiest smile, and hope for a big tip. New Year's Eve was our best night ever. I was standing at one guy's door exactly at midnight. He pressed five dollars into my hand and said, "Happy New Year!" I raced back to Victor to proudly show Keith the spoil, thinking what a happy New Year it was—and what a great way to celebrate the end of our first week of marriage!

Still at work, counting our tips, Keith had another way he wanted to celebrate the New Year. He brought me a pen and a sheet of paper and said, "It's time to write Mark and tell him we're married." I wrote a letter and addressed the envelope. Keith put it in his back pocket to mail on the way home.

On the drive home I pondered my new identity. I was now Mrs. Keith Green. My mother's maiden name, Sosnovsky, indicated that her family in Odessa lived in an area with many pine trees—which are evergreens. Cedars of Lebanon, the hospital where I was born, was also named after an evergreen tree. And now I was officially a Green, hopefully a "forevergreen." Was there a spiritual rhyme or reason to this? Was there a destiny only God could arrange connected with my new name? Anyway, green was the color of hope, and that felt comforting. Maybe my new name was a promise.

We were almost home when Keith spotted a mailbox. He steered Victor to the curb, jumped out, pulled the mailbox lever, and dropped in my letter to Mark. That door was closed forever, and Keith got back in with a big smile on his face.

Besides racing boxes of hot pizzas around, Victor von Van played another important role in keeping our cash flowing. Keith figured we could turn our love for thrift-store shopping into a business by using Victor as a traveling boutique, hippie-style of course. We bought used clothing that still had resale value. Then we'd park Victor on the streets of Hollywood and hang the clothing, scarves, and bags all around the outside. I even made artful displays of items on the ground. It seemed my fashion sense came in handy after all! We set up a mirror inside Victor so our customers could climb inside to try things on. Always looking for a parking place with a lot of foot traffic, Melrose was one of our favorite streets in Hollywood. Once we set up shop in the parking lot of a large mall. Seemed like a great idea since everyone there was a bona fide shopper, but the security police didn't see it that way as they escorted us off the parking lot and told us to never come back.

Overall, we had a lot of fun, especially because we could do it together. And it helped us pay our rent in a non–nine-to-five way while we waited for Keith's big break.

We didn't have a lot of money, but it didn't matter. There wasn't anything more we wanted out of life—nothing that money could buy anyway. The things we were hungry for couldn't have been bought with a million dollars.

It seemed as if all of Southern California was on one big spiritual search just as we were. Not only were we interested in this Jesus Christ—whoever he was—but it seemed like Jesus was getting pretty popular too. On the West Coast there was talk about a Jesus Movement. Lots of people were being baptized right in the Pacific Ocean.

There were several movies out with Christian themes. We drove all the way to Santa Barbara to see *Brother Sun, Sister Moon*. It was about the life of Saint Francis of Assisi, a young soldier from a wealthy Roman family who loved parties and pretty girls. After God touched his heart, he renounced his inheritance and left town literally naked. He moved into a remote mountain church that was in ruins and rebuilt it to serve the poor and needy—even the lepers. He led a life of poverty, totally putting God first in everything. Later in life he visited Rome, and the pope got on his knees to kiss Francis's dusty feet.

We also saw *Godspell*, the life of Jesus acted out by many people our age. Then there was *Jesus Christ Superstar*. We saw that twice when it hit the movie theaters and constantly listened to the soundtrack that climbed to the top of the charts.

Then, of all things, one day in Hollywood Keith met Teddy Neely, who played Jesus in the film version of *Jesus Christ Superstar*. In fact we had him over for dinner. I kept looking at him thinking, *I can't believe it. I'm making hamburgers for Jesus!* I really didn't think Teddy was some kind of mystic, but just getting to know him after seeing him play Jesus, with his long straight hair and flowing muslin robes, really impacted me.

Teddy was full of stories about things that happened while filming the movie in Israel. The cast and crew were camped out in the desert for a while, and Teddy said it was so beautiful how well everyone got along. They were all like one big peaceful family.

One story in particular captivated us. It happened during the crucifixion scene, which Teddy actually filmed in the nude to make it more humiliating and authentic. Keith and I were all ears.

During the month the crucifixion scene was filmed, there was historically very little rain, if any, recorded at their Israeli desert location. The skies were usually clear, blue, and cloudless—as they were this day of filming.

The crew got Teddy onto the cross, tied him down, and took the ladder away. The cameras started to roll for this most agonizing of all scenes. Then, out of nowhere, to everyone's disbelief, from the four corners of the sky dark clouds rolled in. The sky turned almost totally black, and torrents of wind and rain began to ravage the desert sands. Thunder crashed loudly, and giant bolts of lightning were striking from sky to ground. This event was so shocking it literally freaked everyone out. The whole cast and crew dropped everything and ran quickly for cover—leaving Teddy hanging helplessly on the cross, naked and alone.

Teddy yelled and screamed for someone to come back and get him off the cross away from the whipping wind and rain. He called out until he was totally exhausted. No one came. Then, after what seemed like an eternity, someone untied him and carried Teddy's weary body to one of the shelters. Teddy said it was someone he'd never seen before—and never saw again.

"I'm almost certain it must have been an angel," he said in all seriousness.

Teddy was badly shaken for days. But the thing that seemed to impact him the most was the distinct feeling that out there in the Judean desert, they had accidentally tampered with something (or someone) they shouldn't be messing with.

Interestingly, when the crew abandoned their cameras to run for cover, film was still rolling. The next day, Teddy viewed the footage. He said it was unusable because on film the fierce thunder and lightning were so violent that it looked like phony, overdone Hollywood special effects.

When Teddy finished his story, Keith and I glanced at each other with our raised-eyebrow look. We both believed in the supernatural, and we'd both had spiritual encounters we couldn't explain away.

Teddy also told us that after the crucification scene, the tone of the cast and crew was deeply affected. Almost overnight they weren't one big happy family anymore. The Judas character separated himself from the rest, and about half of those on location followed. A different spirit seemed to take control of that group. They seemed to lose their peaceful feeling, which was replaced by loud, rowdy nights and some extra drugs.

The crucifixion scene in the movie had really affected both of us too. We were touched so deeply by that part of the movie. It didn't seem like Jesus had done anything to deserve the way people turned against him or the horrible things that happened to him.

It seemed as if Jesus and the things he stood for were becoming more real and easier to relate to all the time. We really loved the movies with spiritual overtones. Actually, they were more inspiring than some of the real-life people we'd met who said they were Christians. One thing was for sure. We specifically did not want to become like some of the "Jesus Freaks" we were encountering.

Shortly after Keith moved in with me he'd been asked to do a series of concerts in the Pacific Northwest. I'd been laid off from Matrix Image so I went with him. While we were in Seattle, Keith introduced me to a girl who said she was a Christian. She was the first Jesus Freak I'd ever met. Kathy was someone Keith had met when he'd first run away several years before. Something about Kathy made us totally uncomfortable. You couldn't have a normal conversation with her. She'd say things like, "Oh, we're out of milk, praise God," or "It's a beautiful day, praise the Lord." Every other sentence was punctuated with some religious exclamation. It gave me the creeps. We never wanted to walk around uttering mindless phrases like she did. We were content just to call ourselves followers of Jesus and leave it at that. We didn't want to become alienated from the human race!

My own reluctance ran even deeper. I wanted to know the truth, but because I was Jewish it was hard to believe I might find it in Jesus.

Even though I'd gotten more out of reading small sections of his teachings in the Bible than I'd gotten from all the other mystical books I'd read put together, I was still uncomfortable when I thought of following him.

In fact, one night shortly before we got married, Keith and I had a pretty big disagreement at the Bla Bla Cafe about our wedding rings. Keith wanted to get small crosses engraved on them. I dug in my heels. We took a heated walk outside the Bla between sets to work it out. Wearing a Jerusalem Cross around my neck occasionally was one thing, but engraving a real cross on a ring I'd wear every day for the rest of my life was something else. Keith felt having crosses on our rings would be symbolic of our decision to make Jesus our master, and they would be a constant reminder that we were married in his name. I was torn, but for some reason I couldn't explain, I really did want to honor Jesus in our marriage. Letting Keith's faith pull me along, I finally agreed.

We went back into the Bla for Keith's final set and he played a song he wrote with Todd called "War Games." After our "engraving crosses on our rings" fight, the song really touched me. It was so difficult to believe in a God I couldn't see. Sometimes I felt like a war was being fought inside of me for my very soul.

I've been out fighting the war today
The war inside of my head
I thought that I killed my enemy
I thought that my ego was dead
But it's still stubbornly living
In the kingdom of my thoughts
In my state, in my state of mind.
I've been out struggling with everyone
In the arena all day
The views I defend don't seem to matter much
We all could debate either way
Where's the root of my problem

Why does everybody oppose
Every side, every side that I take?
Hey God, where were you today?
You didn't answer my prayers.
Lately I pray and I pray
And lately you are not there.
Maybe my beliefs are all illusion
Created by my mind just for a crutch
Doubt creeps in to make its reintrusion
And sweeps away the faith I need so much

When Keith finished, the audience broke into wild applause. Keith always wrote from a place that was deeply personal, trying to capture in music the things he was thinking and feeling in his heart. I guess a lot of people shared his struggle. I know I did.

As we drove home from the Bla that night, I found myself thinking back to my early childhood. As much as I struggled, it was slowly sinking in that God just might be real.

When I was a little girl, I came down with pneumonia and was delirious with fever. When the doctor came, he became alarmed. He told my mom I was too sick to move to the hospital, and then gave me a shot. Before leaving he said that if my fever didn't break by about four in the morning, I wouldn't survive the night.

My mom never left my side. Through the haze of fever I watched her putting cool, wet washcloths on my forehead—and heard her desperate prayers. I felt bathed in her love and in another kind of love that I seemed to be floating in. Was it just the fever?

When the doctor returned at 6:00 AM, I woke up and ran to the door. He was shocked to see me. He ordered me back to bed and told my mom it was a miracle I had made it through the night. He'd brought a death certificate with him in his black bag expecting to need it.

Since then, I knew that the God my Jewish mother prayed to had answered her prayers. I wondered if the love I felt on that long, hazy night was more than just my mother's love. Could it be that God had reached out to me before I even started seeking him?

There were other influences in our lives too. Shortly after Keith and I were married we began to get closer to some people who were also into music, only it was Christian music. Recently we'd even acquired a new roommate who was sleeping on our fold-out couch— Keith's friend Randy Stonehill. Keith had met Randy one night about a year-and-a-half before at the Bla. Since then they'd had a blast writing and singing together occasionally. Randy had even recorded an album of rock 'n' roll Christian songs, an idea that was really new to us.

Now besides being involved in music together, Keith and Randy had their share of fairly energized spiritual debates. The thing that always upset Keith was the fact that Randy didn't think Keith was quite "there" as a Christian. Except for our question—"Was Jesus really God?"—Keith couldn't see any major differences in their beliefs. But Randy didn't see how Keith thought he could be a Christian without settling what we called the "God question."

"Keith, you can't be a Christian if you don't believe Jesus is God," Randy would say.

"But I believe Jesus is God's son. I believe in what he says. I want to live my life by his teachings. Doesn't that make me a Christian?"

"You're just not getting it," Randy said, shaking his head.

"Well, I totally believe every word in the book of James."

"If you only follow the teachings in the Bible that you happen to like, then you don't really believe—"

Round and round the debate would go.

They developed a deep but rocky friendship revolving around their mutual love of music and their crazy personalities. So it was inevitable that they'd end up doing some concerts together.

The summer before we were married, Randy had invited Keith to do some songs with him at the Salt Company, a Christian club in Hollywood. It was their first performance together and they were great! Their high energy levels made the air around them pulsate.

They were also hilariously funny and kept the crowd in stitches between, and even during, some of their songs.

As a result of Keith's friendship with Randy, a few more Christian concerts were opening up. Keith was invited to play at California Lutheran College and then we made plans to go to Northern California with Randy, who had been invited there to do a few concerts. We thought we simply were going so Keith could do a guest set at Randy's concerts. We had no way of knowing we were about to meet someone who would have a lasting impact on our lives.

The first night of our trip, Keith and Randy played at a small, sparsely attended Christian coffeehouse in Fresno. The following day we drove out to Turlock for the next concert, where they'd be sharing the bill with someone else.

As we drove Randy said, "The guy who's playing tonight will really blow you away. His name's Barry McGuire."

Keith said, "You mean *the* Barry McGuire?"

"The guy who sang the hit song 'Eve of Destruction'?" I added in surprise.

"Yeah, that's the one," Randy smiled.

"The Eve of Destruction" was an intense song from 1965 when it hit the top of the music charts across America. It was during a time of war, and the race to develop nuclear weapons was ramping up. The lyrics expressed very real fears of an apocalyptic "end of the world" just around the corner. We all remembered it well enough to sing it in the car as we drove.

> The eastern world it is explodin',
> Violence flarin', bullets loadin'.

The idea was, how could anyone not believe that the world was on the eve of destruction?

It was hard to believe Barry McGuire was a Christian now, and we were eager to see what he'd be like.

The Turlock concert was held in a high school gym. There were a few hundred people there when we arrived. After Randy's set and then Keith's, we settled back in our seats, anxious to hear Barry.

He'd made a Christian album just like Randy. The very idea of people recording entire albums of Christian songs that weren't hymns sounded outrageous to us.

When Barry stepped out on stage to sing, we were immediately struck by his presence. At first glance, he looked a little rough around the edges—a big, burly guy with long hair and a bushy beard. He looked like he might ride to church on a Harley-Davidson. But as soon as he spoke, I was amazed at his meekness. He sang a few songs, playing the big guitar strapped around his shoulder. We were particularly impressed with one called "Bullfrogs and Butterflies." It was incredible to see this big hulk of a guy singing what sounded like a children's song. He explained it before he sang.

"What do bullfrogs and butterflies have in common? The frog grows from a tadpole, and the butterfly grows from a caterpillar. They both start off as one thing and then transform—or get reborn—into something else. They both get born again. And just like them, we need to experience a spiritual rebirth before we can really know God."

He sang and talked about God in a way that we'd never heard before. He made knowing God sound simple. Barry's manner was so warm and easygoing that we were glued to every word he sang or spoke. When he was finished, we followed him back into the locker room with hopes of talking to him before he had to leave. He was in a big hurry to catch an airplane, but he took a few minutes with us. Up close he was kind and gentle—but it was more than that.

There was something about his eyes. They were like clear peaceful pools. His spirit was far different from his gruff-looking exterior—this was obviously a man who had been transformed. He was married, and he and his wife traveled all over the country telling people about Jesus, often living out of their small vehicle that had a camper shell on it. We were impressed by this singing star who was now following Jesus in such a humble, sacrificial way.

We were also impressed by Barry's exit. He'd lingered with us as long as he could, but had to leave quickly or miss his flight. In the lobby many people, just like us, would want to talk to him. We saw his dilemma and watched as he dragged a bench underneath a narrow transom window high on the locker-room wall. With a twinkle in his eye, he apologized, then wiggled his way outside. Keith absolutely loved Barry's antic and passed his guitar out to him before he raced off to the airport.

After that evening, Keith and I knew Barry McGuire had something we wanted. That special something in his spirit had caused the seed of an idea to burst open in Keith's heart—an idea planted there by another friend, Randy Wimer.

Keith had felt an instant love for Barry, which he compared to the depth of relationship he'd had with Randy Wimer, who played in a band called MU. Keith was taken by Randy's quiet spirit the first time they met. Randy was a Seventh-day Adventist and talked a lot to Keith about Jesus.

As we drove home from Turlock, Randy's discussions with Keith all came back to him. Now some of the things he'd said about Jesus were starting to make more sense. Randy had told Keith that Jesus could take away sins once and for all, unlike the Eastern and occult religions he'd studied.

Many of the Eastern religions teach the idea of multiple lives and that your lot in the next life is determined by how holy you were in the lifetime before. If bad things started happening to you in one lifetime, it was because you were paying for the sins of your past life. If you had "good karma" you'd have a happy life, but "bad karma" meant you should expect hard times. We used to joke around when we saw someone do something wrong, saying, "That's gonna be a few years of bad karma!"

Keith recalled something his old friend Randy Wimer had told him—that Jesus can wipe away your sins so you don't have to pay for them later. When we got back home, Keith grabbed one of his older journals to find his notes from that conversation. He read the quote out loud to me:

> Christ created us, the world, and the universe. His teaching is the way out of the cycle of death and rebirth (re-incarnation) and He is the way.

Keith concluded that he was more open than ever to the idea of Jesus being able to "cut your karma." And after hearing Barry McGuire, I had to admit that the idea of getting a clean slate and being born again spiritually was starting to look as if it might really be possible.

Unfortunately our burst of inspiration was short-lived as the rockiness of newlywed life with no money hit. Keith stopped playing at the Bla because, once again, he wasn't drawing a good crowd. But Keith felt he'd been there too long and needed a break anyway. My mom cheered us up with a beautiful belated wedding reception at her house, where lots of friends and family came and loaded us down with lovely gifts. But even with all those blessings, even with our love, we felt like life was running out between our fingers, leaving us with nothing to show for our days.

Still grasping at straws, Keith took me to a Christian Science lecture, but it was dry. It didn't fill the void. Actually it did the opposite. Keith wrote, "Lecture freaked out my Christian balance more."

Then in March, Keith played with Randy Stonehill at another Christian coffeehouse near the beach in Pacific Palisades. The night proved to be another number on our growing list of disappointments. First Randy played, then Keith. Keith always loved to play new songs to try them out on an audience. This night was no exception. Two days earlier, we'd written a humorous song about the energy crisis America was plunged into. There was a huge gasoline shortage, so if a station had gas, people might wait for hours to get some. Called "Self-Service Mama," it was about a guy who was flirting with a girl he'd met in line at a self-service station. Part of the chorus contained some mildly suggestive images, but we just thought they were funny.

Self-Service Mama
I like the way you wear your clothes . . .
Self-Service Mama
I love the way you hold the hose . . .

After Keith's set, Randy came up to him in a highly agitated state. "What in the world are you doing singing songs like that here? You've offended these people. This isn't the Bla Bla."

Keith was irritated too. "What are you talking about? These people don't know a good song when they hear one. Don't Christians have a sense of humor?"

"You blew it, man."

"Well, excuse me. Are you trying to tell me that 'Queen of the Rodeo' song you sang tonight had some kind of spiritual message?"

"Hey, there's nothing wrong with a simple love song," Randy said defensively. "I'm just trying to help you."

"You can help me by trying to understand where I'm at and by getting off my case."

After that Keith did become more cautious about the songs he sang for these super-Christian and unfunny people Randy was introducing us to. One that they especially seemed to like was a song Keith had been working on called "The Prodigal Son." It was from a story in the Bible about a young man who demanded his inheritance early from his father so he could go out and live on his own:

I was done hoeing,
Out in the fields for the day.
I was thinking of going.
I had to leave right away.
My father was reading
The holy books in his room.
My heart was just bleeding,
I knew I had to go soon. . . .
I said, "Father there's so much to know,

There's a world of things to see,
And I'm ready to go
and make a life for myself.
"If you give me what is mine,
I will go if I can have your blessing.
But if you won't bless my journey,
I'm gonna leave anyway!"

As the story goes, the father gives his son his share of the money, and the son goes out and squanders it on wild living, gets used by his friends, and finally hits rock bottom. Then he realizes what he gave away by leaving a home where he was loved. It was a powerful thirteen-minute-long song with several movements to it. Keith had worked on it for hours on end, and I was often his scribe as the music and lyrics came together. Keith decided we should write a rock opera with this song as the centerpiece.

At that time, I was working on a song with a similar theme but a much different feel. "Run to the End of the Highway" was a song I started for Todd. He had told us he was thinking of splitting from home in hopes of finding the truth about life somewhere out there.

Since I'd gone all the way to Asia on my search, and Keith had rifled through every spiritual option you could think of, it was appropriate that we finished the song together:

Well, you can run to the end of the highway
And not find what you're looking for
No, it won't make your troubles disappear.
And you can search to the end of the highway
And come back no better than before.
To find yourself you've got to start right here. . . .

It was crazy in a way. Here we were writing songs about people who needed to get their lives together, but our lives were slipping out of control again. Despite our heady, spiritual dialogues, we were once again falling back into the same old sloppy habits to deaden the pain of Keith's lack of success—not to mention our inner emptiness.

As Keith wrote disgustedly in his journal:

Took a downer, snorted coke—not good enough— smoked dope till the cows crowed.

Keith was really down on himself, and so was I. But a few days later at a party in a friend's gazebo we did it again. It was a beautiful day, and after a small argument about whether we should or shouldn't, Keith and I ended up smoking large amounts of hash. The drugs made us miserable and only underscored the fact that we were lost and failing in our search for God. We were beginning to realize that all our good intentions were getting us nowhere fast.

Nothing really seemed to be working for us. Drugs weren't enlightening our souls, but we lacked the willpower to quit. We'd given up meat and some of our favorite foods for two years hoping our sacrifice would trigger spiritual revelation. It didn't. Since being vegetarians didn't bring spiritual purity or get us closer to God, we figured why bother? To celebrate our decision to eat meat again, we went out for barbecued pork and scratched one more potential answer off our ever-shrinking list.

We couldn't seem to make it in our own strength, but did we have to know God before he'd help us? We didn't have the answer. We just knew we wanted to be pure and righteous, that we wanted to follow Jesus, and yet we seemed incapable of doing so. That's the way things continued through much of 1974. Keith wrote these two entries on the same day that summer:

July 29, 1974
Still Stoned

Always a rational reason why I can cloud up my clear sky and pretend that I'm getting "high." What a screw up!

Never believing in my will—a snort, a joint, a pill will screw up my head until I let my angel(s) lead me away.

God

> *There is no one to talk about how I feel. I love the Christ always—and Jesus and all the words and works. There's metaphysical Christians—and there's Jesus Freaks that scream, yell, and chant his name. But there's no confused Christians like me that I can see or meet.*
>
> *I love the goal so thoroughly that I'd give up anything to attain it if I were sure about the path. I believe in the virgin-birth, all the miracles, and the ascension, but I don't want to just do lip-service. (But I do see the value in speaking the truth—including names and credit where it is due, to the Master, or/and God.)*
>
> *And metaphysics is so dry and so undigestable to my spiritual heart. Ah! My heart—It wants to break for the truth and its fulfilling substance. It is time to put away diversions and time-wasting-fillers—and seek the truth and speak the truth and love my neighbors, truly love them all.*
>
> *Harness my tongue and mind. Point my every day in God's direction for His service only, only, only, only, not mine!*

It was clear that something had to break for us—and soon.

"THERE IS A REDEEMER"

In 1975, as we stumbled into our second full year of marriage, Keith had that old restlessness about him. Our life seemed to be rushing by at a crazy pace. We ran all over town, delivering the lead sheets we'd been writing and making demos of our new songs. A blind singer, Tom Sullivan, fell in love with one of Keith's songs, and the guy from Helen Reddy's management team picked six of Keith's songs to send to her, including "Love with Me."

Still nothing materialized.

Meanwhile, our relationship suffered many more tense moments. I was earning money with Keith on the lead sheets, and we worked pretty well as a team in everything—well, almost everything.

When it came to the house, we hit our big differences. I didn't want to be responsible for all the cooking, cleaning, and laundry. It didn't seem fair to me, but Keith had other ideas.

We had a fight about Mel cooking for me, and she wants it shared. I was still very mad at Mel cause she wouldn't take care of me. My head was fighting between selfish chauvinism and sincere belief that Mel should take responsibility for the homey things. I don't know. I know I'm lazy and never liked housework, but neither does Melody. Please let me know, God. I split . . . and called her and talked things out. She decided that she'd do the housewife trip for a while. It is resolved—temporarily.

Even more troubling, our spiritual houses needed a good cleaning up, but who did we call for that? It would have been a lot easier if we could have opened the phone book and found the number for "Charlie's Cosmic Clean-Up." We wanted to live a life that would somehow put us in contact with God in a real way, but it seemed as if we were just going backward.

The day after our domestic argument—while I cleaned the house—Keith poured out his spiritual frustrations in a song called "I Gotta Do Better Than This." Once again Keith captured the heart of our spiritual struggles.

Lord I'm not living up to your expectations
I've gotta do better than this
I've got no excuses
No explanations
I've just gotta do better than this
Lord, I've gotta do better than this

That night he wrote in his journal:

January 10, 1975

Mel cleaned all day and I lazied out and worked a little on music. I came up with the melody idea originally written at the Bla 12/14/74—put a verse and melody to it and wrote chorus lyrics.

Keith and I kept fighting the urge to forget everything by smoking dope or dropping a few pills. But it was a battle we kept losing.

One night in early February, after a wild weekend of partying, something strange happened to Keith while he was playing a one-nighter back at the Bla. Albie had been in a pinch for talent, and Keith had agreed to help him out.

We'd smoked some dope to help get us through the evening, and

Keith was really getting off on his performance. He had written one song in particular the year before that I had always loved. It was taken from a Bible story known as the "Good Samaritan." Before, the term "good Samaritan" had symbolized some weak guy who'd always go out of his way for everyone, letting everyone walk all over him—a totally weak and uncool person. But Keith's song, "On the Road to Jericho," gave the story a whole new meaning for me. People sat down with their drinks. I could tell they were really listening as Keith sang with deep emotion:

I left Jerusalem last week for Jericho.
In the afternoon, the sun was getting low.
Then the bushes shook and out they came at me—
They were robbing me half-naked
As they beat me head to toe.
Left me wounded on the road to Jericho.

Lying almost dead and wounded by the road,
Crying out in pain for a sympathetic soul.
First a priest and then another of my kind,
They were men I would have trusted,
But they acted deaf and blind.
They were strangers on the road to Jericho.

As Keith sang, it was as if he was the one crying out in pain. I could feel it and see it on his face as he grimaced while he cried out the words. I could only think of the times I'd felt abandoned by those I'd trusted. It seemed everyone in the club was zeroed in too. And then Keith's lament grew hopeful, as someone came to show mercy to this wounded traveler. Only it wasn't who the traveler expected:

Through the blood and tears I saw a worried face.
He was from Samaria, my people hate his race.

He bandaged up my wounds and laid me on his horse.
Though my memory is cloudy,
I can still feel his friendly glow—
Such a kind man on the road to Jericho!

It was a moving performance, but that's all I thought it was. I hadn't noticed anything out of the ordinary about Keith while he was singing. But as we drove home he said, "Mel, this incredible thing happened tonight when I was playing 'Jericho.' I don't know if I can explain it—but I felt a touch from God."

Keith didn't elaborate so I wasn't exactly sure what happened, but I wondered if he wasn't seeing himself as that wounded traveler. Later that night he confided in his journal:

February 8, 1975

Got stoned again. Made $64 at Bla. Had religious experience while playing "Jericho." Decided to immediately stop smoking. God entered my life again. . . .

Out of the gloomy despair of a dope-clouded mind came the call to New Life—the Christian calling again. After forsaking the Lord to escape from my conscience and my path (my own self-discipline) for the cloudy shroud of constant smoking—and playing so self-assured at the Bla—I felt the despair surround me and the Christian angel called me, saying "Come to my fold."

O Lord, forgive me. Take me in again, please my dear Lord, in Christ Jesus' name.

Praise God who never forgets but always forgives.

My perfect Father, I want to be with you and perfect too.

Once again Keith was caught up in his titanic inner struggle. It continued throughout the month.

Privately, he wrote:

February 23, 1975

The Calling

Oh I feel the calling so strong tonight. To join the holy army and fight the numbness in the world toward God. Even the very belief in the existence of God is a battle. But when I truly believe in God and I have to fight the insidious evils around me—and more horrifying, right inside me—I find myself feeling beaten, and hearing those Satanic words, "Give up. You're too human. Only the saints, priests, monks, and nuns are clean enough from the world and its forms to reach the Lord God and be chosen for Holy service."

Please, God, in Christ's name and teachings I want to be chosen to be with you . . . on your side only! No possibilities of any other master or side or path, or pseudo light, belief, or god. I want to forsake the evil one now!! I want to die for you, God, and be reborn a whole disciple. Living, emulating, and shining Your will, teachings, and bearing fruits everyday to everyone.

I love you, God. And I know You love me! The devil hates me more every day. He despises me more the closer I get to you. He's loosing his grip. Praise you, God. Your light is the only thing I want to see—and the only thing I want to reflect.

Blessed be your will.

In March, about a month after Keith's experience at the Bla, we decided we wanted to go to church. Since church was where most people who believed in Jesus hung out, we thought we'd give it a try. We met Randy Stonehill and another Christian rock musician, Larry Norman, at the Little Brown Church for their Sunday morning service. I took my first communion with soda crackers and grape juice. I left with a very warm feeling in my heart, and Keith had a fairly good experience too. He later wrote, "Stiff service, but great, great sermon on giving."

Going to a Christian church, however, also made us face one of the major problems we saw with Christianity—the supposed deity of Jesus. Spiritual master, yes. But God?

We were reading in our chocolate-brown, King James Bible things like John 1:1, which said, "The Word was with God and the Word was God." But we couldn't quite buy that. The idea even made Keith mad.

Once before, we'd tried going to a little Protestant church in Van Nuys. When we'd walked in, the usher in the back looked overjoyed. I guess not many hippies went to church there. We found some seats way in back, and the congregation started singing hymns. As we opened the hymnal, Keith flipped through it reading various lyrics. Suddenly he stood and said loudly, "Let's get out of here!" By reading some of the words Keith realized these people believed Jesus was not only the son of God, but that he was God. We walked out rather abruptly, and I was embarrassed. Now we were facing the "God question" again.

While growing up Keith had been taught that Jesus wasn't God—but he was a man who possessed the "true idea of God" more than all other men. As for me, I simply didn't see any way that a man who had walked on the earth could be God. There was no way I was going to worship a mere man.

To make things interesting, our old friend Todd started talking about joining a group of Christians who believed Jesus was God. Keith tried to talk him out of it: "It's better to be right with God and be alone, than to be wrong about him and be wrong with hundreds of people."

But Todd was a seeker in his own right and determined to follow his heart. He joined the group, and we started seeing a little less of him.

The Saturday night before Easter, Keith played at the Bla. We decided to go to church the next morning, but where do hippies, trying to find God, go on Easter? We'd seen an ad for a Sunrise Service at the Hollywood Bowl, a huge amphitheater that hosted wild rock concerts and symphonies under the stars. It seemed like our kind of place. Since Keith worked at the Bla until after 1:00 A.M., we decided to stay up all night until the 6:00 AM service.

After work we went to Jay Leon's Laurel Canyon house in Hollywood to wait for dawn. Keith wanted to talk Jay into coming with us, hoping he'd get into Jesus too. After we got there, Keith and Jay got into an extremely goofy mood. I got annoyed. I thought we should prepare our hearts in some way, even though I wasn't exactly sure how. It just seemed like this Jesus, whoever he really was, deserved some respect. Besides, I was hoping for some kind of revelation at the service and felt we needed to be in a more spiritual mood.

By now Keith had done a bunch of spiritual arm-twisting and Jay said he'd come with us. At 4:00 AM we got so hungry we all drove to Canter's Jewish Deli, open 24-7 on Fairfax Avenue. We loaded up on lox, bagels, cream cheese, and other munchies. After eating, Keith and Jay were so tired they got really loud and even sillier. I was laughing and irritated at the same time—and very relieved when it was time to go to church.

We drove to the Hollywood Bowl and found seats. I wrapped up in a blanket to fend off the cool morning air and we eagerly waited for the service to begin. It came and went without fanfare. After an hour of singing and listening to the preaching, Keith and I left feeling disappointed. We were sad that there was nothing about it that captured Jay's interest either. Keith later wrote:

March 30, 1975

Stayed up all night at Jay's. Watched videos til 4 A.M. Ate at Canter's. Dinged out. Mel got bummed cause we had no Easter austerity, but we were out of it. Sunrise services at the Bowl were real traditional. Singing and a weak sermon. Home, crashed until 4 P.M. Parents, dinner. Ten Commandments on TV.

Actually, watching *The Ten Commandments* was more inspiring to us than going to church. We liked the Old Testament stories, and with our growing trust in Jesus, we didn't mind being linked with him. Still, we didn't want to be identified with what we knew as Christianity. Even so, a few days later Keith bought a Bible for his friend Jay and drove over to give it to him.

Just after Easter Keith started to get some measure of success musically. Teddy Neely, our *Jesus Christ Superstar* friend, asked Keith to join his band for one of the hottest TV rock programs, *Midnight Special*, on NBC. Then Keith landed another night spot at a place called Goodbye Charlie's. Our CBS salary, which had been held up for several months because of some glitch, was about to be released, and it looked as if we were going to have more money than we'd know what to do with. Still these rumblings of bigger and better things to come left Keith with an unexpected sense of emptiness:

Dark Before the Dawn?

> *I've felt frustrated and a bit depressed the past few days.*
> *Everything I'm trying to do musically is futile.*
> *Spiritually I have not been high. It is discouraging.*
> *I feel so helpless in my desire to have musical success. It all seems to be on human levels that I desire it. But I know that there are spiritual reasons, and spiritual ways and means, to my life and purpose.*
> *Lord God, I pray to be comforted through this wait. Give me strength in Christ Jesus' name. Help me be patient. I am waiting for the time to arrive for me to reach the people and be accepted to retell the Christian story in parables, but my life is still unpure and not Christlike enough. Help, Lord.*

Then, one evening near the end of April, dawn started to break. Keith's old friend Randy Wimer came over. Todd came over, too, and we ended up having what Keith called "a great Bible debate." The talk centered, of course, on God and Jesus. We were confused. If Jesus was God, did that make him his own father? That wasn't even logical. And why did people worship Jesus when the Bible says to only worship God?

Randy brought up a Scripture we'd never heard. It was out of the New Testament book of Hebrews, a book written to Jewish followers of Jesus, so my ears perked up. "God commanded all the angels to worship Jesus when he was born," Randy said. Then he read Hebrews 1:8: "'But unto the Son he saith, Thy throne, O God, is for ever and ever.'"

Keith grabbed the Bible from Randy. "Let me see that. God calls Jesus God?"

"He sure does. God even calls Jesus 'Lord' a few verses down." Randy took the Bible back and read, "God says, 'Thou, Lord, in the beginning hast laid the foundation of the earth; and the heavens are the works of thine hands.'"

"You mean it says Jesus created the earth? That's something to think about. But I'm still not buying this 'Jesus is God' stuff," Keith insisted.

The next night, Keith drove Randy Wimer to his parents' house, which was about an hour away. All the way there they argued about the Scriptures and whether they were totally accurate and inspired word-for-word. To Keith it seemed impossible that the whole Bible could be absolutely true. How could men write a book that was perfect? Keith later wrote:

> Randy kept claiming the Holy Spirit is the source of his translation and interpretation, and then something clicked inside.
>
> On the way home, tears filled my eyes and I was filled with the Holy Spirit.

A short time later he also wrote:

The Holy Ghost
Last Monday I discovered the knowledge of the existence of the Holy Ghost. As the personal vehicle through which the Son comes into our personal lives. . . .

I feel so strong, my love for the Father and my trust in the Father. I am learning to love the Son and only now seeing the need to acknowledge a third entity, separate in identity, but one with the others in purpose. . . . Please, Father, in Christ Jesus' name, bring the Holy Ghost into my life and baptize me. Amen.

The day after Keith wrote that prayer, we decided, with some uncertainty, to accept Todd's invitation to go to a service at the church he'd joined. Todd had taken a leap of faith and had not only joined this church, but also moved into their small community of believers—the ones who believed Jesus was God.

That evening when we arrived, the hall was fairly crowded and we took a seat on some folding chairs toward the back. Todd sat with us, and I could tell he was really pleased that we made the effort to come. The people looked normal enough, which took the edge off the moment. The last thing we wanted to do was spend the evening with a bunch of religious wackos.

A man went to the front and talked for several minutes. Then a young guy in blue jeans and a football T-shirt, sitting a few feet to our right, jumped up. He had a Bible in his hand and looked as if he was about to read something. Instead he started to shout out passages from the Bible at the top of his lungs!

Keith and I exchanged knowing glances, rolling our eyes a bit, and sunk down in our chairs. Our worst fears were confirmed as people started popping up all over the place, yelling out Scriptures. As soon as the first guy was done, an elderly woman stood and gave him a run for his money in the shouting department. It seemed more like a football game than a church service.

I leaned over and whispered in Keith's ear, "What are these people shouting for?" It was more of a statement of irritation than a question.

"Who knows," said Keith. "But one thing's for sure, these people are straaange."

Todd started shifting in his seat. Our disapproving whispers were not exactly subtle. Besides, Todd could read Keith like a book.

Suddenly, right in the middle of it all, Keith rose to his feet, his chair scraping against the cement floor as he stood. I held my breath wondering what he was going to do. He simply turned and walked up the aisle and right out the front door.

I was so surprised that I wasn't sure what to do. Todd looked deflated. Neither of us said a word, but Todd was starting to cry a little. Finally I got up and walked outside. I found Keith pacing back and forth in the parking lot.

"Something's not right, Mel. It's not just the yelling. I can't put my finger on it."

"I think Todd's kinda upset that you left," I ventured.

"I had to get out of there. I felt like I was going to explode."

"Well, what do you want to do?"

"I'm not ready to go back yet. You go back in and I'll see you there in a few minutes."

I went back inside for what was left of the service, hoping the yelling was over. It was. I hung around the back of the hall until Keith returned. When the meeting ended, Todd slowly made his way over to us. I felt kind of bad for him and could tell he was embarrassed. But Keith didn't cut Todd any slack.

"Hey, Bro, why didn't you jump up and shout with the rest of them?"

"You know me," Todd said meekly, "I'm not one to put on a show."

Afterward we went out to eat with Todd, and he and Keith continued their ongoing arguments.

"What about Philippians, chapter two?" Todd challenged.

He quoted a passage that said Jesus was "in the form of God" although he came to earth as a humble servant. Because Jesus had suffered death on the cross, the Bible said, "God also hath highly exalted him, and given him a name which is above every name—"

"Okay," Keith countered, "so I agree that God has exalted Jesus. But it still doesn't say he was God, directly anyway. You see, I can argue every one of your Scriptures away," Keith said self-assuredly.

"You can argue, but you don't really have any answers. You're just unwilling to believe," Todd replied angrily.

"I'm not willing to believe everything I hear. Todd, how can you live with those people? They're so strange. You need to get out of there."

"Hey, at least I'm doing something spiritual. What do you have that's better?"

As we drove home from the restaurant, Keith and I tried to sort through the whole evening. We decided that we were really turned off by the church service, but we really liked being in a spiritual atmosphere talking to spiritual people. Keith wanted to go back and check them out again the next week. But the last thing I wanted was to get stuck in a group like Todd's.

"Keith, if we're going to start going to church, let's check out some more options," I said. "Maybe we should try that group Randy Stonehill invited us to go to."

Two days after our experience at Todd's church, we called Randy Stonehill and found out where his Bible study was. They met in a private home in Coldwater Canyon on the other side of the mountain in Beverly Hills. Randy gave us directions.

The Vineyard Christian Fellowship met in a fashionable part of town. There were no halls or churches in sight—just palm trees, manicured lawns, four-car garages, iron gates, security systems, and an occasional uniformed nanny pushing a baby stroller. Coldwater Canyon was definitely on the "Map to the Movie Stars' Homes" sold down on Sunset Boulevard. I figured plenty of wealthy doctors and lawyers lived here too.

We drove over and parked in front of a large yellow house that sat in a huge yard filled with flowers and trees. A white picket fence surrounded all of it. We got out of the car and opened the gate. The house was not as fancy as some of the Spanish or Tudor homes nearby, but to me it spoke of family, commitment, and money—lots of money.

Inside, we stepped into a large entryway just off the living room. About thirty-five people were sitting on couches, chairs, and the thickly carpeted floor. We quietly found a spot on the floor, smiled a bit guardedly, and waited for the meeting to start.

A young man with yellow-blond hair, a round friendly face, and warm and smiling eyes went to the front of the room and sat by the fireplace. He introduced himself as Kenn Gulliksen and started speaking. His gentle manner immediately put me at ease. Keith looked relaxed too. As we sat cross-legged on the floor, Kenn led the group in some songs we'd never heard before. Not knowing any of the words, we just listened:

Father I adore you,
Lay my life before you.
How I love you. . . .

The words just flowed over me. People broke into gentle harmonies that all seemed to weave in and out of each other. I felt a strange sense of peace start to wash over me—a peace that was like the intense emotion I'd felt the night, several years before, when I'd seen myself at the foot of the flaming cross. Only this time it wasn't coming from a drug-induced hallucination. I closed my eyes and felt myself relaxing.

Jesus I adore you,
Lay my life before you.
How I love you. . . .

As the group sang about Jesus I could picture him in my mind's eye. It seemed so natural to think about him in this place. A moment ago it had been a fancy Beverly Hills living room, but now it seemed like a place where the disciples of Jesus met. I almost felt as if I could reach out and touch the fringe of Jesus' robe as he walked by. The spirit in the room was contagious, and the song was so easy to pick up that Keith and I started to sing along as they moved into it a second time. I felt so wonderful I thought I was going to fly off into heaven.

Kenn Gulliksen closed the time of singing with a simple prayer and started talking about God. "Just today I felt like I'd blown it with my wife by getting impatient. But you know, I realized that in 1 John 1:9 it says if we come to Jesus and confess our sins, he's faithful to forgive our sins. So I closed my eyes and simply said, 'Lord, please forgive me for offending Joni.' And then I went to Joni and asked her forgiveness too. It was really beautiful."

I'd never heard anybody talk like that before. It just sounded so down to earth. He made Jesus sound like his best friend or something. It didn't seem abstract or mystical at all. I gave Keith a sideways glance to see if I could read his expression. He had that intent look on his face, the one where his eyes got deep and penetrating. He was totally absorbed.

Kenn also talked about how much God loved each one of us. "Just like I love my wife and children, and want to protect them and take care of them—that's how God loves you. He wants to be in a love relationship with you." He said being in a relationship with God would change our lives; that we could become new people by asking Jesus to forgive our sins and welcoming him into our hearts. There was nothing weird or spooky about anything Kenn was saying. The very best part was that he made it seem like getting to know God—really getting to know him—was totally possible. It sure seemed like he knew God.

Then Kenn talked about how God sent his only son down to earth to live among us and show us the way to the Father. But we needed to be cleansed of our sins to be in a relationship with the Father—and that's where Jesus' death on the cross came in. Jesus was the only offering pure enough to be a sacrifice for the wrong things we've all done that have hurt God and hurt others.

I didn't like all the "Jesus on the cross" talk, but my mind was racing. I knew in the Old Testament days God required the Jewish people to sacrifice the best "spotless" lamb, cow, or ram they could afford. This sacrifice, along with their confession of sins, gained them forgiveness for their sins of the past year. Then a new year started. Everyone had a clean slate and a chance to do better.

Kenn's words broke into my thoughts. He quoted the book of Hebrews explaining, "Without the shedding of blood, there is no remission of sins." He said, "The Jewish people being spoken to knew exactly what the writer meant because they were still sacrificing animals: some of their best if they had large herds, and the poor had to buy an animal to sacrifice. Nothing could be taken away for a feast afterward. It was a costly event."

Of course, animals weren't sacrificed anymore, but the Jewish people still confessed their sins to God. For a sacrifice they would fast from food and water for twenty-four hours on the Day of Atonement—Yom Kippur; the day my mom always took me to synagogue.

My mind was spinning. It seemed Jewish people and followers of Jesus—even today—believed sin was real and needed to be confessed. They also believed that some type of costly sacrifice was necessary for forgiveness. As Kenn spoke he was saying that God gave his son Jesus to be that sacrifice—one time, for all of mankind. The only thing was, we needed to receive it.

"It's like a beautiful present from a friend," Kenn said. "If you don't allow them to give it to you, you'll miss the blessing and they'll be hurt. You need to open your heart to Jesus and let him come into your life. Embrace his sacrifice as your own. He made it for you."

Kenn spoke for about forty minutes, and when he was done he asked everyone to bow their heads and close their eyes. He asked, "Is there anyone here who wants to ask Jesus into your heart—to give your whole life to him? When you ask Jesus to forgive your sins, you'll become a brand-new person. It's like being born again—only it's not a physical rebirth. It's a spiritual one."

You could almost hear hearts beating.

Then Kenn said, "Just raise your hand if you want to receive Jesus." I sat with my eyes closed. It felt as if lead balloons had been tied to my arms. My heart was pounding wildly, and I felt a pressure in my chest. The invitation was repeated but I could not raise my hand.

I felt Keith stir, and I peeked out of the corner of one eye. To my surprise—and dismay—I saw his hand raised high into the air. Now I felt even more pressure to do the same thing, but I just couldn't get my arm to move. One part of me wanted to jump up and shout, "Jesus, I want you! Please forgive me!" But another part of me was sitting back, observing the whole scene and saying, "No way am I going to do this! I'm Jewish. We don't believe in Jesus!"

After a minute or so, Kenn prayed right out loud for everyone who had their hand raised and asked them to repeat some things after him. I wanted that prayer to be for me, too, so I said it in my heart, but I knew I hadn't raised my hand. The moment was over now, and I'd missed my chance.

As the meeting closed, we had to leave right away because Keith had a gig that night at Goodbye Charlie's. On the way out the door, someone said, "I'm glad you came tonight. I've been praying for you." It was a guy we'd briefly met at Randy Stonehill's birthday party a few months ago, and I couldn't believe he'd actually been praying for us. I'd never had anybody in my whole life tell me that. I thanked him and wondered why he'd want to pray for total strangers and what kind of things he'd been praying for.

Keith and I jumped into Victor and headed off to work. Keith was elated and talking a mile-a-minute: "Boy, it was really great tonight. I've never felt anything like it. This is really it, Mel. I feel like I finally found what I've been looking for."

I slouched down in my dark little corner of the van, feeling worse and worse as Keith went on. *Yeah, you did it, but I blew it. What if that was my one big chance to get right with God? I should have raised my hand. Oh God, can I have a second chance? What if I go back next week?* I was happy for Keith, but I felt miserable.

At Goodbye Charlie's I wasn't sure I was ready for the evening. This place was a lot more like a bar than the Bla Bla, although it was decorated much better with red velvet cushions and mirrored walls. But the overall feeling was sleazy. I noticed a sexy-looking blonde sitting on a bar stool. Her skirt was hiked up and she was leaning toward some greasy guy who resembled a hungry shark getting ready for dinner. As we passed them, I heard him ask what her name was. It gave me an uneasy feeling to know people came here to get drunk and get picked up. What a switch from our time at the house in Coldwater Canyon.

Keith did his best, but tonight he seemed to be having a hard time. During one of his breaks, he looked at me and said, "I just can't do this anymore. Something's wrong. I don't know what it is, but I just don't fit in here." Keith had been really excited to get this job, but at the end of the evening he said good-bye to Goodbye Charlie's forever. He never went back.

That week was one of the longest I'd ever spent. As I stood in line at the market and ran around town with Keith, I kept thinking, *I want to go back to the Vineyard. I hope he asks us to raise our hands again. I hope it's not too late for me.* My mind seemed stuck, and I could think of nothing else.

I wrestled with so many questions. I thought about Keith and how he was willing to let go of everything in Christian Science that didn't line up with Bible truth. My dilemma was different. I could never convert to another religion or let go of being Jewish. Being Jewish felt like a literal force pumping through my veins, woven into my DNA. But as I pondered what I'd already read in the Bible, along with my new studies, a few simple facts fell into place.

First of all, Jesus was Jewish. A rabbi. He taught in the synagogues. The twelve apostles, the elders, Jesus' family, and essentially all of his early followers were Jewish. This included the five thousand who were fed supernaturally, as well as everyone at the Sermon on the Mount, one of my favorite readings. God sent the Redeemer to the

Jews first because they believed in the one true God while everyone else worshiped stones and idols and things like that.

In fact, when non-Jews—Gentiles—began to receive Jesus, the Jewish leaders already following him had some big arguments. Many thought the Gentiles who wanted to follow Jesus needed to become Jewish first and keep Jewish laws like abstaining from unclean foods. They even considered making every Gentile man who wanted to follow Jesus get circumcised, no matter how old he was! They were serious about keeping it "totally Jewish" to follow Jesus.

But the book of Acts showed clearly that you didn't need to be Jewish to follow the Jewish Messiah. It also seemed clear in the New Testament that following Jesus was the most Jewish thing a Jew could do. I was stunned to realize it was the Gentiles who were making a switch if they wanted to follow Jesus. They were being "grafted in" to the root of Judaism! And Jesus loved us all equally and set us free to love each other.

New believers, 1975

On top of all that, I'd recently learned that Jesus fulfilled more than three hundred Old Testament prophecies about the coming Messiah, including where he'd be born and that he would be rejected.

One prophecy in particular impacted me deeply. I couldn't believe it was actually in the Old Testament. I'd never heard it before. The Jewish prophet Isaiah talked about the kind of punishment and death the Messiah would suffer. That when he died he would be pierced for our sins. *Pierced!* That word blew my mind. If that didn't describe Roman crucifixion, I don't know what did! There was no prescribed

Jewish death penalty that included piercing. Isaiah said that he also carried all of our sins, paying the death penalty for all of mankind to gain forgiveness at once. He was the spotless Lamb of God. Our eternal sacrifice. It's what Kenn was explaining last week. And there it was in chapter fifty-three straight from Isaiah's mouth.

> He was pierced through for our transgressions,
> He was crushed for our iniquities;
> The chastening for our well-being fell upon Him,
> And by His scourging we are healed. (v. 5 NASB)

I read it over and over again all week, and it pretty much sealed the deal for me on the Jewish side of things. But maybe the most important thing I learned was that the closer I got to Jesus, the more my spirit was coming alive. The more I opened my heart to him, the more excitement and genuine peace I was experiencing—more than I'd ever known.

By the end of the week, I had what my heart needed. I'd made what I called the "Jewish Connection." I wouldn't be betraying my Judaism to follow Jesus. I just needed to receive the gift that Kenn talked about. Yes, I would receive Jesus as the promised Jewish Messiah for all of mankind. It suddenly seemed foolish not to. Even if I called myself a "Christian" like the early Jewish believers did, all it literally meant was being "a follower of Christ." It didn't mean I'd converted to anything. It was just stating a fact.

Finally I realized I could totally follow Jesus and still be totally Jewish!

When Friday night arrived and we walked into that big yellow house, the excitement in my heart was at an all-time high. We sat on the floor again, and when the singing started I could hardly wait for all the preliminaries to be over. Kenn spoke again, and then—at last!—he got to the hand-raising part.

"Is there anybody here who wants to give their heart to the Lord?" he asked.

To my surprise I hesitated. I thought, *This is crazy—I've been waiting all week.*

For the next few moments, I went through an inner battle. Something inside was fighting against me giving my heart to Jesus. Other hands were raised, but I was thinking, *Maybe I'll just raise my hand next week.*

Just then a gentle voice broke into my personal war zone.

"I believe there's another person here who needs to receive the Lord tonight," Kenn said patiently.

I knew he was talking about me. Then I thought, *That's impossible. How could he know?*

The room was totally quiet. My heart was pounding in my chest. *It's now or never,* I thought. Something was tugging at me to open my heart totally to Jesus, but something else wanted me to keep my hand down. These forces were working against each other—right inside me! Then I knew that I had to make the choice. *If I don't raise my hand right now, nobody is going to do it for me,* I thought. *I need to choose sides.*

Quietly I slipped my hand high into the air—just as I used to do in bed at night as a little girl. Only this time I knew what I was reaching for. As I made my choice, I heard "amens" whispered quietly around the room.

Kenn immediately prayed for all of us who were receiving the Lord that night, and a rush of peace filled my heart—a peace deeper than anything I'd ever experienced in my whole life.

Clockwise from top: Melody and Keith; Beach baptism; Keith and Melody at the Dolorosa St. house; Keith and Jay Leon

"YOU PUT THIS LOVE IN MY HEART"

We finally did it. It was hard to believe we were really part of a big family following God, but it was true. Even though we were excited about Jesus and the new way we'd opened our hearts to him, we still had a lot of reservations about Christianity in general. We'd spent so many years wading through spiritual counterfeits and wandering down the wrong paths that we were a bit wary of swallowing everything we heard. Just because somebody says something is Christian doesn't mean it really is. We wanted pure, undiluted Christianity—not a slightly modified version. For some time, though, it seemed as if an unseen hand was at work, bringing the right people into our lives and keeping out the people who would draw us away from Jesus.

Keith was painfully cautious about spending time with anyone who might influence him in a wrong way spiritually. In fact, on the very day I raised my hand at the Vineyard Fellowship, an old friend of Keith's had come over to visit us. His name was Doug, and after catching up on old times Keith told him all about what we were going through spiritually and our recent visit to the Vineyard. Doug seemed to lean toward Eastern thought forms, but as we talked about Christianity something seemed to click.

Doug said, "I know somebody who's a Christian! He's really heavy-duty."

"Really?" said Keith. I was interested too.

"Yeah! He's eighty-seven years old and really wise."

"Where does he live?" asked Keith.

"He lives right here in Woodland Hills," Doug answered. Keith and I were still fairly new to this community and the little house on Dolorosa Street. "I was going to go see him tomorrow. Do you want to meet him? His name's Richard Gene Lowe. He's Chinese."

Keith's expression fell. "Chinese? Forget it!"

"Why?"

"I'm not into Eastern religions anymore—all that stuff's occult. Forget it."

"But this guy's a Christian," Doug insisted.

"He's probably into some mix of Christianity—with Jesus, Buddha, and Eastern mysticism all blended together. I don't want anything to do with that stuff."

I thought that was the end of the matter. The day after I'd given my heart to Jesus, however, there was a knock at our door. Keith jumped off the couch to answer it, and I was right behind him. There on our front porch was Doug with a sheepish grin on his face. Standing right next to him was a short, silver-haired Chinese man—obviously his friend Richard Gene Lowe.

It was an awkward moment, but before Keith had a chance to react, they both stepped inside. Once inside the door, Richard immediately gave each of us a big hug. Then both of his hands shot up into the air as he said joyfully, "Praise the Lord! Praise God!"

It was an odd thing. For the first time, those words didn't sound weird at all. And something about Richard's face instantly drew me.

Richard Gene Lowe was radiant. His happy grin pushed his round cheeks up toward his eyes, making them all crinkled and laughing around the edges. It was almost as if there was some kind of a holy light streaming from this little man. He had something special, the kind of inner joy we wanted. Instinctively I knew it was for real. Even Keith seemed to relax at once. I was thankful because it wouldn't have been beyond Keith to throw both Doug and Richard out of the house.

This little man captivated us at once, and we ended up spending the entire day together. Our conversation ranged from music to the deity of Jesus. We also learned from Doug that when he had told

Richard about us, Richard insisted on being brought to our house so he could meet us. Now we were very glad that he had.

We were fascinated by the incredible story of Richard's life. He told us he'd become a Christian in China seventy years before, when he was just fourteen. He almost married, but when he came to America his fiancée changed her mind. He never married, remaining celibate all these years. He also told us he never took any medicine.

"Except an aspirin once," he said. "The Lord always heals me."

Then he told us story after story of how he'd been healed. When he was younger and working with big diesel trucks, he'd jumped up on a running board and slipped. When he grabbed something, his hand wrapped around a hot exhaust pipe. The burn was so bad that his hand was bright red and the skin was peeling off. He prayed and asked God to heal him, then wrapped up his hand.

"The next day," he said, "it was totally healed. There was only a slight trace to show that it had ever been burned."

We eagerly listened to one story after another of Richard's own healings and the healings of other Christians that he'd witnessed through the years. It was beyond mystical; it was miraculous! And he didn't seem to be making these stories up either.

As he talked, Keith kept looking at me with an astonished, can-you-believe-this? look on his face. Keith had been wondering if Christians believed in healing. He had seen healings while growing up, and read in his Christian Science studies that the sick are healed simply "knowing" there isn't any sickness. And when you "know the truth" your imaginary sickness is gone. Just a few months earlier, Keith had written in his journal:

> I will not take any steps to cut myself off from Christian Science until I feel sure that its benefits of healing the sick are as plenty in a Christian's life. . . .

It seemed incredible that, immediately after making a commitment to Christ, Keith's questions about healing were being answered by this unlikely little man—someone who pursued us even when he knew we didn't want to meet him!

During the course of that first day with Richard, Keith brought up something that was weighing heavily on his heart—Todd.

Keith described the meeting we'd been to, where everyone was shouting out Scriptures. He also mentioned the name of the group and their leader. "Ever heard of these people?"

Richard's eyebrows went up slightly and he nodded. "Oh yes, I've heard of them."

"Well, what do you know about them?" Keith asked. "My best friend, Todd, is living with them. The last time we talked he told me he smashed and burned his amplifier and even burned the cross that was around his neck because this group is heavy-duty against materialism. What could be wrong with wearing a cross? It sounds weird to me."

Richard shook his head and said quietly, "It's not good. They are not true Christians. If he's your friend, we need to pray. We must try to help him."

That was all Keith needed to hear. He was off the couch in a flash, dialing Todd's number. As soon as Todd was on the line Keith made him promise to meet us at Shadow Ranch Park the following afternoon.

The next day Todd did meet us at Shadow Ranch Park, and we cut Richard loose on him. We also told Todd all about our experiences with the Vineyard Fellowship and all the neat new people we'd been meeting. This impressed Todd because he'd prayed to receive Jesus too. But this group he was going to had told him they were the only true church. After what seemed like hours of talking and debate, Todd saw that out of his zeal to make a radical commitment, he'd gotten hooked up with the wrong people.

Finally, he said, "All this really makes sense. I'm going to leave the group right away."

Keith was so relieved, and I, too, was elated at this turn of events.

It was amazing to me how much satisfaction Keith got out of

rescuing Todd from that very dangerous spiritual situation. We now knew that the group was a cult. I might have taken a more passive route, figuring Todd would eventually see for himself that he was in the wrong place. But not Keith. He couldn't, wouldn't rest while he knew his friend needed help. That was the way he was. If there was anything he could do or say to help someone he loved, he always went for broke.

Things were really starting to happen fast. We were so grateful for Richard. He became one of our best friends, and the three of us, along with Todd, became inseparable for months. We spent hours and days together running all over town. Richard had never learned how to drive, so we'd pick him up at his little bachelor apartment, which was so stacked with books and newspapers it was beyond clutter. We often went to garage sales and once, for five dollars, he bought a suit that I altered to fit him. We also loved to pick up chili dogs at Cupid's, our favorite local stand. Richard would laugh as he jumped into Victor, joking about how he kept up with us at his age. The whole time Keith, Todd, and I pumped Richard with questions about God and prayer. Richard was especially big on prayer. He loved telling us about the way it changes things.

"Prayer must be a two-way conversation," he insisted. "You talk, God listens. God talks, you listen."

"What do you mean God talks? Can you hear him?" Keith asked.

"Some people have heard his voice. I hear him in my heart. He speaks to me in a still, small voice."

I asked, "How do you know it's just not your own thoughts you're hearing?"

"That's why you need to get to know God intimately. So you can learn the difference."

In the midst of all our questions, we found out that Richard believed Jesus was God. Even though Keith and I were still skeptical on that point, it didn't turn us off to Richard like it might have in the past. In fact, it didn't change the way we felt about him at all. We loved him and there was no question that he loved us.

Since Keith was never one to keep a good thing to himself, he wanted all of our friends to meet Richard too. We immediately started inviting people to our house so Richard could talk to them about God. Todd was usually there and so were some friends from the Bla. Debbie Docis, one of Keith's fans, soon gave her heart to the Lord at one of these little studies.

Since Richard loved to pray, he began teaching us how to talk to God. We'd all sit in a circle and hold hands. Then Richard would pray as we tentatively followed, offering some of the first prayers we'd ever said out loud.

Richard said, "The reason we pray out loud sometimes is so we can all agree with each other's prayers."

Richard was always teaching us, but he did it in a way that seemed natural. He never made us feel bad about all the things we didn't know or as if we needed a lot of help. He just quietly and kindly helped us without pushing us further than we were able to go.

One day Richard told us he'd volunteered for years at Katherine Kuhlman Miracle Services. We insisted on tagging along once. Keith and I sat in the balcony, and Richard went off to help people in the wheelchair section as usual. It was an amazing day.

Not only did we see people who at least looked like they were getting healed, but also unbelieving doctors read medical reports from the stage to confirm healings their patients had received at previous services. At the end, Katherine Kuhlman called people forward who needed a healing. We took the opportunity to get closer and went forward for some minor problems. We stood in the aisle with several hundred others.

When she prayed and waved her arm from one side of the room to the other, we looked wide-eyed at each other. We both felt a strong and tangible power sweep across the room. We didn't get healed like some people, but we were very encouraged to know for sure that Jesus was into healing hurting people.

Richard was an almost daily influence on us, and as we continued going to the Vineyard, Kenn Gulliksen was beginning to help us sort through our questions. It was Kenn who finally helped Keith settle the "God question."

After a meeting, Keith and I walked up to him and Keith said, "I know you believe Jesus is God, but what does that make the Father? There's only one God. Can you help me understand why you believe the way you do?"

Keith and Kenn Gulliksen

Kenn smiled. "Keith, what you're struggling with is called the Trinity—the Father, the Son, and the Holy Spirit. It really is a mystery. But I think I can shed some light on it for you." He picked up his Bible and turned toward the back, running his finger down the page.

"Here, Keith, listen to this," Kenn said. "This Scripture, Colossians chapter two, verse nine, is talking about Jesus: 'For in Him all the fullness of Deity dwells in bodily form (NASB).'"

Keith looked blank. "I still don't get it."

"Well, look at it this way. Just think of water, steam, and ice. They're all made out of exactly the same substance, but all three are distinctly different. God is a lot like that. But the analogy breaks down. An ice cube can't be a puddle of water and a puff of steam all at the same time—but God is all three at the same time!"

Kenn went on to explain that Christians only believe in one God, but that he expresses himself in three persons or personalities called the "Trinity." Jesus the Son was the physical expression of God the Father. He came to earth in the form of a man and lived a sinless life among us so he could show us the way to the Father. The Holy Spirit is the invisible power of God. He's like a breeze rustling leaves in a tree. You can't see the breeze, but when it blows you can see the effects.

As Kenn shared, we realized that the idea in the Bible is not that a man became God, but that God himself came as a man. To us, this made a huge difference! We remembered reading something in the Old Testament, where the coming Messiah was portrayed as coming as a child, but also being a son and a Father. It was in Isaiah 9:6: "For unto us a child is born, unto us a son is given: and the government shall be upon his shoulder: and his name shall be called Wonderful, Counsellor, the mighty God, the everlasting Father, the Prince of Peace."

Nobody had ever made it all sound so simple. I could tell something was clicking in Keith's mind as he listened to Kenn. I wasn't sure how I felt, but as usual I was taking most of my cues from Keith, and he was keeping his thoughts to himself just now.

A short time later we were visiting my mom one evening, and Keith took a walk by himself after dark. When he came back in, he looked very serious.

"I need to talk to you. Alone."

I was in the middle of trying to talk my mom into giving her heart to Jesus and felt a bit reluctant about just getting up and leaving.

"Right now?"

Keith nodded his head. "Let's take a walk."

Once we got outside I could see how serious Keith really was. When we got down the steps and out onto the sidewalk, he turned to me and simply said, "I bought it."

"You bought what? What do you mean?"

"I believe Jesus is God. I might not understand it totally right now, but something in my heart tells me it's true."

Now I was the one who got serious. I looked up at the moon and wondered what Keith's decision would mean for me. I found out in two seconds.

"Mel, you need to accept it too."

"I want to, if it's true. But I don't know if it is."

"Just do it, Mel. Just take a leap of faith if you need to. I think it's the thing that's been holding us back. I want you to believe with me. I don't want to leave you behind."

I stood silently in the darkness, my heart beating wildly. Kenn's analogy came back to me—water, steam, and ice. But there was something else. Since talking with Kenn, a Jewish friend who believed in Jesus told me that while the Old Testament emphasized the oneness of God because of the worship of multiple gods at that time, there were many hints that he is also somehow more than one. The key Jewish prayer is, "Hear, O Israel, the Lord our God, the Lord is One." But the very word used in that prayer to proclaim the oneness of God—*echad*—allows for a plurality within that unity. Also, the common word in Hebrew for God, *Elohim,* is plural in form too.

It did make sense in a mysterious sort of way. Since asking Jesus into my heart, it really did seem like I had a lot more faith. So I mustered up all the newfound faith I had at the moment and simply said, "Okay. I'll do my best to buy it too."

We were over the edge. We were not only Christians, but we'd found a group of people to learn about Jesus with and two men we really trusted to help us along the way—Richard and Kenn.

We launched into Christianity with a bright burst of enthusiasm and optimism. It was like being shot out of a cannon, and we hit the ground running. Suddenly we started noticing Christian symbols everywhere. While driving down the freeway we'd watch for cars with "Praise the Lord" bumper stickers so we could drive by and give them the "one way" sign we'd just learned—pointing our index finger to the sky, signifying there's only one way to heaven. Then we'd wave at them like they were long-lost relatives because seeing a Christian bumper sticker meant someone who loved Jesus was driving that car!

We felt as if we had joined a big club with millions of people already in it, and we were excited about meeting all of them. We also noticed lots of people wearing fish and dove necklaces, pins, and T-shirts. We learned the symbol of a fish was a secret sign for the early church during their times of persecution, and the dove represented the Holy Spirit. I'd seen these secret codes before, but I never knew what they meant. Now if we saw someone wearing a fish or a dove, we'd walk up and eagerly say, "Hi. You're a Christian, aren't you? We are too!"

So many things in our life started changing so fast that it was a real shock to everyone, including us. Instead of going to parties all the time, we started going to Bible studies almost every night. We even went to a Bible characters party. I sewed Keith a coat of many colors, and he went as Joseph. I put on lots of makeup and went as Delilah, with scissors dangling from the belt of my long velvet dress.

Melody and Keith in costume

Besides the Vineyard, our favorite home study was up in the Hollywood Hills at a tiny two-story house owned by the Cramers, a couple in show business. They had a goat tied up on their front porch, and in their loft, in a large circus cage, they had a monkey that chattered through our Bible studies. One regular there was Wendell Burton, who had starred in a movie with Liza Minnelli and was now a Christian recording artist. Another neighbor, Leo, from next door, had a drinking problem, but he was there whenever he was dry. It was a typical Hollywood crowd, only it was different too. These were the kinds of people we were used to getting together with, but this time it wasn't to have a party. It was to learn about following Jesus.

We learned about Jesus everywhere we could. One night we went to Hillcrest Christian Church in Thousand Oaks with Richard and Todd. We heard a man named Hans Christian talk about the suffering church—that is, Christians who lived in Communist countries, those who could not openly worship God. Many of them were murdered or put in hard-labor camps and insane asylums. We were shocked. I felt stirred in my heart, but something far more moving happened to Keith. He wrote:

My heart was speared by the Spirit to compassion. I cried for the suffering church and pledged to help take on some of that burden.

The next night Keith told some friends all about the suffering church to help get the word out and raise prayer support for persecuted believers. Keith also asked Kenn if Hans Christian could speak at the Vineyard.

Two nights later Hans Christian spoke, and Kenn gave everyone an opportunity to give toward this man's work with the suffering church. Five hundred dollars was collected, and Keith was thrilled. He also added the suffering church to his new prayer list.

This led us to some questions about why our pastor lived in such a huge house in such a wealthy neighborhood. We were relieved to hear that Kenn and his family were house-sitting for a friend. It was a big blessing to them because they barely had any money.

All of a sudden, we were also totally gung-ho about getting everyone we knew to meet and receive Jesus.

Keith was still playing at the Bla, and he decided to tell everyone there that he had become a Christian. We called all of our friends and told them Keith was doing something special at the Bla, but we didn't tell them Keith was going to share his testimony. One person we really wanted to come that night was our friend Michelle Brandes, who had been a fan for more than a year. Michelle knew about our spiritual search, but she was a Jewish youth leader at a local synagogue and was not interested in Jesus. She did love Keith's music, so when we invited her to this special night she took the bait.

The Bla was packed that night as Keith played a few older songs about being lost, and a song I had recently written, "Don't You Wish You Had the Answers?"

Look out your window see the earth
Where did it come from? Who gave it birth?
Where did it come from? Where will it go?

Don't you wish you had the answers
Well, I know . . .

Just look out past the stars
Look to the one who put them there
He made them all
He made them for us, for us to share
He made them all . . .
But he's gonna take them all back someday

At the end of his set, Keith talked about finding Jesus. As soon as he finished, Michelle stood up and bolted out of the club. Keith was right behind her. When he caught up with her, they took a stormy walk around the block.

"I came to hear you sing, not preach! Why didn't you just tell me you'd become a Christian?"

"Mich," Keith said, "Jesus has really changed my life. He can change yours too."

"I don't want my life changed! Besides, have you forgotten I'm Jewish?"

"So am I!" Keith said.

"Please, Keith, stop bothering me with this Jesus stuff!"

We struck out that night with Michelle, but we stayed good friends. We didn't stop bothering her about Jesus either.

At first we had better luck leading strangers to the Lord than we did our friends. Except for our friend Debbie Docis, who was so radiantly excited about Jesus we called her a "lightbulb on legs."

One night in June we had a late dinner with some of our new Christian friends, then we all played penny-ante poker for fun. We were on a winning streak and Keith started joking about driving to Las Vegas.

"Hey, we're on a roll," Keith said, with a gleam in his eye. "Let's go to Vegas!"

One of the guys said, "You're crazy. It's already after ten."

"Come on. It'll be fun. I can make it there in four hours."

Keith was starting to sound more serious, and I was a little worried because I didn't know if real gambling was okay now that we were Christians. But I was always up for an adventure.

Keith ended up persuading everyone and even phoned Debbie and talked her into calling in sick the next day so she could go with us. We headed out and by midnight hit the desert. We were all praying and singing as we drove. One guy picked up his Bible and it happened to fall open at Isaiah 42, which talks about praising God in the desert. He read it out loud, and we really got excited then. Just as he closed his Bible, we saw two hitchhikers barely visible in the dark night.

Keith prayed, "Lord, please send someone to pick them up."

Immediately he hit the brakes and pulled off to the side, saying, "God just told me the someone was us!"

A young couple climbed into the back of Victor. Keith laughed and said, "You just fell into a den of Christians!"

"We don't mind," they said as they got comfortable. Their names were Scott and Lori, and as we drove on we learned that they weren't married but were living together. I noticed that Lori was holding her head in pain. She told us she had a blood clot on her brain that was too big to remove. The doctors only gave her about six months to live. We all glanced at each other and started praying silently.

After a while Scott said, "Hey, this is kinda strange, but for the last couple of days I've had a terrible backache. When we got in, it was killing me. But suddenly—just like that—the pain disappeared." We told them we'd been praying for Lori, and he must have got a healing instead! We talked to them nonstop about God's love on the whole ride up north.

When we got to Las Vegas, we headed straight for the casinos, then left them a few dollars richer. Near dawn we all checked into one room and just lounged around. Scott and Lori were still with us, and it was natural to start praying for each other. One guy had a cold, and after our prayers he said he felt better. My heart started pounding as

I thought about praying for Lori. What if God wanted to heal her blood clot? I finally said, "Lori, do you want us to pray for you?"

"Oh, yes. Please—"

We gathered around her and laid our hands on her back and shoulders and prayed for about five minutes. When we stopped Lori started to cry.

"Why are you crying?" Keith asked.

"It's gone! The clot is gone! It was really big and I can't feel it anymore!" she said. Then she began to sob.

All the time she was talking she was hitting the back of her head really hard—on the spot where apparently the blood clot had been. When we realized that God had healed her, we all started crying for joy.

Lori got up and took a prescription bottle out of her purse and walked into the bathroom with it. I saw her pour some little pills that thinned her blood into the toilet. "I won't be needing these anymore," she announced.

We were all in awe of what had just happened. We'd been talking to them about becoming Christians on the whole drive up. Lori's dad was a minister. She'd slipped away from God, but now saw that she needed to make a new commitment. Scott wanted to receive the Lord too. Then Keith tackled another subject.

"You know, it's wrong for you to be living together without being married. If you really love each other, you need to get married."

To our surprise, they decided to get married on the spot. Keith opened the phone book and found a preacher who did house calls. He came and married them under a palm tree by the pool of the Thunderbird Hotel where we were staying. What a time! Getting two people saved, healed, and married in less than twenty-four hours! We didn't see how it could get much better than that!

After the wedding, Keith drove Debbie to the airport because she had to get back to go to work. When he got back he told us about a robed Hare Krishna guy, shaved head and all, selling books in the terminal. Keith said, "He was at the bottom of the escalator, and at first I didn't want to talk to him. But God had other plans!" Keith later wrote in his journal:

> I really didn't want to [talk to him] . . . I just told him that Jesus loved him. And then I walked away until I couldn't bear it any longer. God just turned me around and walked me right to the bottom of the escalator and I refused to go. He [God] pushed me on it, so there I was. The guy wouldn't listen to me until I almost started crying. I got so intense, he finally did listen a bit and then we talked about half an hour. Then I told him I would pray for him. It was something.

Before heading back south so we wouldn't miss Friday night fellowship at the Vineyard, we gave the newlyweds some extra cash. Then we dropped them off at the freeway entrance so they could continue their journey north.

On the way home Keith picked up another hitchhiker who, by the time we got to L.A., wanted to pray to receive the Lord. We took him to the Vineyard with us, but we arrived just at the end.

Debbie rushed up to us and said, "Guess what? I confessed to my boss that I lied to him and he didn't fire me! I quit smoking too!" We told everyone our Las Vegas story over and over again. Then we left and went to the Little Brown Church and had a very emotional prayer time over our new hitchhiker friend before we all said good-bye and went our separate ways.

It had all been very exciting. But later as I went to bed, something bothered me. It was a girl I barely knew. She had run up to me earlier that night at the Vineyard, all smiles as she said, "Too bad you missed the meeting. Kenn talked all about modesty, not stumbling the brothers. You know, wearing a bra and stuff."

I instantly looked down at my little halter top—two small triangles of fabric in front—with string ties around the back. I felt kinda bad.

Now I was mad. I liked the way I dressed. So did Keith. I thought, *What's wrong with these goody-goody Christian guys anyway? If they're so spiritual, why can't they control their eyes?* But God began to talk to me. The guys did need to be careful, but I was responsible to not make it more difficult for them. I argued with God for a while, but I knew he was right. The next morning I said good-bye to all my little halter tops and sheer gauze blouses, and I told Keith I needed to go shopping—soon.

Two weeks later, Scott and Lori came to visit us and we took them to the Friday night meeting at the Vineyard. Kenn gave Lori a few minutes to share and tell their incredible story—along with the clincher.

"I went to see my doctor and didn't tell him about the healing. He took an X-ray as usual and I waited for the results. Then he came in and clipped the film on the light board in front of me."

"Tell me what you see," he said.

"Nothing."

"That's right, nothing! But these things don't just go away."

"I know, but it's gone!"

The doctor had called in three other experts, and Lori told them the whole story about how God healed her. "They all walked out shaking their heads," she reported, smiling.

Then her doctor told her to make another appointment, but when she got into the reception area, the nurse gave her another doctor's number. "The nurse told me my doctor was so upset that he didn't want to see me anymore! I just give God the glory for my healing. My doctors gave me no hope, but Jesus gave me new life!"

The whole room burst into cheers and applause for the goodness and faithfulness of God. Keith and I were so thrilled to know that the healing had been verified by her doctors. Scott and Lori came to our house after the Vineyard to spend the night, and we began to sense that things weren't going too well in their relationship. Scott went to bed first, and Lori confided that he didn't want to follow Jesus anymore. He was getting drunk and saying he didn't want anything to do with God. Lori was heartbroken.

We spent quite a bit of time encouraging Lori and praying with her before we went to bed. But once we were alone, we tried to make some sense out of the situation.

Keith said it first. "How could this happen? How can Scott turn from God?"

"I don't know. When he prayed with us in Las Vegas, it seemed like he meant it."

"He saw God heal Lori too."

"I can't figure it out," I replied.

The next day Keith wrote, "Lori is still on fire, but Scott has fallen away."

The next day, Keith talked with Scott but didn't feel he got through to him. We told Lori we'd be praying for them and to keep in touch with us. We expected everyone who loved Jesus to be as excited as we were. We never dreamed that there might be some Christians who weren't really excited about God. Even though we couldn't figure out what went wrong with Scott, it didn't stop us from telling others about Jesus.

The next evening we invited Debbie and her parents over for dinner so they could meet Richard. Another guy we'd already led to the Lord was there too. He called his mom who lived on the East Coast and led her to the Lord over the phone. Later, Matt and Bonnie, two fans from the Bla, came over. Frank, a Christian we'd picked up hitch-

hiking and who was staying with us, helped tell them about Jesus.

River baptism by Keith

Keith wrote, "Frank got Matt to pray with him and I got Bonnie to pray with me, but something was trying to stop her from saying the name of Jesus. She split after being totally freaked out." This kind of evening was quickly becoming typical at our house.

Soon we were having all-night prayer meetings in our living room a few nights a week—inviting those who believed and those who didn't.

We kept several crosses and Bibles on hand to give to those who received the Lord. We never minded it when we had to buy new supplies because it meant we'd gained a new brother or sister in the Lord.

Yet Keith and I were aware that just a few short weeks before we'd been lost and seeking too. Keith was so sensitive on this point that he penned this prayer:

July 27, 1975
Not a Fanatic

> *Please, Lord, keep me sensitive to the spiritual needs of those who need your salvation. . . . People can get wary of my company if I go off the deep end and only witness from my "plane" instead of going to where they are and showing them I care for them individually. Lord, change me, get rid of any radical tendencies. Help me control my overwhelming enthusiasm. Make me unselfish, unproud, quiet, and full of humility and gentleness.*
>
> *Father, I love you—you showed your gift to me—Jesus.*

If we ever thought our lives might cool down a bit, we were mistaken. What we were going through was nothing compared to the fire we were headed into.

Not A Fanatic

Please Lord, Keep me sensitive
to the spiritual needs of those
who need your salvation. Please
keep making me wise as a serpent
and harmless as a dove Lord. Praise you.
    People can get wary of my
company if I go off the deep end
and only witness from _my_ place, instead of going to where they are,
and showing them I care for them
individually.
    Lord, change me, get rid
of any radical tendancies. Help me
control my "over-whelming enthusiasm".
Make me unselfish, unproud, quiet, and
full of humility and gentleness.
    Father I Love you. You
showed me your gift to me —
    — Jesus —
    Praise you Lord God - You
are truely one — My Soul Blesses (Amen
your will, your Plan & your salvation. †

"WHEN THERE'S LOVE"

Shortly after we became Christians, Keith and I took two of our favorite people to one of our favorite places—Sequoia National Park. Keith had known Peter and Cag for years. He even lived with them for a while in their large rustic hilltop home overlooking downtown Hollywood. Peter was a record producer, but we had more than music on our minds as we wound up the mountain roads toward Sequoia. A big moon had already risen high over the redwoods when we arrived. As soon as we got into our cabins we made chili dogs and got down to business. We started to tell them why they needed to know Jesus.

Peter and Cag were Jewish and two of the most genuinely kind and loving people we knew. We had become very proud of being Jewish once we became followers of Jesus and realized the spiritual blessing of knowing our Redeemer. In our eagerness to explain all we'd been learning about being Jewish and believing in Jesus, we unloaded both barrels on this beautiful couple. Keith took the first shot.

"The Old Testament talks about the Messiah coming in two ways. First as a humble servant who is despised, rejected, and dies for the sins of the world. Then as a glorious king who sets up his throne in Jerusalem and the whole world comes to bow at his feet. Both descriptions are of the same person—Jesus. He's already come as a servant, and he's coming again as a king!"

I jumped in. "Yeah, even the crucifixion was foretold in Jewish Scripture."

Keith explained: "When Jesus walked on earth the psalms weren't numbered. Instead the first lines were used as titles to direct listeners to the right portion of Scripture. So when someone wanted to refer to, say, Psalm 23, they'd say, 'The Lord is my shepherd, I shall not want.'"

I continued. "So, when Jesus was hanging on the cross and said, 'My God, my God, why hast thou forsaken me?' he was pointing every Jewish person to Psalm 22, which begins with that line."

Keith grabbed his Bible and read out loud, "Psalm 22 says, 'They pierced my hands and my feet . . . they look and stare upon me. . . . They part my garments among them, and cast lots.' Jesus was telling them, 'Hey, what King David prophesied centuries ago is happening to me—right now, before your very eyes!'"

Peter and Cag were their polite and loving selves, quietly enduring, unable to get a word in edgewise.

Keith was on a roll. He turned to Zechariah 12:10. He said, "At the second coming, Jesus will be recognized as the Messiah and deep remorse will be felt for crucifying him." Then Keith read: "'And I will pour upon the house of David, and upon the inhabitants of Jerusalem, the spirit of grace . . . and they shall look upon me whom they have pierced, and they shall mourn for him, as one mourns for his only son, and shall be in bitterness for him, as one that is in bitterness for his firstborn.'"

We so wanted them to understand that the life and death of Jesus was talked about in the Old Testament . . . but we didn't think they could handle much more. Keith took a deep breath and fired his last shot, closing his plea with Isaiah 53.

"This whole chapter is amazing," Keith said. "It talks about how Jesus was rejected by men and was silent before his accusers—even that he died with the wicked and was buried in a rich man's grave. Most importantly it tells us what his death accomplished. It says, 'He was wounded for our transgressions . . . bruised for our iniquities . . . with his stripes we are healed,' and that 'the Lord hath laid on him the iniquity of us all.'" Keith wrapped it up by saying, "The price of sin is death. You see, Jesus paid the ultimate price, once and for all—not only to secure forgiveness of sins for any Jew or Gentile who receives his atonement, but to give us peace, healing, and an intimate relationship with the Father while here on earth."

Keith looked Peter and Cag deep in the eyes and said, "We love you guys so much. We want you to have the same peace and freedom we've finally found by knowing God. Our lives are totally changed. Jesus might return at any minute; that's why it's so important that you accept his sacrifice and his love. We want you guys to be in heaven with us." He took a deep breath and said, "We'd really like you to pray with us and receive Jesus into your hearts as your Messiah. That's all you need to do. It's as simple as that to be born again!"

Keith's last words just hung in the cold mountain air seeping through the cracks of our little cabin.

I don't think Peter and Cag had ever heard a message quite like that. They looked at each other, then kindly but firmly declined our invitation. Instantly we knew we had overwhelmed them. If they hadn't loved us as much as they did, we could have totally destroyed our friendship in that one evening. We had applied quite a bit of pressure. As it was things were a little tense between us for the next few days of our trip.

After we got back home, we remained very good friends. But we were disappointed that we couldn't get them to pray the sinner's prayer and find what we had found.

We had just learned about this thing called "the sinner's prayer," and our goal was to get everybody we knew to pray it with us. It could be said in several different ways. It just needed to contain a few important things. People had to recognize they were lost without Jesus, repent of their sins and of living a life without God, ask for God's forgiveness, and ask Jesus into their hearts as their personal Savior. We thought if someone believed those things enough to pray the prayer they'd be saved. We had begun to lead people to the Lord that way—assuring them that was all it took.

It was so exciting to see these baby Christians come to fellowship meetings and start to learn about Jesus and the Bible. If they started to miss some meetings Keith would always call them to remind them to come, to offer them a ride—anything that would encourage them to keep their commitment to God. Some people seemed to blossom once they became Christians, their lives opening up like beautiful, scented buds. That was wonderful. To us there was nothing better than being able to help someone come to that place with God.

Everything had such a sense of urgency to it, especially when we discovered what a crucial moment in history we were facing. We'd been told that Jesus might return at any moment to catch all the Christians into the air with him and take them to heaven. Time runs out for mankind after that. No one can get right with God past that point. We'd even seen a movie about it called *A Thief in the Night*. There wasn't any time to waste when so many of our friends would not be with Jesus if he returned soon.

In fact, there was one day when Keith and I got separated in the supermarket and I began to panic. My heart started to pound as I hunted up and down the aisles but couldn't find him. I thought maybe Jesus had returned and taken Keith, but I didn't get to go because I wasn't really saved after all. To my great relief, I finally found Keith in frozen foods with a tub of Häagen-Daz chocolate ice cream in his hand, but that frantic, lost feeling stuck with me as a reminder to keep telling others about Jesus.

Keith and I got more and more involved with the Vineyard, and we soon found out about a spiritual gift God would give us, just by asking. After one Friday night meeting, some people from the study told us about how we could get more of the Holy Spirit in our lives. They said it would give us greater personal power to be stronger Christians, and that we'd also be more effective when we told others about Jesus.

"We want everything God wants to give us!" Keith said instantly.

We needed somewhere quiet to pray. It was a warm summer night so we went into the garden. Under a beautiful moon our new Christian friends gently lay their hands on our shoulders and prayed, asking God to baptize us in the Holy Spirit. They asked Jesus to give us more of his power, presence, anointing, and more of his spiritual authority. It felt so wonderful to have them reach out and touch us while they prayed. It was incredible that these people we hardly knew had hearts to pray such beautiful prayers for us. Then they also asked God to give us our own prayer language.

"What's that?" Keith quickly asked.

One of the girls said, "Well, sometimes things are so deep in our hearts we can't find the words to pray, or we aren't sure how to pray—then we can pray in the spirit."

A guy grabbed his Bible. "I'll read what Paul said." He opened to 1 Corinthians 14:14 and read, "'For if I pray in a tongue, my spirit prays, but my mind is unfruitful . . . I will pray with the spirit, but I will also pray with the understanding.'" He then said, "Paul prayed to God with words he understood, but he also allowed the Spirit to pray in a way only the Spirit understood—and he did it all the time. It's mainly for our personal worship, or our private times of prayer and praise to Jesus. It makes us stronger in the Lord and builds up our spirit."

For a moment, Keith and I gave each other that raised-eyebrow look. It sounded kind of mysterious and a little strange too. But these people were so filled with the love of Jesus, we just wanted to have what they had. Besides, they didn't seem strange at all, and the more we learned about Jesus, the more we realized that there was indeed a beautiful spiritual mystery about him. We gave each other our secret nod of consent.

"Okay, hit us with the prayer," Keith said. "I have a feeling we're going to need all the strength from God we can get!"

As we drove home that night, our hearts just swelled with our growing love for God. Keith wrote:

It Happened!
Well, the Holy Spirit has entered our lives and we have a fellowship to go to. New faith and miracles!!

It's wonderful. I know the Father so much more personally through knowing Jesus so much more personally through knowing the Holy Spirit for the first time.

We love his holy name and he's bestowing us with so many new friends and so much new music, so many holy songs. Our purpose is becoming so much clearer. My ministry is coming into view.

Bless you, Jesus, cause you've blessed the Father by saving us all through your death. Amen.

Keith had purposely held off doing any kind of concert for the people at the Vineyard as he normally would for a new group of people. He wanted to just be accepted for who he was without his music. But he still needed to do some gigs to pay the rent. One night he was hired to play two sets at a house party in the Hollywood Hills. Cars were parked all the way down the hillside, and people were streaming toward the door. Once inside, it was jam-packed and loud. Lots of dope was being smoked, but we passed. The piano was in the middle of everything. Keith was like background noise in the room. He tried to get everyone's attention so they could hear the words, but without luck. After the first set Keith was glum.

"I hate this, Melody. It's just not us anymore."

"I know babe, hang in there. Only one more set to go."

Keith's eyes drifted over my shoulder, and I turned to see what caught his attention.

"See that guy, Mel? I'm gonna go talk to him."

We wandered over to a tall, lanky guy leaning against the wall. He was blond, and he had the biggest brown eyes I'd ever seen.

"You look as bored as I feel," Keith said for openers. And then I saw it. I knew what had caught Keith's eye. There was a wooden cross on a long cord hanging around his neck.

Keith asked, "What's that cross meant to you?" Their conversation went way past Keith's break time. Keith found the guy who hired him and said, "I'm not playing the second set and you don't have to pay me for the first set either."

We took off with our new friend Terry and went to Pinks, our favorite Hollywood hotdog stand. It was almost midnight but we had a forty-five-minute wait in line. We talked about God and Jesus and our mystical experiences. Finally, we ordered two chili dogs each, then sat on the curb to eat. Before we left, Terry prayed the sinner's prayer with us, and we made plans to get together the next night. We didn't make any rent money, but Terry had become a new brother in Jesus.

By now the Vineyard meetings had moved from the fancy house in Coldwater Canyon to a school auditorium—with a piano. After about a month in the new building, Keith felt it was okay to play a song for our new Christian friends. He played at a Sunday morning service and picked a song he figured was fit for church. Keith sat at a little upright piano and from a very deep place in his heart sang "The Road to Jericho." People were riveted and some even cried at the end.

That Sunday was the first time our new friend Terry came to church with us—and the first time we heard Kenn talk about water baptism. As soon as we heard about it, we knew it was our next step. We figured the Pacific Ocean was a good place to lay our old lives to rest.

That afternoon we met Kenn and about fifty others, including Terry, at Lifeguard Station 15 just north of Sunset Boulevard. As the baptism service began, we all stood in the cool ocean mist and sang worship songs. It felt so awesome to praise God out in the open, under the canopy of a pale blue sky. It was a little chilly, but our hearts were warm as we prepared to take this step of commitment.

When our turn came, Keith and I went together, wading into the gentle waves. Keith was first. Then me. Kenn repeated, "I baptize you in the name of the Father, the Son, and the Holy Spirit." I leaned back and was momentarily submerged. As the crisp salt water washed over me, I felt like I was being cleansed head to toe, washed clean of my past. When I popped up, Keith immediately grabbed me and gave me a big slippery hug. Still embracing, we walked back to shore, amazed at how fresh and energized we felt. Keith later noted:

We all went down to the beach and we got baptized. It was so fantastic—Mel and I were baptized together. We were all so close. I'll never forget it.

At the beach that day, we found out the Vineyard was about to lose its temporary building and move again. Since the weather was really nice, Kenn announced that we'd start having our Sunday services at that very lifeguard station—with the ocean and sky as our backdrop! We met there for several months, which was great with us. People would ask, "Where do you go to church?" And we'd say, "We go to church on the beach!" It was unconventional, and most people thought it was pretty cool. However, we found that there were some rules we didn't want to see broken.

One day we overheard some of our Christian friends talking about a party. We were immediately curious. One of them said, "Keith, we don't think you'd be interested in going. It's pretty wild."

"What do you mean 'wild'?"

"It's at Leo's house. Sometimes he has lots of booze and dope around. Some people from the study will probably be there."

We knew Leo had a drinking problem, but we thought he was fighting it. We didn't believe he'd throw a wild party and invite other Christians. The next night Keith and I decided to go and see for ourselves.

As we walked up the stairs, we heard blasting music. Inside, people were wall-to-wall, mostly lying on the floor or lounging on big pillows. Carefully stepping over the guests, we took one sweep through the house. There were a few kegs of beer, some people smoking dope and, sure enough, a few people there from the Bible study—and they weren't just passing through. We left right away feeling very upset.

"I can't believe it," said Keith as we drove.

"What can we do?"

We had strong feelings about seeing Christians getting loaded, but we felt helpless. We wondered what we were supposed to do when we saw other Christians making wrong choices.

A short time later we felt like we found some answers at the Cramers' Bible study. Their monkey was chattering in the background, but we were tuned in to the message. It was from the Old Testament book of Ezekiel, a passage about a watchman who had the job of sitting on the wall of an ancient city. The watchman was to alert the people in the city if he saw danger coming. If the people heard the watchman's warning but ignored it, then it was their own fault if they ended up getting hurt. The Bible said their blood would be on their own head. But if the watchman fell asleep and neglected to warn the people about approaching danger, it was the watchman's fault if they got hurt—and the blood of the people would be on the watchman's hands. He would be held accountable.

The Bible teacher went on to say that as Christians we are the watchmen. God wants us to warn others if we see disaster coming their way—and what could be more of a disaster than living in a way that would separate you from God eternally? We left the study feeling like the weight of the world was on our shoulders. We felt especially troubled for our Christian friend Tom, whom we really loved. We knew he was having a hard time breaking off with an old girlfriend, and they would sometimes sleep together.

The thing that made it so heavy for us was that Tom sometimes helped lead Bible studies in another church where he was really outspoken about the need to accept Jesus. He sometimes came to the Vineyard, too, and Kenn knew him. It was only because of our close friendship with Tom that we knew what was going on. What if Jesus returned tonight, before Tom had a chance to repent? He might be separated from God—*forever*—and his blood would be on our hands. We knew we were responsible for saying something right away.

So, Todd came home with us. He was fully following Jesus, too, and as troubled as we were. We all sat on the floor in Keith's music room wondering what to do. In front of the old upright piano, Keith came up with an idea: "One of us should phone Tom and warn him right away."

I thought Keith should be the one, since he had the most nerve. Besides, it was his idea. But Keith's eyes lit up. "Let's draw lots," he said. "They did that in the Bible."

Keith rifled through the scattering of half-finished lead sheets on the piano and found three different-sized pencils. He tucked them into his hand, making them all even at the top. Wouldn't you know who came up with the short one? Me! I protested that one of the guys should phone, but I knew that we all had equal responsibility before the Lord in this situation. Anyway, I was never one to back down from a challenge, and if God had chosen me to sound the alarm I was determined to do it. I dialed the phone.

My heart was pounding as it started to ring. After the first ring, I thought, *Maybe I should hang up. . . .* It rang again. I said, "Keith, it's late. He's probably already in bed."

Then someone picked up the phone. A groggy voice said, "Hello."

"Uh, hi. It's Melody. Did I wake you?"

"It's okay. What's up?"

I could feel my face getting warm. "I'm sorry I woke you, but we went to this Bible study tonight. It was about being watchmen and . . . well . . . uh . . . of course we know what's going on . . . and, well, we just wanted to tell you that the Bible says you really shouldn't be doing that."

"Yeah, I know," Tom said softly. "I'm getting some counsel from my pastor. And I'll be taking care of it really soon."

"Okay. I just wanted to tell you. Good night."

"Thanks. Good night."

I hung up the phone and couldn't believe I'd really done it.

Keith said, "Wow, I'm really proud of you, Mel. You did great!"

I was just relieved that it was over. I knew I'd done the right thing, but it was really hard, and I was a bit puzzled. I couldn't figure out why Tom was getting counsel. What was there to get counsel about? The Bible was clear on the subject of having sex outside of marriage. What was there to talk about?

The next time we saw Kenn, the following Friday night, we were excited to tell him we'd taken the watchman teaching we'd just heard to heart.

"Did you hear we called Tom?" Keith said expectantly.

Kenn paused for a minute and looked thoughtful. "Well, actually, I did hear about it."

Keith happily went on to explain about the Bible study and the watchman and my phone call.

Then Kenn said gently, "You know, you probably shouldn't have called."

Probably shouldn't have called? We were shocked.

"What do you mean?" Keith asked incredulously.

"Well, maybe it would have been better if you'd just prayed."

As we drove home that night, we were really confused. Just pray? What kind of advice was that? If Jesus came back before Tom got things right, he'd be separated from God forever—and we were supposed to "just pray" and not even talk to Tom? We were hearing all these things about living holy lives, practicing what we preach, being watchmen . . . and now this? It seemed to us that watchmen were supposed to sound an alarm, not just pray about sounding one!

We loved Kenn so much—and really respected him. We knew he was a man of God, and that he understood God's unconditional love. But we were confused. Did unconditional love mean that you ignored sin? Maybe there were things he and Tom's pastor knew about the situation that we didn't. Still, it didn't make sense.

"First the wild party at Leo's. Now Tom. I can't believe this," Keith said. "The church is just filled with sinners!"

I couldn't believe it either. But something told me Keith's reaction might be a little too strong.

"We've met some really great Christians in the past few months," I countered. "It can't be all bad."

"I know, I know. But I'm beginning to feel like this is just the tip of the iceberg," Keith said thoughtfully. "I know we're not perfect, but we're trying. It's not just Tom. It's a lot of people. They know the right words to say, but their lives don't match up."

As I said, in the beginning some people just seemed to blossom and grow. But after several months, it appeared that quite a few of those blossoms had already withered. After leading some people to the Lord, we'd run into them weeks later at Topanga Plaza and they didn't even want to look us in the eye. Then we'd learn that they were back on drugs or sleeping around, as if they'd never even seen the light. Keith was never afraid of confrontation, and he'd try to reason with them. We convinced a few to return to God; others we couldn't. Still most of those who returned to church kept living the same old lives.

Why was this happening? They'd prayed the sinner's prayer, but they weren't acting very saved. Why did some Christians stick and others just fall away? We started to think that just giving your heart to the Lord in a prayer might not be enough.

One day a Christian friend named Robin asked me to pray for her brother. We really looked up to her because she'd already known the Lord for eight years—which, to me, seemed like forever. I asked her why we needed to pray for her brother.

"Oh, he's saved," she said. "He's just out of fellowship. He used to come to church all the time. But he's living with his girlfriend now and back on drugs. I know he'll go to heaven, but he won't have any rewards in heaven if he keeps this up. I really want to see him back in fellowship. I know he'll be happier then."

I wondered about this. Is losing a heavenly reward the only thing we need to worry about after we pray the sinner's prayer? What about living for God now?

I told Robin I'd pray, but I felt really odd inside. I figured she knew what she was talking about since she'd been a Christian a lot longer than me, but something didn't add up.

Later Keith and I talked about it, voicing the questions that were collecting in our minds. If you prayed and asked Jesus into your heart, was there ever a point where he might leave you? What if you decided to leave him? And if you asked Jesus to save you, could you keep living in sin and just be automatically forgiven of everything? All we knew was that we were getting really frustrated with what we were seeing around us.

After trying to figure out how to pray for Robin's brother, Keith spent one whole morning telling Feather, a young hippie girl, about the Lord. In fact, that day it brought all our questions to a head.

Feather was very skeptical about Christians, and she gave Keith a run for his money. "I don't think they're any better than I am," she said. "The Christians I've known have all been a bunch of hypocrites. They say one thing and do another."

"Real Christians aren't like that," insisted Keith. "They really love the Lord and they live holy lives."

"Well, I don't need a list of dos and don'ts in my life. I believe there's a supreme being, but I don't want anybody telling me what to do."

"If you had a child, you'd want to protect him, not control him. God loves you so much that he doesn't want you to do things that will cause you pain. I know. I really blew it before I was a Christian. I hurt a lot of people, but mostly I hurt myself."

As Keith started to share from his own life, I could tell Feather really started listening. We both knew exactly where she was because we'd been there ourselves. The more open Keith was about himself, the more I could see she started to believe him.

Keith said, "God wants to be in a relationship with you. I think he's been speaking to you for a long time. You need to start listening."

Her attitude grew softer and Keith really encouraged her to open her heart to the Lord. "Just pray with me," he said. "You don't have anything to lose—and you have everything to gain."

Finally, after a few hours, she came to a point where she was willing to pray and ask Jesus into her life. Keith led her in a really precious prayer, and then wanted to take her to meet some of our friends. He said, "I want to introduce you to some of your new brothers and sisters who really love God. We want you to meet some real Christians."

We jumped into Victor, drove up to Hollywood, and ended up at the home of our friends the Cramers, but they weren't around. The Cramers happened to live next door to Leo, and now we heard some noise coming from Leo's backyard, so we walked over. There were a few people from the Bible study swimming in Leo's pool, and we pulled up a few chairs at poolside, all the while telling our new sister, Feather, how great it was being a Christian. She was starting to look more relaxed, and I knew we were getting through to her at last.

We were only there a few minutes when the sliding glass door from Leo's house flung open wide. A new Christian we'd met at the Cramers' home came charging out at full speed. He ran across the concrete with his arms raised over his head, yelling, "Praise the Lord!" and dove into the pool. There was only one problem. He was totally naked.

Now there he was, swimming around in front of us with nothing on but a big smile. I quickly glanced at Feather. She looked upset.

Keith immediately jumped to his feet. Standing on the edge of the pool he said firmly, "Get out of there right now!" Then he had immediate second thoughts. "No! Don't get out. Where are your pants?"

The guy didn't want to tell Keith where his pants were, but Keith insisted. He gave in and Keith went into the house to get them. Then he brought them out to the pool and handed them to this happy streaker.

"Put them on!"

He did.

Leo was really angry when he heard what Keith had done. He thought Keith had a lot of nerve to tell a guest at his house that he needed to put his clothes on, but we were really upset too.

The incident had unraveled our whole testimony to Feather, who was just hours old in the Lord. Even though nudity was widely accepted among hippies, we'd told her Christians were different. We never saw her again after that day, and we knew it was because of what happened at the pool. Everything we'd told her about Christianity had been ruined. We didn't know if she'd ever believe another Christian again, and our hearts really hurt for her.

This, coupled with the time we raided Leo's beer blast, served to fuel Keith's quickly growing reputation as some kind of radical. It also earned us the name the "God Squad." The name didn't stick, but these things stuck in our minds and caused us to be really troubled.

It was apparent now that the attitude of many Christians was pretty lax. It seemed like you could be a Christian and do almost anything you wanted—sleep around, smoke dope, and swim nude in mixed company—and it seemed as if nobody was objecting.

Keith fell into a real depression over what we were seeing. "Something's really wrong here," he said. "I've struggled too long and too hard to find Jesus. I'm not gonna quit now, but I'll tell you one thing—I'm not going to compromise what I know is right, no matter what people around us are doing."

"It seems so crazy to play games with God," I added.

"Yeah," Keith concluded, "we have to give God more than lip service. We need to give him life service."

We were wrestling with some big questions, like what it meant to really be a Christian. The Bible says if you confess Jesus with your mouth you will be saved, but we wondered if just saying you were a Christian was enough. Anybody could do that. Did something more need to happen to prove you were a Christian?

Even though we had a lot of unanswered questions, something in us really began to hurt for other people who'd been just like us—people who were trying to find something real in life, a reason to live. We had an aching desire to reach out to those who were looking in all the same places we did—drugs, the occult, free love. We knew how they felt and understood how hurt some of them were. We wanted to help them find the peace and hope they were longing to find.

Since Keith loved to tell people about Jesus, we usually made a point of going out to find people to talk to anywhere. One Sunday a few friends were over and we argued about where we should go to find some hurting people to lead to the Lord. It was between Muscle Beach in Santa Monica and Tapia Park in the foothills. The beach came out the winner and off we went!

True to its name, Muscle Beach was filled with flexing masses of manhood—posturing, lifting weights, and balancing girls in very small bikinis far above their heads in swan-dive positions! We plopped ourselves down on the grass right in the middle of all this and Keith started playing some worship songs on his acoustic guitar. We all sang out loudly and with a lot of enthusiasm. A small crowd started to gather around us as Keith's energetic playing drew people like a magnet.

After singing for a while, I noticed one blonde girl who was sitting several feet away. Her head was down, and it looked like she might be crying. I got up, went over, and sat down by her. She was crying.

I sat there for a minute, unsure of what to do. Finally I said softly, "Excuse me. You seem kind of upset. Is there anything I can do to help?"

She lifted her head. Her eyes were red and questioning.

"I know you don't know me," I ventured, "but that's my husband playing the guitar over there. I just felt like I was supposed to come over and talk to you."

Her lip quivered a little as she started to speak. "I . . . I just don't know what to do. I'm pregnant and I don't want this baby."

"Why don't you want it?"

A sob caught in her throat. Then she said, "My husband and I are separated, and I can't take care of a baby by myself."

Her light hair and delicate features made her look too young to even be married, let alone pregnant. She continued with her story and I played with the grass, silently praying that God would help me to help her. Bit by bit, her story unfolded.

Her name was Cassie, and she and her husband had gotten involved in some kind of strange group that was very repressive, especially toward women. She could only wear a certain type of clothing and had extremely limited privileges. To make things even worse, her husband started beating her.

She dropped her face into her hands and started sobbing. "I went to the leaders and told them he was beating me and that I was afraid. But they told me I couldn't separate myself from him. I was so afraid. And . . . and then I found out I was pregnant."

She really broke then and just wept. I looked away. Muscle men were still tossing around tanned bathing beauties. Little kids were running by with corn dogs and lemonade. Keith was still playing his guitar and singing about Jesus.

Cassie lifted her head in a moment. "In spite of all the threats, I left and moved into a Salvation Army unwed mothers' home in Los Angeles. The reason I'm so upset is because today's Sunday."

"What's so upsetting about that?"

"On Tuesday I'm scheduled to have an abortion."

My heart broke for her. Before becoming a Christian, I would have thought getting an abortion was a good solution to an unwanted pregnancy. Now I knew better. Destroying her baby was not Cassie's answer. I talked hard and fast, knowing I might be her last hope. I told her to not get an abortion, but that bit of advice seemed kind of empty considering her whole situation.

Hoping that Keith might know what to do, I went and told him everything. Keith immediately got up and went to her side. His eyes were filled with compassion as he said a few comforting words of encouragement. She really responded to his kindness. Then I heard him say, "Why don't you come home with us? Come and live with us. We'll help you."

I was probably as surprised as Cassie by Keith's invitation. I thought, *Come and live with us? Is he serious? We don't even know her.*

But as I thought about it for a minute, I realized Keith saw exactly what she needed—someone to love her enough to take her in and walk through this terrible time with her. There was also a second little life at stake. It really seemed like God brought us together so we could help her, and I was glad Keith asked her to move in with us.

We drove to the unwed mothers' home to get her things. It was a very depressing place filled with some really young girls, who were very pregnant. We helped Cassie pack and took her to our house in Woodland Hills, assuring her she'd have a nice room all to herself.

Cassie looked relieved as we turned onto Dolorosa Street. She could see it was a nice family-type neighborhood. She appeared to love our little house with its warm, sunny-yellow kitchen and big picture windows in the living room. We had three bedrooms off a narrow hallway, with the only bathroom at the end. We showed Cassie to her room and helped her get settled.

By Tuesday we had actually talked Cassie into canceling her abortion. On Wednesday her baby was still alive. We led her to the Lord and talked for hours on end about Jesus and her husband and baby.

Then one morning, Cassie was nowhere to be found. She returned late that night and told us she had hitchhiked down to Muscle Beach. After she'd been with us about two weeks, we woke up and she was gone again—only this time she didn't come back.

We often wondered what happened to her and worried that she might have scheduled the abortion after all. We had no way of knowing.

Cassie was gone, but we soon learned that God had big plans for our little house. At a Bible study we met a young mom named Cindy, whose husband had moved in with another woman. Cindy was raising her three-year-old daughter, Kelly, alone. Kelly was really cute and looked like a miniature version of her very pretty mom. We became friends and did a lot of things together. Cindy was sweet and vulnerable. As a new Christian she was always trying to help others.

One night when she came out of the bar where she worked, there was a drunk guy by her car. She talked to him about Jesus and picked him up the next night to bring him to a Bible study. He got angry at the teacher and stormed out in the middle of the study. Cindy started to chase after him, but Keith blocked her way at the door.

"Let him go," Keith said firmly.

"But I brought him. I feel responsible to drive him back home," she insisted.

"He's a big boy. He can find his way home. It's just not safe."

Later that night, we all sat down and had a talk. Cindy had recently looked up an old boyfriend who wasn't a Christian, and she was struggling to keep strong in the Lord.

"You know, it would really be good for you and Kelly if you lived in more of a Christian environment," Keith offered.

"The only people I could think of living with are you and Melody."

"Well, we'll just pray about that!" Keith told her.

Keith and I did pray that night, and the next day we told her that she and Kelly could move in with us if they wanted. They did. As soon as they moved in, Keith sat down with her and they had a long discussion far into the night. There were a few guys wanting to take

Cindy out, but Keith told her he didn't think she should be dating anyone because she was still a married woman. He also pointed out that she should look for another job because by working in a bar she was helping people get drunk. Cindy really wanted to do what was right, and she took his counsel on both points. Now she and Kelly shared one of our three bedrooms, leaving one remaining bedroom for us, and a music room.

But there was still more room at the inn.

A short time later, I struck up a conversation with a young woman at the health club where Keith and I belonged. We were always trying to keep in shape, but I admit I spent most of my time in the Jacuzzi. In fact, that's where I was when I met Maureen. She looked sad and told me she was going through a crisis in her marriage. Later she confessed that her husband had been shoving her around, hitting her. She was very open when I started to talk about Jesus. Later, Keith and I invited her to church with us, and, well, one thing led to another. Pretty soon I was asking Keith if she could come and live with us too.

Some people thought we were crazy for having so many people move in with us. We'd often hear comments from people at church like, "You guys are nuts. You haven't even been married that long. You need time alone." It was true we were young in our marriage, and even younger in the Lord, but it just didn't seem like the urgent needs of these people were going to wait. Where else were they going to go while we made sure we got our time alone? So we did what we felt the Lord wanted us to do—we kept our home and our hearts open to anyone who needed help. It gave us a deep sense of joy to know we could be used to make a difference in someone else's life.

In the process of seeing other people's lives change, our lives were changing radically too. We used to go to all-night parties and run around doing whatever we wanted. Now that people were moving into our house, Keith and I were spending a lot more time trying to help them grow in the Lord and overcome the effects of the past.

Cindy, for instance, seemed to be having problems with her jobs. After she'd quit her job at the bar, she started waitressing in a deli. But now her boss told her if she wanted to keep her job she'd have to stop reporting the full amount of her weekly tips to the IRS. The other waitresses were complaining because Cindy was consistently reporting a much higher figure than they were, and they were afraid they'd get caught cheating.

Once again, Keith sat up late at night and talked with her.

"What am I going to do?" Cindy asked, desperately. "They want me to lie."

"You can't lie. And it wouldn't be right to cheat the government."

"I don't want to lie. But I need my job."

"It's more important to do what's right."

After much discussion Cindy came to a firm resolve and a decision that made us all really proud. Keith wrote in his journal:

> *Cindy came home from her last day of work. She had to quit because they wouldn't let her be honest.*

Not only were we staying up half the night counseling people, there were also other meetings taking place at our house, as loving Jesus soaked into every nook and cranny of our lives. One night, after a Friday meeting at the Vineyard, Kenn announced, "Everyone's invited to an all-night prayer meeting at Keith Green's house!" Keith's natural leadership was starting to surface again.

So here we were, having all-night prayer meetings when we barely knew how to pray ourselves! But Keith had read books about giants in the faith who prayed all night. One man used to go out in knee-deep snow and pray all night for the Indian tribes he was trying to reach. Another man would crawl into a hollow log in the woods to pray all night. We figured if all-night prayer helped make them strong, it would help make us strong too—even in our comfortable living room!

One night something unusual happened. Sometime in the gray, predawn hours, we had lost ourselves singing songs of praise. Gently, slowly, it seemed as if the whole atmosphere in the room changed as we worshiped the Lord with our friends. An overwhelming sense of peace settled on us. The air was thick with it. At one point we all looked at each other and saw what looked like a misty fog gently hovering in the room. We all saw it at the same time. The Holy Spirit seemed to be with us in a very sweet way, and we could feel the closeness of God. We were learning to discern God's presence and enjoy the peace that came with it.

When we weren't meeting at home or the beach, we often could be found at one of Keith's favorite restaurants talking about Jesus with friends while trying to tell our waitress about him too. That's how we met Susan.

Susan was a waitress at Nappy's, Keith's favorite burger place. Taking Keith's burger order was always interesting—blood-rare with nothing but mustard, ketchup, and grilled onions. It was usually a conversation starter too. Susan was young and pretty and kept brushing strands of white-blonde hair away from her cool, gray eyes. But for all her prettiness something seemed wrong.

Keith noticed immediately and said, "You look a little sad. Is everything okay?" It seemed like she'd been waiting for someone to ask.

"Oh, I'm kinda worried," Susan said. "I'm going up on some old drug charges pretty soon. I might end up in jail."

We both were shocked at how open she was and at how someone with such a sweetness about her could be in such trouble. Every time she brought something to our table, we asked more questions. Her story quickly unfolded. She had given her heart to the Lord recently at a rehab center in Hollywood but left before finishing the program.

When we told her we knew Jesus too, her walls just melted. She showed us faded needle marks on her arm and said she'd even tried to kill herself a few times.

"Why didn't you want to live?" I asked.

Susan told us rather matter-of-factly that she'd been really neglected and sexually abused repeatedly as a child. "I've been on and off drugs since I've been eleven, and, well, I've done some pretty horrible things to make money," Susan said, looking down. "I'm gonna go to jail for a long time unless God spares me." Before we left, she asked us to pray for her day in court. "I've got a six-year-old daughter. If I go to jail, I can't take care of her." We exchanged phone numbers before we left.

"She is so sweet," Keith said, shaking his head. "I can't believe she's had such a rough life. It doesn't seem fair."

Susan's court date arrived, and God did intervene. A short time later, we got a shocking phone call. A hit-and-run driver ran over her daughter as she sat on the curb right in front of her apartment. The child was unconscious, and the doctors didn't give much hope. We prayed over the phone, but I had a very disturbing impression that her daughter was not going to survive, which I did not share with Susan. Tragically, her daughter did die, and Susan was going off the deep end. She didn't want to live.

Keith said, "Let's invite her to come live with us so we can help her." She needed permission because she was on probation, so Keith sent me to Hollywood to talk to her probation officer. Susan was there too.

"She is a thief, a con artist, and a liar," the officer said deliberately. "You don't want her to live with you."

"But we do," I said. "We love her, and she's been through so much."

"She will just use you like she's used everyone else."

"We're Christians," I said. "We'll take responsibility for her and help her get her life back together."

Miraculously, he gave his consent. But within a few months, Susan got sick and couldn't shake it. When she realized she was pregnant, she tried to hide it. But trying to hide things from Keith was usually an exercise in vanity. Quite often Jesus showed Keith what was going on. When Keith confronted Susan on it, she flipped out and started yelling. She ran through the house and stormed into our tiny laundry room. Keith and I followed right behind her. She tried to run out, but Keith stubbornly blocked the door.

Trapped in the laundry room, Susan cried, "I can't have this baby!"

"Well, what are you going to do?" asked Keith.

"I'm splitting," she cried. "I'm not fit to be a mother!"

She was crying hysterically and the story came out bit by bit. After her daughter died she nearly lost her mind. She spent some time very high to try to numb the pain. That was when she got pregnant.

"But we love you," pleaded Keith, still leaning on the laundry room door. "We'll take care of you and your baby. Where would you go? Back out on the streets?"

"I've got friends—"

"They don't really love you, Susan. Not like we do. Not like Jesus does," Keith implored.

"Why did you have to figure it out! I could've left here without anyone knowing I was pregnant," she said angrily.

As they were arguing, suddenly out of nowhere, a very clear thought just popped into my mind. I'd heard that voice before, most recently when we were praying for her daughter who died. I didn't understand it, but my impression was so strong I had to say something.

I started with the easy part. "Susan, I know the circumstances are far from perfect, but God wants you to have this baby—not to replace your daughter, but I believe God is really going to bless you with this child." My heart was pounding now. I took a deep breath and went out on a limb. "Susan, I think God just told me you're going to have a baby boy. A beautiful son. And he is going to be part of your healing."

Susan calmed down and Keith just stared at me. The tug of war ended as suddenly as it began. Five months later, right before Susan left to live with relatives in New York, we threw her a big baby shower. Not long after that we got a sweet note from the East Coast. Susan was still in love with Jesus, and she had given birth to a beautiful baby boy.

One thing I was learning about my husband was that he would go anywhere, anytime, if it meant being able to tell someone about how he or she could know Jesus.

Keith even went so far as to drive a guy we'd just met all the way to Arizona. We met Ray Ware through some Christian friends, but he wasn't a Christian. He was a genuinely nice guy—a clean-cut, all-American type, but that didn't matter to Keith. Ray still needed the Lord.

When Keith heard Ray was taking a Greyhound bus to Tucson the next day, Keith announced, "God just told me to drive you!"

Everyone, including Ray, kept telling Keith he was crazy. But Keith thought, *How could anyone measure a few days' drive against the value of someone's eternal soul?* A mutual friend, Jerry Houser, an accomplished actor, went along so Keith wouldn't have to drive back alone—or maybe he went so Ray wouldn't have to be alone with Keith!

At any rate, Keith returned a few days later, road-weary, but excited. "We've got a new brother in the Lord!" he announced, bursting in the front door.

Even though we saw lives being turned around—like Ray's, Cindy's, and Susan's—we were still troubled by the believers who didn't stick. A few more had dropped out and weren't around anymore. We wondered where they went, and, more importantly, why they went. What made them fall away? Was there some attitude in their hearts that they hadn't dealt with? It made us question our own hearts and attitudes.

Keith could be painfully self-examining. Quite often he was much harder on himself than anyone else. He would say, "If they could go cold toward God, what about me?" We realized that outward changes were the easiest—things like giving up drugs and drinking or cleaning up our language. The inner changes were the most difficult. Some of our attitudes were a lot more subtle and harder to detect. Were there things we hadn't dealt with in our own lives?

In particular Keith started to question his music. He asked me, "If my life is going to be totally submitted to the Lord, what does that mean about my music?"

I was amazed that he was even open to this question. For years he'd believed part of his destiny was to use his music as a platform to deliver a spiritual message. It was a sense he'd had long before he was a Christian. But now that he really knew the Lord, Keith felt he needed a new go-ahead from Jesus. Singing for people seemed like the natural thing to do for someone with Keith's talent. But he didn't want to assume anything.

This was an excruciating question, since Keith's music was more than a hobby. He'd been singing all his life. Music was imbedded in the very fiber of his being, and it was most certainly our means of support. A lifetime of hopes and dreams were wrapped up in his music. Was it possible that after so many years of searching for acclaim and musical success that Keith might not ever sing before an audience again? We talked about it more than once.

"You know, Mel, since I was a little kid, music has been a part of my life. My grandfather taught me my first rock-and-roll chords, my parents have stood with me. . . . But I'm not sure anymore if God wants me involved in music."

"Keith," I countered, "God gave you your music. Wouldn't he want you to use it?"

"I don't know. Why should I think Jesus wants me doing music just because I've always done it? Because it's the thing I do best? That's not enough of a reason. Maybe he wants me to go get a job flipping hamburgers at McDonald's."

I didn't know what to think. How could he not do music? On the other hand, I knew it was always important to obey God. Still this seemed like a pretty high price to pay.

"You need to do whatever you think God's telling you to do," I said finally.

Keith spent many hours, even days, agonizing over what to do. Finally he announced his decision. "Mel, the only way to know for sure if God is giving me my music is to give it up. I need to let it go. I think it's okay to keep writing for CBS and to play at home—but I'm laying down all of my public performing at the foot of the cross. I won't pick it up again unless God tells me to."

I swallowed hard. "Are you sure?"

"I'm sure," he replied. "I don't want to presume upon the Lord." Then he got an intensely serious look in his eyes. "Mel . . . I don't really know if God will ever let me pick it up again. Once I lay it down, that may be it forever."

If anything left me with an uneasy, open-ended feeling, it was this decision. We were getting down to the roots of big issues. It was really scary. But Keith had made his mind up. As far as he was concerned, Keith Green would never play in public again. The old Keith, the one with the dream of being acclaimed as a well-known singer, was dead.

Keith loving our dog

8

"YOUR LOVE BROKE THROUGH"

Throughout the summer of 1975, Keith turned down any concert offers that came his way. He confined himself to his upright piano at home. This put a bit of a strain on our finances, but Keith was determined not to budge from his decision.

For me it was really a strange feeling to have something that was such a part of my life be dead. I was surprised to find how much I missed the music, but it was obviously a much greater sacrifice for Keith.

One starry night we took a walk to the neighborhood donut shop. Holding hands on the way, we looked up at the moon and stars and began to wonder about what might happen in the future. Of course, Keith's music was one of the first things to come up.

"Music is such a part of who you are," I began. "It's hard to imagine you without it forever."

"I've been thinking about that," he agreed. "But you know, maybe my music has been a crutch."

"What do you mean, a crutch?"

"When I was growing up, my talent always opened doors for me. I never really had to work at making friends or having social graces like other people did. I knew I could win people over if I could just get to a piano. Music has always been my calling card."

"You sure blew me away when you played for me on our first date," I said, squeezing his hand.

"That was the whole idea," Keith said with a grin. "But now I want to be accepted because I reflect the Lord, not because I blow everyone away with my music."

We reached the donut shop, and we were in luck. They had some hot ones cooling on racks. We got several in a bag and went outside to sit on the curb. It was such a nice night and, with other people always in the house, we had so little chance to talk alone.

"All the talent in the world won't buy me a godly character," Keith was saying, "and that's what I want more than anything."

I agreed. That's what I wanted too.

After we got back home, Keith went into his music room and closed the door. I could hear him playing a beautiful new melody on the piano. I could tell Keith was playing it just for the Lord, and I silently wondered if the Lord and I would be the only ones ever to hear it.

Keith's twenty-second birthday came and went in October, and we were busier than ever with the new people in our lives.

Just before we'd become Christians, about six months before, our good friend Karen Bender had come over with her daughter, Dawn. Karen had met a guy she really liked, and he wanted her and Dawn to move to Colorado with him. They'd come to say good-bye, and we'd sat on our front lawn to smoke a "good-bye joint" together.

Now Karen and Dawn were back from Colorado. Karen came back first and moved to Hollywood, but Dawn stayed in Colorado with her grandparents. When Karen returned without Dawn, she rented an apartment in an adults-only building. Since then, however, Dawn had returned so she could be with her mom, which presented two problems. First, no one under eighteen years old could live in the building, and the manager told Karen she was going to have to find another place now that Dawn was back. Second, Karen was working a split shift at the phone company, which meant little Dawn was home alone many evenings.

Since Keith and I wanted to spend some extra time with Dawn now, we decided to take her with us to some evening Bible studies. She really wanted to go.

"When I was living with my grandma and grandpa," she told us happily, "I went to church with them on Sundays. I told them I wanted to be a Christian, so they phoned the pastor to come over and pray with me. I got baptized too!"

We took Dawn with us to as many meetings as we could over the next few weeks.

One night I was standing at the sink doing the dishes when Dawn phoned. Keith spoke with her a few minutes and then came into the kitchen to announce, "Dawn's moving in with us."

I stood there silently for a moment, the tap water still running.

"Moving in with us? What do you mean?"

"Dawn called to say good-bye," Keith explained. "Since Karen can't keep her in the apartment, she was going to send Dawn to live with some of her relatives." When he told me which relatives, I winced. Karen had told us about them. They had a lot of problems—drinking and smoking dope at all hours of the day and night.

Keith, Dawn, and Melody at Santa Monica Beach

"They're leaving tomorrow morning to move up north into the woods somewhere, and Karen wanted to send Dawn. Mel, you should have heard Dawnie's voice. She didn't want to go. She asked if she could come and live with us instead."

"And you said—?" I just wanted to confirm what I'd heard.

"I told her she could."

I was silent again for a moment. I could feel something rising up inside of my chest. On one hand I really loved Dawn and had a lot of compassion for her situation. On the other hand, Keith didn't even ask me how I might feel about it. True, it wouldn't be a good thing for Dawn, so young—and young in the Lord too—to go off to the woods and live with people who were struggling with major addiction problems. I just wished Keith had talked to me before telling her she could move in. After all, she was a minor, and the responsibility was pretty big. But in the same moment, I resolved to not even mention it to Keith. I knew I would have said yes anyway. I really loved Dawn and felt very protective of her. It was obviously the best thing to do. In those few moments of silence, I felt a sense of peace rush into my heart. Maybe that was the Lord's way of telling me we were making the right decision.

Dawn moved in with us just a few weeks after her eleventh birthday. She said happily, "I've always wanted to live in a real house with a backyard and a dog." Even though we told her to just keep calling us Keith and Melody, she started calling us Mom and Dad right away.

Mom and Dad . . . Keith and I had talked about having children, but it was a short conversation. Neither of us had any burning desire to be parents just yet. Now, here we were, the parents of a beautiful, bouncing, preteen daughter. We knew zero about being parents, especially to an eleven-year-old, but we loved Dawn. She had taken root in our hearts.

So Dawn moved into Cindy and Kelly's room, and now there were five of us in the little house on Dolorosa Street.

About this time, Keith was asked to perform at a benefit for the Hollywood Free Theater, which was made up of a group of Christian actors who met to encourage each other in the Lord and to work on their acting skills. Keith and I had gone to a few classes there. Neither of us showed any star quality, but it was fun.

It had been nearly three months since Keith had put aside performing music. He'd quickly turned down other opportunities. But this time he felt torn. He wasn't trying to slip out of his commitment, but he did have a desire to help raise money for this group of Christians. Finally he felt it was okay to at least ask the Lord about it. He prayed a lot because he didn't want his own desires to get in the way of hearing God.

At last Keith thought he had some direction. "I believe God is giving me the go-ahead to accept this one invitation," Keith told me. "He didn't tell me to pick up my music again. I think maybe he's letting me do this because it's for a good cause. It's a one-time thing. After that I'm totally going back to my commitment."

The benefit was going to be held in the heart of Beverly Hills at a very "in" night spot called the Daisy. On the night of the benefit, late in September, we jumped into Victor and headed up Wilshire Boulevard, past the famous Brown Derby restaurant, then turned onto North Rodeo Drive and into the parking lot of the Daisy.

The place was packed when we arrived, but not with the usual crowd. We immediately saw many familiar faces from the Vineyard—Randy Stonehill, Larry Norman, Jerry Houser, and a Christian recording artist named Jamie Owens. Then there were famous faces we were seeing up-close for the first time—Pat Boone, Dale Evans, and Julie Harris, who'd just starred in the movie *The Hiding Place.*

The Daisy was alive with energy and excitement. Light glittered off the chandeliers and mirrors, and Christian music played in the background. The long, mirrored bar against the far wall held only trays of fruit juice and soft drinks that night.

Keith and I found a small table for two. He was slotted near the end, just before Pat Boone and Julie Harris. Keith usually had nerves of steel, but I knew he felt a lot of pressure. He wanted his performance to bring glory to the Lord—and only to the Lord.

When Keith's turn came at last, he walked into the bright spotlight and sat down at the piano. The room fell into a polite hush. He looked out at the audience as he started playing softly on the piano and talking. "This song I'm about to sing is my song. This is your song. It's for everyone who's ever left the loving arms of their heavenly Father to go out on their own."

"I was a prodigal son," he explained. "But I'm not running anymore. I came home covered with mud and dirt from the world, and my Father in heaven picked me up, washed me off, and sat me on his lap."

As Keith launched into "The Prodigal Son Suite," the meandering conversations ceased. I remembered being the blurry-eyed transcriber as I copied the lyrics into our songbook during those long hours Keith put into writing it during a stony time almost a year-and-a-half earlier. Now people set down their soft drinks and turned their attention to the stage. I sensed at once that something was happening up there with Keith. This wasn't just a performance. It was as if, through Keith, God was portraying his heart to us—a Father's heart that longed for his children to come home.

When Keith came to the part where the now-broken prodigal son returns home, there was such a trembling cry in his voice that my throat tightened. At the table next to me, a woman cried.

> I was near home,
> In sight of the house.
> My father just stared—
> Dropped open his mouth.
> He ran up the road
> And fell at my feet,
> And cried . . . and cried . . .
> Father I've sinned.
> Heaven's ashamed.
> I'm no longer worthy
> To bear your name.
> I've learned that my home
> Is right where you are
> O Father, take me in . . .

People all over this beautiful ballroom were dabbing at their tears. Then Keith broke into the last movement, the part where the father responds. His words were unexpected, but they were the very words the lost child in everyone longs to hear. With joy and a heart full of forgiveness the father calls for a celebration . . .

> Bring the best robe
> Put it on my son!

Shoes for his feet—
Hurry! Put them on!
This is my son
Who I thought had died!
Prepare a feast
For my son's alive!
My son was lost
My son was dead
My son's returned,
In the hands of God!

When the song ended, Keith threw his head and body forward over the keys to emphasize it was finished. There was a moment of stunned silence. Then the whole room exploded in applause and cheers. Many people jumped to their feet in a standing ovation. But Keith got up from the piano at once and quietly made his way back to our table, barely looking up.

Once the program ended, many people came up to Keith to encourage him and tell him how the Lord touched them while he was singing. Keith looked pleased, but he was a bit reserved. Later, on the way home, I found out why.

"I wasn't sure how to respond when everyone was so excited," he said, shaking his head.

I was elated. "Keith, you were incredible. I really saw the Lord in you in a more powerful way tonight."

"I felt the Lord in a new way too." Then he hesitated for a moment. "Mel, I think the Lord gave me back my music while I was playing tonight. I was in the middle of the song and I just felt a peace and an assurance that I was right in the center of God's will—doing exactly what he created me to do."

"That's wonderful!"

"Yeah. It's hard to believe, but I think God really wants me to play for him and for his glory—and only for his glory."

When Keith received his music back, it was the go-ahead from the

Lord that he'd been waiting for, but it was another three months before he really picked it up and started running with it.

When he did, word about his music ministry quickly spread through our friends in Christian music. By the end of 1975, Keith was getting asked to do concerts in some churches in Southern California. It was a whole new world. Except for the few concerts he'd done with Randy Stonehill, Keith had only played his music in nightclubs, colleges, hippie vegetarian restaurants, and recording studios—along with a few television appearances when he was younger. Playing in churches posed some new challenges and interesting transitions for us.

Our first big question was, how much money do you ask from a church that invites you to do a concert? In the secular world, everyone always struggles to make more money. Besides the money itself, the amount you receive is a yardstick to measure your worth and popularity. The better you are, the more you get. Even though Keith was never in it just for the money, it was his trade and it paid our bills—and we still had bills to pay! Our CBS salary helped, but our growing household had become a hub of activity, and we were often busy with what seemed to be a continual "feeding of the five thousand."

We were just learning about finances from a Christian point of view. Keith had always had the highest integrity when it came to money, but the idea of tithing was new to us. In fact, we got a fiery baptism on tithing when a seven-month delay in our CBS salary eventually came in—a check for seven thousand dollars! After we got over the initial shock of giving away seven hundred dollars in tithe all at once, we were glad to follow biblical principles about giving. At least they were clear. But what were the biblical principles about charging for concerts? Where were they found in the Bible?

Our inquiries didn't help much. Other Christian musicians were all over the map when it came to this matter. Some sold tickets, some asked for a certain amount up-front, and others went for love offerings. We heard stories galore. They weren't all good. We had a few tough experiences of our own.

There was the time Keith was called at the last minute to play at a very large church about an hour and a half away from us. He was told on the phone they would give him twenty dollars to come. Keith balked because he figured that would just cover his gas for the three-hour round trip. It was such a large church, he felt the people could afford to give a little more. But they stood firm, probably thinking the opportunity to play for a few thousand people would help give Keith's ministry greater exposure. Keith didn't feel it was the brotherly way to do things. By the standards we were used to, we wouldn't have run an errand that far away for that price, let alone do a full concert. But this was not show business. This was ministry. We were confused, but Keith felt the Lord wanted him to go, even though we didn't think they were being fair. Besides, it was a good opportunity to minister to a lot of people.

So we set out, feeling our way along in the dark. Now that we were Christians we instinctively knew the money rules had changed in some way, but we really didn't know exactly how. Keith's music was no longer a career. He considered himself a minister, and we wanted to see people come to the Lord. But music was Keith's trade and we had big household expenses every week. Keith was an accomplished performer, so it seemed like he should ask for more than somebody who'd just taken a few guitar lessons. Yet as a minister, should Keith even care about how much he made? It was a question we'd have to wrestle with for some time.

Even with these questions, our excitement about Jesus continued to grow and touch every area of our lives—especially our music. We were so full inside and grateful to finally know the Lord after so many years of searching. All we wanted to do was tell the whole world that there really was a God and that he could be found. One of the best ways we knew to do it was through music. New songs just tumbled out one after another.

Keith was constantly writing—either alone, with me or Todd, or with some other new musical friend. Sometimes a combination of us wrote together, which made it even more fun. Many songs were inspiring calls to worship God in Spirit and truth. Others were lighthearted expressions of joy—and then there were the funny ones.

Keith didn't believe that being a Christian meant you lost your sense of humor or your ability to have a good time. We didn't sign up for that!

One day our friend Wendell Burton came over, and he and Keith ended up in the music room. Wendell went to the Vineyard and usually led worship at the Bible study at the house where the monkey lived. He also was a very talented singer and songwriter, and he and Keith decided to try and write something together. What resulted was "He'll Take Care of the Rest," a funny song about some heroes of the faith who trusted God even when the odds were against them:

You just think about Moses
In front of the burnin' bush,
Barefoot on the holy ground,
You know, he must have been thinkin,'
Hey, what's an old dude like me
Gonna tell 'em all when I go down?
(Go down, Moses!)

But the Lord said, "Hey, Mo!
Don't you worry 'bout your going down south,
I'll be saying every word that comes out of your mouth!
"You just keep doin' your best
And pray that it's blessed.
Hey, Mo, I'll take care of the rest
I'll get you through it, Ol' Pharaoh blew it!"

You just think about Noah,
Totin' his umbrella
When there wasn't a cloud in the sky.
All his neighbors would laugh
At his pet giraffe
And they would (ha, ha)
Snicker as he passed by.

But the Lord said,
"Hey, Noah, be cool.
Just keep buildin' dat boat.
It's just a matter of time
'Til they see who's gonna float!

"You just keep doin' your best
And pray that it's blessed.
Hey, Noah, I'll take care of the rest—
I'm the Weather Man!"

Then there were a few songs that Keith wrote right away to express his own pure joy at finally finding the truth that set him free. Now Keith was shining a light that drew people. He wrote this song to the Lord to tell him that whenever anyone asked why he looked so happy, he had the honor of pointing the way to the source of that light and simply saying, "It's because of you!"

It's because of you, people smile at me
And they say, "What a lucky guy!"
Because of you, I can raise my hands to the sky
And say, "I'm only happy because of you!"

Another song Keith wrote during this time talked about the supernatural touch from God he felt in his heart. "It's like chocolate ice cream," Keith said. "How do you describe the taste to someone who's never tasted chocolate?" To express his gratitude for that miraculous touch he wrote "You Put This Love in My Heart."

Is all this real or a dream?
I feel so good I could scream!
You put this love in my heart.

Well, I know the loneliness I had before
Is gone now, I'll never feel it anymore.
'Cause your lovin' has released me
From all that's in my past,
And I know I can believe you
When you say I'll never be forsaken
Your love is gonna last!

One day, Keith walked into the music room while I was working on a new song. He listened as I played what I had of it on the piano—and sang the few sketchy words.

When I hear the music start, I wanna sing it for you
Music that will fill your heart, I wanna bring it to you

"Pretty good so far, Mel."

I showed him the chords I was playing and he started fiddling with it. A few days later, Keith sat down to write, but nothing was coming. He was walking around the house pretty frustrated. After he went back into the music room, I had an impression. Words seemed to form in my mind. Was the Lord trying to say something to Keith through me? I wrote down the words and took the piece of paper to Keith. He opened the note and read, "Rest quietly before me, and I will give you a song."

Pretty soon I heard music. Keith was singing a song, with the same chorus melody I'd written, but it had a whole different theme. Keith walked out and said, "The Lord just gave me a love song, from him to me."

My son, my son,
Why are you striving?
You can't add one thing
To what's been done for you.
I did it all while I was dying.

Rest in your faith
My peace will come to you.
When I hear the praises start,
I wanna rain upon you
Blessings that will fill your heart.
I see no stain upon you
Because you are my child
And you know me.
To me you're only holy,
Nothing that you've done remains,
Only what you do for me.
My child, my child
Why are you weeping?
You will not have to wait forever.
That day and that hour is in my keeping—
The day I'll bring you into heaven . . .

Another song we wrote together was inspired by something we read in the newspaper, the story of a priest who was trying to cast demons out of a woman who was possessed. The priest said that one time the demons started laughing and talking to him through this lady. He claimed that they were boasting, saying, "We have all the power because nobody believes in us anymore!"

As soon as Keith and I became Christians, we knew there was a real God—and a real devil. It certainly explained the dark force that took control of Harmony outside the Bla Bla that hot night a few years ago. And one night from our bedroom we heard a loud noise, like heavy chains scraping across a hard surface, then a loud crash. We rushed into the living room to find that our large double-globed table lamp lay smashed to pieces—on the soft carpet. Weird. So many people in Southern California, and across America, were dipping into occult and New Age philosophies without realizing the demonic powers behind them. Most of it had looked pretty innocent to us before. Even with my vow to never get into satanic things, I did without realizing it. But now we knew that Satan was a hardball-playing, totally evil, spiritual entity. Satan put enough truth into darkness for it to appear as light. The more you hung out in the devil's territory, even in ignorance, the more power you gave to him—and he was determined to capture and destroy every unsuspecting soul he could.

I drove to the market after reading about the priest, and his words kept coming back to me. I found myself scratching lyrics on a scrap of paper with one hand while driving with the other. After I got home I put a fresh copy of the words, to be sung from Satan's point of view, on Keith's piano. He added a few more words and some music. The result was called "Satan's Boast."

> Oh, my job keeps gettin' easier
> As time keeps slippin' away.
> I can imitate the brightest light
> And make your night look just like day.
> I put some truth in every lie
> To tickle itchin' ears.
> I'm drawin' people just like flies
> 'Cause they like what they hear.
>
> I'm gainin' power by the hour,
> They're fallin' by the score.
> You know, it's gettin' very simple now
> Since no one believes in me any more.
>
> Oh heaven's just a state of mind
> My books read on your shelf.
> Oh, have you heard that God is dead?
> I made that one up myself!
> They're dabblin' in magic spells,
> They get their fortunes read,
> They heard the truth but turned away
> And followed me instead . . .

Everyone likes a winner.
With my help you're guaranteed to win.
Hey, man, you ain't no sinner, no!
You've got the truth within.

And as your life slips by you believe the lie
That you did it on your own.
But I'll be there to help you share
Our dark eternal home—
Our dark eternal home.

Another influence was the Christian literature we were discovering.
Keith was constantly reading, and one of his favorites was a classic
allegory called *Hind's Feet on High Places* by Hannah Hurnard. Keith
was thinking about the trials and testings the Lord had brought him
through when he wrote the song "Trials Turned to Gold."

He's brought me low
So I could know
The way to reach the heights.

To forsake my dreams
My self-esteem
And give up all my rights.

With each one that I lay down,
A jewel's placed in my crown.
Because his love
The things above—is all we'll ever need.

He's brought me here
Where things are clear,
And trials turn to gold.

He later wrote this journal entry:

Where Things Are Clear

> *We are nothing but dust. Our lives are not ours. Our bodies are not ours. Our future is in your hands. The Lord is making me ready to die—completely—I don't deserve to live—so come Spirit of the holy God—live instead of me. There is no joy left in life but to realize I am nothing and let God be what he is—all.*
>
> *Tears cannot express nor laughter his grace/gifts. I am his. Please Keith! Don't ever go back—look up. It's time to go.*

Probably the greatest boost to our growth as songwriters was meeting other Christian musicians. Keith's first Christian recording session was playing piano on the *Growing Pains* album by Jamie Owens. Then, through Jamie, Keith met a guy named Terry Talbot. Keith and Terry hit it off immediately.

Terry and his brother, John, had been in a famous rock band called Mason Profit. Terry was working on a musical called *Firewind,* and he asked Keith to sing one of the lead vocals on a song called "Walk and Talk." Interestingly it was going to be a duet with Barry McGuire. Keith couldn't believe it, since Barry had made such an impression on us a few years before in Turlock. Now Keith was going to sing his first recorded Christian song with him! It seemed that so many little threads were starting to weave together.

Keith was really excited about this recording session because he was going to get to meet so many other Christian artists. From the story I heard later, Keith must have made quite a first impression.

Before Annie Herring from the Second Chapter of Acts even came to the session, Jamie Owens had told her, "Wait until you meet Keith Green. He's so filled with energy and his heart is just full of the Lord. You're going to love him!"

When Annie walked into the studio, Keith was working on his

solo with the recording engineer. She suppressed a laugh because Keith was trying to sing his lines with energy and feeling—and at the same time trying to explain to the engineer where to punch between words. The engineer finally got it and did it just as Keith said. Annie thought, *Boy, he sure knows how to take charge!*

A little while later Billy Ray Hearn of Sparrow Records showed up since *Firewind* was going to be released on his label. Keith did what he always did when he met the president of a record company. He dragged Billy Ray over to the piano and said, "Listen to this!" Then he proceeded to play a few songs. That wasn't all. Keith told him, "You gotta come to one of my concerts! There's a whole different spirit during a concert!" Billy Ray told Keith he'd try to come to a concert—sometime.

Besides getting to know Terry and Barry much better that day, Keith met Annie and the rest of Second Chapter—Annie's brother and sister, Matt and Nelly Ward, plus Nelly's boyfriend, Steve Greisen. They all had a great time getting to know each other and joking around. In fact, Annie made a lasting impression on Keith.

In jest, Annie, who was used to holding her own in a large family full of brothers, gave Keith what she considered to be just a loving punch. But when Keith came home he said, "Annie slugged me in the arm—hard!"

A week later, Keith met Annie's husband, Buck Herring, who was the producer for Second Chapter. He learned Buck and Annie had only been married for a few years when her dad died. It was then that Annie's youngest brother and sister, who had been living with their dad, came to live with Annie and Buck. Sharing a home Nelly, Matt, and Annie discovered they could harmonize together.

The first time I met Second Chapter, I was so new to Christian music that I'd never even heard of them although they were famous. Keith took me to their house in Northridge, and when we walked in, Buck was listening to one of their albums. I was blown away. I walked into the kitchen and Annie was standing at the sink with an apron on doing dishes. I didn't know what to say, so I said the first thing that came to my mind.

"I just heard your album. I've never heard you before. It's incredible. You . . . you all sound like angels!"

"Oh, thank you!" Annie said with great delight.

Immediately I felt really stupid. How embarrassing to tell a famous singer that you've never even heard them! I wanted to fall through the floor. But I was really in awe of this beautiful woman with elegant, high cheekbones and dark, dancing eyes—a woman of God who sang like an angel and did dishes like a normal person! Standing in her kitchen, I wasn't sure how to act. But Annie was so kind and warm and seemed genuinely encouraged by my remarks. I guessed she was used to people getting a bit flustered around her. She made me feel welcome at once.

Meanwhile, Keith and Buck were off in the corner talking about music, producing, and making albums. Keith had so many questions, especially about who he was supposed to sing to. I could hear them talking in the background as I helped Annie wipe the counter.

"I really believe I'm supposed to make an album." Keith was picking Buck's brain. "But I'm not sure if it's supposed to be a Christian album or not. What do you think?"

"What else would you do?" Buck said.

"Well, I want to lift up the name of the Lord. But it seems like Christians have plenty of music already. Why sing about Jesus to Christians? They already know him."

"Evangelism is important, Keith, but it's not the only reason God gave us music," Buck responded.

"I know, but it's the thing that's most important to me. I really want to do an album with a Christian message—for people who don't know the Lord yet."

"We tried it, brother. Our first contract was with MGM, and the secular machinery didn't know what to do with an album full of Christian songs."

"Maybe so, but at least the album will have a better chance of making it. I can always tell when I hit the Christian radio station even before I hear the words. It just really bothers me that Christian records have such low budgets you can't get good sounds."

"It won't matter how good your album sounds," Buck said as he shrugged. "A secular label still won't know what to do with it."

"I'm not into singing just for Christians. I really want my music to bring people to the Lord."

"Then I'm sure the Lord will show you what he wants you to do," Buck said simply.

As we drove home that evening, Keith was deep in thought. I could tell his conversation with Buck didn't convince him. Keith wanted to reach people outside the church. I knew he wouldn't rest until his questions were settled.

Our musical family kept growing as we met people like Chuck Girard, Phil Keaggy, Mike and Kathy Deasy, Kelly Willard, Karen Lafferty, and Andrae Crouch. We also listened to tons of tapes by people like Bob Ayala, a group called Mustard Seed Faith, and a girl with the name of Honeytree. We were totally impressed that they'd given their talent to sing only for the Lord—and yet we were still torn over what path Keith's musical ministry might take.

It was during this time, too, that one friendship in which there had been long-standing tension was finally resolved.

Keith bumped into Randy Stonehill unexpectedly one day at the Vineyard offices. They were both glad to see each other, and Keith invited him over to our house. Because of some heated conversations before we were Christians, the friendship had been strained. They were still friends, and Keith even played at Randy's wedding, but things hadn't been quite right.

When Randy arrived with his guitar case, he and Keith headed straight into the music room. I was in the kitchen with Cindy, Kelly, and Dawn, and I could hear them laughing, talking, and playing music. Then it got very quiet for a long time.

"Things between me and Randy finally got worked out," Keith told me later that night. "I told him how upset I've been, thinking that I would have become a Christian a lot sooner if he would have really shared more about Jesus with me."

"What did Randy say?"

"He said he did try to tell me, but because he wasn't living out his faith consistently he knew his words probably didn't have a lot of power. He said he knew actions speak louder than words sometimes. Randy said he was sorry."

"That was pretty neat of him to be so open with you. What did you say?"

Keith smiled. "My heart just melted, and I saw some of my mistakes. I know sometimes it was hard for him to have a two-way conversation with me. I'm not always the best listener. I forgave him, and I asked him to forgive me too."

"Well, it was Randy who invited us to the Vineyard."

"Yeah. We were both teary-eyed. Then we got really excited. I ended up pulling out the melody Todd and I wrote a few days ago, and we worked on the words together. It's called 'Your Love Broke Through.' It's really hot!"

Later, Keith wrote:

March 21, 1976

Randy played me some new songs, and then we started talking. One thing led to another and it finally ended up in a big confession. . . . IT WAS A MIRACLE and an answer to prayer.

The Lord really seemed to be starting to tie some loose ends together. We were hoping the next thing God would tie together would be Keith's music. It always amazed me that some major record company didn't snatch Keith up after one listen. I'd often seen him play his heart out for some executives, giving a performance that would take their breath away, but nothing ever came of it.

Now I wondered if something had been blocking the way. Had the Lord been waiting for Keith to become a Christian before letting his career take off? What if, now that we were Christians, God would blow open doors, unplug ears, and help Keith find a record company that believed in him?

The dream of making it musically was not dead. It just had a slightly different slant to it now. Keith continued to make demos of his songs and run them all over town still trying to get a record deal with a secular label.

Then it seemed like our dream was going to take off. About two months after meeting Buck, Keith went into Hollywood one afternoon to meet with the people at Arista Records. Arista was a well-respected secular label turning out hit records with top-name artists. Keith played some of his songs for the Arista folks and they got very excited.

When Keith got home, he bounced through the door. "Melody! Guess what?"

When I hurried into the living room, Keith was smiling from ear to ear.

"Mel, Arista wants to send me to New York next week!"

"New York! You're kidding!"

"They want me to meet with Clive Davis! God is sending me straight to the top!"

Playing for Clive Davis in person was nothing short of a dream come true. He was one of the most powerful men in the industry. He signed Janis Joplin; Santana; Sly & The Family Stone; Bruce Springsteen; Blood, Sweat & Tears; and Billy Joel to mention a few.

Keith continued excitedly, "They're paying my way out and everything. This might be it. Maybe God is going to open some doors after all!"

The following week I drove Keith to LAX and gave him a kiss good-bye, wishing I could go with him. Keith was so charged up I knew that when he sang he was going to blow Clive Davis out of the water. I wished I could be there to see his face. That long-awaited record contract seemed to be finally at Keith's fingertips.

Once Keith arrived in New York, he settled into his hotel room anticipating his big meeting with Arista the next day. After his meeting Keith wrote:

April 9, 1976

> *Clive Davis . . . kept me waiting for almost two hours. It was a failure, but I took it so well I couldn't believe it . . . kept telling myself that the Lord wanted me to do a Christian album. It depressed me, but I kept my chin up.*

The following afternoon my phone rang. Keith was calling from New York.

"How'd it go?" I asked eagerly.

"Well, I think God wants me to do a Christian album."

"You're kidding?"

"No. My interview was a flop. I was really upset at first, but I'm kinda starting to feel relieved now. At least I finally have a clear answer from the Lord. Hey, do you want me to bring a New York pizza home?"

"That would be great!"

Keith later wrote:

> *Called the cab after ordering a genuine Pizza Stop pizza for Mel. At the airport I discovered some Krishna people and a bunch came on the flight. It bothered me so much that I decided to write one of them a note which read: "Only Jesus Christ Is Lord of All." Then the Lord gave me a melody, and I will have a song soon. Went home and had pizza and brownies.*

While the brownies were baking, Keith grinned and told me the smell of his warm pizza in the overhead made all the passengers drool.

Keith did have a song soon. He called it "Jesus Is Lord of All." More than anything I felt his lyrics were a personal statement that even in disappointment he trusted that Jesus cared about, and was involved in, every aspect of his life:

Jesus is Lord of all
Jesus is Lord of all

> No sin is too big
> No problem too small
> Jesus is Lord of all.

The dream was dead—the one that had been in Keith's heart since he was a child. Some dreams are so deep they seem to become a part of the very fabric of your being. When they die, a part of you dies too. This should have been the biggest disappointment in Keith's life. But it wasn't. I saw the grace of God in Keith in such a strong way. After the initial depression lifted, he was actually excited. His prayers had been answered at last.

Now Keith knew why things never really had come together with his secular music. He saw even more clearly how his life plans needed to be anchored in the reality of God's will. Otherwise they would never be anything but fantasy. The song "Your Love Broke Through," which Keith had written just a few months earlier with Randy and Todd, had an even deeper meaning now.

> Like a foolish dreamer
> Trying to build a highway to the sky,
> All my hopes would come tumblin' down
> And I never knew just why.
> Until today, when you pulled away the clouds
> That hung like curtains on my eyes.
> I've been blind all these wasted years,
> When I thought I was so wise.
> But then you took me by surprise . . .
>
> All my life, I've been searching
> For that crazy missing part,
> And with one touch you just rolled away
> The stone that held my heart.
> And now I see that the answer
> Was as easy as just asking you in,

And I'm so sure
I could never doubt
Your gentle touch again.
It's like the power of the wind!

Like waking up from the longest dream
How real it seemed!
Until your love broke through.
I've been lost in a fantasy
That blinded me,
Until your love broke through!

Keith was sure at last that the Lord wanted him to sing his music to Christians and probably even make a Christian album. Mostly he wondered what God might want him to say to all these Christians. We'd seen some glaring inconsistencies. A lot of people were going to church and to Christian concerts—but not many of them seemed really excited about Jesus. Keith wondered how God felt about that.

And his heart was heavy whenever he thought about it.

9

"FOR HIM WHO HAS EARS TO HEAR"

After the doors slammed shut on the record deal with Arista, Keith launched out in a whole new direction. He still didn't know if he was really ready for the church. Or, for that matter, if the church was ready for him—and the unorthodox way he looked. He didn't even own a suit or a tie. But Keith figured since Jesus took him as he was, the church would have to do the same.

Since Victor wasn't really cut out for the road, we bought another vehicle that we tagged the Pregnant Blue Guppy. It was an old blue van, and the previous owner had extended the back about four feet. The extension kind of bubbled out, which gave it the pregnant-fish look. It had a big bed in back and bucket seats in the front. Now we were ready to go on the road—only we weren't sure where!

Neither of us had a church background, so we had no idea where to start. Other musicians told us which churches did concerts and helped us get going. Chuck Girard, the lead singer of the group Love Song, gave Keith a jump start. Love Song often had to turn down invitations because of so many requests, so Chuck would recommend Keith. We got all Love Song's overflow, which was a big help.

By spring 1976, Keith was ready to go out on the road, doing church concerts up and down the West Coast. He had a lot of different kinds of songs—serious, funny, inspiring. We were about to find out what being in a public music ministry was all about.

Keith did a concert one night in a church of a few hundred people. At the end, the pastor stood and encouraged everyone to give generously because it was all going to be given to Keith. "Let's bless him back for the great time of ministry!" A big pillowcase was the offering bucket. About half an hour later, we wandered out to the Blue Guppy and opened up the envelope we'd been given. We were stunned by the amount inside. We obviously hadn't received all that was given. Keith didn't know what to do.

At first Keith said, "I'll just let it go. I'm not going to make a big deal out of this."

But after a few minutes he realized he couldn't drive off without talking to the pastor. It wasn't just the money. It was the principle. Keith felt he should be given the whole offering because that's what people were told. Everyone gave with that in mind.

When Keith told me he was going to go back in and talk to the pastor, I nearly died. I probably wouldn't have gone because I'd be afraid to look like I was just being greedy. But Keith was determined.

"We always take all of our expenses out of the offering," the pastor said in reply to Keith's inquiry.

"Then you should have told everyone that was going to happen when you took the offering. Then it would have been fine."

"Well, no one's complained before—"

Keith stood firm. "I just don't think it's right. Everyone was told the offering was going to be given to me, and that's who they thought they were giving to."

I could tell he felt awkward, knowing he was probably being misunderstood.

"I'm not trying to be greedy, but I feel the givers were misled— whether it was intentional or not," he concluded.

I don't remember if Keith was given the rest of the offering, but he did what he felt was right. I knew he did it from a pure heart. In fact, a few months earlier he had written an entry in his journal where he was reflecting with disgust about the love of money he used to have:

I would stop at nothing to work at a stupid money-making scheme!! I had so many of them that I wouldn't have to worry even if I wasn't a musician. I figured out lately that we could be very rich if we wanted to. All we'd have to do is really hustle and save. Hustle for lead sheets and studio gigs and perform gigs and write really sell-out songs about sex and double-meaning stuff. Praise the Lord, we don't want to.

Our real concern about finances was centered in the fact that we had more and more people floating through our home. A woman in her forties, who was extremely depressed and suicidal, moved in for a few months. Another guy who was on and off heroin stayed with us, along with his wife and two little kids. He robbed us, then showed up at our next prayer meeting to pray for the robber. Later his wife told on him and we forgave him. Then there was the young Spanish girl who was kicking an addiction to Seconal—or downers. And then a friend of ours met a girl in Beverly Hills who was selling roses for the Moonies, a group run by Sun Myung Moon. Our friend phoned us immediately.

"Hey you guys. There's a girl with me who wants to find Jesus. She's traveling through from out-of-state. I don't know what to do with her and I don't know who else to call. Can I bring her over?"

Keith said, "Of course!"

That evening, our friend showed up with one of the tallest, prettiest, and most exhausted girls we'd ever seen. Patricia Forrester, or Podie as she called herself, came from the East Coast in a van with several other Moonies. To make money, they sold flowers along the way. But Podie was starting to feel more like a captive than a disciple.

On this day, the leaders dropped off Podie in Beverly Hills with a bucket of roses. As usual she had no money and no idea when she'd get picked up. After several hours, Podie slumped on a bench in despair. That's when our friend noticed her. He sat down next to her to see what was wrong. When he talked to her about Jesus, her heart opened up. He said he knew a place where she could stay, and she jumped at the chance to escape.

That evening Keith stayed up half the night talking with Podie.

She was open to Jesus because she'd recently had an experience with him. One night back East she felt like she was cracking up under the grueling Moonie work schedule. She snuck out in the middle of the night and ran into the woods behind their compound. She told Keith that as she cried out to God, "God came to me and it felt like warm butterscotch pouring over me, coating me with a tangible soothing peace. I knew it was Jesus." With her renewed sense of peace, she had the strength to go on, but with increasing questions.

Leading Podie to the Lord was easy for Keith—compared to convincing her that she could stay with us and get some rest, no strings attached.

Everywhere we turned, there were desperate or wounded people who needed help. While Keith was wrestling with the question of what it was the Lord wanted him to actually say to the church, we'd been having message-shaping experiences. Some were pretty vivid. The nude-bathing incident was definitely one of them, and so was our experience with a young woman who went by the name Mistiana.

Keith and I had flown up to Seattle, where a lot of people were already into his music because of all the clubs he'd played every time he ran away from home. Keith capitalized on his popularity by doing a concert at Everett College, surprising the students by preaching a strong evangelistic message. We then went up to Bellingham, where Keith did a concert at his old Washington State college hangout, Mama Sunday's. But this time, instead of playing songs about searching, he sang and talked about what he had found.

It was during this trip that we met Mistiana. You couldn't miss her when she walked in a room. At first glance, she looked like a gypsy, with her long flowing skirt and black velvet jacket. Her dark, flashing eyes, framed on each side by long feathered earrings, caught our attention with interest. We talked to her for a long time and found out she was going to be driving home to San Francisco. We wanted more time with her and asked if we could ride along as far as Portland. She agreed to take us.

During our drive, Mistiana told us she was into witchcraft. Actually she was a bona fide, spell-casting witch. Keith began talking so hard and fast about God that she became angry, feeling like she was a prisoner in her own car. To make matters worse, after a few hours Keith had insisted on driving the whole way, so Mistiana was stuck in the backseat. Before we pulled into Portland, however, Keith was leading her in a prayer to receive the Lord.

We wound up riding all the way to California with Mistiana. We also talked her into coming to our house instead of returning to San Francisco right away. She didn't know any other Christians, and we knew she might not be able to stay strong if she went home alone. For hours in the car we talked to her about our past involvement in the occult and drugs and all the wonderful ways God had set us free.

Melody, Keith, and Mistiana at the Vineyard

When we got to Sacramento, we phoned a pastor we knew and we all went to dinner. He invited us all back to sleep at his house and he spent some time ministering to Mistiana. Later Mistiana slipped out and smoked some pot. It was obvious, but no one said anything. Keith later wrote:

> . . . [she] smoked a joint and we all knew it, but she did not confess it for a few days.

We left in the morning, and just a few hours out of Los Angeles saw something in the clouds we could hardly believe: a Holy Spirit dove and a cross. We all saw it at the same time and kept blinking in surprise. Whatever it was, it was the sign Mistiana was looking for. It convinced her she was heading in the right direction with Jesus. But even though she'd prayed to accept the Lord, something about her still seemed kind of strange.

Immediately when we got back home Keith grabbed a book off our shelf. It was called *Jesus Is Coming Soon* and was about the end times when Jesus would return. But Jesus wasn't going to return for everyone, the book said. Anyone involved in idolatry, fornication, or witchcraft, to name a few things, would be swept away in the Day of Judgment.

As Keith read from this book and quoted from the Bible, Mistiana's dark eyes got bigger and bigger. Suddenly she put up her hands and said, "That's enough. I have some things I want to get rid of—right now."

Keith closed the book. "Sure! Let's do it. What do you want to get rid of?"

"Well, I've got my astrology chart, some tarot cards, and some books. They're in my trunk. I'll get them, but what should we do with them?"

Keith thought for a moment, and then his eyes lit up as they always did when he had a good idea. "Let's burn them!"

Mistiana grabbed all her occult trappings, and we piled them in our front driveway. As Keith set them on fire, we rejoiced at the goodness of God and at Mistiana's obedience. I don't know if our suburban neighbors driving by on Dolorosa Street were rejoicing or not, but they were at least getting used to seeing strange happenings at our house.

In a couple of months, however, Mistiana moved to another small Christian community led by a very special pastor named Reverend Glenn. He pastored the Topanga Canyon Community Church up in the mountains. It was real hippieville up there, and Reverend Glenn had a heart that was open to the people many other Christians ignored. It was a sacrificial, bare-bones kind of ministry. Reverend Glenn lived with his wife and kids in this old beat-up church, and he hardly owned anything. But they kept their doors open day and night. Often there were kids sleeping in the pews because they had no place else to go, and no one else who cared.

Not too long after Mistiana moved to Topanga she got engaged to a guy she led in the sinner's prayer in a bar. He was an alcoholic and untested in his Christian commitment. It didn't seem like either one of them was ready to get married, so Keith tried to talk Mistiana out of it. When that didn't work, Keith went to Reverend Glenn, who was going to do the ceremony.

"Please, don't marry them," Keith begged. "They're both new Christians. They barely know each other. I'm telling you this guy is not committed. Counsel them against it. Please tell them to wait."

For whatever reasons, Reverend Glenn decided to marry them. Keith hoped his hunch was wrong and the newlyweds would live happily ever after, so we went to the wedding. We loved Mistiana. We still loved Reverend Glenn too, even though we were afraid he might have missed it on this one. Only time would really tell.

Meanwhile we continued to wonder if there was anything we could have said to Mistiana that would have prepared her to make wiser decisions. We didn't know, but more than ever the experience underscored our question—why didn't leading people in the sinner's prayer revolutionize their life right away?

Our house was continually swelling with people. Cindy no longer had an outside job. Keith and I told her we'd take care of both her and Kelly if she wanted to stay home to help us cook and run the household, which was now a full-time job. With so many people in and out, I didn't know what our neighbors thought—especially if we were going to have bonfires in our driveway! But it looked like they were going to have to get used to us because we decided to buy our house.

Now the question of what to charge for a concert was becoming more of a pressing issue. We tried several different ways. Sometimes a church wanted to take a love offering for Keith, and sometimes they wanted Keith to tell them how much he'd charge. In these instances, Keith set a small fee for going. One night he asked for about fifty dollars, but later he really struggled, knowing other, less-accomplished music ministers got a lot more. He was trying to figure out if he should start asking for seventy-five dollars or even one hundred dollars a night. At least then he'd know what he'd be getting and didn't have to worry about scanty offerings. On the other hand, an offering gave the Lord a chance to bless you where a set fee did not. Keith was trying to figure out where all the boundaries were. Did you not go minister somewhere because they couldn't pay you enough? And how much was enough?

In some ways, the Christian music ministry was beginning to appear similar to the secular music business we'd just stepped out of. Record companies, contracts, concert tours, even a pecking order of artist popularity were similar in Christian ministry and secular industry. But in other ways the Christian music scene was a whole new animal. When you were invited somewhere, what should you expect to receive in return? Some churches were obviously wealthy. Others were poor. How did you deal with the differences?

We wondered if asking for a minimum amount would settle the issue.

"And yet," Keith said, "I can't imagine Paul telling the Corinthian church, 'Sorry, guys. I can't come unless you promise me five thousand shekels and two first-class chariot fares!'"

The money issue, however, was not going to immobilize Keith from delivering the things in his heart. The work seemed so urgent. In June 1976, when Keith did a concert in Ashland, Oregon, what he told the audience impressed me because I saw how much Keith was changing.

"It's getting darker outside," he said during one of his piano rambles. "I drive down the freeway everyday in L.A. and I see a million people passing who don't know their Creator. They don't know God. What is this? How can they go through life? How can they go through forty, fifty years and not know the Lord?"

"There's a high suicide rate, a high divorce rate, and the insanity rate keeps increasing—all in proportion to the population, but the darker the world gets, the brighter the light of Jesus gets. Twenty years ago, you couldn't tell the difference between a Christian and a moral heathen. There were a lot of upstanding people and they had high moral codes. . . . But today if you don't live with someone before you get married, you're considered stupid by the world. . . .

"In L.A. right now on the streets there are rows, and rows, and rows of pornographic newspapers for sale cheap—right at the eye level of little kids. There are women lying with women right on the front covers, men lying with men . . . magazines that you would have been put in jail for even possessing five years ago. It's Sodom and Gomorrah time!

"Jesus said, 'It shall be in the last days as it was with Sodom and Gomorrah.' The only sin listed [for Sodom and Gomorrah] was homosexual gang rape. . . . Two months ago, there were two crimes never before recorded in the history of Los Angeles crime—two homosexual gang rapes! We're standing at the door. The Lord is returning soon."

Keith had strong convictions about homosexuality, but we really had a heart of compassion for anyone caught in that lifestyle. After a concert in Seattle, a young guy named Neil drove us to the airport. Keith noticed that he was struggling with something and drew him out. Within minutes Neil was confessing. Even though he was active in church, he was living a hidden homosexual life, about which he had mixed feelings. Keith reached out to him and asked when it all started.

"I was about ten and . . . my uncle molested me. It was scary and confusing, but then I kept experimenting with guys my age . . . and well, now—"

"Are you happy?" Keith asked.

"Well, I would be if I didn't feel so guilty sometimes," Neil said. "What's wrong with being gay, anyway? It's my sexual preference. God made me this way."

Keith said, "God didn't make you gay, but he did create all of us as sexual beings. Because of that, in fairness, God gave us reasonable boundaries because he is not into confusing people. If we're single, no sex before marriage. If we're married, no adulterous affairs. And no sex with the same sex."

I jumped in. "He also banned rape, incest, and sex with children and animals."

Keith continued gently, "We might be violated by someone in a sexual area, but it really breaks God's heart and arouses his anger against the one who hurt us. We may even be tempted to dabble in some of those areas, but we've been given advance warning to treat them as taboo. God always has a good reason if he says something is wrong."

I added, "For example, God also banned some animals as food, and science later proved those boundaries wise because of health risks, especially with pork. We can eat those animals freely now if we choose, but only because God lifted the boundaries. But he's kept his sexual boundaries. God lists giving in to homosexual desires right next to giving in to adultery and other things he doesn't want us doing."

Keith grabbed his Bible and read 1 Corinthians 6:9–10 (NIV): "Neither fornicators, nor idolaters, nor adulterers, nor homosexuals, nor sodomites, nor thieves, nor covetous, nor drunkards, nor revilers, nor extortionist will inherit the kingdom of God."

"Wow," Neil said, "I never realized living a gay lifestyle was lumped in with those other things too. I felt like being gay was the worst, most unpardonable sin in the Bible. If it's so wrong, why doesn't God just change me?"

I jumped in. "Hey, why doesn't he change all of us so we're never tempted again? It doesn't work that way. God doesn't take away desire and turn us into blank, unfeeling beings. We need to decide to make better choices and ask God to help us change by his power—but we also need to practice self-control. We need to cooperate with the power of God. That's what makes us like Jesus."

Keith looked at Neil intensely and said, "You just want what everyone wants—a loving, intimate relationship that will bring you real joy and happiness. But you won't find it in sex—gay or straight. You'll only find it in deep relationship with God, and you can only have deep relationship with God by getting the things out of your life that grieve him. For you, that's living a gay life. For me, it's something else. But we've all got something."

I said, "When we meet Jesus, some things change instantly. Other things might take a little time. We just need to ask God for extra help to get free in those areas. Even if it's two steps forward, one step back, at least we're moving in the right direction."

Keith concluded, "The main thing is that we decide to live differently. After we make a firm decision in our heart, God gives us more power to walk it out, and I think the temptations get less intense too."

"Look, it's God who gives us the desire for intimacy. He gives us our sexual desires. It's just that he sets boundaries," I added.

We were near the airport and Keith wanted to offer some ongoing practical help. He said, "You shouldn't have to be alone in this. I know some Christians who would help you get free."

Neil looked at Keith and seemed on the verge of tears. He said, "Thanks for caring and not condemning me. When I confess my struggles, I find out some guys have the same problem because they hit on me—and the straights, especially in the church, avoid me. I really am pretty lonely and miserable. I really wish I could change."

As soon as Neil sounded open to getting help, Keith had him stop at a pay phone. Keith called our friends at Jesus People USA in Chicago to see if they had room to take in Neil. We knew they'd had success in helping others out of the same situation. As we got back in the car and kept talking, all I could see in Keith's eyes was an overwhelming concern to help Neil get set totally free.

Early in 1977, Billy Ray Hearn of Sparrow Records offered a record deal to Keith. A short time after the *Firewind* session, where they first met, Billy Ray took Keith up on his offer to come see him in one of the many church concerts he was doing. Billy Ray slipped in unannounced. He was shocked to find the place packed to overflowing. He even had to crawl over people just to find a place on the floor in an aisle. It was not protocol for record company presidents, but Billy Ray stayed to see what it was about Keith that drew so many people.

It was a powerful night of music and ministry. Billy Ray was more than mildly interested, and that kicked off a long process of conversations and negotiations with Keith and his father over the proposed contract. Keith asked Todd to play bass on the album, but who would produce it? Earlier Keith had asked Buck Herring to produce him, but Buck figured that he and Keith were both too intense to try working together. A young man named Bill Maxwell was suggested. Bill was a hot drummer and an excellent producer who coproduced with Andrae Crouch on his albums. He was also a committed Christian. When Bill came over to our house to meet us, we were taken with his warm, open manner. He looked like he was in his late twenties, with light brown, shoulder-length hair and a Southern accent. He was decidedly unassuming for someone who came so highly recommended.

Keith played Bill all of his demos and then played some songs on the piano for him. Bill's response was very direct: "You sound so much better in person than you do on your demos. You've got so much more energy and style in person. That's what needs to come across in the recording."

Keith and I had noticed that before too—but how could we capture Keith's style and energy on tape? More importantly, how could we capture the unusual sense of what God was doing inside Keith as he sang? Could it be done?

Keith and I were learning the value of prayer, so at his concerts Keith began asking people to pray for the album project. "I really need your prayers more than anything," he'd say, "because I've pretty much got the songs picked out, and the producer, and some of the musicians. But in the studio, a spiritual song can sometimes lose its anointing. I want the Holy Spirit to come through. I want to make sure the Spirit is producing it and recording it. If you all would just put me on your prayer list . . . I need that!"

Getting ready to record an album forced Keith to seriously examine a new teaching we'd heard. Soon after we gave our hearts to God, Kenn had encouraged everyone to attend some seminars addressing the basic conflicts young believers face. We drove excitedly for ninety minutes to a stadium in Long Beach. The first half of the seminar was filled with great teaching, and we took notes like crazy in the large notebooks they gave us. After lunch the teacher began to talk about music. He believed some instruments should not be used in Christian music—such as drums and electric guitars. He went on to explain that certain sounds were evil and conjured up demons. I glanced across at Keith who sat like a rock, and then I glanced down at his notebook. He had stopped writing. After a few more minutes, Keith began to write. In large capital letters diagonally across the whole page he wrote: WRONG!

I caught my breath and thought, *Oh no! We can't be rebellious—* Keith leaned over and said, "This guy's out to lunch on music!"

Before recording, we discussed the "demonic instrument" issue with Bill over and over again. Keith concluded that no instrument was inherently evil in itself, but it was the intent and spirit of the player that made the difference. Even so, we decided to go easy on the electric guitar.

By the time we went into the studio some months later, Bill had seen Keith in concert several times. He knew exactly what Keith could do and was committed to capturing it on tape if it could be done.

Bill and Keith in the studio

Usually the instrumental tracks are laid down before a singer overdubs his vocals. Keith made his demos that way too. So he put on his headset, stood in front of the microphone, and began to sing the first song.

Bill commented, "Keith, you're sounding just great, but something is missing."

"What? What do you want me to do?" asked Keith.

"I don't know," said Bill. "I just know you can do better. Let's try that vocal again. This time make me believe what you're saying."

It was nearly impossible to get a bad vocal from Keith, but Bill was looking for that fire he'd seen ignite in Keith during a concert—the quality that set Keith apart from so many others. Keith stood in front of the microphone and tried again.

Bill shook his head and said, "Keith, I've heard you do this song much more powerfully in concert." Then Bill got an idea. He told Keith, "We're going to do this 'live'!"

Bill sat Keith at the piano with a headset and a mike and said, "Just sit here and play while you're singing like you do at a concert." Then Bill came into the control booth where I sat watching through the glass.

The tapes were rolling now, and Bill gave Keith the nod. Keith was only halfway through the first verse when Bill and I exchanged wide-eyed looks. Something sparked! The song definitely had life! Bill had pinpointed that indefinable something that made the difference between the slick, homogenized demos Keith had produced for years and a vibrant, exciting recording.

Of course! Keith always sang and played at the same time. His voice played off of the energy and rhythm he was feeling from the piano—and vice versa. Now we were cooking!

As Keith expected with making a Christian album, there wasn't a big budget compared to the tens, and often hundreds of thousands, that go into a secular album. We only had fifteen thousand dollars to work with. But there are some things money can't buy.

Together Bill and Keith were capturing Keith's raw energy, emotions, and spiritual heart cry. The songs were fresh and the delivery was powerful. Listening, you had an uncanny sense that you were hearing from Someone other than just Keith Green.

We knew that "something more" we were feeling in Keith's music was because of the intense prayer we were getting. Besides the prayer Keith had requested at his concerts, the people living with us formed prayer teams and prayed faithfully at home during every studio session. There was one thing at the very top of their prayer list—that the anointing of the Lord would come through on the recording of each song. Keith wanted God to touch people in a deep and powerful way. And we knew, no matter how good a song was, without God's anointing it would never be more than just a good song. We were after far more.

While Keith and Bill were mixing the tracks one afternoon, Keith said confidently, "God told me this is going to be one of the biggest-selling Christian albums ever!"

Bill raised an eyebrow skeptically. "How do you know that?"

"Because I told the Lord I'd give the money I made back to him to use for his work—and not just put it all into my own pocket. So I know he's going to bless it."

Bill could sense Keith wasn't speaking out of arrogance, but from a sincere desire to help others. This really touched Bill—but a history-making Christian album? Only time would tell.

Keith fittingly named the album *For Him Who Has Ears to Hear,* taken from Revelation 2:7, "For him who has ears to hear, let him hear what the Spirit is saying to the churches."

Who has ears to hear what God is saying? Obviously it is supposed to be the church. But was it possible to have the right equipment and still be deaf to the voice of God? Keith wanted to sing to the people who were in tune with God—or be used as a tool to help unplug the ears of the ones who weren't. His dedication on the album jacket read:

This album was born through much prayer in the Holy Spirit and is totally committed to the glory of God and His Son, Jesus, who can give you ears to hear.
    Matthew 11:15
    —Keith

By the summer of 1977, Keith's debut album was in the bookstores. We had a big mailing party at our house to send out the albums to the six thousand people who had pre-ordered it at concerts during the past several months. Keith told everyone he'd send it to them hot off the press—and he did.

Rather than just throw away the names of six thousand people who seemed to be interested in receiving further encouragement and ministry, Keith said, "Let's just keep in touch with all these people and put together a little newsletter to encourage them in their walk with the Lord." And so the *Last Days Newsletter* was born.

Just before Keith's album was released, he started working with Steve Greisen, who was engaged to Nelly Ward of Second Chapter of Acts. Buck Herring and Steve wanted to help lesser-known artists with valid ministries get on the road. Steve would do the bookings, and they took on Keith. Buck wrote a letter of recommendation, which was a big help because Keith was only well-known on the West Coast. As usual, Keith had big ideas.

"I want to tour the whole country this summer!" Keith directed Steve. "Can you set it up?"

Steve set up a fifty-two-city tour, and off we went! We'd even retired the Blue Guppy and bought a thirty-two-foot Titan motor home that we dubbed the Ark. Now we had enough room to take several new Christians along with us. Keith's old Jewish friend, Jay Leon, had finally given his heart to the Lord and he, along with Podie, formed the core of our little road team. During our nine weeks on the road, we had plenty of time to counsel everyone and encourage them in the Lord. Of course they were a big help to us too.

What a tour! Keith's album had just been released so he was still unknown. He ended up singing to a lot of built-in audiences at coffee-houses, youth group meetings, and regular church services. Often Keith would joke about his hair, beard, and faded blue jeans to relax all the gray-haired saints who came not knowing what kind of music Keith was going to play.

"Somebody dragged his grandmother here tonight," he'd say, "and she's looking over at me saying, 'Do you bear witness to this?' I just wanna say that God works in mysterious ways, and I am one of his mysterious ways. I know you haven't seen this much hair up on the pulpit before, but God doesn't look on the outside to see what kind of a Christian you are. He looks on the inside.

"Now I don't wanna upset anybody who's used to listening to waltz and polka music a lot, because I do get into the piano. Aren't you glad I'm not playing electric guitar? This sound system scared me too when I walked in. I mean, I bet you expected gladiators to come out!"

By this time he'd usually put everyone at ease. But there were some very difficult aspects to this tour.

Some nights the promised housing didn't happen, and we had to rent our own rooms unexpectedly. Adequate sound systems and tuned pianos were usually rare commodities. Overall the audiences were sparse, and some nights we'd make little or nothing. One pastor who brought in Keith told Steve in advance, "He can come, but Chuck Girard is in town the same night and I know who I'd rather go see."

Our Titan motor home was living up to its name. Keith constantly needed to tighten screw after screw. Seems it was made to go somewhere once a year and sit for a few weeks vacation. We were giving it a pounding.

God was teaching us to be grateful in all things—the big and the small. There was one concert, however, that was a real eye-opener.

We were in the Deep South, a part of the country we'd never been to before. When we arrived at the church where Keith was going to minister, we lightheartedly commented that the inside looked like a giant wedding cake—tall, white pillars, pastel icing-colored walls, and lots of large artificial flowers. We soon realized there was something else about the church that was different from what we were used to. Something serious.

When we went out to eat with the young couple who'd brought us in, Keith spoke up. "Hey, was I missing something at my concert tonight, or were all the people at the church white?" Keith asked with an inquisitive but steady gaze.

The young guy said, "Yeah. All white. There's still a lot of prejudice in the South."

Keith and I were both stunned by this dose of reality. We knew prejudice still existed in some places, even in the "melting pot" of Southern California. But we'd never seen it so overtly displayed. It made us sick.

The young couple, leaders in the church, were really hoping God would change things, but they didn't have a solution or a lot of hope.

"It seems like it's been this way forever," the guy said. "Lots of people our parents' age still look down on black people—consider them servants, call them demeaning names behind their backs."

Keith interrupted. He was visibly agitated. "This is crazy," he said emphatically. "No, I take that back. It's evil. Especially in the kingdom of God. People who say they love Jesus are supposed to act like Jesus. Christians should know better!"

"You would think so," the young wife added with sadness. "But one of the unfunny jokes I heard growing up was that the reason God made some people black and some people white was so they would know what church to go to."

Keith was steaming by now. It wasn't the sponsors he was mad at, but the ignorance and the injustice. "I'm never ministering in a church like this again," he said. "And if I ever land in one by mistake and notice in the middle of my concert, they're going to hear about it on the spot!"

Returning home after being gone so long was a total reentry process, but it was great to be back. Keith reflected on the highlights of how Jesus had touched people during our tour to a concert crowd in Southern California.

"I just got back from the road," he told them. "I've heard people say, 'It's worth it when only one person comes forward to receive the Lord.' I say, 'Yeah, it is worth it.' There were some real humbling concerts, like twenty people. One person would come forward. I'd sit down at the end of the stage and I'd say, 'You're the whole reason why I came to this town.'

"And then there were other really beautiful times. I played at an army base in Fort Leonardwood, Missouri, for some 500 young recruits. They felt a little bit out of place. They didn't have any hair, and they were all about eighteen. It seemed under their breath they were saying, 'I want my mommy!' and they were freaking out about being in the army. The Lord got to them in that state, because 350 got up and received Jesus!"

We had learned at the Vineyard that every trial was an opportunity to grow. Through all the blessings, as well as the challenges, we certainly grew on that nine-week tour.

We were growing at home too. Now there were more than a dozen new Christians with us. So as money came in from Keith's concerts, studio sessions, and album sales it was poured back into helping the people who had come to live with us.

We'd moved Keith's piano into our bedroom and turned his music room into a dormitory. Counseling, helping, encouraging, witnessing—it pervaded every part of our life. The best part about it was how much fun it was—like an adventure every day! We often wondered what would happen next. If someone wanted to give his or her life to the Lord or serve God in a deeper way, we'd do whatever we needed to do to help make it happen. I knew I needed to stay as flexible as possible, since Keith was so naturally spontaneous.

One night after a concert a young guy wanted to give his life back to the Lord. Keith was frustrated because he didn't have enough time to finish counseling him, so he said, "Hey, we've got room in the motor home. Why don't you come hang with us on tour!" He came on the road with us for a few weeks and Keith constantly ministered to him. By the time he left to go home, he was on the right track.

Meanwhile, as every available sleeping space in the house slowly filled, Keith had a growing desire to move out into the country. We thought it would be wonderful to get the people who needed help out of the big city and into a place that would be peaceful and rest-ful—somewhere that wasn't filled with so many glaring, easy-access temptations. Besides, we didn't know how long our neighbors would put up with our endless streams of what, by their standards, probably looked like a group of aliens.

Keith and I both loved the Pacific Northwest, and we thought for sure we could find a farm or ranch for sale up there. Keith really wanted to live in the woods, and I wanted to live by the ocean. We always argued about it. I hoped we could find a little place nestled in the trees with an ocean view!

On our next concert tour to the Pacific Northwest late in the summer, we continued to spy out the land for possible places to move. One of our stops was in a little town called Sweet Home, Oregon. A family from the small church where Keith was playing opened their home to us. They lived on a beautiful farm. It was haying season, and they were out on their tractors wearing straw hats and bonnets, pray-ing it wouldn't rain between the time they cut the hay and got it baled. In spite of our hippie, whole-earth orientation we were really new to being in the country, so it was an incredible scene to behold. We felt like we were staying at the little house on the prairie!

The family loaned us their motorcycle and told us we could take it for a ride in the woods. There was only one problem—the roads weren't paved and we kept getting stuck in the mud. We also got lost, and the motorcycle kept dying on us. So there we were, lost out in the backwoods, with a dead, muddy bike.

Just when I started to think, *Oh, Keith, what have you gotten us into now?* a guy came wandering out of the woods. He was very thin, with shoulder-length blond hair. The only thing he was wearing was a leather headband and a very skimpy loincloth, but he was carrying a clipboard and a pencil. He was actually talking to the trees, obvi-ously high on something. His name was Rick. We talked with him for a few minutes and he told us he lived alone in a tepee in the woods. He also told us about a nearby river that Keith wanted to check out.

We pushed the dead motorcycle down a narrow trail. As soon as we got to the river, Keith wanted to go skinny-dipping.

I said, "No way, that guy might be around here somewhere."

Keith was convinced we'd left him far behind. "Come on, Mel, it'll be so much fun . . . just for a few minutes, please."

The next thing I knew we were splashing around in the chilly river having a water fight. Then I got totally paranoid and rushed for the rock where I'd left my clothes, insisting it was time to go get ready for that night's concert.

On the trail back, we started wondering if maybe God had plans for Rick. We regretted not talking about Jesus with him when we had the chance and prayed we'd run into him again. Sure enough, a few minutes later Rick was walking toward us. Right there in the middle of nowhere Keith and I told him all about the God who created the trees, sky, and animals Rick loved so much—the same God who wanted to create a new heart in Rick. By the time we had to leave, Rick was clearheaded enough to tell us how to find our way out! We invited him to the concert and prayed like crazy that he would come. He did! He'd even put on some jeans and a red flannel shirt. We were grateful for that! Still, he was one-of-a-kind in that country congregation. I prayed he wouldn't panic and leave before Keith shared about how to meet Jesus.

Rick did give his life to the Lord that night and—you guessed it—he came back to Southern California with us. The only place for him to sleep, however, was in our garage because our house was packed full of women—with the exception of a young neighbor boy who was only twelve. We'd led his mom to the Lord, and she felt her son was having some demonic problems, so she asked if he could live with us temporarily. Perhaps we could help him. The only place for him was in a sleeping bag on the floor of our bedroom.

So now we had something like fourteen people living with us in our little three-bedroom, one-bathroom house! You couldn't go anywhere without literally running into someone. With everyone trying to figure out how to get closer to God, it seemed we were constantly counseling someone.

Outside the house, we still kept meeting people who needed a place to stay so they could escape a bad situation and get grounded in their new faith in Jesus. Only there wasn't any place left in our home. Not only did Keith no longer have a private place to write music, he could barely get a turn in the bathroom with all the women! What could we do? Our answer was unexpected.

When Dawn had come to live with us a few years earlier, we had needed some type of legal authority to enroll her in school. Karen approved of us becoming Dawn's foster parents, but the State of California needed to approve us as well. We didn't accept the regular foster parent money the state provided, which meant they wouldn't visit us as much. But we still had to pass a housing inspection because government standards required a certain amount of "airspace" in Dawn's bedroom. We had passed everything with flying colors back then.

Now it was time for another visit from Dawn's social worker, and knowing our crowded living conditions would make her eyes bug out, we were in quite a dilemma. There was no way we were going to lose Dawn, but we couldn't put everyone else out on the streets either.

"What are we going to do?" I asked Keith when we had a rare moment alone to talk. "We need more space. That's all there is to it."

"I've got an idea," Keith said, his face brightening. "Let's rent another house."

"It might work," I replied thoughtfully, "but wait a minute. We've been here almost three years, and I've never even seen a house for rent in this neighborhood. Everybody owns their own home."

Keith's brow was furrowed in thought. "There are those apartments about a mile away," Keith said. "But they'll never rent one to a bunch of wild-looking single hippies. Hey, I've got an idea. Why don't we rent one for us?"

"You mean move out of our own house?"

"Yeah, they'll for sure rent one of those places to a nice couple with a teenage daughter!"

We did have some extra money because of Keith's new album. Later that day, we drove over and looked at a two-bedroom apartment. It wasn't far away so we'd still be close to people back at the house, and Dawn could have her own room, which would make the State of California happy. We put a deposit on the apartment and went home.

The whole thing seemed kind of crazy, but it was also really exciting. We were scheduled to move in a few weeks and my mind was getting into gear for packing.

Then, driving though our neighborhood one day, Keith suddenly said, "Mel, look! A 'For Rent' sign!"

Sure enough. It was right in front of a nice-looking house with a big tree in the front yard. Unbelievable.

We rented it immediately. It was a pleasant three-bedroom place with a den. We moved all the singles over there and cleared out a bedroom for Dawn in our house. Dawn's social worker came and went—and so, by the end of 1977, we had become a two-house family.

We needed a name for the new house so that when we talked about it we'd be able to separate it from our house on Dolorosa Street. The new house was on Sale Street so we just called it the Sale House.

In no time, it seemed, we had filled up both houses again.

These were powerful times and innocent times. We just did what was in our hearts to do, and we were always on the run, unaware of how our lives were about to change one more time.

Keith closed the year by playing at the Daisy again, but this night in particular was strangely different. It was a New Year's celebration, and I was sipping some kind of fruit juice, watching Keith minister. He was only about twelve feet away so I could see him clearly. By now I'd watched Keith play hundreds of times, but this night burned into my memory.

The spotlight was bright white, flooding Keith's face with light. His eyes were aching as he sang, overflowing with unspoken feelings as he poured out his very soul. But as he sang, he was not looking at the audience. He was looking up into the light, as if looking directly at God. He seemed transfixed in time . . . like there was something holy or significant about the moment. His eyes were the bluest of blue, sparkling, yet crying out. His skin like milk. He looked like a little boy. His eyes were haunting as he looked up into the light. I had the strangest sensation watching him.

When the thought first came I shook it away. But it came back. I sat and watched and was captured by the moment. I thought, *Keith Green—you're not long for this earth. . . .*

Immediately I wondered where that thought came from. It was crazy to even think such a thing.

I didn't know what Keith was thinking or hearing from the Lord in those moments. I never asked him—and I didn't tell him what I had thought, either. But it would not be the last time I had feelings like that about him.

10

"ASLEEP IN THE LIGHT"

Keith was right about his album *For Him Who Has Ears to Hear.* Very quickly, it moved up the chart of bestselling Christian records to become the biggest debut album in the history of Christian recording—with more than three hundred thousand copies distributed!

The net effect was that by the end of 1977, requests for concert bookings started flooding in from all across the country. It was incredibly exciting. In the space of a few short months, Keith rocketed from being an unknown to becoming one of the most popular and sought-after singers on the Christian scene.

But very little of the flap about his popularity reached Keith at all—not in his heart anyway. He disliked being referred to as a "recording artist" since that term seemed to imply that he was some kind of celebrity. First and foremost, Keith considered himself to be a minister of the gospel—one that used his music as a tool to get his message across.

Keith would often say, "If someone writes a great story, people praise the author, not the pen. People don't say, 'Oh what an incredible pen . . . where can I get a pen like this so I can write great stories?' Well, I am just a pen in the hands of the Lord. He is the author. All praise should go to him."

I could tell Keith was starting to get caught up with inner questions that, for him, held more importance than his popularity rating.

"Mel," he said to me one morning as I packed his clothes for another concert tour, "I feel like the Lord is calling me to make an even deeper commitment to him. I don't want to get caught up in everything that's happening to us and become some kind of star in the church. I can already feel the pull to go out there on stage and manipulate the crowd by saying things I know will move people emotionally. I don't want to get soulish."

Keith quickly found a way to respond when people tried to put him on a pedestal. He'd just say, "Jesus is the only star!" He said it so much someone made him a T-shirt with those words boldly lettered across the front—and Keith wore it often.

Rather than let the attention go to his head, Keith was challenged to go deeper with the Lord. He felt he needed to count the cost in a greater way if he was really going to be a true follower of Jesus. In particular he was beginning to struggle with the thought that something might happen to me. There had been this rumor kicking around about a devastating earthquake that was going to hit Southern California soon. It was supposed to destroy Los Angeles. Whether or not there really was going to be an earthquake, Keith considered what he would do if something happened to me.

While Keith was on the road alone for a few days, he wrote a prayer to the Lord:

January 22, 1978

I only pray you let me keep my wife Melody for I need her love and help, although your grace is sufficient unto me. Please spare her to stay with me, I will give you far more love than I give her, and all my love for her is for you, Jesus. Take anything, but leave my Melody. Please God, but I am willing to suffer all loss if it is your precious will. I am yours.

Bye bye Lord—your baby.

Keith returned home thoughtful. He wondered if a tragedy might cause him to lose his faith. If he wasn't willing to lay even the deepest loves of his life before God, what did that say about the roots of his faith?

When Keith told me what was bothering him, he said firmly, "I've decided that whatever it takes to get deeper with the Lord I'm going to do—even if it means praying and saying, 'Lord, Melody's really yours.'"

Keith's wrestling with giving everything to the Lord had another dimension to it, too, because we'd just had some great news. I was pregnant! Shortly before I'd had an early miscarriage, but this time it looked like there were none of the distress signs I'd had with my first pregnancy. We were really thrilled! Now all we had to do was wait out the nine months.

Those nine months weren't spent passively, however. We were on the road, running through airports to catch planes and staying up half the night to counsel our ever-growing community in Woodland Hills. We were never at a loss for things to do—and never alone. I wasn't alone in my pregnancy either. We had two other pregnant women with us at about the same stage! One was married and her husband was helping us with the community. The other mother-in-waiting was Dinah. After a difficult childhood, she married and divorced at a young age. She'd recently given her heart to the Lord and was planning to be the best single mother on the planet.

We had a lot of people living with us who were badly in need of help, so it was a relief to have some stable people joining us too, people who needed a place to stay while learning how to make a full commitment to the Lord. Kathleen Griffin was one of those. Her thick blonde hair, laced with fresh flowers, and California-girl complexion made her one of the prettiest, too. More than that, Kathleen represented the kind of Christian commitment we wanted to encourage others to make since she was one of the most caring people we knew.

After you become a Christian, what do you do about it? Do you keep the blessing to yourself? Or like Kathleen, do you pour yourself out for others? These questions came more and more into discussion for us.

There was already talk about a second album, and Keith believed it was supposed to be more than a nice collection of upbeat, inspiring songs. A stray comment he made one day made me think about these issues of living the Christian life that we were confronting every day.

While talking about how necessary it was to pray, Keith offhandedly said, "Our whole life should be a prayer!"

The words rang in my ears. I kept hearing the phrase over and over in my mind, "Our whole life should be a prayer!"

Later, alone in our room, I sat down at the piano and just started playing. A melody and some words came to me, flowing together with unusual ease. I played the few simple chords and started to sing what Keith had said, only now it was in the form of a prayer.

Make my life a prayer to you.
I wanna do what you want me to . . .

I reached for a pencil and pad of paper to start jotting down the lyrics as fast as I could. Then I started playing the piano again. There were a few false starts, but basically the whole song flowed out in about twenty minutes.

When it was finished, I was overjoyed. I'd never before experienced the Lord's help and creativity in my writing quite like this. I almost felt like I had just taken dictation. "Make My Life a Prayer to You" seemed to be born of the Spirit in a special way.

Keith loved the song and started singing it in concert right away. Then it really came alive because it was, of course, Keith's prayer too.

The night Steve and Nelly—now Mr. and Mrs. Greisen—came to a concert, Nelly was so moved by the song, she asked me if she could sing it on the next Second Chapter of Acts album. What an encouragement! I couldn't help but remember my days of tears and wadded-up lyrics in the trash.

Through the months of April, May, and June 1978—while *Ears to Hear* was number one on the charts—we were in and out of the studio recording Keith's second album. The only problem was he still didn't have an album title that felt right. Sparrow was eager to release the album, and we needed a concept so the artists could get busy with a cover. Nothing was clicking. One day Keith was looking through all the song lyrics for what seemed to be the tenth time. He suddenly glanced at me with excitement.

"Hey, Mel, what about these words in your song?" He quoted:

Make my life a prayer to you.
I wanna do what you want me to.
No empty words
And no white lies,
No token prayers,
No compromise . . .

"No token prayers, no compromise," he repeated. "Let's just call the album *No Compromise!*"

It seemed to capture the heart of what Keith wanted to say—how important it is that believers quit compromising with the world and start living radically committed lives.

Even the artwork was going to reflect the *No Compromise* theme. One lone man would be standing up in the midst of a crowd that was bowing in worship to an earthly king. A guard was angrily pointing out the man standing alone with a look that said, "You've had it!" The picture reminded us of Daniel in Babylon.

Keith wanted to shake believers awake from the comfortable slumber we'd seen. Most of us weren't faced with anything as obvious as the choice between bowing to a false god or being killed. But we are continually tempted to bow to other false gods—to go with the crowd, be ashamed of our convictions, stay silent instead of speaking out for what is right. So we compromise. We harbor secret sins. We bow to invisible idols of fear, pride, lust, greed—and just wanting to be accepted by others. Just as Keith was facing the need to clean these things out of his own life, he wanted to challenge other Christians to do the same.

Keith was so convinced of the urgency of this message that, just like the first album, people were rallied to intercede. Keith asked everyone at his concerts and those reading our newsletter to cover the recording in prayer for God's anointing and power. The most strategic of all praying happened within our little community. In the houses people signed up to pray in shifts during each recording session. Then at each session, day or night—sometimes all night—there were community people right in the studio with us. They engaged in quiet but constant on-the-spot intercession.

If the recording engineer was having trouble getting the right sounds, everyone prayed. If Keith was trying to hit some difficult notes, they prayed. If we were working on guitar parts or background parts, they prayed. There was constant prayer—asking for God's help, anointing, and grace. We sensed this was a special project that would convey a difficult message. The soothing oil of the Holy Spirit was needed if the message was going to touch hearts.

As always, I was right at Keith's side. Even with his immense talent, somehow Keith trusted my judgment. He'd often ask, "Mel, how was that?" Or my favorite, "Do you have any ideas for background vocals?" And Bill Maxwell was so pitch-sensitive he could always tell if any notes were even slightly off-key. Bill seemed to know how to bring the best out of Keith. And our Jewish friend Peter Granet—the one we'd dropped our gospel bombs on in Sequoia a few years ago—even came to lend his support as Keith's recording engineer. It was one big happy family!

Speaking of family, I was very pregnant by this time. Whenever Bill played the drums, my baby kicked me without mercy—often right in time with the music!

But there were a few points on which Keith and I were not side-by-side. One of Keith's new songs was called "To Obey Is Better Than Sacrifice." Actually, I loved the song, but one line really bothered me. It was sung from God's perspective, as if it were the Lord speaking.

To obey is better than sacrifice
I don't need your money I want your life

And I hear you say that I'm coming back soon
But you act like I'll never return
Well you speak of grace and my love so sweet,
How you thrive on milk but reject my meat
And I can't help weeping at how it will be
If you keep on ignoring my Word

Then, at the end of the third verse, there was that line that especially troubled me:

To obey is better than sacrifice—
I want more than Sundays and Wednesday nights.
'Cause if you can't come to me every day,
Then don't bother coming at all.

Don't bother coming at all? I wondered. In the studio, Keith and Bill had a long discussion about it before the final vocal was laid down.

"Keith, I really feel like that statement is going to make people feel condemned," he objected, "especially people who might not know the Lord."

"It's mainly for Christians who should know better," Keith replied. "I really believe I need to say it that strongly to make the point."

"But it's a hard line to draw," Bill came back, shaking his head.

"Well, it's the line I'm walking," Keith replied.

I had already voiced my concerns about it to Keith by this time. I knew he wanted to make a strong statement, but I wondered if there was another way he could do it. Some people were going to be offended, but even that wasn't my main concern. The bottom line for me was whether the statement really represented God's heart toward us. Of course he wants us to come to him every day. But even when we blow it, I couldn't imagine God saying, "Don't bother coming at all!" I felt really torn. I knew Keith was trying to shake people spiritually like he would if they were sleeping through a fire that would destroy them if they didn't wake up. He felt such a strong sense of urgency.

He'd told me, "If you saw a child about to get hit by a truck and the best you could do was kick him out of the way just before impact, you'd do it. He might end up with a few broken ribs, but at least he'd be alive. Any parent would thank you for saving his life—they wouldn't be angry about the broken ribs! You did the most loving thing you could do."

In the end, Keith made the decision to record the song as it stood. Even though the lyric never really sat right with me, I also wanted to see religious apathy shaken at its core—even in my own life. So I totally supported Keith's heart in the message he wanted to convey.

Another song with a strong message for believers was called "Asleep in the Light." We had no trouble with the lyrics in this one.

Keith got the idea from a phrase in the book *Why Revival Tarries* written by Leonard Ravenhill, who had come to America in 1950 after being involved in many revivals in Great Britain. Keith just happened to find the book on someone's coffee table during a time when he was asking God to help him be less intense. After finishing it he said, "What is God doing? Letting me read this book was like pouring gasoline on a fire!" So stirred by the book's concepts, Keith hoped it's message put into a song would spread like fire.

Do you see, do you see,
All the people sinking down?
Don't you care, don't you care,
Are you gonna let them drown?
How can you be so numb,
Not to care if they come?
You close your eyes
And pretend the job's done. . . .

Open up, open up, and give yourself away
You see the need, you hear the cries,
So how can you delay?
God's calling and you're the one.

But like Jonah you run.
He's told you to speak
But you keep holding it in.
Oh, can't you see it's such sin.

The world is sleeping in the dark
That the church just can't fight
'Cause it's asleep in the light.
How can you be so dead
When you've been so well fed?
Jesus rose from the grave
And you—you can't even get out of bed.

It was true that Bill and I, and many others we knew, were behind the warning Keith was trying to sound. But what about the Christian public? What would they think about this message that was growing stronger in Keith's heart every day?

That July, while the album was being pressed, Keith had been invited to sing at a major Jesus festival. The organizers wanted Keith to be the closing person, on the last night—which was quite an honor.

The festival was called "Jesus Northwest," near Salem, Oregon. It normally drew about twenty thousand people, but this year an estimated thirty-five thousand people were there! As we were driven in, it was exciting to know so many people wanted to get closer to God. And we loved hearing that a traffic jam had clogged the roads for two or three miles, which had the police frantic! Once inside the festival area, we saw the campsites overflowing with thousands of tents jammed up side-by-side. It was all one big, glorious mess of confusion and excitement. Because the festival continued for several days in open fields under a blazing sun, many had stripped down to the bare minimum to beat the heat. Keith and I thought it looked like a mini-Woodstock hippy gathering.

It was great that so many people were there enjoying the Lord and enjoying each other, but as we began to feel more of the vibe, something seemed amiss to us. It was a huge success, and the promoters were blown away. But the real question was what the outcome would be from an eternal perspective. Would everyone go home thinking, *Wow, that was a lot of fun!* Or was there something God wanted to say to everyone?

Inside the hospitality trailer, the man who put the festival together expressed his concern to Keith: "We have a success in numbers, but I'm not sure what's happening in the Spirit."

On the last evening of the event, several of us gathered in the little trailer to pray before Keith's turn to go on stage and close the evening. Our friend Winkie Pratney, who lived in East Texas, was there with his wife, Fae, and son, Billy. Winkie had been one of the main speakers and had stayed on to be a support to Keith. By now Keith and Winkie had developed such a close friendship that Winkie was like an older brother and mentor to Keith.

In fact, Winkie, a night-owl himself, was probably the only person who would have put up with Keith's late-night phone calls—sometimes at one or two in the morning—just to say, "Hi, what are you doing?" A New Zealander, Winkie had a quick, brilliant wit and keen mind. His dark eyes flashed brightly when he laughed, and he laughed often. But beneath the humor was a drive to see men, women, and young people not only commit themselves to Jesus, but also to follow after him hard. For years he'd written books and articles and traveled around the world speaking and teaching as a true ambassador for the Lord.

But just now both Winkie and Keith were troubled—not about what had happened at the festival, but what had not happened. We'd all heard that the emphasis of the festival had been on music—lots of it and loud. There were some speakers, too, but hardly anyone had given a challenge for change or commitment. The place was packed, but some were saying there had been no real move of God, that it was just one big party. Keith and Winkie felt strongly that if nothing happened it was a waste of a festival.

There was a piano in the trailer, and Keith crawled under it to get alone with God and pray. He'd be closing out the festival in just a few minutes. From where I was praying I could hear Keith softly crying.

There was a tentative knock at the trailer door. Someone summoned Winkie outside to see a young blonde girl who had asked to speak with him. She had tears in her eyes. Winkie recognized her from the Youth With A Mission booth there at the festival. She was timid, but at the same time had a gentle boldness as she spoke.

"Excuse me, but I've felt a little grieved during this festival because it doesn't seem like God has been given a chance to speak what's on his heart. There's been no breakthrough. We've had counseling tents and prayer meetings, but nobody from the stage has said anything about getting right with God." She looked shyly at Winkie and pressed a folded piece of paper into his hand, saying, "I don't know if you can give this to any of the leaders, but I was praying and, well, I really felt like God gave me this Scripture."

While Winkie was outside, I looked over at Keith. I could hear loud weeping and choking sobs coming out from under the piano. In between the sobbing, Keith prayed out loud, "O God, what do you want me to say? What do you want me to do?"

When Winkie walked back inside the trailer, he was reading from a small piece of paper in his hand.

At the same moment, Keith's head popped out from under the piano and he said, "Winkie, isn't there a Scripture somewhere about festivals?"

Winkie looked up from the paper in shock. "Yes," he said. "I just happen to have one. A young girl just gave it to me."

When Keith read the slip of paper, his mouth dropped open. A few minutes later, he carried it on stage with him.

When Keith walked into the spotlight, the crowd burst into a prolonged roar of applause, whistles, and cheers. Keith sat at the piano and adjusted the microphone, waiting for things to settle down a bit. Then he turned to the crowd and, still wiping a few tears away, started talking.

"Have you ever felt the Lord was sad? Most people think, 'No, no, the Lord's always happy.' Well, tonight I was praying and I kind of felt the Lord inside me, weeping. So I started to cry.

"I got to thinking about all the people that give God one day a week. How would you like it if your wife gave you one day a week? 'Well, dear, I'm here for the weekly visit.' People like to visit God from ten to eleven on Sunday mornings. Like visiting time at the local jail. 'Lord, how ya doing in there? Are they treating you all right? Is the food okay? We're working on getting you out. Well, I'll see you next week!'"

I'd gone over to the side of the crowd to watch Keith on stage. As with any outdoor event, the crowd was a little restless and distracted. And tonight it didn't help matters that an afternoon thunderstorm left two inches of squishy mud on the ground. I could tell people were waiting for Keith to start singing, and eventually he did. But the song he chose to open with was anything but lighthearted, the newly recorded "To Obey Is Better Than Sacrifice." Ending with those last two lines: "Cause if you can't come to me every day, then don't bother coming at all." As soon as he hit that last lingering chord, he started talking again . . .

In the Old Testament it says, "These people draw near with their words and honor me with their lips, but they remove their hearts far from me." I was listening to everybody singing worship songs before, and nobody deserves praise and worship but Jesus. It's a beautiful thing.

But what if your wife said "I love you" but you knew she didn't honor you and love you in her heart. That you weren't the most important person on earth to her, and in fact, she had a couple of other men she liked to look at and think about more than you? How sick would it be for you to hear, "Oh, darling, I love you!" What do the words "I love you" mean? If you praise and worship Jesus with your mouth, and your life does not praise and worship him, there's something wrong.

I want you to go away from here broken and blessed in that

order. I don't want you to go away from here under condemnation. But I want you to get broken before God because unless you're a broken vessel, he can't put you back together the way he wants you.

The crowd was totally quiet now. I noticed one young guy toward the front wearing cut-offs and a "Jesus Is Lord" T-shirt. He leaned forward with a serious look on his face. It was then that Keith reached into his pocket and pulled out the slip of paper Winkie had given him. I suspected things were going to get even more serious as he started to read.

This Scripture is out of Amos. "Thus saith the Lord, I hate, I reject your festivals, nor do I delight in your solemn assemblies, even though you offer up to me burnt offerings. . . . I will not accept them. . . . Take away from me the noise of your songs, I will not even listen to the sound of your harps. But let justice roll down like waters, and righteousness like an ever-flowing stream."

Does anybody understand what that means? Some of you do. Among thirty-five thousand so-called Christians there's always a remnant of real ones peppered in. My job as a minister is to make sure that every person here leaves a real one. But I can't do it. I'm nothing but dust.

Keith looked to the sky and said, "I depend on you, Lord Jesus . . ." His words had the effect of a shotgun blast. The crowd sat in stunned silence—the first silence I'd heard all night. I glanced quickly at the guy in the Jesus T-shirt again. He was just sitting there with his mouth open. I wondered what he was thinking as Keith continued:

How many of us care about the people living next door to us? How many of your neighbors have never seen anything more than a little fish on your car? They think you work at the fish market. If you get really bold, you put the Greek letters in there—in case you run into a Greek truck driver! What's going on?

As for me, I repent of ever having made a record or ever having sung a song unless it's provoked people to follow Jesus, to lay down their whole lives before him, to give him everything. It doesn't cost you much to follow Jesus—just everything!

Keith talked about reaching the world—not just being responsible for what we see but for what we know. He really hit hard when he compared the average Christian to a three-hundred-pound baby growing overweight on the teachings of Jesus but never exercising his faith.

"The best exercise I know is hitting the streets for Christ—door to door, ghettos, prisons, old age homes, orphanages, high schools, colleges—why don't you do it? You say, ' 'Cause I don't feel led.' You feel lead all right, it's just a different kind of led."

Keith had been preaching for more than thirty minutes, and he knew people were wondering if he was going to sing any more songs.

"Hey look," he said, "I've heard all my songs and God's heard all my songs too. I don't think he's that interested. Don't worry, I'm gonna sing again, but it's the least important part of what I've got to do tonight."

He did sing a few more songs—"The Sheep and the Goats" from Matthew 25, and "Asleep in the Light"—but they only served to underscore his hard-hitting message. Then he prayed:

> Lord Jesus, I repent for our sin of not caring about all the lost souls, for not caring about all the hungry people. Lord Jesus, I repent for all of us . . . for playing church and not being Christians, for being part of religion but not being your children who are broken before your throne, and put together in your Spirit.

When Keith sang "My Eyes Are Dry" and taught it to everyone, he started to weep, his voice cracking with emotion.

My eyes are dry, my faith is old,
My heart is hard, my prayers are cold.

And I know how I ought to be—
Alive to you and dead to me.
Oh, what can be done with an old heart like mine?
Soften it up with oil and wine!
The oil is you, your Spirit of love,
Please wash me anew in the wine of your blood. . . .

Then with tears streaming down his face, Keith prayed again, "Lord, we're sorry! Lord, we're sorry for having such deceitful hearts and such weak flesh. For being children of our own desires instead of being children of your desires—children of religion rather than children of truth. Lord Jesus, please save us from ourselves and from institutions . . . Lord, corner our flesh—crucify our flesh, kill our own desires."

He turned back to the crowd.

> Do you know that the rich young ruler would be accepted in any church today? But Jesus wouldn't accept him. Why? Because he had an idol in his life.
>
> Do you know who the Christian idols are? I happen to be one of them. So are Andrae Crouch, Evie, and B. J. Thomas. You can even idolize your pastors. They don't want to be idolized. They never asked for it. Remember that applause you gave me when I walked out? I didn't hear you applaud the Lord like that anytime today . . . We're more excited about a Second Chapter of Acts concert than we are about the Second Coming! *Sin!*

This was tough stuff. I wondered what everyone was thinking about Keith's message. How did a bunch of people who thought they were Christians feel about having their salvation challenged? It seemed to me it needed a good challenge. And if the young fellow I'd been watching was any indication, the Lord was doing good things. He had his arms wrapped around his legs, his head bowed on his knees. . . .

Keith continued,

The rich young ruler came to Jesus, and Jesus said, "You still lack something. Go away. I can't take you right now." Who today would say, "I'm sorry, brother, I can't lead you in the sinner's prayer. You've gotta give up your dope, your selfishness, your love of possessions, your clinginess to family and friends—and your life"? Aren't you a little disappointed at how Jesus handled such a sinner? Didn't the Lord know how to lead a soul to himself?

The requirement for salvation is not just a prayer. The requirement is an open, totally empty heart that's ready to be full of Jesus Christ. After saying the sinner's prayer, if in a few months your friends can't tell that you're born again, if your relatives can't see a change in you, if your teacher can't see that you're a Christian, you're probably not!

Because let me tell you something, when someone's born again they get excited! It changes the way they live, what they do, how they speak, how they act, what they do with their money, their cars, their girlfriends—it's all different! Then how come it looks the same? How come Christians are trying to ride the line?

I challenge anybody who calls himself a Christian, which means "little Christ," to live as Jesus did. Or else sometime Somebody might say, "I never knew you." I'm gonna get on my knees every day and say, "God, search my heart and see if there be any wicked way in me. I don't want to go astray. I want to be with you."

You can't get to heaven by being a nice guy. You might end up to be the nicest guy in hell!

Finally, Keith gave a challenge to everyone in the audience—first to people who had never given their lives to Christ, and then to people who considered themselves Christians but had never given Jesus every hope, dream, possession, every friend and loved one.

If you're here tonight and you don't know Jesus it's because of two things. One, because of your sin. Two, because of the hypocrisy in the people around you, including me. If you don't know Jesus, you've got two choices—and I'm not gonna say "heaven or hell." I'm gonna say you can follow Jesus or you can hate him. You can't sit on the fence. Those who are not with him are against him.

Then Keith asked people to bow their heads and he prayed, "Lord, we ask you for a miracle. There are no words I can say, no song I can sing, to convict the sinner. Only your wonderful Holy Spirit can do anything. Send your Spirit . . . touching hearts to repent."
Keith turned to the crowd.

If you want Jesus Christ to completely take over your life, you're willing to die for him, give him every possession, every friend, every loved one, every plan, every hope, every dream. You're willing to give it all up if necessary. I'm not saying that's what he wants you to do, but you are willing. If you're willing to come before his throne empty-handed, raise your hand. If you can't look him in the eye and know you've been living a pleasing life before him, get your hand up and make it right. Jesus Christ is not your Savior unless he's the Lord of your life, and Lord means he owns and controls—lock, stock, and barrel—your destiny, your future, and your present. And he throws away your past as far as the east is from the west.

I looked at the young guy I'd been watching to see if his hand was up. Instead he was flat on his face right in the mud along with many others! Other hands were up everywhere. Thousands of them. Not only that, weeping and loud crying broke out all across the open, grassy field. It was awesome. I could hear people sobbing and choking out prayers to God.

Then Keith asked everyone who was making Jesus Lord of their life for the first time to stand. To my shock, almost everyone in the crowd stood. Keith was so surprised he thought they must not have understood him. So he clarified it.

"This is not a rededication. This is the first time, the first time you've ever understood what making Jesus Lord really meant. Do you really mean it? Wow! How many people here realize that when they get home they have a lot of things to get rid of and a lot of things to change in their lives? A brother down front here says he has to remodel his whole bedroom. You've gotta remodel your whole heart, then the outside's gonna change!"

Then Keith called Winkie, Fae, and me up on the stage, and we all led worship with Keith for about half an hour. That's the way the festival ended. Keith slipped quietly down from the stage, raw and totally exhausted. He had delivered his soul.

I was the first one to encourage him about how powerfully the Lord used him, but there were many others waiting to tell him the same thing. For Keith it was totally overwhelming.

As we drove across the festival grounds on our way back to our motel, we saw lots of people lying before God out in the fields or on their knees—praying. It felt like a holy hush had descended and was still lingering . . . gripping every hungry heart.

Even with awesome results, Keith came away from the festival quite disturbed. What was the purpose of a festival anyway? Was it just a place for Christians to get together and have a party? Or maybe it was just another way to market the gospel. The promoters did seem to have good hearts, but were the people who came receiving it in the right way? Or did the responsibility of the spiritual tone of the event rest with each invited minister?

Personally, Keith's night of ministry left him with many questions. It took raw obedience to tell thirty-five thousand people, who were all having a good time, that God hated their festival. The pressure to please a crowd that large is overwhelming—to be popular, loved, and invited back, even to sell a lot of records or make a good name for yourself. In obeying God, Keith figured his hard message would turn people off. That would have been easier for him to live with. But to become like a celebrity in spite of his strong words, or to be seen by some as a hero because of them was, in some ways, frightening.

"Mel, I left all that stuff behind three years ago when I became a

Christian. The groupies, the fans, the praise of men—I don't want to get sucked back into that again."

Keith's quick rise to popularity had been unsettling enough. He was worried about getting entrenched in a system that might eventually cause him to forget about God—or cause others to focus on him instead of the Lord. Keith was also worried about the power of his own natural charisma. He knew it was a gift from God, but what if he was unknowingly making things happen in his own strength even though he didn't want to? How did he know if people at any given concert were responding to a move of the Lord or if they were just responding to the performance skills he'd acquired over a lifetime of training?

For Keith, these were more than passing questions. They were deep concerns. He had major questions about the Christian music industry, but even more troubling were the questions he had about himself. Keith really felt he needed to take some time off to sort through everything. We'd been on a nonstop schedule of traveling and recording for months. Besides, Keith figured it would be a great time to do some studying.

Winkie Pratney had recently bought Keith a whole library because of his hunger for the Lord and confusion over the intensity of his feelings. Winkie felt that Keith needed to study church history. Winkie told him, "Lots of Christians have felt like you do. They've written some really great stuff. You need to read what they had to say." Then he took us to a bookstore and bought Keith a whole shopping cart full of books.

So, shortly after we returned home from Jesus Northwest, Keith announced, "I'm taking a sabbatical—starting right now!"

"For how long?" I asked.

"I don't know. Maybe a year. I might do a few concerts but no major touring. I need some time. I want to get into the Word of God more—and all those books Winkie gave me. I just need to figure some things out."

It was nice to have Keith at home more as my September due date approached. We were so excited about this baby. We'd already read several books, along with flipping through the Bible, to help us find names we liked. We were taking natural childbirth classes to learn how to survive the unknowns of my first labor. Keith's mom even gave us Keith's original baby dresser! He'd painted it with a bunch of hippie stuff several years ago, so I spent a few days stripping off the paint, oiling it, and putting on a smooth satin varnish. Things were coming together!

Preparing to be parents brought us to a whole new level of counting the cost of living the type of life that we had chosen. We both were excited about raising our child in a busy ministry. It seemed that the best way for a child to have an understanding of how to serve God would be to grow up doing it.

Up to this point, we both thought producing an album was a much harder task than producing a baby. But that idea, at least from my point of view, was about to change drastically.

My labor pains hit on a Sunday, two weeks early, in the middle of a hot fudge sundae at Solley's Deli. My discomfort was only eclipsed by Keith's excitement. He told the waitress, "My wife is in labor!" Within a few hours, he drove me to our doctor's house. We'd become good friends with Dr. Paul Reisser and his wife, Terri, who taught our childbirth classes, and Keith could not wait for him to check me. I was in labor for sure, but only the earliest stage, so Paul and Terri invited us to sleep over that night. Keith groggily coached me through each contraction.

By morning, against my protests, he called for reinforcements, and about twenty people from our community came over to pray. They also brought a bunch of gifts since my early labor preempted their planned baby shower. Between contractions I unwrapped gifts, but it sure was hard to smile!

That night Keith wanted everyone to camp out with us at Paul and Terri's house, and it started to feel like a three-ring circus. As I walked from room to room all night to speed up my labor, I passed little clusters of people praying. All the while I kept hoping my nightie was as opaque as everyone said it was. In the morning, I finally went to the hospital. Keith was by my side watching the contractions on the monitor—telling me to breathe and relax. I was beginning to wonder if this baby was ever going to be born. I was totally exhausted, but Keith kept encouraging me.

"Pretty soon we're gonna have a baby to hold!"

"Really?" I was beginning to have my doubts.

"Hang in there, honey. We'll have our baby in no time. Just think! Our baby!"

After a full forty-nine hours of labor, I made it through the final few pushes and heard Paul say, "It's a boy!"

He had lots of curly hair, and Keith kept exclaiming, "Wow, a boy! Honey, a little boy! Oh, thank you, Jesus! Thank you!"

Keith and newborn Josiah, 1978

Doctor Paul wrapped our little blond-haired baby boy in a blanket. I was in awe as I inspected his little fingers and toes and looked into his blue eyes. As soon as he could, Keith gently lifted our son out of my arms and almost danced around the delivery room, posing for pictures and grinning from ear to ear. Then Keith and I just stared at each other. How did God do this miracle?

We named our son—our son!—Josiah David, after two great kings. Josiah was the child-king, and the Bible said he always did what was right in the eyes of the Lord, never turning to the right or to the left. David was known as a man after God's own heart. Josiah David looked a lot like Keith, who looked a lot like his dad. Keith was thrilled about that because of his deep love for his father. The feeling of being wheeled out of the hospital with my baby in my arms and getting to keep such a precious gift was one of overwhelming joy.

Meanwhile, our other family was growing too. By now we had become an official nonprofit ministry, and naming our ministry was nearly as difficult as naming our son. We settled on Last Days Ministries because it reflected the urgency we felt about the times we were living in. As we compared current news events to Bible prophecy, it sure seemed as if things were lining up. But even if they weren't, every person on earth would face their last day sooner or later and we hoped when they did, they would know Jesus. We wanted Last Days Ministries to help at least some of those people meet the Lord. About this time people with the same desires began to come and help us build the ministry.

The day Wayne Dillard drove up was a big event. He was the only one who'd ever shown up driving a new car! He'd written us from South Carolina after being deeply moved at one of Keith's concerts, saying, "My friends call me 'Mr. Fix-It' and I'm willing to do anything you need." We told him to come right away!

And Jerry Bryant, who had a radio program called *Jesus Solid Rock* in Illinois, came with his young son, Andy, after sponsoring one of Keith's concerts in Carbondale. Not everyone came from such a great distance. Carol Hoehn was also from our area, along with Francine Weisberg, and Pam Wible.

Our friend Dinah had had her baby—beautiful dark-haired Elizabeth—and she was helping me learn some basic new-parent skills. Keith and I had also taken in a teenage girl who had a background of physical abuse and who needed parenting. She shared a room with Dawn.

Michelle kept coming around too. She dropped in one unseasonably hot night. Keith was determined to hold her attention as long as he could so we could tell her more about Jesus. We'd just installed a small fireplace so Keith set the air-conditioner on freezing and built a fire for Mich. This little mood-setting event worked. We watched the flames with her until dawn, talking about the dark and light side of spiritual truth—and about who killed Jesus.

Keith said, "You're either walking with God in the light or walking with Satan in the dark—whether you realize it or not. There's no in between."

"Satan isn't real," Michelle said. "The idea of Satan is just a 'Christian thing.'"

Keith opened his Bible and said, "Not true. Satan is a 'Jewish thing.' In the first two chapters of the book of Job, Jehovah God and Satan are having conversations."

"Well, the only 'Jewish thing' I've ever heard from Christians is that we killed Jesus. I mean, Hitler's photo hung in every Catholic school in Germany while he was doing 'God's work' because 'we killed Jesus.'"

"Now that we really know God," I said, "and know his heart, we realize many have done horrible things in the name of Jesus. Anybody can say they follow Jesus, but their deeds prove whether they really do or not. Hitler was flat-out evil! He wasn't even close to being a Christian. People who really love Jesus love the Jewish people too. Mich, Jesus was born in Israel to a young Jewish mother. He was Jewish, Mich, and he came to his own people first."

"Yeah, well what about the killing Jesus thing?" Mich asked.

Keith put things into perspective. "There were four reports from eyewitnesses in the New Testament and they all agree. Sure, some Jewish people didn't like Jesus. Especially some leaders who were jealous. But most of the Jewish people were following him. The other factor was the Romans, who saw Jesus as a political threat who might overthrow their government. Even the so-called 'Jewish' high priest was a corrupt political puppet of Rome. Scripture says they 'plotted to take Jesus by trickery and kill him.' But they said, 'Not during the feast, lest there be an uproar among the people.' Who do you think those people were?"

"The Jews?" Michelle guessed.

I jumped in, "Yeah, like the five thousand Jesus miraculously fed, and the people at the Sermon on the Mount, and all the multitudes the Bible says followed him constantly."

"So who was to blame?" Michelle asked.

"Well," Keith said, "there was an actual conspiracy between corrupt leaders on both sides—the Romans and the Jews. The few Jewish leaders involved didn't represent the majority of their people—and it was a handful of Romans who tried Jesus and killed him. Crucifixion was a Roman form of execution. Since Jewish law only allowed stoning, Jesus would have been stoned, not crucified, if the Jews killed him. Besides, Jesus himself said, 'I will be delivered to the Gentiles . . . to be mocked and scourged and killed.' "

"Ultimately," Keith continued, "we are all to blame. It's our need of a savior that caused Jesus to die. However, he really gave his life willingly—as the Passover Lamb. He said of his life, 'No one takes it from me, but I lay it down myself.' The handful of people involved weren't guiltless, but Jesus forgave them at the cross—just like he forgives all of us."

Michelle took everything in that night. She didn't want to pray with us when she left before dawn. But before we went to bed, Keith and I prayed that the Holy Spirit would keep wooing her.

Keith and I didn't know the exact moment Michelle finally and wholly gave her heart to her Messiah. For her, it had been a two-and-a-half-year process of personal prayer and searching the Scriptures—and even she wasn't sure of the exact moment it all came together. But when it did, it was obvious to everyone that it was the real thing.

A short time later, Michelle moved in with us and became Keith's administrative assistant, but more than that—she became one of our closest friends.

Some of our discussions that late night with Michelle fueled Keith and Kelly Willard's song, "How Can They Live Without Jesus?"—especially the lines:

How can they live without Jesus
How can they live without God's love
How can they feel so alone down here
When there's so much more up above
Well, maybe they don't understand him
Or maybe they just haven't heard
Or maybe we're not doing all we can

Living up to God's holy Word
For phonies have come, and wrongs been done
Even killing in Jesus' name
But if you've been burned, here's what I've learned
The Lord's not the one to blame
For he's not just religion, or steeples and bells
Or a salesman who will sell you
The things you just want to hear
His love is just
And he loves you so much
To cause some of us
Just to follow . . . follow

Meanwhile a lot of people were wanting to follow Jesus—and many of them landed on our doorsteps! There was an almost continual flow of people showing up to give their hearts to Jesus or to help us minister to those who had. Along with this people explosion, of course, we needed a housing explosion as well. As usual, names were needed to clarify which house we were talking about.

Our little house on Dolorosa Street became the Green House. Then we bought the house next door from a guy named Harvey. We made a gate through the side fence, and turned that house into a girls' dorm even though it bore the unlikely name of Harvey's House. Another house we rented on Dolorosa was called the Rental. We also rented two houses on Sale Street—the first we named the Sale House, and the second was the School House because it was across the street from a school. The Pool House was named for obvious reasons, and the Glass House got its name because it was full of sliding glass doors and windows. Within a short space of time we went from twenty-five people in three houses to seventy people in seven houses!

Although we were experimenting with community living and everyone living out of one pot, Keith and I were underwriting almost 100 percent of the expenses with our own money. God was really blessing us financially, so we wanted to bless him by pouring it back into ministry. There wasn't a lot left over, but for everybody to have at least a little feeling of independence every month we gave everyone a little cash for mad money. We did a lot of things together like going bowling, miniature golfing, and eating at Solley's Deli, Baskin-Robbins, or Little Tony's for pizza. Keith beamed like a proud papa every time he'd take his big family out for fun.

To bring in some extra money, we put together a housecleaning service with teams of girls, while the guys had a gardening service.

We kept leading more people to the Lord, and we'd baptize them wherever we could—in swimming pools, at the beach, in Jacuzzis. Carol even got baptized in the bathtub at the School House! Everyone crowded into the small bathroom for the event, and I stood on the toilet lid to watch as Keith did the honors.

Mealtimes were always interesting because much of our food was donated. We ate things like squid, tongue, and graham crackers spread with cake frosting for dessert. Sometimes we'd just open a bunch of unlabeled cans to see what was for dinner. As we shuffled from house to house for meals and almost nightly Bible studies, I wondered more than ever what our neighbors thought about us. We were such a motley crew of ex-bikers, unwed mothers, and ex-drug-users. We'd walk along the street in groups of ten or fifteen, past kids on skateboards and dads mowing the lawn in Bermuda shorts—a bunch of post-hippies trying to follow Jesus.

We decided the neighbors must think it was all pretty strange. So we went in teams door-to-door throughout the whole neighborhood to let them know who we were and what we were doing. We also invited them to come to any of our Bible studies or Friday night potluck dinners. We'd say, "We're always available to pray with you. If you ever need help with anything, just let us know." We left them little business cards we had printed up with our address and phone number, as well as a Xeroxed schedule of our activities.

At our Friday night potlucks, we'd usually have some type of concert after dinner. Sometimes Keith would play, or one of our friends like Randy Stonehill or Phil Keaggy. Then Keith, Richard

Gene Lowe, or Reverend Glenn would preach. We saw dozens of people come to the Lord, even whole families with their children. Todd's mother and father received the Lord as well.

But there was another side to community living. Because many of the people who were staying with us had come from some pretty rough backgrounds, their lives were generally out of control. We had to make a lot of rules to build in some strong structure. For instance, everyone had a buddy to go places with because some people couldn't go to the corner store alone without sneaking cigarettes, beer, or scoring drugs.

Some of the rules even seemed kind of crazy, but we needed them—it was against the rules to pull wheelies on the bicycles because the tires got bent and people got hurt. It was against the rules to eat some of the better donated food without permission because it was set aside for pregnant moms. And to keep some semblance of order and cleanliness, we actually had to hand out demerits when people didn't make their beds or clean their rooms.

Even though we knew other rehabilitation-type ministries had similar rules, Keith was really struggling with having so many people under his authority. He confided to his journal:

> I'm so afraid of power. Not God's power . . . my fleshly desire to rule others. In my heart of hearts, I only want to serve. To present the babes as mature men and women of God! I want more than anything else to pour myself out for them, for Jesus. But then there's my old nature that wants to control everything.
>
> Lord, I repent of my old nature and I give my fear of power to you. For you are the only true power, Jesus!! Control my life with your Spirit. Control the sheep's lives with your Spirit—and if you use me, let me give thanks to you!! For you're the only true God and Savior!! Hallelujah! Let me continue to grow less important to me. I am so blind. Help me see.

In the midst of all this, Keith continued to explore the questions that had risen after Jesus Northwest. He plunged into a time of soul-searching and reflection, praying for revival in his own heart. He was also fasting regularly as he buried himself in the Word and the writings of Christian leaders of the past and present. The pages of many classic books were worn and underlined by the time Keith got done with them. He'd often grab the nearest person and read the good parts out loud to them.

Keith was exceptionally fidgety and restless now too. When he wasn't fasting, I'd catch him poking his head in the freezer looking for his favorite chocolate ice cream. Then he'd pace the floor—the carton in one hand and a spoon in the other. He hated it when his weight was out of control, but his nervous energy got the best of him sometimes.

Early in October 1978, I dressed our son, Josiah, for his first big outing, only the event wasn't exactly what we'd have chosen. Richard Gene Lowe, our first teacher and our dear friend, had been on his way home from a big conference somewhere. It was late at night, and he was sleeping in the passenger seat of his friend's car. A truck coming in the opposite direction hit them head-on. The doctors said Richard never knew what hit him, but we were shaken—even though we knew Richard was with the one he betrothed himself to years ago, his beloved Jesus. Keith really thought the Lord took Richard home in a merciful way.

"Boy, that's the way to go!" he said. "No lying around in a hospital with some long drawn-out disease. You just fall asleep and wake up in the presence of the Lord!"

"Yeah, Richard didn't feel a thing," I said.

"When my time comes, that's the way I wanna go," Keith said as he snapped his fingers. "Earth to heaven in an instant!"

Keith's words went right by me at the time. There would come a day, though, when they would come back. For the moment, I busily tucked the blanket around Josiah as we headed out the front door for Richard's memorial service.

One day a short time later, Keith walked into our bedroom looking more serious than usual—and that was saying a lot. He was
holding the book *Rees Howells: Intercessor* as he flopped on the bed.

"Did you know Rees Howells and his wife gave their infant son
away so they could go to Africa as missionaries?"

"They gave him away," I repeated flatly. Already I didn't like the
sound of this.

"They gave him to relatives," Keith continued, "and God told
them they 'could never claim him again.' Years later, after their son
graduated from college, he joined his father in the ministry in Africa.
But he was already all grown up."

"That's really heavy," I said, but silently I thought, *Isn't there something else we could be talking about?*

"Yeah. God told him to do it."

"I sure hope it was God," I said, and now I bit my lip, wondering
what Keith was leading up to.

"Mel, what if God told us to give Josiah away?"

"I can't see how that could ever be the Lord's will," I shot back at
once. "I mean, do you really think he would ask us to do that?"

"I don't know. He might. God can do anything he wants."

"Well, I always want to obey the Lord, no matter what it costs.
But that would be a hard one. Are you saying you would be willing?"
I pressed him.

"It would be the hardest thing I've ever done," he said seriously.
"But if I were 100 percent positive it was God, I'd do it."

By now my heart was so heavy it could have burst. I was afraid
Keith was going to do something crazy. *What if he tells me he thinks
God wants us to give Josiah to somebody else?* I was thinking. *What
would I do? You don't just give kids away, do you?* I did not want to lose
my son. My emotions were rocking.

Things had been so much easier when it was "just us and our
stereo." We'd always said we would give the Lord everything, but it
seemed a lot easier to give God things like money, comfort, and time.
How do you give your child? Rees Howells found out. So did

Abraham, with his son Isaac. The enormousness of their commitment was staggering to me.

Fortunately it wasn't a question we needed an immediate answer to. We weren't going to put Josiah up for adoption or anything. Still, our parent-hearts were being painfully tested. For the next few months Keith, in particular, was going through a deeper testing than I knew about until much later.

January 15, 1979
Lord, Help Again!

My Jesus, please pour your strong life out on me because I've grown so hard, cold, and "spiritual." I'm almost dead . . . I need and desire to be close to you. I want it!! So bad! Just to please you. I need to know your heart, Lord. I don't want to be a Pharisee!!! Please, God, you know I'm serious about this. Send your angel to answer.

One evening in February 1979, Keith was poking through his bookshelf—pulling out books, scanning a few pages, then putting them back. I noticed that he kept at it, until one book seemed to capture his interest. Keith carried it over to his favorite chair, a five-dollar Naugahyde recliner we scored at the thrift store. He kicked back to read for a while. I smiled and shook my head. Keith was always tackling books that frightened me off just by their size. He was probably only half a chapter into it when he called me over.

"Mel, do you remember this book?"

It didn't look familiar. "No. What's it about?"

"It's all about revivals! Real ones!"

I did remember what he was talking about now. The book was called *Revival Lectures,* written by a nineteenth-century revivalist named Charles Finney. One night about a year before, Keith had phoned me from the road, sobbing. He had read me a whole chapter of that book over the phone! Keith had been reading more Finney lately and tonight he had rediscovered this particular book.

He went back to his reading now—no long passages to read out loud, I guessed—and I got ready for bed.

When I walked out into the living room to say good-night, Keith was still engrossed in reading. But by this time, his expression had changed from excitement to total sobriety. Keith was so absorbed that he barely looked up as he mumbled a good-night to me. I went in our room and turned out the light.

The next thing I knew Keith was shaking me awake. I was so groggy I could hardly understand what he was saying. "Mel, wake up! You need to get up."

"Uh . . . what? Why?"

"It's happened! Get up. We're gonna have a special meeting right away."

Our voices woke Josiah up and he started to cry for my attention. It was barely daylight, and through my drowsy haze I wondered what on earth Keith was talking about.

"I've got to go to the other houses," he said. "I'll be back."

As I turned my attention to Josiah, the front door slammed and Keith took off in the gray morning light. One of the first places he went was one of the men's dorms. Wayne Dillard and a few other guys were awakened the same way I'd been. Later on Wayne told me what happened when Keith shook him awake.

"As soon as I got my eyes halfway opened, I could see his face—it was like he was smiling from the inside out. He was radiant."

"Wayne, wake up!" Keith said. "We've got to have a meeting."

"Okay," Wayne mumbled, "but what time is it?"

"It's about six. Listen, I was out in the Ark praying all night. And I just got saved."

"You what?"

"I just got saved!"

Clockwise from top left: Podie, Cindy (standing), Michelle, and Annie Herring (seated); Keith and Josiah; Keith, his father, and Josiah; Keith, Melody, and Josiah; Keith and Josiah with Dinah

11

"RUSHING WIND"

By the time all seven houses heard about the special meeting, our community was buzzing with curiosity. Having an early morning meeting was in itself a shock. Usually no one even saw Keith before 10:00 AM because of his late-night schedule. I watched everyone quietly drift into the School House throwing questioning glances at each other. It looked like all seventy of us were there, crammed into the living room and spilling into the hall and kitchen, anxiously waiting to find out what was going on. As soon as I saw Keith's face, I knew something big was happening. His eyes were clear and bright, and his whole face was lit with a broad grin. Something had happened to him!

"You know I've been struggling with a lot of questions about my ministry and the Lord's will for my life," he began. "I've been really wanting God to be more real. I've wanted to be closer to him, to feel his presence more. Well, I was up all night in the Ark and God showed me so much sin in my life that I spent the whole night weeping and crying out to Jesus. I told the Lord I wasn't going to leave the Ark until I had a breakthrough—no matter how long it took. Finally it happened. I had a touch from the Lord like I've never had in my whole life, and, well . . . I know I just got saved—I just got saved last night."

Keith's words stunned everyone as much as they stunned me. I could see it in their faces. *Just got saved?* I thought. *What have you been if you haven't been saved?* But Keith just kept talking, either ignoring or not noticing the wide-eyed surprise on everyone's face.

"Last night I was reading Finney, and I just couldn't get past a chapter called 'Breaking Up the Fallow Ground.' God convicted me of so much fallow ground in my life—ground that's hard and crusty and needs to be broken up for him. . . ." Now the happiness in Keith's eyes clouded over as they started to fill with tears. Blinking them back, Keith pulled out some sheets of paper from his Bible, unfolding them as he talked.

"I've already gotten these things right with God. Now I want to confess them to you and ask for your forgiveness because my sins have affected you. First of all, I know I haven't been a very good leader. I've wounded some of you with my words and my crummy attitudes. . . ."

Keith broke and started to cry, but he controlled himself enough to go on.

"The Lord has also shown me areas of pride and unbelief in my life. I don't read my Bible enough, and I don't pray enough either. And I'm so undisciplined. I've been a bad example to all of you. I have no excuse except for being lazy and loving myself more than I really love God. . . ."

He went on for several minutes, pouring out his heart and crying.

"Another area God has convicted me in is not trusting him for finances. When we offered the cassette of my Jesus Northwest concert in the newsletter, we said we'd send it for free or for a donation. The Lord showed me we shouldn't have even mentioned donations after promising not to solicit funds, so we're going to send everybody's money back to them right away. God also convicted me about the envelope in the center of the newsletter that says, 'This is not a request . . . just a convenience in case you feel led.' One of the only reasons for including the envelope was hoping they would feel led.

"I know my sin has broken God's heart. I know it's hurt you too—and I'm really, really sorry. I'm not worthy to bear the holy name of Christian. Please forgive me."

Then Keith picked up his Bible and read a Scripture to us from Hosea: "Break up your fallow ground, for it is time to seek the Lord until he comes to rain righteousness on you."

Keith explained, "Fallow ground is ground that was once tilled, but has since gotten hard and unusable. Before it can receive seed, it needs to be broken up and made soft again. Finney says to break up the fallow ground of our heart we need to examine our motives, actions, and state of mind very carefully."

Then, picking up the Finney book, Keith read to us: "'Many people never seem to think about doing this. They pay no attention to their own hearts, and never know whether they are doing well in their walk with the Lord or not—whether they are bearing fruit or are totally barren.'"

Keith explained the two kinds of sin Finney talks about. Sins of commission are the things we do that we shouldn't. Included on Finney's list were lying, cheating, gossip, wasting time, slandering others, love of possessions, vanity, envy, bitterness, hypocrisy, having a bad temper, and hindering the usefulness of others. Keith added in a few areas that Finney didn't list because they weren't as prevalent in his day—things like sexual sin, drugs, and involvement with false religions.

If that wasn't enough, there were the sins of omission—the things we don't do that we should. Included in these were lack of love for God, for the Bible, for prayer, for the poor and needy, and for the lost all around us and in foreign lands. Also listed were the sins of ingratitude, neglecting to be careful about our words and actions, and a neglect of self-denial.

Keith quoted Finney again. "'There are many professing Christians who are willing to do almost anything in religion that does not require self-denial. They are so far from realizing that self-denial is a condition of discipleship that they do not even know what it is!'"

As Keith was talking, an awesome sense had been coming over me. Instead of thinking that the things he'd done were so terrible, I found myself starting to examine my own heart, thinking, *If God put the searchlight on Keith, what does all this mean for me?* By now I was starting to make a mental list—a long one.

Keith read the whole chapter out loud to us. It was a real outline for a point-by-point examination of our own hearts. Finney said that general confessions of sin are not good enough. Since our sins were committed one by one, as much as possible they need to be repented of one by one—confessing to God those sins committed against him, and confessing to other people the sins committed against them. No shortcuts allowed! Then Keith paused and took a deep breath before he continued.

"I believe God wants to do something powerful in all of our lives. What God did for me, he wants to do for you. He wants all of us to have pure hearts that are soft and open to him. We all need to humble ourselves and break up the 'fallow ground' of our hearts so God can be glorified. I believe we all need to have a breakthrough with God. I really think we all need to pray now."

Everybody bowed their heads and closed their eyes. Then Keith started praying a very powerful prayer and a hush fell over the room. In just a moment something began to happen.

Suddenly one of the women burst into tears. She'd been sitting on the floor and now she was on her face, her whole body heaving with deep, uncontrollable sobs. A few others started to weep, and the next thing we knew we were all on our faces, crying and calling out to God. Actually, some of us could do little more than moan. The feelings were so deep it was hard to even put them into words. It was a gut-wrenching time of conviction and soul-searching. The sound of wailing started to rise and fill the room—and it went on and on.

After a long time, Keith asked everyone to go and take some time alone with God. "Go home and make out a list. List every area of sin that the Lord is showing you and will continue to show you. List it in detail. Let the Lord shine his spotlight into your hearts."

We met again later that evening and during the next few days—day and night. We had hours of prayer, weeping, and humble open confession. Everyone was being broken. People would read their list of sins and ask forgiveness of God and those who had been affected.

There was such an awesome sense of God's presence in the room. Sometimes it was so overwhelming. And more often than not, after someone shared, tears of sorrow ignited into tears of joy and even laughter as many broke through to God at deeper levels than ever before. People said they felt cleansed and refreshed in a brand-new way, as if their souls had just come alive and the weight of the world was lifted off their shoulders. It seemed that, one by one, this was happening to everybody.

Everybody, that is, except me.

After a few days, so many people had experienced their break-through that I started to worry about when I'd get mine. Keith was beginning to worry about me too. He'd walk over to me while I was lying on the floor praying and ask, "Do you think you might be getting close?" He was so excited and had waited so long for this to happen that he wanted to be sure it happened for me too.

One of the first people Keith phoned was Winkie. "It's happened!" he told him. "We're having a powerful move of God!"

Meanwhile word was getting out locally, and some people from the Vineyard showed up at our ongoing meetings. All with the same results: deep conviction of sin and a fresh touch from the Lord. Even some neighbors came. One in particular was deeply moved. Sandy lived across the street from the School House. We met just after Keith and I moved in, and she asked about our Jesus bumper stickers. She attended Van Nuys Baptist, and with more than ten thousand members it was one of the largest churches in the nation. Sandy was uncommonly hungry to know the Lord more deeply. She'd been coming to our evening Bible studies for many months, and we loved her even if she didn't look like the rest of us on the outside.

Sandy always drove her fiancé's brand-new Mercedes Benz and wore a gigantic diamond engagement ring. She was a blonde-haired, blue-eyed California beauty with college and career goals. Her fiancé, Ron, was from a large wealthy family at her church, where they'd met six years earlier. Sandy had been only fifteen then, but she and Ron had been together ever since. Everyone said they were the perfect couple. But we couldn't tell; we'd never even met him.

Ron was always working and was preparing to enter medical school. Keith and I wondered if he was the right guy for her. Sandy had been going all out for God with us, but where was Ron? Then one night Ron came with Sandy to a meeting. I watched Keith look over at them during worship. Sandy's arms were raised, and huge tears were streaming down her cheeks as she praised God. She was like a golden sunbeam, but Ron was more like a giant iceberg. He sat like a stone by her side, coolly indifferent. Did he even notice the presence of God?

The next day Keith and I took Sandy aside, but Keith did the talking. "You need to break up with Ron immediately. He doesn't love Jesus. Not like you do anyway." Sandy looked a little shocked as she fiddled with her diamond engagement ring, but it didn't deter Keith. "God has a calling on your life, Sandy, and you're not going to find it being with that guy."

Things were moving quickly and with great intensity. One night a brother from another ministry came and taught us about God's sacrificial love. At the end of his teaching he shared a story with us.

There was a man with the job of raising and lowering a drawbridge so passenger trains could cross a deep canyon. This man had one child, a son, whom he loved very much. One day the little boy wandered toward the bridge without his father noticing.

Soon the father heard a train whistle. As he started to pull the lever to lower the bridge, he looked out the window and saw that his son had crawled down into the big heavy gears. If he pulled the lever, his son would be crushed!

There were only seconds to decide. Hundreds of people would die if he didn't lower the bridge—all sons and daughters loved by someone. He took a deep breath and, his heart screaming with pain, pulled the lever.

The bereaved father stood helplessly at the window, beating on it with both fists and screaming out in anguish, as the train zipped quickly over the bridge. The passengers saw him and thought he was waving so they waved happily back without realizing the price that father had just paid for them.

When the story was over, every face in our room looked stricken. As the meeting was dismissed, I started crying. Running into the dark night, I fell on my knees in the backyard with my face pressed into the grass. I still hadn't had a breakthrough like all the others, but with this story I'd felt the heart-crushing pain of the father. In my mind's eye I could only see my curly-haired Josiah in those merciless grinding gears.

"Oh, Lord," I cried, "please give me a clear picture of what it cost you to send your only son to earth. I'm so sorry for taking your sacrifice for granted, and for not loving you the way you deserve to be loved. Please forgive me!"

The next day I left the meeting and went to sit in a car parked near the School House. I decided I wouldn't leave that car until I got my breakthrough. That worked for Keith when he wouldn't leave the Ark, so maybe it would work for me. I didn't know what else to do.

I'd already made a long list of my sins and shared them with the ministry, repenting to God and man. I confessed to everyone that sometimes I got really tired of living in community. I also acknowledged that I was still striving for recognition in my songwriting and how much pride I had when Keith would say in concert, "Melody and I wrote this song together." My prayer life and my time in the Word left so much to be desired too. I also confessed that I took the best baby clothes for Josiah before sending some donated clothing off to Mexico. I knew I'd hurt people by not speaking the truth in love sometimes or by being judgmental. To be honest, I was even judging this revival. I was mad at Finney and jealous of those who were starting to look happy while I was feeling totally miserable. I felt like such a mess.

Maybe I'm not repenting in the right way, I thought as I sat in that car. I was devastated by the blackness of my heart. I thought I loved God. Maybe I didn't love him at all. Maybe I never did. But the thing that scared me the most was the fear that I might be incapable of loving God. So why should he love me—or forgive me for that matter? I started to question every motive of my heart, and I felt as if I was tumbling down a dark shaft of despair.

After a while Keith came out to talk to me. As much as he wanted to see me have a breakthrough, he didn't think camping out in a parked car was the answer. "Mel, why don't you come back into the house now?"

"I can't. I don't even know if I love God. How can I go to a prayer meeting?"

"Mel, you love God. I know you do. Maybe it's not gonna happen the same way for you. Come on back in."

I went back into the house, but I wasn't comforted. I saw the wickedness of my heart and I felt torn from the inside out. I didn't understand why I seemed to get passed over by the Lord.

There finally came a point where I just had to let it go and go on without the happy feelings and the thought that maybe I wasn't a Christian. *Perhaps God doesn't deal with everybody in the same way,* I reasoned. But then, maybe I only felt like I'd been left behind in the darkness. I decided I would serve God in that darkness as fully as everyone else was serving him in the light, whether or not I was really saved. I still believed that living God's way was the best way to live.

When the intensity of it all subsided, it seemed that the Lord had drawn near to our community in an incredible way. Later we would refer to this time as "the revival." Charles Finney defined revival as "a new beginning of obedience to God," and that was definitely what happened. It was a life-changing time for all of us, myself included—even though my memories were a bit painful.

Keith also knew that his statements about "just getting saved" came from his black-and-white way of looking at things. It was just that he'd glimpsed a walk with God that required a much deeper commitment. It was almost as if he'd never given his heart to the Lord before. He said, "It's like getting born again . . . again!"

Even Michelle had a powerful experience. God had mostly been dealing with our sin and she, too, had shared her list—but she also got especially transparent about her biggest fear. "You guys know I wore blue jeans to my baptism," Michelle began. "I never let anybody see my legs. It's not just the scars from my birth defect. I see everything that goes with them—the surgeries, the pain, the kids making fun of me in school."

As Michelle started to cry, many of us cried with her.

"So today," she continued, "I went to the park by myself and wore a pair of shorts in public for the first time. Jesus is healing me of my shame. He's giving me the courage to not be so self-conscious about my scars and my limp."

Later that night, some of us went to Solley's Deli and Michelle came along—wearing shorts.

Jesus was so amazing! This move of God was setting us free as well as purifying our hearts. We knew this was what people everywhere were longing for.

Keith believed the Lord wanted the spirit of revival we'd just experienced to sweep the nation. It just happened that the very next concert Keith had scheduled was at the end of March in Oral Roberts University's 11,500-seat Mabee Center. Tulsa seemed like the perfect place to start, with its clusters of well-known ministries, and ORU was one of the best-known Christian universities in America. When revival broke out there, it would resound across the nation! Keith marveled at God's perfect planning.

It seemed that with the revival Keith had also found his answer to our long-standing questions about finances. He bounced into the kitchen one afternoon and said lightly, "Mel, we're just gonna go wherever God sends us and not worry about money."

"Well, usually you just go for offerings anyway." I wasn't sure why Keith was making this sound like it was so different from what we were already doing.

"Yeah, but we're not going to worry about how much of an offering or honorarium we get," he replied, "or even if we get one at all. I really feel like God is telling me we need to pay our own way into these cities and not ask for anything from the churches!"

Now that did sound different.

Keith's new financial decision and desire to see our revival spread had an immediate effect on his scheduled time at ORU. Since the university didn't usually take offerings at the Mabee Center, they were going to bless Keith with two thousand dollars for one concert. But now the plans needed to change. Keith didn't want the two thousand dollars, and he wanted to minister for at least a week.

In Keith's thinking, when Finney went into a city it wasn't for a one-night stand. He stayed until the Lord finished doing what he wanted to do. If revival broke out, Finney could be in the same town for months. With what had just happened to Keith and our community, it sure seemed like God was up to something big.

The first person Keith phoned in Tulsa was the ORU student body president who had initially invited him. Keith explained to him what he felt God's new direction was—that we were to come for a week for free. The guy's jaw must have dropped.

A short time later, we received a return phone call from this brother who said we had a green light. Instead of going to the Mabee Center, Keith could preach for a week in the ORU chapel! We were all so excited we could hardly see straight. So we made plans to go to Tulsa and had no idea when we'd be back.

Keith said, "If revival breaks out, we might even end up moving to Tulsa!" He wrote a "Prayer Bulletin" and mailed it out to the twenty-two thousand people who were now receiving the *Last Days Newsletter*. Keith asked readers to pray because we were going to Tulsa and he believed God wanted to pour out his Spirit, bring repentance, and put a spirit of prayer and conviction upon the whole city. Keith wrote:

Last Days

Prayer Bulletin

There have been so many wonderful events the past few weeks that we haven't been able to think about really starting our next newsletter. God has brought a true reviving of His Spirit and purpose to our ministry and we really want to thank the Saints who have been faithful to lift us up continually before the Throne of Grace! Since it might be a while until the next issue of our newsletter comes out, we had to get this bulletin off to you so that you can pray specifically . . . (that is if the Holy Spirit has given you the burden to pray for us, of course.) God has had us under a spirit of conviction about many things wrong with our personal lives and our ministry as a whole. He has shown us His wonderful grace by giving us His spirit to help us truly repent of these inconsistencies and hypocrocies. In the next newsletter we will be more specific about the areas God is chastising and disciplining us in.

The main reason for this "Prayer Bulletin" is, we will be going to Oral Roberts University in March from the 19th to the 24th. God has promised us that if we are faithful to obey His direction to pray and seek His face, that He will send a spirit of true revival upon those on campus, and even surrounding Tulsa, Oklahoma! We also ask you, His people, to be faithful and join us in prayer, for without prayer nothing can, or will be accomplished. Everytime in the Church's history when God brought a renewal of obedience and holiness to His people (which is what true revival is), it always started with God's people storming the Throne of Grace through prayer and supplication, interceding for the luke-warmness and carelessness of those professing to be believers. It is our reponsibility to pray "without ceasing" for God to send His Holy Spirit to convict the Church to "repent and do the works you did at first!" (Rev. 2:5). If we ever want to see sinners saved from their chains, then we have to seek the Holiness of God, so that the world will be convicted by our love and our zealous fire for our Precious Saviour Jesus.

Please pray! We beg you! Without prayer we're helpless! If you believe that God can do all things then beseech Him to pour out His Spirit on the hearts and minds at O.R.U. and the people of Tulsa. Don't think that your little prayer means almost nothing! That means that you're calling God a liar when he says "Ask and you shall receive, knock and the door shall be opened, seek and you shall find!!" (Luke 11:9) Dare to take God at His promises! If we believed that your prayers meant so little, then why would we be taking the time to ask you to pray? We need your prayers, so please ask Jesus to prepare the way for our little team of 20 to 25 people (who will be arriving up to a week before the scheduled start of the meetings). They are arriving early so that they can pray the way through the enemy lines and make way for a move of spirit that can rock the devil's kingdom from coast to coast if we are faithful! (For we know that HE

always is!) I will be doing evening concerts and preaching, and there will be other men of God to pray and minister also, including Winkey Pratney, Toney Solerno, and the Group Candle from Agape Force. Besides the evening meetings, there will be around-the-clock prayer vigils, teachings on prayer, repentance, restitution, and true conversion during the day. And an explicit call for God's people to **repent of their prayerlessness!!!**

We expect the harvest of souls fully-converted to be far too many for us to follow-up on, so Jesus has promised us that if we are faithful in prayer, He will restore the churches who love Him, to full-fire!.

Please do not doubt, but pray with the faith that God supplies "for without faith it is impossible to please Him!" (Heb. 11:6) This is such an opportunity! Tulsa, as you know, is right in the middle of what is called "The Bible Belt", and at O.R.U. there are so many church-kids from around the world who could be so used of God to go back to their home towns and preach the gospel! My mind boggles when I think of the possible fruit of a Spirit-filled student body, faculty and city. If we believe, then God will spread this fire throughout the country (and even the world!) "For I say unto you, all things for which you pray and ask, believe that you have received them, and they shall be granted you!" (Mark 11:24) "And this is the confidence which we have before Him, that if we ask anything according to His will, He hears us. And if we know that He hears us in whatever we ask, we know that we have the requests which we have asked from Him. (I John 5:14,15) AMEN!

WE LOVE YOU!
YOUR BROTHER IN PRAYER

KEITH GREEN
and
THE "LAST DAYS" COMMUNITY

Keith was also really excited about God picking ORU in particular as the place to begin. As all ministries do, ORU had experienced some financial difficulties. Keith hoped that if the Lord birthed this spiritual reawakening in what seemed to be the cradle of so many other ministries, it would open the door for fresh blessings to pour in. Keith said, "God is really going to bless ORU once this revival breaks out there!"

Keith sent Wayne Dillard and a few other guys to Tulsa two weeks ahead of the chapel meetings to meet with the local pastors so they could get ready and start praying. Keith had also planned a pastors' luncheon when he got to town so he could meet them and share his heart about the citywide revival.

After Wayne had been in Tulsa for a week, though, Keith received an upsetting call from him.

"Keith, they don't want you to come."

Wayne explained that the student group that invited Keith had neglected one critical detail—to go through the proper channels with the change of plans. The administration was surprised when they first found out about the upcoming revival on campus by reading the school newspaper.

"The ORU administration said they didn't invite you in, so you shouldn't come," Wayne explained.

Keith figured their concerns were understandable. After all, they didn't really know him or his ministry very well. From their point of view, uninviting him probably seemed like the responsible thing to do.

Yet we did wonder if maybe the administration had heard about Keith's steamy message the previous year at Oklahoma Baptist University. There had been a tremendous response from the students, but it did cause some real shock waves when Keith told them: "Going to church, or a Christian college, or to cemetery—I mean seminary—doesn't make you a Christian any more than going to McDonald's makes you a hamburger! If there were that many on-fire people in all of Oklahoma, there would be headlines all over the nation: 'Oklahoma Has Revival'!"

For whatever reasons, Keith's time in Tulsa was cancelled. Keith wasn't convinced, however, that the decision reflected the Lord's heart. He was going to pursue getting it reversed. He immediately set up twenty-four-hour prayer chains at Last Days, and everyone started fasting. The next day he was on the phone back and forth to Tulsa from 8:45 AM until dinnertime, trying to work things out. But he was told, "We're sorry, brother. We don't really know who you are. We're responsible to protect the students here. We can't let you come."

Keith finally told them he understood their position, but he felt the Lord wanted him to come anyway. That day he wrote:

March 10, 1979

ORU is cancelled. We're going anyway. In my spirit, I know it's right, but the rest of me is scared! Had the best prayer/cry in a month. Oh! Did I cry!

Keith did have some misgivings. He wondered if he'd really heard from God about going. He didn't want to be propelled by any false desire of his own to bring a fiery message to Tulsa. But he received what he believed to be confirmation from the Lord. The Vineyard was going to send us out with its blessings. Also, a Scripture passage came to us from Jeremiah 23, convincing Keith he should go with the right motives. Keith struggled up to the very last minute.

March 11, 1979

In an hour and 15 minutes the Vineyard will lay hands on us to go to Tulsa and I'm not sure totally we're supposed to go! Oh, my pride, reputation and false faith all say "go." My mind and heart are divided. I can't find my spirit! . . . I must go for the right motives. God said, "Go!"

We loaded up the Ark with about twenty-five of our Last Days family, including Carol, Kathleen, Sandy, and Jerry, who Keith had recently appointed as LDM pastor, and drove all the way to Tulsa. When we arrived we had no place to stay, but the student body president told us about a house for rent. It only had a few pieces of furniture and most of us slept on the hardwood floor, but it met our needs. We immediately started two things: a twenty-four-hour prayer chain and a series of meetings with the ORU administrators, who were shocked that Keith actually came after being told not to.

At the first meeting with the administrators, Keith told about the mighty move of God we'd just experienced and how he believed God wanted it to spread across the nation—right from ORU's chapel!

Keith was emphatic about what he felt God had told him. He

even asked if he could rent the Mabee Center, though at two thousand dollars a night that would mean taking out a loan. He told them, "We're kinda expecting a revival so we need room for lots of people."

Though ORU had rented the arena in the past to many secular artists, including Billy Joel, Keith was told they wanted to continue to pray about it over the weekend before giving a final decision.

That night when Keith got back to our little rented house, he announced, "It's not over yet! But we need a miracle."

Keith kept the 24–7 prayer chains going that whole weekend, and he also called everyone to a fast. We weren't new to prayer and fasting. We knew we needed to do everything in our power to show God we were serious. We wanted to move God's heart. We needed him to give us favor with ORU so they'd rent us the Mabee Center. In the meantime, some of the local pastors were very open to Keith. In fact, when Keith sang and shared his vision for the city at a pastors' luncheon, it turned into a prayer meeting, with many tears and heart-rending prayers. Keith, determined to reach the city one way or another, also scheduled meetings in some other churches and schools.

That Sunday morning Keith preached at a local Baptist church in West Tulsa. The service usually ended like clockwork at noon, but because of the powerful move of God it didn't dismiss until 2:30 P.M.—and Keith was invited back for another service.

That night Keith was given the evening service at Tulsa Christian Fellowship, the oldest charismatic fellowship in the city. His message and songs centered on God's broken heart over the hypocrisy of luke-warm Christianity. Keith often said, "Christians don't like to talk about hypocrisy any more than turkeys like to talk about Thanksgiving!" That night he was driving the point home, and his preaching was even a bit abrasive. He'd come with a burden to shake the congregation into a confrontation with themselves and with God, and I knew he was about to pull out all the stops.

"You don't like it, do you?" he asked. "You came to hear a concert, and you're getting cornered. The Christian walk is a bunch of squirm-ing flesh getting nailed down to a cross. 'Hey, man, I want a padded cross. You know, a Posturepedic cross with nice springs in it. Something comfortable.' The gospel is a no-compromise, absolute sellout for Jesus, 100 percent walk!"

Keith had been pacing the floor as he spoke, his piano long forgotten. "I hate to say this to you, folks. I really love you but—"

Instinctively I braced myself. I could feel something coming. Turning to the congregation, Keith pointed and said in a booming voice, "You brood of vipers and snakes! . . . who call yourselves Christians and halfheartedly serve him!"

Instant shock ran through the place. Some people in the congregation had obviously been going to church before Keith was born, let alone born again. Even I couldn't believe my ears.

Suddenly it didn't seem to matter. An overwhelming sense swept through the room. Keith had gone back to the piano, and as he began a song, he prayed, "Lord, these people can't know how much I love them. They've heard me yelling and screaming at them. But Lord, you know the heart you've put in me that hates sin and hypocrisy and compromising so much. You know how much I love these people and want to see them turn into blazing, glowing Christians. O God! Please bring a revival!"

Without hesitation, people started rushing forward to the altar rail, weeping and sobbing as they came and fell on their faces. The pastor joined Keith, and they both led the congregation in a very powerful time of personal and corporate repentance. Keith recalled something the pastor had said in an earlier prayer and spoke it out like a battle cry: "Lord, let there be a revival and let it begin in me!"

It seemed like revival was, indeed, going to break out in Tulsa!

... individually ...
... of any radical ... or over-whelming ...
... control my ... make me unselfish, unproud, quiet ...
... me humility and gentleness.
... Father I love you. You ... gift to me —

Keith performing

12

"I WANT TO RAIN UPON YOU . . ."

On Monday morning we were still waiting to get word on the Mabee Center. Keith rented a place called the Caravan Ballroom, a country-western dance club, to use in the meantime. It was only open on the weekends, so we rented it for Tuesday and Wednesday nights, still hoping we could rent the Mabee Center later in the week. By Monday afternoon Keith went to get the final verdict from ORU. I waited in the lounge and prayed.

He returned with an extra bounce in his springy step.

"Guess what?" Keith said with a gleam in his eye.

"They're going to let us rent it!" I said.

"Nope. We can't rent it. They're going to give it to us."

"For free?"

"Yeah. This is it, Mel. God did it!"

Not only was the administration going to let us have the Mabee Center for free, but ORU would officially sponsor the concerts! We would have the Mabee Center on Thursday, Friday, and Saturday. After that it would be up to ORU if Keith carried on for more nights or not. Keith agreed that if ORU said "that's it" by Saturday night, we would go home. The administration also told Keith he could give an altar call. The only other person up to that point who had been allowed to give one at the Mabee Center was Kathryn Kuhlman. On top of this, ORU would provide housing for us and let us eat our meals in the campus cafeteria!

We were amazed by all of this and very grateful to the Lord and to ORU. It was the miracle we'd been praying for.

Now we had five nights scheduled in Tulsa, and we started getting the word out, especially about the events at Caravan Ballroom since those were coming up fast! We printed posters, and some ORU students helped us put them all over town. Meanwhile, Jerry Bryant put together some quick radio ads for the local stations.

Keith was being careful not to presume upon the Lord, so he wasn't about to announce a revival. Keith said, "Let's not call it anything. Let's just say it's a free concert!"

Keith had come to Tulsa with the attitude that he didn't want to take anything from the people of this city. He felt God had told him: "Freely you have received, freely give." He was beginning to have a strong conviction that the gospel was supposed to be free. Whether it was a gospel concert, recording, or tract, Keith felt he couldn't deny those things to anyone just because they might not have money.

So not only did we pay for everything ourselves, Keith determined not to take offerings at any of his meetings. At this point, according to the major Christian music surveys, Keith's *No Compromise* album had risen quickly to number one on the charts, and *For Him Who Has Ears to Hear* was now number four. Keith had brought about two thousand of his albums to town, and they were not for sale. They were only to give away at the concerts. Another thing we brought to town was a little bit of Charles Finney. Keith and I had paraphrased the "Breaking Up the Fallow Ground" chapter in Finney's book and had it printed to give to people at the concerts to take home as an outline for repentance.

On the Tuesday and Wednesday evenings, the Caravan Ballroom, with an eleven-hundred-person capacity, was packed with people from churches and colleges in Tulsa.

Keith's basic theme was the same—getting Christians saved. "This country is full of unsaved Christians," Keith said, "and this city is probably full of more of them than almost anywhere else in America."

Both nights the dirty dance floor was filled with people on their knees making commitments to Jesus Christ. I could sense that things were starting to build toward the coming ORU meetings.

During this time Keith struggled with a sense of weakness and inadequacy. He wanted to be God's voice, and yet he saw how he didn't measure up to what it took to speak for God. In what few quiet moments Keith had that week, he wrote a little in his journal:

> The meetings have been good, but the anointing is no heavier than last year, because I am not praying more than last year.

> 3:15 A.M.
> Can't sleep. An angel wants to burn my lips with the coal. I must count the cost. Isaiah 6:7–8—Here am I. Send me!
> Prayer is the key. Make me a man of prayer!
> Put power in my words. Your word is powerful! Make your word my word, make your power my power. I want to be God's voice, full of love, mercy and fire! But I must be dead! I am ready for death! Kill me, destroy me, burn me beyond recognition. I know now that you would never hurt or harm me. You only want me dead! Let it be done! I don't want greatness. I want you to be great! Lower me down, humble me. Teach me to humble myself, O Lord! I love you so much, but not as you love the Father. I want to love you that way!

Keith wanted to gather some elders around him, so he phoned Leonard Ravenhill, whom he hadn't even met yet, and offered to fly him to Tulsa. Leonard was unable to come. But on Wednesday afternoon, Winkie Pratney arrived with several other leaders we knew, including an elder from the Vineyard, to give us moral support and prayer power. Keith wrote:

> O God, I was frightened, but now I'm feeling better. This is God's revival. His will, his burden, not mine. Lord, let me pray! Help me prepare a message in the furnace with you!
> Not by power, not by might, but by my Spirit! Amen.

I could see the mounting pressure taking its toll on Keith. He looked like the weight of the world had settled on his shoulders. He wasn't eating right, and he wasn't sleeping much either. Emotionally he was under tremendous strain. Now that the administration had given its okay, Keith felt he had to be on target with God. He said, "If God didn't really tell me to come here, then I'm not a Christian and I've never heard God's voice at all." So he paced and took long walks, wondering out loud, "Did I really hear God's voice?"

On Thursday afternoon we went to the ORU campus to pray and prepare for the evening's meeting. The Mabee Center was the largest arena in Tulsa and probably one of the nicest. It had plush, folding theater-type seats and the whole arena sloped downward toward the stage, which was the lowest part of the arena. There was a long, beautiful floor-to-ceiling curtain that separated different-sized sections of the arena.

That evening about one thousand people showed up. Just before going out on stage Keith wrote:

March 22, 1979
6:15 P.M.
Dressing Room

Here goes—burn me now, God—send a Pentecost!

That night Keith talked about how not to grieve away the Holy Spirit. He centered on how often we ignore the things God wants us to do. "He doesn't need to use any of us," Keith said, "but he wants to use all of us—to our fullest potential. The greatest argument against Christianity is Christians! The world is tired of hearing 'Praise the Lord.' People want to see it!"

By the end of the evening more than half of the people responded to Keith's challenge to be totally sold out for Jesus. Many were down on their knees in front for the altar call, weeping and repenting. Someone even got healed when Keith sang "Easter Song," which often happened at Keith's concerts.

Afterward Keith was uncertain about how things had gone. He didn't feel anything. He didn't feel really good, and he didn't feel bad. He just felt kind of neutral.

But Winkie and the others were very excited. Winkie told him, "God's presence was powerful tonight. These meetings could really break into something wonderful if things keep going like this!"

Winkie reminded Keith of Asbury, a Methodist college, where a number of years before, revival had broken out in a chapel service and went on for weeks. People would walk on to the campus and sense the presence of the Lord so strongly that they'd start weeping over things that weren't right in their lives. Classes were shut down while everyone was in the chapel weeping and repenting. It was a small college compared to ORU, but it affected Christian colleges across the nation. If revival broke out at ORU, the impact could be phenomenal.

Friday night there were twice as many people at the Mabee Center, and Keith was feeling more confident. He preached a powerful message on "faith without works is dead."

He said, "I'm not here to preach salvation by works. No such thing. God chose Abraham because Abraham had a godly heart, and then God gave him the grace to do godly works to prove his godliness."

Keith used a simple analogy: "An apple tree becomes an apple tree as a gift of God, but it proves it's an apple tree by making apples."

Again there was a dramatic response. More than one thousand people came forward to get right with God and quit playing Christian games with their faith.

Keith came away from that evening feeling terrific. But when he asked Winkie and the others what they thought, he was surprised at their consensus.

"Well . . . it was great, Keith," Winkie said. "But to be honest, it didn't have the same touch of God on it as last night. It was great preaching, and the Holy Spirit moved . . . but it wasn't revival preaching."

Now Keith didn't know what to think. Thursday night he didn't feel anything and was surprised to hear how powerfully God was there. Then the next night he felt wonderful, but the presence of the Lord was not as strong. Keith knew he couldn't trust his feelings, but he was really off-balance now, especially going into the third night. If God didn't move powerfully on Saturday night, it would be all over.

Keith fasted and prayed all day Saturday. He kept jotting things down on some kind of list he was making. And right up till the Saturday night meeting he kept noting in his journal:

March 24, 1979
6:00 P.M.
Dressing Room

> *I'm so tired. My flesh is rebelling so hard. It doesn't want to have a prayer life. Help me, oh God. Tonight, I either live gloriously or die shamefully. Oh Lord, I'm so lazy. I don't see how I can handle this kind of life for very long! Help! Please, Jesus, help me to do good only for your glory. Let me not entertain any other reasons for they are not holy! I want your name to be great.*

As Keith paced backstage, occasionally peeking through the stage curtains, it was obvious the crowd was going to be the biggest yet. The floor-to-ceiling curtain partitions were pulled back totally to accommodate the surprise crowd of forty-five hundred. The audience was mainly from ORU, but we learned there were many people here from local churches and colleges as well.

When Keith walked onto the stage, he lost no time in getting to the heart of the matter.

"Tonight we're gonna speak about holiness. What is *holiness?* It means 'to be set apart.' It doesn't mean you live in a monastery. It means you don't do worldly things. First John says if any man loves the world he is an enemy of God."

Keith went on to talk about the importance of the law and why it needs to be preached—so that sin can be exposed for what it is.

"Rules are beautiful because they tell you you're breaking something. Without the law, there is no knowledge of sin—and without knowledge of sin there's no salvation from sin. That is pretty simple and I have a definition of *sin* that's pretty encompassing—'anything that causes God pain.'"

I knew the concept of being able to hurt God would be new to a lot of people. I looked around to see how this audience was responding.

Everyone seemed to be listening closely as Keith continued. "God is the most loving person in the universe. That means he's also the most sensitive person in the universe. Love is making yourself vulnerable. The more you love, the more you can get hurt. How would you like to have eyes that saw every sin that was ever committed every single day? The Bible says, 'The eyes of the Lord are in all places watching the good and the evil.' Our sin hurts God.

"God is the most patient person in the universe, but time is running out. The Bible says there will come a day called the Day of the Lord. It will come as a thief in the night. In that day no flesh will be justified or glorified before the Lord. That means we'd better get out of the flesh quick!"

Keith reached for his Bible to pull out the list I'd seen him working on all day. "Now I've got a list that the Lord gave me of sins on this campus. Specific sins."

My heart started to pound. The atmosphere noticeably shifted, and a few people started to shift in their chairs as well.

Keith started reading. "There is worldliness on this campus. How many people believe that?"

A good number of hands went up, but not all.

"Oh! Only half of you," Keith laughed. "What about the worldly half? Don't you think so?"

"There is sexual immorality on this campus," he went on, "and there is homosexuality on this campus."

Now the audience was as still as a roomful of tombstones.

"There are people who waste the time and the money God gives them," Keith continued. "But the time is short. 'For we must work the works of him who sent us while it is still day, for night is coming when no man can work.' Nobody who believes the Bible would dare waste his precious time.

"And I'm telling you, there's dope being sold and smoked around here. There are people going out and drinking. There's an honor code here, right? No dope allowed. People have to be in by a certain time. No one's allowed to lie or cheat and so forth. There's a spirit of deception and self-deception among the students with their lying and cheating and hiding things."

Keith went on to tell the story of Achan, from the book of Joshua, and what happens when there is "sin in the camp." When the walls of Jericho tumbled, a man named Achan got greedy and took a bit of the spoil for himself—some things devoted to idols, which God had forbidden people to touch.

Keith explained that in Joshua's very next battle, many men died and God told Joshua why: "The sons of Israel cannot stand before their enemies. . . . For they have become accursed in my sight."

Now Keith faced the audience squarely.

"There is sin in the camp! Oral Roberts has a dream, and it's of the Lord. His dream is to send out men and women of God from this campus all over the face of the earth. But every sin in your life produces a curse, because sin brings a curse. I'm telling you, according to this principle, if there is sin in the camp—there's a curse upon the whole school!

"Tonight it's time for us to stare our sin in the eye with the light and the grace of God. You know what the difference between condemnation and conviction is? Condemnation is always general. But God always speaks to us specifically to heal us. We can't walk around with this spiritual-white-washed-hallelujah-praise-the-Lord cover-up anymore!"

Keith went on to compare sin to venereal disease, saying people get it having what they call fun. The first symptoms are subtle and almost painless. Then it incubates in their system and drives them mad, blind, and finally dead. Keith told everyone, "Sin is fun to get, but it's like sugar-coated, long-acting cyanide!" He encouraged every-one to quit playing deadly games with God.

"Maybe if we get holy and put aside our sin, Oral's dream will come true. How many people here are guilty of mocking him? Gossiping about him and his family? I wonder how many of you prayed for him today or yesterday? I had to repent before I could come out and preach this because I've laughed at him and judged him too. I'm not saying there's nothing to repent of in the administration or in Oral or in me. But if there's something wrong with someone, the biblical way of changing it is to submit and pray. God can speak to them. I learned that last week."

Then Keith asked those who felt they needed to commit their lives to Jesus to come forward. He also called forward those who God was dealing with about sin.

"Come and repent of your sexual sins, your homosexuality, your self-gratification, your bitterness, cheating, lying, deceitfulness, gos-sip, rebellion, hypocrisy, disloyalty, vainglory, pride, and your vain attempts at being religious.

"Let's come and return to the Lord. 'For He has torn us, but He will heal us.'"

People from every part of the arena were starting to stream for-ward, filling the stage around Keith and pressing right up against the piano. As the stage area filled, people started lying in the aisles and across the front of the stage area. It looked like a bomb had gone off! There were bodies everywhere—people on their knees or on their faces, broken and weeping. It was an incredible sight.

Keith was softly playing the piano, not even looking at the people. His gaze was focused upward, on the Lord. No one was focused on Keith either. People were on their faces crying out to God.

In a moment, with his head resting on the piano, Keith began to sob. The response had been tremendous. It looked like twenty-five hun-dred people had come forward to get their lives right with God. But Keith's burden was for more than that. He believed God wanted to bring a revival, and suddenly he burst out with a tearful, pleading prayer.

"Lord Jesus, send your Holy Spirit, and honor your Word. My preaching is garbage! I don't know what to say. The songs I've sung are all trash without your Spirit! God, send your Spirit, for without it we're all dead! Coming forward doesn't mean a hill of beans to you unless we've come forward in our hearts. God, send your Spirit upon us to break our hearts."

Then Keith honored his own prayer of a few days earlier—to let the revival begin with him. He prayed, "Lord Jesus, I just personally repent for trusting in my own talents, my own strengths, my own abilities. God, I know they're just in vain. So, Lord, before this whole body, I just repent of being self-confident and self-sufficient, and, Lord, I ask that you crush that spirit of pride and ego. Replace it with your sweet spirit of humility, God, because without you we are nothing."

As Keith openly poured out his heart, the night seemed to ignite with an even stronger sense of God's presence. Then he said, "I feel there is somebody here that the Lord has told to share before this body. It might be a faculty member, administrator, or student. I don't know. But if the Lord's told you that you're to share, come now and do it. And make sure it's Jesus. And Holy Spirit, I ask that you'd control it. That you don't let this turn into soulishness."

As Keith opened up the microphone, it was almost as if the very atmosphere caught its breath for a moment. There were already thousands of people lying in the aisles and on the floor, or on their knees with their faces buried in their chairs. I could hear a few nervous coughs around the arena, and it seemed like an eternity until the first person made his way slowly to the microphone to say, "God has shown me tonight that I'm not really a Christian. I've gone to church all my life, but it's been a farce. There was no real commitment. I had everyone fooled except God."

As this person was sharing, several more people made their way to the front, slowly picking their path over everyone on the floor. Each person took turns repenting for things like gossiping, not supporting the faculty, lack of prayer, being lukewarm, or being a phony

Christian. Most were weeping, and there was a very tender spirit moving through the whole place.

For the next half hour or more, the confessions started getting more serious and more personal. The weeping that accompanied these confessions was also getting more intense—maybe because the students realized they could be expelled for what they were sharing, especially the confessions about using drugs. Two or three people confessed to smoking grass or using drugs of various kinds. But these young people seemed more concerned about getting right with God than the possible consequences of their sin. Still, I wondered what the faculty members present were thinking.

Over and above all this, though, it felt like the Spirit of God had settled on us in a thick cloud. It was a brightness you could almost see—something gentle and tender, yet infinite. I knew something powerful was taking place.

So did Keith. He'd crawled under the nine-foot grand piano to pray and cry out to God. I sensed he was getting himself out of the way to let the Holy Spirit do his work. I could barely see Keith from where I was sitting. And people kept going up to the microphone, crawling over a sea of bodies to get there.

In a few more minutes, one young man got up and confessed an area of sexual immorality in his life. He was very broken and extremely sorry. This threw us into an even deeper level of God's dealings.

Pretty soon a clean-cut, neatly dressed young guy took the microphone. He was trembling and weeping so much before he spoke that I just knew he was going to say something pretty heavy. He started off slowly. Haltingly.

"You . . . you all know who I am. You think I'm one of the most spiritual students on campus. Well, I'm not. I know what I have to say may get me kicked out of school, but I believe God wants me to share it anyway. . . .

"I don't know how to confess this, except to just come right out and say it. I've been involved in homosexuality here on campus . . . and God has broken my heart tonight. I see how much I've been hurting him, hurting you, and hurting the school. I really need God to forgive me. With his help I'm going to change."

His confession sent shock waves across the arena. Many people burst into fresh waves of sobbing as this precious brother continued to share. It was apparent that we were just coming to the deep level of breaking we'd been praying for since God had told Keith to preach revival in Tulsa. The Holy Spirit was so strongly present. He had been raining on us all night, first in a gentle sprinkle, then in a steady shower.

Now it felt as if the very floodgates of heaven were about to burst wide open. Whatever was about to happen, we were all willing to do what was needed, even if it took hours, all night, or all week to walk it through. What Keith had seen in his spirit was starting to take shape before our eyes.

Then I saw one of the men in pastoral responsibility at ORU threading his way across the stage toward the young man who was still sharing. He came alongside the student and put an arm around his shoulder.

This man took the microphone and assured the student that he really appreciated his sharing and that the Lord forgave his sin. He also told him that ORU would take no disciplinary action against him, which I thought was really neat because the student seemed so sorry. Then the ORU official gave some guidelines for the rest of the meeting, in essence saying, "We feel things like this are to be confessed privately, and we don't think it's a good idea for any of you to share personal sins openly." It seemed like a good principle, and it was given in a loving way. But the second he was done speaking, something happened.

The change in the atmosphere was so immediate it was staggering.

Keith crawled from under the piano and looked around the arena with questioning eyes. I could tell he didn't know what to think. He talked a little bit and tried to encourage everyone, but he seemed at a bit of a loss. He even said, "I don't know what happened. Everything seems different. . . ."

Something had obviously changed, but it wasn't clear what. There was a tangible sense of a loss of conviction, and nobody else got up to share. The Holy Spirit, it seemed, had been quenched in some way, and there was nothing you could do to whip him up or bring him back. It was over. Keith managed to close by leading everyone in a few songs of praise and worship.

As I stood to sing "I Have Decided to Follow Jesus," my heart felt like a bag of cement. There was a sick feeling in the pit of my stomach. I felt a sense of terrible loss. Like something great had almost happened.

Keith closed with "Easter Song" and went straight to his dressing room. By the time I got there, he was on the floor—sobbing.

After a while, Winkie came in to talk.

"What did I do wrong?" Keith cried. "How did I grieve the Holy Spirit?" Keith was devastated. He told Winkie that he hadn't felt anything while he was ministering, that he had no sense of what God was doing. Then at the end, he knew something went wrong, but he didn't know what. He figured he must have blown it in some way.

Winkie tried to comfort him. "You're not to blame because you didn't feel anything. You preached, you sang, and then you got out of the way to let God do what he wanted to do. What happened was something totally out of your hands—the power of it and the disappointment of it. You were just a vessel God wanted to express revival through."

"Revival? Winkie . . . was it revival?"

Winkie had been in at least two real revivals. In answer to Keith's question, he nodded. "The exact same thing was starting to happen tonight that I've seen happen before, when whole communities were broken wide open to God in short periods of time. The same sense of the presence of God. The same conviction. Tonight was awesome, a sovereign move of God. I feel like it could have gone on—not just in time, but in effect. But something grieved the Spirit of God."

"I know," Keith said. "It seemed to change after people were told what to say and what not to—"

Winkie interrupted him. "Keith, we need to be careful. We can't sin the sin of judgment. We just have to leave the whole thing in God's hands."

Winkie did say he had thought a bit of teaching as the confessions were going on probably would have been good—that perhaps everyone who needed to repent of sexually related sin could have been asked to stand along with the last guy. Then one person would not have had to stand alone to confess a sin others probably shared, and they all could have been prayed for together. Winkie thought the move of God would have continued then.

"But it was almost impossible to get to the stage," he said, "with all the bodies everywhere. And you were under the piano. I didn't feel a sense from the Lord to say or do anything, and neither did any of the other leaders I came with. It was God on the loose, and none of us wanted to interfere. When God moves like that, you don't even want to breathe wrong—"

There was a knock at the door. The ORU administration was ready to talk with Keith about the possibility of further meetings. Keith and Winkie met with them backstage. They expressed their appreciation for what they said were wonderful meetings. But they didn't think things should go any further.

They were right. It was over.

Talking after a concert

ORU Altar call

Top: Melody and Keith in Hawaii

Left: Keith in concert ministry

Keith and
Loren Cunningham

13

"GRACE BY WHICH I STAND"

Our mood was a bit glum as we left Tulsa. We'd decided to stop in and visit Winkie in East Texas on our way back to California. We were in need of a little rest and an encouraging word. Keith seemed especially down, and I wondered what it would take to bring him out of it. As we headed toward Lindale, eighty miles east of Dallas, the interstate highway was bordered on each side with huge vistas of open green fields. There were enough truck-stop diners, backyard oil pumps, and herds of cattle to remind us every mile we drove that we were in the Lone Star State. When we turned off into Lindale, we were amazed that Texas was so lush. There were big beautiful oaks hung with clumps of mistletoe, piney woods, and many little lakes. There wasn't a tumbleweed in sight!

Winkie had told us all about this unique little community out in the middle of nowhere. Several well-known ministries had chosen to put roots down in the area: Youth With A Mission, David Wilkerson and World Challenge, Dallas Holm and his band Praise, the Agape Force, and Calvary Commission. Even Leonard Ravenhill and Barry McGuire lived out here. We didn't know if God had some kind of master plan for the area, but we were interested in making the rounds.

One of the very first people Keith wanted to visit after we arrived was David Wilkerson, whose story was told in *The Cross and the Switchblade*. He was also known internationally for founding Teen Challenge, a successful rehabilitation ministry for teens. We'd read another of his books, *Debs, Dolls, and Dope,* which had inspired us to keep helping people with difficult life-controlling problems at a time when we had felt like giving up. David Wilkerson also had just rocked the Christian world on its heels with his prophetic book *The Vision,* which was about God's coming judgment of America and the church.

As we drove through the iron gates of Twin Oaks Ranch, we were very impressed. Nestled on a few hundred acres of lush green pastures with three lakes, there were more than twenty ministry houses, several offices, and even a gymnasium. We met David Wilkerson in his office, quite a bit in awe that this man who was being so mightily used of God had agreed to see us.

David greeted us warmly. He was tall and thin, and his glasses had dark-to-light shading, which gave him a hip, big-city look. Keith got right to the point. He told him what had just happened at ORU and shared his concerns. Keith believed the Lord was brokenhearted over what happened on that last night, and he was confused about how to respond. David seemed to agree that God probably had much more in mind than actually happened, and he encouraged Keith to unburden his heart to the Lord in prayer.

Next we went over to meet Leonard Ravenhill. After reading his books for two years and talking to him on the phone from Tulsa, we couldn't wait to meet him face-to-face. I must admit I was a little apprehensive. I thought, *This man is so spiritual he'll see right through me. He'll know every sin I've even thought about committing.*

When we met Leonard, however, my fears melted immediately. Leonard Ravenhill had such warm fatherly eyes! And he looked so distinguished, with a full head of thick gray hair and a friendly smile.

When he invited us into his living room, Keith stepped right up to him and gave him a big bear hug.

"I've wanted to meet you!" Keith said exuberantly.

"Well, I've wanted to meet you!" Leonard said, returning Keith's embrace.

When we met Leonard's wife, Martha, she was wearing a freshly pressed, shirtwaist dress and her grey hair was pinned up in a neat little bun. She immediately offered us some English tea and an assortment of delicious homemade cookies.

We sat on their sofa, and Keith began to pour out his heart right away. Keith's upset over what happened at ORU had been brewing, and he was very agitated now as he recounted all the details.

"Leonard, let's you and me drive back up to Tulsa and kneel before the Prayer Tower and ask God to throw it down!"

"Oh, no!" Leonard said with a bit of a chuckle in his voice. "If we did that, it might fall on us!"

Leonard told Keith that even though the move of God may actually have been hindered, the Bible clearly warns us not to raise our hand against God's anointed.

"When you were at ORU, you bared your heart, Keith, and the ones God was working on in that meeting—even if they live to be older than I am—will never forget that Saturday night when God spoke and men began to confess."

We must have stayed for more than an hour, and by the time we left we knew it wouldn't be our last visit with the Ravenhills.

Besides the personal turmoil Keith was feeling about his time at ORU, by now some shock waves from Keith's time there had started to fan out across the nation. In Tulsa itself, the secular newspaper *Tulsa World* ran a report on the last night of Keith's ministry, mentioning the way the confessions were suddenly stopped. Christian magazines would also run reports, and some were labeling Keith a fiery young prophet.

For now, all Keith wanted to do was put ORU behind him and enjoy the fellowship of all the wonderful people we were meeting in Lindale, Texas.

Only by this time, we'd found out that we really weren't in Lindale. That's just where the nearest post office happened to be. We were actually in an even smaller place called Garden Valley, a good ten miles from Lindale. We still hoped to move out of the city so we decided to look around as long as we were in the area. Still it was hard to imagine moving to Texas, of all places, when we'd grown up on the West Coast.

Actually we'd heard that an old friend of Keith's had a ranch in the area, and we decided to go see him. Keith first met this friend when he was a Hollywood hippie and record company executive—and before either of them were Christians. After this guy became a Christian, he'd lived in his van in front of our house on Dolorosa Street for almost three months while we helped him pull his life together. Eventually he'd come here to get some training from the Agape Force and then bought some land in the area.

Keith got directions to the property, but we got a little lost and just drove around enjoying the beautiful countryside. We came upon a large sweeping field and out in the middle of it was a huge wooden waterwheel. Right behind it sat a log ranch house. What a picture! Keith and I both spotted it at the same time.

"Look at that!" Keith exclaimed.

"Beautiful!"

Spontaneously, Keith prayed right out loud. "Lord Jesus, that property needs to be used for you. We claim it for your kingdom!"

Then we had a good laugh because we usually didn't run around claiming things, but that was how the prayer had sprung out of Keith's heart. We drove on and kept looking for his friend's property.

When we finally found the right driveway, we pulled in and his friend gave us a tour. There was a beautiful ranch house with three bedrooms sitting on 140 acres. As we walked around, we found out it had a small chicken coop and two barns, one of them two stories high. Then, we came around the south side of the ranch house, and we were about to leave when we saw it!

"Look at that!" Keith nearly shouted.

"It's the waterwheel!" I laughed.

"Can you believe it? This is the land we prayed for a few minutes ago!"

Since the property bordered two highways, we hadn't immediately seen this side. We looked at each other, wondering if it was just an unusual coincidence or if the Lord was trying to speak to us about moving into this area. Keith, never lacking for boldness, went back to see his friend later and told him he thought the Lord wanted us to buy his property. The only problem was it wasn't for sale.

We had so many things on our minds at once, but in the midst of all the intensity one of the funniest moments we'd had in a long time just dropped on us out of nowhere. Maybe it was a little humorous gift from the Lord. Keith and I were lying around in our hotel room talking about how Christians, us included, could be so fickle in our faith. God miraculously delivers our souls from the jaws of destruction, and as soon as the going gets tough we quickly forget how bad our lives were before we knew the Lord! The first thing we do is look back to our old life with longing eyes.

"It's just like the people of Israel," Keith said. "They're oppressed and dying in Egypt, so God sends Moses to deliver them. God even parts the Red Sea and feeds them manna from heaven every day, but all they do is grumble and complain!"

"Boy," I said, "that sure sounds like me sometimes."

"I can just hear them out there on their way to the Promised Land," Keith said, chuckling. "Walking around and whining, 'I wanna go back to Egypt!'"

Then Keith put on his best Jewish God accent and said, "So . . . you wanna go back to Egypt?"

That started it! We began throwing verses back and forth at each other, laughing ourselves silly over the trivial things that sometimes turn our hearts away from the Lord . . .

So you wanna go back to Egypt,
Where it's warm and secure.
Are you sorry you bought the one-way ticket
When you thought you were sure?

You wanted to live in the Land of Promise,
But now it's getting so hard.
Are you sorry you're out here in the desert
'Stead of your own backyard?

Eating leeks and onions by the Nile.
Ooh, what breath! But dining out in style.
Ooh! My life's on the skids.
Give me the pyramids!

Well, there's nothing to do but travel.
And we sure travel a lot.
'Cause it's hard to keep your feet from moving
When the sand gets so hot.

And in the morning it's manna hotcakes.
We snack on manna all day.
And they sure had a winner last night for dinner,
Flaming manna soufflé.

Well, we once complained
For something new to munch.
The ground opened up
And had some of us for lunch.

Ooh! Such fire and smoke.
Can't God even take a joke? . . . Huh? . . . (No!)

We didn't know it at the time, but this song would play a very important part in Keith's next album—a subject that was starting to become a cause of real concern for him.

After we got back to California, Keith was once again trying to sort through some major questions. Moving was one of them. We still had the dream of having a ranch in the country to help people get their lives together. Was it supposed to be in Texas?

Another big question for us was what to do about Keith's next record. Keith's contract with Sparrow had been fulfilled, and his ministry was soaring with huge record sales between his first two top-selling albums. He wasn't unknown anymore and could negotiate a very sweet deal with Sparrow or with another company if he wanted. Only now he felt very strongly that the Lord wanted him to downplay money and not even charge for his ministry.

Keith also had mounting questions about the Christian recording industry and his involvement. Sparrow wanted him to sign on with them again, and other record companies were vying for his next album as well. Keith really needed to hear from the Lord because one thing seemed certain—he was going to be making more records.

In April, just a few weeks after the event at ORU, Keith decided to go away for a long weekend to fast and pray. He drove a few hours up to Big Bear, which was high up in the San Bernardino Mountains. When he came home, he shared his journal with me. I could easily see in my mind's eye what the few days had been like for him.

Keith had checked into the hotel and made a long prayer list. His core question was, "What is my calling and ministry?"

The weight and responsibility of trying to be a full-time pastor to seventy people, many with great needs, and at the same time trying to fulfill his call to the church at large was crushing him. Keith was wearing many hats at once, and he wanted to know what his priorities should be. He listed everything he was doing and asked God if he should scratch anything off—evangelist, revivalist, musician, singer, pastor, overseer, organizer. Keith also prayed about the future of the Last Days community, a possible move to Texas and who would go, the recording situation, and the motives and priorities of our ever-growing *Last Days Newsletter*.

Texas, somehow, was beginning to seem right, but would Keith's friend even sell us his ranch? And if he did, where would we get the money to buy it? We'd poured almost everything back into keeping everyone fed and paying the rent on all the houses.

Keith was also concerned about me. He prayed about my ministry and calling and for a certainty of my salvation, since I'd never had a breakthrough during the revival.

It was a long, tough weekend since Keith was feeling more bored and cold in spirit rather than on fire for the Lord, which he'd been preaching about.

April 17, 1979
1:30 A.M.

Royal Knight Hotel. Help. I flattered myself with the whole armor of God knight stuff and got a sleazy room. I'm so brave until the war starts with my flesh. "I buffet my body and make it my slave, lest possibly after preaching to others, I myself may become disqualified." Help me buffet my body.

5:00 P.M.

Here I am, waiting. Scared, bored, hungry. Unbelieving, frustrated, even mad at God for making me go through this. I preach against easy grace and then when it isn't easy, I get mad at God for making it just the way I preach it!!! Oh! The total hypocrisy of it all!! Please forgive me. Daddy, break me and for your sake speak to me now, please!! Lord Jesus, please. I want answers and help with these areas. I've never been a follower. I've been a leader all my life, but now I want to follow you.

8:40 P.M.

I have begun to feel the Holy Spirit's presence. I have such a long way to go. I have no idea what it must be like to live without talents, possibilities, chances for greatness. It is a curse, I know. But I must employ them for they are gifts of God. Parable of talents and minas.

O God, what great blessing you could have through my life if I were totally dead and a clean, sanctified vessel. This blessing for you, this glorification of your throne and name—I want. But if you would get more joy from me doing other things, from being obscure like Rees Howells. . . . What do you want of me?

10:00 P.M.

I cried a great cry at the hopelessness of it all! Good break, but now what? Your pleasure is all I seek, nothing else matters. I still am embarrassed when you tell me to witness.

Keith had to fight through it for a long while, but in the end the sense of God's presence finally came:

I am helpless, more than since I first got saved. Even more so, because I have no Christian hope in myself. I write. I can't pray. I scream inside, but not enough to cry. When I cry, I get so excited I'm finally crying that I quit crying. Help! I'll try and pray again. Glory to Jesus . . . Angels are here with me. The room is full. . . .

What God really seemed to be after on this weekend was more of Keith himself. Was he willing to lay down everything for the Lord, including me? Including Josiah? What Keith had read several months ago, about Rees Howells giving up his own son, came back to him. Keith had to struggle with being willing not only to lay down his own life for the gospel, but also being willing to lay down his love for Josiah and me.

Another quote, by Joseph Parker, whom Leonard Ravenhill had written about in *Why Revival Tarries,* came to Keith: "The man whose little sermon is 'repent' sets himself against his age, and will . . . be battered mercilessly by the age whose moral tone he challenges. There is but one end for such a man. 'Off with his head!' You had better not try to preach repentance until you have pledged your head to heaven."

Keith's retreat encompassed the day of Josiah's seven-month birthday. Keith wept for a long time about the question of his willingness to let the Lord have full rights to Josiah—no matter what. But when he finally came to the place of willingness, he wrote a song on his guitar in the form of a prayer—weeping the whole time.

The song lyrics were written in Keith's journal, but he didn't want me to read them. He took his journal back and opened it to the right page, then grabbed his guitar and sat cross-legged on the floor in front of me. He wept again as he sang:

Well, I pledge my head to heaven for the gospel.
And I ask no man on earth to fill my needs.
Like the sparrow up above,
I am enveloped in his love.
And I trust him like those little ones he feeds.
Well, I pledge my wife to heaven for the gospel.
Though our love each passing day just seems to grow . . .

Tears were misting my vision now, and a hard lump tightened in my throat. He kept singing:

As I told her when we wed,
I'd surely rather be found dead,
Than to love her more than the one
Who saved my soul.

I'm your child,
And I wanna be in your family forever!
I'm your child, and I'm gonna follow you
No matter, whatever the cost,
Well I'm gonna count all things loss.

Well, I pledge my son to heaven for the gospel,
Though he's kicked and beaten,
Ridiculed and scorned.
I will teach him to rejoice
And lift a thankful, praising voice.
And to be like him who bore the nails
And crown of thorns.

Well, I've had my chance to gain the world
And to live just like a king,
But without your love
It doesn't mean a thing!

Well, I pledge my son . . . I pledge my wife . . .
I pledge my head to heaven.
I pledge my son . . . I pledge my wife . . .
I pledge my head to heaven for the gospel.

When Keith finished singing he looked at me, waiting for my response. But how do you respond to a song like that?

I told Keith, "The song is incredible."

I was always proud to be married to a man so committed to God that he would pay whatever price obedience might require even if it cost him his own life. But this was different. Now God was dealing with things much closer to Keith's heart than his own life. It was unthinkable for Keith to do anything that might harm me or Josiah. It went against all of his natural instincts. Yet it seemed Keith was being asked to give his most treasured gifts "back" to the One who gave them in the first place.

This new song was a powerful declaration of Keith's devotion to Jesus. It was a promise too. No matter what happened in life, like Job in the Old Testament, Keith would never, ever turn his back on God.

On the other hand, it wasn't some abstract ideal of commitment some stranger happened to be singing about. It was my husband, singing about our son and me. I understood it. But my mother's heart cringed at some of the words Keith used about Josiah. Still, I knew when Keith entrusted us to God, it didn't mean he'd neglect us or not take care of us. It just meant he wouldn't live in unreasonable fear of losing what he loved the most on the earth. That he trusted God with absolutely everyone and everything . . .

But later I realized my level of trust was not a strong as Keith's, especially when it came to *my* firstborn son. I prayed that God would give me the same grace to let go of Keith and Josiah if I ever needed to.

One of the conclusions Keith announced when he came back from Big Bear was a surprise to everyone. Keith said he sensed that God had prepared some of our family to take their next step forward in their journey with the Lord. So Keith started meeting and praying with each person to find out who was supposed to stay and who was being called on to their next place. I was surprised to hear Cindy, who was the very first person to come live with us, was feeling called to Agape Force in Texas for more discipleship training. And Sandy told Keith she broke off her engagement with Ron because she was being called to go to Agape Force too. Jacob Damkani had also moved on, telling Keith the Lord was calling him back to Israel to share the Messiah's love with the Jewish people. They butted heads a bit on this. Jacob was such a fearless evangelist, Keith thought he could reach more people in the States.

Because of Keith's deep love for each person, the process seemed to be more painful for him than anyone else. But things were changing fast. Keith felt he was supposed to concentrate more on the *Last Days Newsletter* and getting back out on the road to minister. The questions about Texas were still up in the air.

He also made a vow to the Lord to read ten chapters of the Bible and spend one hour in prayer every day. He realized the spiritual foundation in his life had to be strengthened to support the weight of the ministry God was giving him.

April 22, 1979

> *I'm not listening to my flesh which says, "Oh, you're becoming legal! God won't honor this forced prayer stuff!" Well, there are times when the Spirit's grieved by my clock-watching soul, but there are good times of prayer and I believe they will form into godly habits. Lord, please help your servant be consistent. . . .*

Lack of prayer is sin.
Legal prayer is sad.
Freedom is best.

During the next few weeks, with constant interruptions and distractions, Keith didn't always meet the required reading and prayer time he'd set for himself. When that happened he knew he was breaking his vow to God. That was too much for him to handle. He started slipping into depression.

May 13, 1979

Oh what can I do? Sure. concerts, records, ministry, but worthless trash compared to the potential. O God, do something. I'm here begging you.

Please give me that love for Your Word and prayer or free me from the bondage of this predicament. I want so to obey you, to be disciplined, but you've got to help me. It's my fault, but Your move.

I'm stagnating, limp and powerless, I'm defeated. Numb and tearless, waiting for a word, a miracle, please free me Jesus. I'm desperate, yet nonchalant. I'm in a hypnotic state, "oh everything will work out." I'm getting to the end of my long rope. Corner me Lord!

A few days later, God gave Keith some much-needed assurance.

May 15, 1979, 5:00 P.M.

On Sunday I felt the Lord say that the cloud was gonna lift soon. Praise God.

A short time later, Tony Salerno from Agape Force dropped in unexpectedly. He helped Keith see that, although God wanted to spend time together with him each day, the vows Keith had made were keeping him under condemnation. Tony taught Keith about meditating on Scripture as a way to focus in on the Word. Keith wrote:

> *My vows were too hard. . . . Please Jesus, let me out of them "legally" and let me develop into a man of God through your discipline. My intentions . . . were to get to know you and I want to do that any way I can. Please lead me into an hour of prayer a day without me timing it. God doesn't want me serving him under obligation, but out of love.*

Even with this new bit of understanding, Keith seemed to alternate between feeling like he had no vision and feeling like his vision was too big to really be of God.

I was still stuck back at the place of wondering if I was ever going to have a breakthrough or if I would ever feel confident that God accepted me. The beginning of our answers came totally unexpectedly.

In his typical way, Keith picked up the phone one night at about 11:00 P.M. and called Winkie just to say hi. It was 1:00 A.M. in Texas, but Winkie was still awake, packing for a ministry trip to Hawaii. Keith immediately said, "Wow, can me and Mel come with you? Do you want me to sing?"

Winkie understood Keith's heart and knew he wasn't into dropping hints or trying to manipulate his way anywhere. Keith just really wanted to spend some time with Winkie. So, like a little kid, he kind of invited himself along. Somehow Winkie managed to put together a few last-minute concerts for Keith to help us justify the trip, and within days we were off to Hawaii.

After we landed in Hawaii, things started happening quickly. At the Honolulu airport someone met us and, in true Hawaiian style, hung flowered leis around our necks. We went directly to a pastor's house to rest and catch up on our jet lag. Keith took a nap in the bedroom while I rested on the living room couch. I was amazed at the beauty of the Hawaiian scene just outside the window.

I could see tall, flowered palms and hear lots of birds chirping away at the crystal clear sky. I wasn't thinking about anything in particular. Then a thought came to me. Actually it seemed like more than a thought. It seemed like a still, small voice, and it said, "I am going to give you the desire of your heart. You're going to have a little girl."

I didn't hear it audibly, but it was so clear and direct I was taken aback. I wasn't even pregnant—or at the moment even thinking about that subject. I thought it might be the Lord, but I wasn't sure. Especially since I'd recently been wondering if I knew how to hear God at all. I figured it could have just been my own drifting thoughts, but it was the kind of thing that only time would tell.

Keith's last-minute concert in Honolulu that night was packed with people. I decided to do a little exploring while Keith played, and I found a room upstairs in the back of the sanctuary.

It was the singing that first drew me there. Peeking through the half-open door, I saw several beautiful Hawaiian women in a time of worship and praise. They were praising God with Hawaiian dance too. The gentle flowing movements of their bodies and their delicate footwork seemed to me to be what God must have intended when he created dance. It was pure and sanctified for him. Their hands were speaking adoring words of worship like a beautiful, holy sign language. It was evident they were enveloped in God's presence. I'd never seen anything like it.

Then they burst into a jubilant song of praise and celebration. Their dancing and joy just exploded with energy and excitement! I tore myself away, feeling a little guilty for sneaking off from the concert, but I could have stayed there all night.

It was ironic to me that I was in ministry, traveling all over the country with my husband who was a top Christian recording artist— and yet I wished I could break free and worship the Lord in joy and freedom like these ladies—hidden in the back room of a remote church.

Next we went to Maui and then on to Kona to visit Youth With A Mission, which provided housing and hospitality for us on their base. In the process of starting a Christian university, Loren Cunningham, the founder of YWAM, spent some time with us. We'd never met Loren before, but immediately we were impressed with his gracious warmth and breadth of vision. He walked us around the campus, which he saw more clearly in his mind at that moment, since everything was in the beginning stages.

Loren would point and say things like, "Over there will be the Plaza of the Nations representing every nation on earth!" It was actually a big rocky field, but he went on to paint such a vivid picture I could imagine it finished as he was talking. Keith and I both were excited about Loren's desire to equip Christians from around the world—spiritually, culturally, intellectually, and professionally—to use their God-given abilities to communicate the Good News in all nations.

Something in our hearts leapt just listening to Loren talk. Was it just that he had confidence in what God had shown him? Or was God stirring something else in our hearts? Before we left, Keith told Loren he'd been struggling in some areas and knew he needed men of God to speak into his life.

"Loren, would you be open to me calling you sometimes, when I need counsel or advice?"

With a warm smile, Loren said, "Keith, I'd be glad to help you in any way I can." We could tell Loren said it from his heart—especially when he moved toward Keith and wrapped his arms around him in a big bear hug.

Loren's response blessed Keith so much. For years Keith's heart had been crying out for somebody to come along and be a father in the Lord to him, and he sensed such a father's heart in Loren. Keith left the YWAM base with an extra spring in his step.

We spent the last few days of our trip at the home of some friends of ours from California who lived about twenty miles from the

YWAM base. We'd first met Jimmy and Carol Owens through Buck and Annie Herring. They were the parents of our friend Jamie Owens. We arrived to a big spaghetti dinner and stayed up late laughing and talking. I really liked them and felt especially close to Carol. Her maturity in the Lord and spunky directness, laced with humor, made her easy to talk to—and I sure needed someone to talk to.

That next morning, I got up before Keith and slipped into the kitchen. Carol was alone, making coffee. We sat at the kitchen table in the warm morning sun. Within minutes I was pouring out my heart to her.

"I asked Jesus into my heart four years ago," I confided, "and even stood up at your musical *If My People* to make my first public declaration of faith. But I don't know if I really love the Lord."

Then I just started crying. This was the first time I'd said out loud the words that often drove me crazy in the middle of the night: "Carol, I don't even know if I'm saved—"

"Why would you feel that way?" she asked evenly.

I told her that since the time of the revival, I'd been feeling more and more lost. I knew my heart wasn't pure enough and that I still was undisciplined in many areas. I wasn't living up to God's standards and I knew it.

"I usually mix sound for Keith at his concerts," I went on, "so I've heard his message over and over. Sometimes I just want to crawl under the soundboard and disappear. I've stood for so many of his altar calls I'm sure God must think I'm crazy by now. I just don't know what to do."

When I finished, Carol reached over and laid her hand on mine, giving it a gentle squeeze. She said, "Melody, don't you hear what you're saying? This is so much law. Where's the grace?"

"Grace . . ."

Then she picked up her Bible, which had been lying on the kitchen table, and turned to Galatians.

"Listen to this," she said. " 'You have been severed from Christ, you who are seeking to be justified by law; you have fallen from grace.'"

"Yeah, but so many people just trample on God's grace—running around in sin and thinking it's okay."

"Maybe so, but that's not what you're doing. Melody, you need to receive God's grace—not deny it."

I knew that "easy believism" grieved the Lord. I certainly didn't want to be too easy on myself. But on the other hand, I didn't want to reject his gift of grace and grieve him in another way. I wondered if God was trying to tell me something through this trip—first, through the freedom of the beautiful worship dancers in Honolulu and now through Carol.

Later that day, Jimmy and Carol talked with Keith and me, repeating much of what Carol had shared with me—and more. They listened to Keith's many difficult questions and patiently gave him answers from the Scriptures. The spirit of it was kind of like Mom and Dad having a heart-to-heart talk with their kids.

Something was getting through.

Jimmy and Carol's in Hawaii

The cloud is lifting! I have been under the law. Vows, promises, self-improvements, and discipline. God's proved it to me. I'm incapable. I can't do it.

Grace, not works! I've got to abide and let Him do it. There is a balance in this. Prayer, faith equals works, fruit.

Only Jesus saved me the first time, and only Jesus can save me now. I believe He is beginning a great redemption.

We returned home with high hopes. Something had happened to us in Hawaii—meeting with Loren, our special time with Winkie, the talk with Jimmy and Carol Owens. Just the beauty and grace of the islands helped put Keith a little more at ease from all the confusion he'd been feeling. I had such wonderful memories of graceful, dark-haired women worshiping the Lord so freely.

A short time later, Keith wrote:

> For the first time in months, I awoke with peace—Real Peace. I can seek the Lord now, for an angel from God has come to minister to me. I love God so much. My heart overflows with quiet, gentle joy. My eyes water with tears for the peace in my soul. My faith is refreshed. My desire to commune with God and intercede for souls is renewed with power! My thirst for God's word has greatly increased. The prison doors have swung open of themselves. The shackles have fallen off to the ground. My heart is bursting with joy and hope! Oh! I can hope again.
>
> Jesus, I'm so grateful that there was no formula—no secret way to regain my peace. No amount of Bible reading or forced prayer time (on my part) brought this state on. But you, in answer to the desperate crying out of my heart, came and rescued me from the bondage of works and self-spirituality. I want to glory in your presence. You want me to share your glory—but only as a gift, not as a result of my efforts, but as a result of your goodness, mercy, and love for me.
>
> Thank you for helping me hang on!

Soon after returning home, Keith received a last-minute invitation to a new California festival called Jesus West Coast in the university town of Chico. Nestled at the base of the Sierra Foothills, Chico was about one hundred miles north of Sacramento. At first Keith was unsure about going, even though he knew his friend Winkie would be there, but when he prayed, he felt a "yes" from the Lord. What Keith didn't know then was that the festival organizers had been unsure about even inviting him.

The founder of the festival was Bob Maddux, a pastor with a hippy past who now only liked Christian folk-style music, unsure if God could really use Christian rock music. But Winkie, without us knowing, had convinced Bob to invite Keith to come sing. Bob trusted Winkie enough to invite Keith, but not enough to give him a well-attended slot.

When Keith and I arrived at the festival grounds, we were amazed to see that something like a mini-city had been built—with streets, a market, and a store. And the campsites even had showers! We were told it was set up like old-time Bible camp meetings. It was all very cool, but what wasn't cool was the festival schedule.

When Keith saw he'd been given an afternoon slot, he was unhappy. We both knew afternoons were times when people ate and napped to get ready for the big evening meetings. Keith felt the more people he could minister to at the same time, the better it was. I wondered if Keith felt a sting of rejection as well. Still, on his appointed afternoon, Keith poured out his heart as if there were thousands, although, as we had expected, it was poorly attended.

The next day Bob pulled Keith aside and said apologetically, "I was really touched by the anointing on your life Keith . . . and on your songs. I'm sad not many people got a chance to hear you." Bob realized that the men who mentored him had personal issues with Christian rock music. Issues that were cultural but not scriptural. That day a deep friendship began to form between them.

Several thousand people attended the three-day festival, which was great, but even better, the Lord visited with awesome signs in the sky. On the first day there was a literal ring around the sun for the whole day. The front-page headline in the local newspaper read, "Halo Surrounds Sun at Jesus Festival."

Then on the last night, Loren Cunningham, our new YWAM friend from Hawaii, was giving his message when he was given a note onstage that a huge thunderstorm was moving directly toward the festival, threatening to rain it out. So Loren stopped his message and led everyone in prayer, asking God to redirect the storm and protect the festival. It was hard to believe, but the gathering clouds began to part, revealing brilliant blue skies. Even more incredible, two rainbows appeared—one rainbow on each side of the festival grounds.

Absolutely no rain fell that evening, and a local newspaper ran another story the next day saying, "You can't argue with rainbows."

Those rainbows reminded me of driving across the Nevada desert one night as new believers. The sky was pitch black when—of all things—we saw a huge rainbow of pure white light arching fully across the desert. It touched land at both ends. We stopped the van and piled out, blinking in unbelief. It was unreal. A perfect rainbow of white light! Keith and I still talked about it as one of our "signs from God in the sky" stories. Now at the festival there were not only remarkable signs in the sky, but thousands decided to follow Jesus, and we made wonderful new friends. It was a huge success as far as we were concerned. Afterward we went to dinner with Bob and his wife, Claudia. They confided to us that they were left with fifty thousand dollars of debt from festival costs. They weren't wealthy people, and that was a huge amount of money for anyone to owe.

Keith said compassionately but clearly, "I believe the reason you guys lost money on the festival was that you charged people to get in. If you'll do it again next year and let people in for free, I'll give you ten thousand dollars!" I swallowed hard. We weren't rich either, but I was so proud of Keith's heart.

Not waiting for Bob's response, Claudia boldly jumped in and declared, "Okay, Keith, we'll do it!"

A short time later Keith and I went out to do two benefit concerts. We'd take offerings to help get Bob and Claudia out of debt. One concert was in Sacramento and one in Castro Valley. Sacramento had a great response. But the one in Castro Valley was something else. The freeway off-ramps were backed up for miles! We jammed Church of the Crossroads with as many people as we could without the fire marshall shutting it down. But there were hundreds of people left standing outside, with carloads still arriving.

Keith said, "Awesome! I'll just do two concerts tonight!" Keith loved seeing so many coming to be ministered to and, as usual, he couldn't bear turning anyone away. We looked at each other, knowing his decision would take double energy. But also that it would reap double ministry for the Lord. And being able to take two offerings that night for our new friends' festival debt was very exciting.

Just before the first concert, we walked down to a little pizza place with Bob and Claudia for a quick meal. When we returned to the back entrance, the security guard wouldn't let us in. Keith didn't say something like, "Don't you know who I am?" or "Hey, I'm Keith Green." He smiled and simply said, "We're with the band," and they let us in. I loved what God was building in the heart of this man I had married.

Keith raised twenty thousand dollars in three concerts, and the only thing he would take away was our airfare. With our concerts and people responding to letters Bob sent out to cover the JWC losses, Bob got totally out of debt and started plans for a free festival the following year. This time Bob gave Keith an advance invitation saying, "Next year, bro', I hope you'll take an evening spot to minister."

Melody and Josiah

The year was speeding by so quickly. It seemed we were going through bigger and faster changes than anyone we knew. It was exciting for sure, but was it normal to have so much happen so fast? Did God have us on some kind of warp-speed pace? And if he did, I wondered why?

14

"I WANT TO BE MORE LIKE JESUS"

Keith wrote in his journal in August 1979, "We're moving in about a month to Texas!" A quick phone call from Keith's friend in Texas set the wheels in motion. He prayed and felt he was to sell the ranch to Keith. Now the only problem was where in the world would we get the money?

We needed a down payment of $31,500 in thirty days, but we knew if the Lord wanted us to move, he would provide the money by the time we needed it.

Never in a million years would we have expected to move to Texas. Yet, besides the fact that we'd finally be able to move out of the suburbs of Southern California, the main draw was the opportunity for relationships with others who understood the call on our lives. Keith felt like he'd finally found spiritual fellowship with men who were brothers in the Lord and some who were even fathers in the faith. The small YWAM base, a few miles away, was neat because of the bonding Keith had felt with Loren Cunningham in Hawaii.

There were also many practical reasons to move to East Texas. We could get a lot more land for our money than we could in Southern California. And Texas was centrally located, which meant all of our telephone and travel expenses would be much less. Most important, it seemed that God was leading us there. The Lord impressed Keith with a Scripture from the book of Isaiah about enlarging the place of our tent and spreading abroad to the right and to the left. An unlikely excitement about Texas was growing in our hearts. But the question of the down payment remained.

So to lighten the load for our move to Texas, plus make some much-needed money, Keith and I went back to our financial roots. We had a big yard sale!

Actually the sale spilled out over the entire lawn of our house and onto the lawn of the Harvey House next door. We went through everything we owned to see what we could do without—and so did the rest of our Last Days family. We ran ads in the newspapers and put signs up on all the nearby street corners. There was too much stuff to set up and tear down every weekend, so we stayed open seven days a week.

We had clothing, furniture, books, records—you name it. I sold my two-hundred-dollar rabbit coat for seventy-five dollars, and all of my silver and turquoise jewelry for almost nothing. We kept marking down everything until we were almost giving it away. It must have been one of the biggest, longest-running yard sales in history.

As Keith and I spent many hours talking to customers and making sales, Josiah was just learning how to walk. In his little cloth diaper, we'd send him back and forth between us on the front lawn, with wild applause for every faltering step he took. We also spent a lot of time keeping him from eating the rocks he kept picking up. People never stopped commenting on how adorable he was, with his full head of flaxen blond curls and his big blue eyes. What they didn't know then was that he had a little brother or sister on the way! I had now officially discovered I was pregnant with our second child. I couldn't help but wonder if what I thought the Lord had spoken to me in Hawaii would really come to pass.

While we were trying to raise money, we'd also been fasting and praying for a miracle. We'd even talked about getting a bank loan if we needed one—and as the deadline approached, it looked as if this would be more than just talk.

One day I noticed Keith was pacing much more than normal. I finally asked him about it. "Keith, are you okay?"

"I'm going to have to apply for that loan. Today's Thursday, and the money's due on Tuesday. We've only got five days left. But I don't want to get a loan. I seem to have lost my peace about it. I need to pray more today."

That night we had a special prayer meeting, and the Lord spoke to Keith out of the book of Malachi. Keith was surprised, but excited, as he read: "Test me now in this . . . if I will not open for you the windows of heaven, and pour out for you a blessing until there is no more need."

He said, "I think the Lord's telling us to forget the loan and trust him to supply the money by Tuesday."

Everyone was really excited, but I was apprehensive. How could we know for sure that Scripture meant God was saying no on the loan? I wondered how Keith could feel so certain. I did my best to believe.

During the next few days, the Lord did fulfill his promise to provide. To our surprise, some of our good friends became part of the answer to our prayers. We were blessed and humbled to receive $4,000 from Buck and Annie, $4,500 from Matthew Ward, and $1,000 from Sparrow Records. What generosity! Sure enough, by Tuesday the Lord had supplied the full $31,500.

The day the moving vans came we were, as usual, in a frenzy of activity. What was left of seven households of furniture had to be moved, and there were mountains of large cardboard boxes on our front lawn. It took two whole days for the vans to load up everything.

People-wise, we were a pared-down remnant of about twenty-five, including Wayne and Kathleen, who were now engaged to be married, thanks to a bit of matchmaking by Keith; Francine, who helped me with Josiah; Pam; Podie; Carol; and Michelle. Carol and Michelle had become the dynamic duo of all things administrative, and we breathed a sigh of relief when neither of them felt called somewhere else.

A few newer people were moving with us too, in particular the DeGraff brothers, Larry and Terry. Larry came to Last Days Ministries first, but we met Terry at ORU in an odd way. When we went to ORU, Larry stayed in California to work on the cover art for our "Revival" issue of the *Last Days Newsletter*. He told Keith he'd had a little art experience, so Keith gave him a shot. We missed Larry, so when I saw him backstage at the Mabee Center I was startled and said, "Hey, I didn't think you were coming."

He replied, "Oh, you think I'm Larry. I'm Terry."

We talked in circles until Terry convinced me he was Larry's twin who had come to check out Keith. Larry had never mentioned he was a twin! After ORU, Terry was so touched he came to serve at Last Days Ministries with his brother, and we got a double blessing. They were both graphic artists who did a great job keeping the *Last Days Newsletter* looking amazing.

Several people were leaving to get training at Agape Force, including Jerry Bryant and his son, Andy, along .with his radiant new fiancée, Cindy, with her daughter, Kelly. Keith was elated they were engaged. We met Jerry when he sponsored a concert in Carbondale, Illinois. He told us his wife had run off with his best friend, and he was raising his little boy, who looked just like him, all by himself. Keith told Jerry, "You gotta meet Cindy! The exact same thing happened to her, and she has a little girl who looks just like her." A short time later we intentionally took Cindy to Chicago with us on a ministry trip, and Jerry drove up so the four of us could share a meal.

When telling their story, Keith loved to say, "And the rest was history, folks!"

Finally, with everyone on their way somewhere, it was time to say good-bye to the house on Dolorosa Street, and the other houses too. In fact our old friend Jay Leon had gotten married and ended up buying Harvey House. Our little homes had all served us well as we stretched their walls with people, prayers, and lots of activity.

I stood in the empty living room of our little yellow house and looked around with a twinge in my heart. We'd be renting it out now. I thought of all Keith and I were leaving behind—our families, many close friends, and all we'd known as a couple. Yet we had new hope and vision for the future. We also had our children—Josiah, Dawn, and a new baby on the way—and there were all the beautiful people who wanted to come with us.

As I turned to walk out of our front door for the last time, I really wasn't sad after all. I felt ready for the future, whatever it might hold.

All twenty-five of us arrived in Texas fifteen hundred miles later and poured into the Ranch House on our new property. It was quite a change of style from California with its high-pitched wooden ceiling in the living room, new bright-red carpeting, and exposed rustic logs all through the house. The kitchen was huge, with a long counter that would make a perfect serving line for all of us—and speaking of all of us, it was going to be quite a squeeze after living in so many separate houses in California!

Fourteen single girls in three-high bunks and two with babies in cribs all shared the large master bedroom. Right next to them, Keith and I shared a bedroom with Josiah and his crib. The single guys lived upstairs at the other end of the house, while the other married couple and their kids shared the Fish Room, a tiny enclosed den with a huge built-in aquarium you could see through from the kitchen. They put a Velcro curtain on their side for some privacy. It was a cozy beginning, to say the least.

Along with everyone else, Keith and I faced some new and interesting challenges. With fourteen girls behind the main wall on one side of our bedroom, we certainly couldn't talk very loud. On the other side of another wall was some extremely loud bundling and mailing equipment that often ran all night. We shared the blue bathroom with the Fish Room family and whoever else needed it. It was across the hall from our bedroom, right off the main living room, which had become offices. In the morning, the trick was to slip into the bathroom without being stopped by someone in the office who had a question.

We put the printing press in the garage—the Multi 1250 we'd purchased to handle the ever-growing newsletter—along with the collating machine Wayne invented out of an eggbeater motor and some nylon line.

Ranch living was also light-years away from living in the suburbs. As city folks we had a lot to learn. We quickly found that the neighbors didn't take kindly to people who don't tend their land, and mowing 140 acres was no small chore!

We swiftly acquired some ranch machinery—tractors, a brush hog, and a few funky old trucks. Still a city boy at heart, Keith bought one tractor with an enclosed glass shell, which allowed for air-conditioning and a stereo! So we were off and running. The land was planted in hay, and Keith loved to get out there and help cut and bale. There was always work to be done—keeping the fences mended and fields fertilized.

Our long-standing dream of living off the land seemed to be on the verge of finally coming true. But throughout the months, lots of crazy things happened to show us just how inept we were at trying to become Texas ranchers. For instance, the first time we burnt our fields, which is what farmers do in Texas, we nearly had a runaway fire!

Then Keith went to a local auction and bought thirty-five head of cattle, and in a short time we had more than one hundred head. We were going to raise our own meatloaf! One day a few of our guys tried to perform what they thought was a simple gender-specific surgery on one of the bulls. The poor bull died from shock. We didn't want this perfectly good bull to go to waste, but no one would come out to butcher it because it's illegal for a butcher to cut up an animal that dies before he gets there. We decided to do it ourselves.

The bull was hoisted upside down by a tractor, and soon the guys started carrying huge chunks of fresh meat into the house. It was quite a scene! We had chunks of beef in all the sinks and in our blue bathtub, washing it and getting it ready to freeze.

But there was one other complication. Just before the bull died, he'd been given a shot of penicillin, which some people were allergic to. So we labeled the penicillin leg in a special way. For months, if we ate beef, we'd have two kinds! As you walked through the food line you'd see a little hand-lettered sign that said "Penicillin Meat" for those who needed to avoid it. We especially loved to share the history of this event with any dinner guests.

Then there was the Great Chicken Massacre. Keith bought a

bunch of chickens so we could have fresh eggs. Everything was fine, until they got bad throat infections and couldn't swallow. We had two choices: kill them or let them starve to death. Keith decided to make the slaughter a ministry event, sort of a cross-cultural experience for all of us city folks.

Keith gathered us in the kitchen to make the announcement: "Death is a reality on a ranch. If we want fried chicken, a chicken has to die. We've only seen the sanitized, supermarket version covered in plastic wrap with a price sticker on its belly. Someone else did the dirty work. If you're willing to eat a chicken, you should be willing to kill one!"

All I can say is I was glad I had to go see my baby doctor the morning of the slaughter! But I saw the pictures and heard the stories, and it went down in LDM history as the day the feathers flew!

We also did some crazy things just for fun, since entertainment was limited out in the country. We bought a few riding horses, and one day Keith decided it would be interesting to bring one of them into the kitchen just to see what would happen. We found out real quick. We walked the horse through the sliding patio door and decided to memorialize the moment with a photo. The flash unsettled her and, well, she had a rather large accident on the carpet. Everyone laughed themselves silly, even though we had a big mess to clean up afterward.

Then there was the first tarantula Keith found—it was huge and hairy. Keith put it in a jar and wondered what to do with it. It wasn't poisonous, but it was big enough to seriously bite the kids and needed to be destroyed. Keith decided to put the jar into the microwave. Everyone in the kitchen immediately took sides. The that-would-be-a-horrible-yucky-thing-to-do side consisted mostly of us girls. But the boys won out, and Keith did the honors. Luckily the jar had a lid on it. (And yes, it was a horrible, yucky thing to do.)

Keith always kept his sense of humor. One day he shaved off half his beard. Then he spent hours entering rooms and the barn beard-side first. Then he'd turn around and shock everyone!

Once someone took a video camera into the barn all night to try to tape a calf being born. But mom refused to go into labor with the bright lights and gathering crowd. After having a baby myself, and feeling very big with this second pregnancy, I didn't blame her. I went home to bed! But getting a good night's sleep at the Ranch House was getting increasingly difficult, especially in the girls' dorm.

The grace was starting to lift for having two babies between eighteen and twenty-four months old in the dorm. One always woke the other one, who woke up everyone. It was also difficult for the moms who didn't have enough space to make a little home for their children. Keith decided to rent a house in Van, the small town a few miles away, for one of the moms. Dinah was pretty extroverted and seemed to do better in cramped quarters, so Keith planned to let Barbara have the rental.

Barbara came to LDM just before we moved to Texas. Her son was about the same age as ours and, amazingly, his name was Josiah too. We'd always laugh when our "Josiahs" were out of sight because when we asked if anyone had seen Josiah, the next question was always, "Which one?" The same question arose when anyone mentioned anything Josiah said or Josiah did. So Barbara and I got an idea to cut down on the confusion.

Barbara was a beautiful black girl with dark ebony skin. Her Josiah was a milk-chocolate color because his dad was white. My Josiah was blond and very fair. We took an upbeat approach and told everyone at the ranch that when they needed to clarify, they could say "Chocolate Josiah" or "Vanilla Josiah." We thought it was cute, and no one was offended. All the offense was saved for the owner of the rental when he saw Barbara.

On moving day Keith got an abrupt phone call from the owner who said, "You didn't tell me you were putting a black girl in my house. We don't let blacks live on the main road in town. Off on a side road is okay, but not on the main road."

Keith said, "I'm coming over right now." In a flash he peeled out of our driveway.

He was gone for more than an hour. As soon as he got back, I ran up to him and asked, "What happened?"

"Well, I let him know we were living in the real world now, and there were actual laws about housing discrimination. This guy huffed and puffed and got all red in the face arguing with me. He kept saying it had never been done."

"Well, go on, what happened?"

"I just told him, in no uncertain terms, that it was illegal to deny Barbara housing because she was black—and that I was a Christian minister and I'd have no problem taking him to court and putting Texas housing laws to the test if he didn't let Barbara move in!"

Then a big grin spread over Keith's face as he said, "Barbara will be the first black person to live on the main highway. She'll finish moving in tomorrow!" I was so proud of Keith I could have screamed. In fact, I think I did.

We were certainly learning a lot living out in the country. One thing was for sure, we were enjoying having a lot of land and animals to play with, but we knew Jesus had brought us here for greater purposes. One purpose, we'd thought, was to open another home to help people needing rehabilitation, and we intended to do that right away. But after praying, we just didn't have a sense of peace about it. In fact, God seemed to tell us specifically to go into a holding pattern, like an airplane circling a runway without landing.

That left us with a big question mark. Working in rehabilitation was our main reason for wanting to get out of the city. Now what were we supposed to do with all this land, besides farm it?

Since we weren't doing rehabilitation anymore, a lot of the rules we'd needed for people coming to us right off the streets were no longer necessary. Right after the revival in California, we got rid of things like demerits and buddies. But relaxing things was a continual process as we grew in understanding. In California, many people who decided to leave ended up back on the streets, taking drugs or just forsaking the Lord, so Keith's first instinct was to try to talk people into staying. In Texas, he came to a point where he told me, "The next time somebody wants to leave, I'm just gonna help them pack their bags. I won't even give my opinion unless they ask for it!"

Even if the ranch was a question mark, God's other purposes in bringing us to Texas quickly became clear. The fellowship with other Christians who had the same type of broad vision and drive was an enormous blessing to Keith, especially his friendship with Winkie Pratney. Keith was especially glad for Winkie's advice on an area that plagued Keith—his lack of self-discipline.

Once, when they went to New Zealand together for a few weeks on a ministry trip, Keith shared his concerns. "I just can't get my act together. I feel so lazy sometimes. If I really loved God, I'd have more discipline, right?"

Winkie, who by now had a chance to observe Keith up close, just smiled. He then gave Keith some serious advice. "There's nothing wrong with your spiritual life. But your physical laziness is bringing you down."

He pointed out that Keith had developed a Bohemian night-person lifestyle—up too late, in bed too long, not eating right, rarely making a bed or washing a dish.

"I can see how the enemy can attach a lot of lies to those areas of weakness, but your bad habits don't prove you don't love the Lord," Winkie encouraged him. "They're an open door for you to feel condemned—that's why you need to work at changing them."

When Winkie gave Keith his first instructions—to get up at a reasonable hour like 9:00 AM and to make his bed—Keith flinched. "That's what maids are for," he protested. After all, they were staying in hotels at the time of this decision.

But Keith did it, and every morning Keith called Winkie in to inspect his room to keep himself accountable.

At Winkie's advice, Keith also tried to eat a more balanced diet and pick up after himself. These were simple things. But as Winkie told him, "The grind of the road can be destructive to your spiritual life, Keith. It's important to be disciplined—and it's got to start with the basic areas, or else you burn out or you'll shallow-out."

All this went against Keith's natural grain. Keith didn't even like to practice the piano! Sometimes at the opening of a concert, he'd sit at the piano and let his fingers run all over the keys. People would clap, thinking, I guess, that the Spirit was moving him, but he was just loosening up his fingers! When it came to discipline, Keith was always trying to hit the ultimate high note, but he'd miss the mark, of course, and crash. Winkie's advice to take faith-sized bites struck a chord, and Keith was willing to do whatever it took. He wrote:

> I used to think discipline and self-control was a natural by-product of a supernatural holiness and revival. But now I see that lack of self-discipline is keeping my holiness (which I already have in Jesus) from controlling my life and coming to the surface. This is a brand-new view, and I believe I've isolated the enemy's greatest stronghold in my life at this time. . . . Discipline is not holiness, nor the way to holiness. It just helps you maintain it.

Keith and I were also continuing to write new songs and felt another album coming together. Besides the songs "So You Wanna Go Back to Egypt" and "I Pledge My Head to Heaven," there were songs like "Lies," "Unless the Lord Builds the House," and "I Want to Be More Like Jesus," which we wrote with Kelly Willard. It was time to go back into the studio.

Keith already knew that we were supposed to do something very different with this third album. But what? He had already decided not to charge anything for his concerts because that was ministry, but his recordings were being sold in bookstores all across the nation. Were they "products" or "ministry"? Keith could see where his recordings might be a bit of both, but his reason for doing them was definitely ministry. Keith wondered if it was right for some people—mainly the poor—to be excluded because they couldn't afford to "buy" his ministry.

Actually, one big decision about this album had been made just before the move to Texas. Keith was going to be producing and distributing it totally on his own. It all came about in very unusual circumstances. Keith had come across some pretty strong Scriptures that seemed to confirm what he was already feeling in his heart. He wrote the gist of them in his journal:

> *"Israel's priests instruct for a price, and her prophets divine for money: yet they lean on the Lord, saying, 'Is not the Lord in our midst?'" Micah 3:11[NASB]*
>
> *"For from the least . . . to the greatest of them, everyone is greedy for gain." Jeremiah 6:13 [NASB]*

On top of those Scriptures, Keith came across another one—Isaiah 55:1 (NASB)—that really blew his mind. He excitedly read it to me. "'Ho! Every one who thirsts, come to the waters; and you who have no money, come, buy and eat. Come, buy wine and milk without money and without cost.' Isn't that heavy?"

"Yes, but what do you want to do?"

"I'm not totally sure yet, but I think the Lord is gonna tell me soon," Keith said thoughtfully.

Keith got his answer in Atlanta when he went there to play at a music festival. Some good friends were there too. Jamie Owens-Collins was also doing a concert, and her husband, Dan Collins, was with her. Sparrow Records had just hired Dan as their A&R guy (Artist and Repertoire Director) as well as being their in-house producer.

Dan and Jamie were surprised when Keith phoned their room early in the morning asking them to come talk. When they got to his room, Keith said, "I've been praying all morning and I just got my answer from God. I'm not supposed to charge for my music! What do you think?"

The three of them had a hearty discussion-debate. Dan and Jamie understood Keith's heart and knew his motives were good, but they also had a few cautions to share. In the end they could tell Keith was certain he'd heard from the Lord. Since Keith was playing that night, Dan offered one last piece of advice before they went back to their room.

"You know, Keith, this might be the Lord speaking just to you. Telling you how to do *your* ministry. It might not apply to every Christian artist," Dan stated simply.

"Maybe you're right," Keith replied.

"So it might be best if you didn't talk about your decision tonight during your concert. Let it brew in your spirit for a while," offered Dan.

"Yeah. I should probably just wait."

Waiting was not easy for Keith. Especially if he had something fresh burning in his heart. That night he was a few songs into his ministry time when he spilled the beans about his decision not to charge. He also shared a lot of his reasons why and spoke with all the passion and conviction he felt in his heart.

When Keith got home, he was so relieved to have finally received an answer to this all-consuming question.

"I really want to give the gift God gave me in music freely as Jesus has commanded, 'Freely you have received, now freely give.' "

Keith had been ordained by the Vineyard and, as an ordained minister of the gospel, he believed that his music was just a tool to present the ministry.

Then one day Keith came to me, looking as white as a sheet.

"Mel, I've been praying, and I believe God just told me I blew it! He was wanting me to start my own company so I could give my records away and I shouldn't have re-signed with Sparrow."

"Are you serious?" I asked. "What are we going to do?"

Keith had just signed a new contract with Sparrow. He had done it mostly as a reaction to being chased by other companies. One record company was offering to set up a fund with one hundred thousand dollars in it for each album Keith would do for them. The cost of making each album would come out of that fund, and whatever was left over from the one hundred thousand dollars per album, he could take as a personal bonus. That meant if Keith could produce an album for, say, forty thousand dollars, he could put sixty thousand dollars in his pocket—each time he did a second, third, fourth, or fifth album! On top of that, Keith would get a hefty cash bonus just for signing. This was an incredible offer and major temptation for him because we needed money for the vision and goals of Last Days.

Another company was also pursuing Keith and, of course, Sparrow wanted him to stay. Keith had seen all this as a temptation, and he reacted. He signed with Sparrow again for a ten-thousand-dollar bonus. He figured it must be God because it wasn't as good of a deal.

That's when Bill Maxwell told Keith that one record company had even offered him thousands in cash under the table if he could persuade Keith to sign with them. Bill told them he didn't want any part of something like that, but that he'd be glad to set up an appointment for the company to talk with Keith for free.

But following his convictions, Keith was really in a bind. He was legally and spiritually bound to fulfill the contract he signed with Sparrow. He'd been beside himself wondering how he could stay faithful to what God was asking him to do. Finally he phoned Billy Ray and asked if we could go over to see him.

Billy Ray lived in a large house in Northridge, and he answered the door. With his sandy hair and freckles, he looked boyish. As we walked into his living room, he looked very relaxed, but we were nervous. Keith had a sense that his destiny was somehow going to be affected by this man's response. It would be crazy for Billy Ray to release his biggest artist from a legally signed contract. We had no way of knowing what would happen.

Billy Ray and his wife both had the gift of Southern hospitality, and invited us to take a seat on the huge semicircular couch in their spacious living room. I stared at the Chinese screens and shifted anxiously. Keith had come, not entirely sure what he would say. After a few moments of small talk, he launched in. "I guess you're wondering why I wanted to see you tonight."

"I hope everything is okay. What's on your mind?"

Keith was never one to beat around the bush. "I need to ask you to let me out of my contract."

Billy Ray just looked at Keith silently.

I focused on a small water lily down at the corner of one of the Chinese screens. Keith went on to share his heart with Billy Ray.

"I blew it. God just told me to start my own label and give my records away. I'm really sorry. I don't know what to do. I know I signed a contract and I'll honor it if I need to, but I'm asking you to release me from it. I'm not going to another company. I'm starting my own. I won't even be selling my records in the bookstores."

This definitely broke the ice. They talked back and forth for a few minutes, and, finally, Billy Ray said, "If God doesn't want you at Sparrow and I try to keep you, then I'd be fighting against God. That means God will be standing against me and the whole company."

We waited to see what more he'd say.

"Keith, if you want to be released from your contract, I won't hold you to it. I'll let you go."

Keith was totally relieved. So was I. This couldn't have turned out better. Keith was very encouraged by Billy Ray's immediate willingness to release him.

Now Keith was ready to record his third album and do whatever the Lord had in mind for it. As the February 1980 due date approached for our second child, so did the date Keith and I were scheduled to go to Los Angeles and work with Bill Maxwell. We decided it would be easier, and much less expensive, for us to go to California to record than to fly Bill and all the musicians out to Texas. I'd had an early labor scare that took me to the hospital for an afternoon, so Keith immediately flew me to California a bit ahead of him. He wanted to be sure I'd be there to have our baby and not get stuck in a hospital in Texas without him.

Keith left the ministry in the capable hands of Wayne and some of our upcoming leaders while we were gone and, a short time later, flew in Michelle for some much-needed administrative assistance.

As it turned out, I went into labor nine days early. My doctor thought I might need some blood, and I was moved to tears when Michelle walked into my hospital room and told me she had just given blood in my name—just in case.

February 7, 1980 6:45 A.M. Recording in L.A.

Bethany Grace. My new daughter is keeping me awake.

*She was born at 10:19 A.M. on February 5, two days ago,
to God's glory*

Our second child arrived to very happy parents, who were right in the middle of making an album! Bethany Grace—a little girl just as the Lord promised me in Honolulu! Her middle name symbolized some of the precious lessons the Lord had taught us during that time because now I knew for sure he really had spoken to me. I took it as a very special sign of his love for me.

My delivery was much easier than with Josiah. I left the hospital within a few hours, and that night Keith and I even went out to dinner. We went to Nappy's, still his favorite burger place, where he proudly told our waitress, "My wife had our baby girl today!" Amazingly, within days I felt good enough to go back in the studio—with Bethany Grace snuggled in my arms.

By this time, we'd decided to call the album *So You Wanna Go Back to Egypt*. We were really excited about being able to give this album away, but it was an enormous step of faith. Keith and I talked about the money it was going to cost.

"Do we have enough to even produce this album?" I asked.

"We may have to mortgage our house back in Woodland Hills to press about twenty-five thousand albums. If we give them all away and run out of money, we'll just consider the album a limited edition. At least I'll know I've obeyed the Lord."

Even with the prospect of having to mortgage our house, we were still excited about the album. Nobody was going to be left out because of a lack of funds, and the messages of the songs were fresh and powerful to us. As Keith said, "I think I can sum up the theme of the whole album in one word—*grace!*"

"Grace?" I prodded him. "I can see that in some of the songs, but others are very convicting."

"Yeah, but look how patient God is. He doesn't give up on us, even when we grumble and complain, or give up on ourselves!"

Keith said he knew some people might think the album seemed a bit sad at times but that it was completely honest.

One night at the studio I was sitting in a beanbag chair, cuddling Bethany Grace during what seemed like a fairly typical evening. Then Bob Dylan showed up to play harmonica on "I Pledge My Head to Heaven." It was, all at once, totally incredible! We'd spent some time getting to know Bob on various occasions before moving to Texas.

We'd first met Bob through an elder at the Vineyard sometime after our revival time in California. Apparently Bob's girlfriend had gone to a Vineyard service, where she gave her heart to Jesus. After receiving some basic Christian counseling that she shouldn't be living with her boyfriend, she decided to move out. The elder at the Vineyard had no idea that the boyfriend was Bob Dylan—that is until Bob called to set up an appointment and talk about why his girlfriend was encouraged to move out. In the process of conversation with the elder from the Vineyard, Bob, who was Jewish, heard all about Jesus.

Somewhere along the way, he also got turned on to Keith's music and loved the rawness, which is why he wanted to meet Keith. By the time we actually met, Bob had already been studying the Bible and learning about Jesus. We had invited him over for dinner, and I cooked him hamburgers at our house. The unrealness of it far surpassed cooking for Teddy Neely of *Jesus Christ Superstar*. Bob Dylan was one of the most famous people in the world, and here we were just having a casual meal together on the secondhand fold-out table in our living room!

The most memorable time we spent with Bob was at his apartment and office near Santa Monica. It was during the time he was writing the songs for his album *Slow Train Coming*, and Bob pulled out some lyric sheets for us to read. He wanted to know what we thought and we told him—the lyrics were great.

Then Keith and I exchanged glances, both thinking, *Can you believe one of the world's greatest songwriters is asking our opinion?* Maybe it was his vulnerability that bonded our hearts to his in a special way.

At any rate, Bob seemed to want to know what Keith thought in other areas besides music. Although he was one of the most well-known musicians in the world, he was also the same as anyone who wanted to know more about God—full of eager questions and fresh excitement about his spiritual discoveries. He told us that he loved to pick up hitchhikers and tell them about Jesus. They never recognized him because he drove a beat-up old car and wore a knit ski hat over his famous curls. He also told us that he didn't like to get out of bed before reading ten chapters of the Bible. We were impressed!

Keith really loved Bob, and they talked a lot. Once, however, Keith felt he went too far in trying to make a point. Later, in his journal, Keith wrote with deep regret: "Tried to be the Holy Spirit to Bob Dylan today. . . ." But there seemed to be something very special taking place between them. Keith had the greatest admiration for Bob and once said to me, "He's a prophet waiting to get saved."

One night we took Bob over to Buck and Annie's house along with Bill Maxwell. We listened to Second Chapter's latest album as well as some rough mixes from Bob's latest album, *Saved*. Bob fell in love with Second Chapter's music and asked them to open for him on his upcoming tour. They prayed, but didn't feel a release to do it. We were a bit surprised. Had Bob asked us, we would have gone with him in a heartbeat just to hang out this man who had written the musical soundtrack for our generation. Besides, like us, Bob was Jewish, and we could have talked a lot about his new relationship with God.

One of the main things Keith counseled Bob to do was to try and get some time off the road so he could rest, study, and grow in the Lord. Bob did attend a Bible school at the Vineyard for a while, but it seemed impossible for him to get away from all the ongoing demands on his life. Nevertheless, Bob had kept in contact with Keith after we moved to Texas, and when Keith asked him to play on this album, we were thrilled that Bob said yes.

This night in the studio, Bob got ready to play the harmonica and he talked with Bill for a few minutes. He told Bill that *For Him Who Has Ears to Hear* was one of his favorite albums of all time! Bob was hoping Bill would use a similar production style for Keith on this album. As they set up the microphones and Bob began to play along to the track, I closed my eyes and held Bethany Grace close to my heart. It seemed like a dream as I listened to the familiar sound of this world-famous harmonica playing on a song about the possibility of my husband, my son, and even me, losing our lives for the sake of the gospel.

With Keith there was never a dull moment. We worked in five studios while recording the album, and one was in the guesthouse of a well-known recording artist. One day no one was there to let us in. After standing around with Bill Maxwell and several singers (for background vocals), including Kelly Willard and Matt Ward, Keith decided to break a small window in the door so we could get inside.

We all tried to talk him out of it, but Keith figured it was cheaper to replace the window than pay everyone for standing around. It all went fine until someone who didn't know us drove up and saw the broken glass. Keith had some quick explaining to do, and of course he later replaced the window as planned.

It did seem, as Keith said, that all the songs tied in to the theme of grace in one way or another, especially grace when we are not doing as well as we would like in our walk with the Lord.

Keith wrote "You Love the World (and You're Avoiding Me)" while we were in California working on the album. He told me, "This may sound like the happiest song on the whole album, but it's really the saddest, for me. I wrote it as if the Lord was talking to me!" It was all too easy for Keith to plop in front of the tube sometimes and get caught up in the program schedule. It's not that Keith was against TV or movies, but when those things got in the way of his relationship with the Lord, he knew it was no good. So he wrote:

> I want you here with me
> But you've been keeping other company.
> You can't sit still!
> It's plain to see, you love the world
> And you're avoiding me.

My word sits there upon your desk,
But you love your books and magazines the best.
You prefer the light of your TV
You love the world
And you're avoiding me!

You used to pray. You were so brave.
Now you can't keep even one
Appointment we've made.
Oh I gave my blood, to save your life.
Tell me, tell me is it right?
Will you leave me here
Alone again tonight?

Another song, "Unless the Lord Builds the House," was all about being busy in ministry, which has its own special temptations like doing things that seem spiritual but really aren't. Someone had written to Keith and told him, "Don't get so caught up in the work of the Lord that you forget the Lord of the work!" So Keith wrote this song:

Unless the Lord builds the house,
They labor in vain who try at all,
Building anything not according to his call.
Unless the Lord wants it done,
You better not work another day,
Building anything that'll stand in his way.

You love the Lord
And it seems like he's been leading,
You've asked him to bless all your plans
But are you so sure
You're not just doing what you want to,
Building your house on the sand . . .

Working so hard at the things that you believe in,
No one can tear you away.
But don't you lose sight
Of the very one who calls you,
You may be sorry some day . . .
Some day.

For wood, hay and stubble,
Will all burn up in the fire.
But to love the Lord with all your heart,
Should be your one desire.

Keith started writing "O Lord, You're Beautiful" while we were on the road one time, but he didn't finish until a long time later at our old house on Dolorosa Street. I woke up to the sound of Keith softly playing the piano, which was then in our bedroom. I didn't know how long he'd been playing, but the presence of the Lord was strong as I lay there listening to the beautiful melody. Keith was weeping, and he told me, "The Lord brought me right into the throne room, and I sang to him and just worshiped." He hoped others would be drawn into worship when they heard this song.

Oh Lord, you're beautiful.
Your face is all I seek.
For when your eyes are on this child,
Your grace abounds to me.

I wanna take your word
And shine it all around.
But first help me just to live it, Lord!
And when I'm doing well,
Help me to never seek a crown,
For my reward is giving glory to you.

Oh Lord, please light the fire,
That once burned bright and clear.
Replace the lamp of my first love
That burns with holy fear!

Keith loved to write with other people. Just before we moved to Texas, Kelly Willard and her husband, Dan, came to visit us. Besides the great time we had just hanging out together, Kelly had a little tune she played for Keith to see if he could add anything to it. It was beautiful! They worked on it a bit that night, and later Keith and I finished the lyrics to "I Want to Be More Like Jesus."

Kelly sang with Keith on the background vocals for the album, and when it came to this song, she came up with some really beautiful "answer back" parts that seemed to give the song the perfect touch it needed.

As each day passes by,
I feel my love run dry.
I get so weary worn and tossed 'round in the storm.
I'm blind to others' needs
And I'm tired of planting seeds.
I seem to have a wealth
Of so many thoughts about myself.

I want to, I need to
Be more like Jesus.
I want to, I need to
Be more like him.

Our Father's will was done,
By giving us his son
Who paid the highest cost,
To point us to the cross.

And when I think of him
Taking on the whole world's sin,
I take one look at me,
Compared to what I'm called to be.

Remember, there's no greater love
Than to lay down your life for a friend.

The end of all my prayers,
Is to care like my Lord cares.
My one and only goal
His image in my soul.

Yes my weakness is revealed,
But by his stripes I'm healed!
He's faithful and he's true,
To complete the work he begins in you!

The first time I heard "Grace by Which I Stand," the hair stood up on my arms. I knew it was a song I needed to hear. I also knew that Keith wrote it to himself because he needed to hear it too. God had done powerful things in our lives in Hawaii, but the message of grace was still being transferred from our heads to our hearts.

When Keith first wrote this song, he was almost embarrassed. He knew most people thought he almost entirely ignored the subject of grace in his preaching and ministry. But for the liner notes Keith wrote, "The whole last year has been one endless lesson on the holy grace of God, and I praise him for the opportunity to share it with you!" In this song Keith points out that, apart from God, our own efforts for holiness are absolutely futile. As Keith sang this song in the studio, there was a hush as he poured out his emotions in a very personal and abandoned way.

Lord, the feelings are not the same,
I guess I'm older—I guess I've changed,
And how I wish it had been explained
That as you're growing, you must remember . . .
That nothing lasts—except the grace of God
By which I stand in Jesus!
I know that I would surely fall away,
Except for grace by which I'm saved.
Lord, I remember that special way
I vowed to serve you
When it was brand-new.
But like Peter I can't even watch and pray
One hour with you, and I bet
I could deny you, too!
Well nothing lasts—except the grace of God
By which I stand in Jesus!
I know that I would surely fall away
Except for grace by which I'm saved . . .

After about two months in California, the album was finally finished. We were all ready to go back to Texas. Francine and Dawn, who were also with us, had changed about a million diapers, and I was looking forward to getting back home and adding Bethany's bassinet to our little bedroom with Josiah in the Ranch House. On the airplane back, Keith summarized our trip in his own way: "I feel like we both just gave birth. You had a baby and I had an album!"

"Hey, I've got an idea," I said with a laugh. "Next time you can have the baby and I'll make the album!"

Keith gave me a silly you-know-I'd-never-survive-childbirth look, and we settled in for the flight home. We were excited to get back and show off our new little brown-eyed, dark-haired baby girl—and play everybody a tape of the new album.

By May 1980, the Egypt album had been mastered and pressed,

and we were out on the road doing our first concerts with our new price policy. We wondered if, after all our efforts, it was really going to work.

At one of the first concerts we did, Keith had us keep the record tables covered with drop cloths as usual until the end of evening's ministry. This in itself was a very nontraditional approach as far as Christian concerts went, since album sales really helped cover the night's expenses. But Keith refused to sacrifice the tone of the evening's ministry just so he could make more money in sales. He went into each city with a burden to minister to the people there. He didn't want to provide a diversion in back by giving them an excuse to go and shop while his ministry was going on.

I was out in the hallway of a large arena, stacking albums and tapes as high as I could on the table. The only thing separating me from the throngs of people inside were a few sets of swinging doors. After the altar call and the last worship song, I could hear Keith starting to make our new price policy announcement from the stage.

"My records are in the back. We don't feel good about selling them or setting a price. You can give whatever you want for them, even nothing, if you don't have any money."

Suddenly I heard the pounding of feet as people started piling out of the bleachers. Then the swinging doors burst open, and masses of people charged toward me at the record tables.

"How much are these?"

"Wow, are they really free?"

I tried to respond as best I could to the many questions coming from a wall of unfamiliar faces.

"They're offered for whatever you can afford to give. You can take one for free if you don't have any money—"

While I was answering one person, who was clearly wondering what to do, others just started grabbing albums. Some were handing me money, others weren't—and to my total amazement, some people were scooping up armloads of albums and taking off with them at a run. It was loud and crazy, and I couldn't answer everyone at once. A sea of faces surrounded me—people reaching over and around each other to get to the records.

As the crowd pressed in, the record table kept inching its way backward. Every few minutes I would push it forward with all of my strength, but I was continually losing ground because of the press of bodies against it. I was slowly being backed up against the wall behind me until the inevitable happened.

I was literally pinned between the wall and the record table, wondering when Keith was going to show up and rescue me—and whether we were going to lose our shirts on our new way of distributing this record.

Last Days staff on our way to Texas

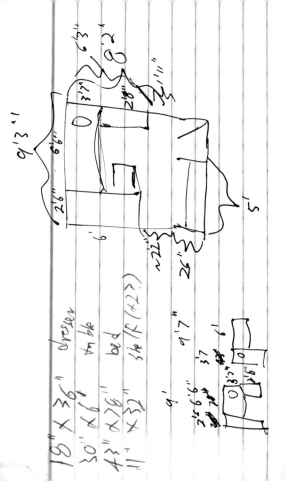

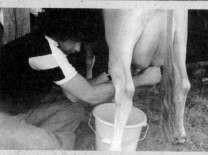

Clockwise from top left: Texas baptism; Recording session. We broke the window to get into this studio. Left to right: Keith, Jay Leon, Kelly Willard, Kathy Emond, and Matthew Ward; Keith shaves; Melody (pregnant with Bethany), Grandma Helen and Josiah; Milking duty

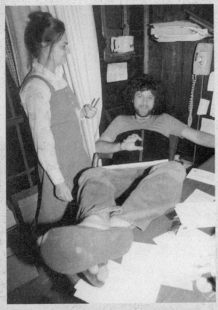

Top left: Keith and Carol Hoehn in the ranch house office

Top right: Ranch house living room/office

Above: Keith with Josiah and Bethany on his lap enjoying a tour bus trip

Left: Melody pregnant with Rebecca, holding Bethany with Josiah and Helen

15

"UNLESS THE LORD BUILDS THE HOUSE"

After our first few concerts, when the record tables were wiped clean and I was nearly trampled in the rush, Keith knew he needed to define his price policy a little more clearly. From the beginning, he knew there would be some people who would take advantage, but he still wanted to minister to people who honestly couldn't afford to buy his records. Even though some of the responses were discouraging, Keith didn't want to give up on this idea.

Eventually, at the end of his concerts Keith would make his announcements a little more specific. "Those who don't have anything can get an album for nothing, and those who have little can get it for little. We believe the gospel's been getting a little too commercial, so we wanted to uncommercialize our part of it. We just ask that you don't take more than one free album per household."

Keith was also offering the Egypt album through the *Last Days Newsletter* for whatever anyone could afford—and he was letting bookstores help distribute it in their stores without actually selling it. If a store wanted to help distribute the album, we would send them a pad of order blanks with a place to stamp their store's name on them. Then, for every order we received with the store's stamp, we would send the store one dollar as a thank-you—even if the person ordering from us wanted the album for free.

Keith figured most people knew the going price of recordings in the bookstores and understood that making records was very expensive. What he actually set up was an honor system of payment, trusting that if someone could afford to buy one they would. When people did get his recording, they found an unusual statement printed on it. They were told it was okay to make copies to give (never sell) to their friends.

In an interview with *Contemporary Christian Music* magazine about this, Keith said, "My whole reason for giving the album away is that I love people! Of course I don't want to see fifty thousand people send in nothing. At the same time, I don't want people to feel that I'm doing this to get a donation, or that they have to send in a donation."

In the same interview, the magazine writer said with a skeptical edge, "If people are too poor to buy an album, they probably are too poor to own something to play it on." The question implied was, just how committed was Keith to helping people receive ministry?

Keith said in the interview that he would respond to a sincere request. "I wouldn't buy [them] a $2,000 stereo, but I think it would be a Christian thing for me, on an individual basis, to offer somebody something they could listen to ministry on."

That was just the beginning of misunderstandings over his new price policy. Keith was being viewed skeptically and as very unconventional. But he always was better at breaking the mold than he was at fitting into it, especially when it came to following traditions. So he just pressed on throughout the rest of 1980, doing what he felt the Lord was telling him to do and continually clarifying his position.

Keith also started taking some rather unconventional steps with his concerts that summer. A local church in a given area usually sponsored concerts, but Keith started running into some boundaries that concerned him. Sometimes he'd receive a phone call from the church he was about to go to, and he'd be questioned about where he stood on certain doctrinal issues. Quite often before a concert, Keith would be approached by someone in authority who would tell him things like, "We invited you in to sing, but we don't want you to preach," or "Don't give an altar call," or "Don't talk about the Holy Spirit or speaking in tongues or healing." Keith respected these wishes. Yet he found it difficult to limit what he felt God had sent him there to accomplish, and he struggled with these constraints.

Once when he was told not to give an altar call, he told me, "It feels so unproductive to pour out my heart to minister to people and then not give them any opportunity to respond to the Lord in some way."

Also, there were times during a concert that Keith would have a strong impression that Jesus was healing people. He told me, "It's like I can *see* the form of a body with an area that's highlighted, and I believe God wants to touch someone there." Sometimes he'd call out specific healings from the stage and even ask people to stand at the end and tell everyone what had happened if God had healed them.

One night really stands out to me. It was in Anaheim at Disneyland's "Night of Joy," where only Christian musicians played. During that outdoor concert, Keith boldly spoke out that he felt Jesus was healing someone's heart. Afterward we mingled in the crowd as usual, and a girl named Janie came up to us.

She was weeping as she said, "I'm twenty-three and I was born with a hole in my heart. Every breath I've taken my whole life has hurt me, but as soon as you called out that healing, I could instantly feel the pain in my heart disappear!"

We questioned her over and over again. Actually it was more like an inquisition. How did we know she wasn't just making up that story just to get some attention?

But Janie insisted, "I am telling you the truth! I have been in pain all my life, and it doesn't hurt anymore!"

"Are you sure?"

"Yes! I can breathe without pain now!"

"Show us," we insisted.

So she stood there taking several very deep breaths . . . in and out . . . in and out, then jumped up and down saying, "Praise God! There's no pain. No pain!" We rejoiced together for a few minutes, then gave her our phone number and told her to call us after her doctor confirmed what she was feeling. She went to the doctor and came up to some of our Bible studies with a praise report. We kept in contact with Janie for more than a year, and it seemed that Jesus had indeed healed the hole in her heart!

People getting healed like Janie didn't always happen. Not every healing Keith called out resulted in a testimony at the end. Why wasn't everyone healed? Keith began to wonder if the healings were really from God's holy touch. Maybe the source was metaphysical—coming from the dark side, like the healings he'd seen growing up in Christian Science. We'd never heard any practical teaching on healing. Kathryn Kuhlman was our only example, but she had such a mystical "other realm" feeling about her ministry. If anything, we were down to earth. Not wanting to take a chance he might be grieving God when healings took place, Keith made a hard decision.

Keith told me, "I know for sure God loves seeing people healed, and that he is totally able to heal. I just don't know if I am tapping into him, or if it's just my own hopeful imagination connecting with the dark side that I want nothing to do with anymore. I'm not going to call out healings in public again, Melody."

I said, "Are you sure Keith? It sure seems like it's the Lord touching people."

"I'm sure," Keith continued with a sigh of sadness. "I wish I knew if it was okay, but no one can give me a clear answer. So I'm not only quitting, but if I start to *see something* again, I'm going to ask God to totally take it away."

I felt sad, too, but knew it wasn't worth taking a chance on. We knew the healing of someone's hurting soul was really the greatest miracle of all. There were other pressing issues too. When Keith went into a city to minister at a church, he wanted to reach the church at large in that city. He wanted Christians from other churches in the city to come too, if they wanted. But people in one denomination would not always tell people in another about a concert at their church, and even if they did, it was not often that other church would pass the announcement on to their people anyway. In fact, there didn't seem to be much cooperation at all between the different bodies of believers. Then, even when different churches did come together for a concert, another problem arose. If Keith gave an altar call, people always gave their hearts to the Lord. The different churches wanted to know which church got the new believers? Which church would Keith direct them to attend?

This simple gospel of following Jesus was not so simple on the road. Keith believed Jesus would want everyone to come together, but we were discovering there were several different camps of believers, and they didn't seem to fellowship together much.

The way the congregations were separated by doctrinal issues was very difficult to deal with, since Keith might be in seven different churches in the same number of days. It was mind-boggling really. It wasn't just about fulfilling an itinerary of concerts. It was about having to face a whole nation full of Christians who emphasized different things in their teachings or worship—or both. Sometimes Keith didn't know which camp he was walking into—the faith camp, the evangelicals, or the charismatics, just to name a few. Keith believed every Christian should be full of faith and charismatically evangelistic—but it wasn't that simple. It could wear you out just trying to figure out where people were so that you didn't offend them. It felt like spiritual whiplash. Keith did try his best, but diplomacy did not always come easy for him.

All of these things started adding up—the limitations on what to say and do, the tone of the meetings, and the frustration of trying to get several denominations together at any one church. Keith was remembering his unhindered time of ministry at the Caravan Ballroom in Tulsa. We'd just rented a hall and invited the city. Keith began to get the idea to use what he called "neutral auditoriums," places every church in town could feel comfortable sending their people to.

Keith said, "We'll be able to reach the whole city at once and no one will feel they got their toes stepped on!"

From then on, whenever it seemed right, we paid our own way into cities. We'd rent an arena and take an offering to cover our expenses. There was still one thing, however, that kept bothering Keith about his ministry—his growing celebrity status.

Most nights, after pouring out his heart, almost begging people to get right with God, there would be long lines of people waiting to meet Keith at the foot of the stage. He would stand there sometimes for hours to speak to each person in line. Some wanted counsel and prayer—or to tell Keith what the Lord had done in their heart that night. But it became evident that the majority just wanted to get close to him or just wanted to talk about sound equipment, how they could break into the music ministry, or how to get a record deal. Keith saw the same shine he used to have in his eyes—the hunger to be popular and be up in front of people.

For a long time Keith didn't talk to anyone after his concerts because he was so upset by the hero worship he saw in people's eyes. Not wanting to encourage anyone in idolatry or to allow someone to cause him to stumble, Keith simply slipped backstage. He was so concerned over this issue that a few years earlier he'd even written an article called "Music or Missions," about churches full of "star-struck" Christians and what that did to the Lord and the ministers themselves:

> Can't you see that you are hurting these ministers? They try desperately to tell you that they don't deserve to be praised, and because of this, you squeal with delight and praise them all the more.
>
> How come no one idolizes or praises the missionaries who give up everything and live in poverty, endangering their lives and their families with every danger that the American dream has almost completely eliminated? How come no one lifts up and exalts the ghetto and prison ministers and preachers? Because we are taught early on 1) that comfort is our goal and security and 2) that we should always seek for a lot of people to like us.

There had recently been a slaughter of some missionary nuns in Africa, and Keith made the comparison between the lives they had lived and the life the average music minister lives.

Who lives more comfortably and has more fans than the latest bright and shining gospel star? Who lived less comfortably and had fewer friends and supporters than the selfless missionaries who recently were raped, mutilated, and butchered to the glory of God in Africa?

Quit trying to make gods out of music ministers, and quit trying to become like those gods. The Lord commands you to "deny yourself, take up your cross daily, and follow Me." My piano is not my cross. It is my tool. I'd never play the thing again, if God would show me a more effective tool for proclaiming His totally demanding gospel.

In spite of all the adulation, Keith kept fighting to keep his eyes on eternity—holding up his life in the light of eternal priorities. Thinking ahead he knew what he wanted to hear on the day he arrived in heaven.

The only music ministers to whom the Lord will say, "Well done, thou good and faithful servant," are the ones whose lives prove what their lyrics are saying and the ones to whom music is the least important part of their life. Glorifying the only worthy One should be most important!

One big area Keith felt he needed to focus on was the Christian music industry itself. Now that he had made a break from the usual way of doing things he felt he could speak to those involved in every aspect of Christian music.

Sometime before this, Keith had gone to a meeting of the Fellowship of Contemporary Christian Ministries (FCCM), which consisted of artists, promoters, producers, and record company people. At one point Keith stood up and, with a broken heart, told everyone that they were making too many demands on each other and on the concertgoers—demands that were not holy and not blameless. Keith said they all looked too much like the world and not enough like Jesus—

himself included. He ended up on his knees before them all, weeping and saying, "From now on I will not come into any of your communities unless I come as a servant." He stayed on his knees pledging himself to be a servant to the body of Christ and openly repenting for wrong attitudes that he'd held. This triggered a very powerful move of God, with many openly weeping and repenting to the Lord and to each other. At the end everyone took communion together.

The next time Keith went to an FCCM meeting, it was with something different in mind—ticket sales. Keith felt that selling tickets to a night of ministry was equal to a pastor who would only come pray for the sick if you promised to pay him in advance. This FCCM meeting didn't end as sweetly as the last one.

Keith had been pressing Buck Herring pretty hard about the fact that Second Chapter of Acts was selling tickets to their concerts. Buck thought they had clear direction from the Lord to ask each person to pay three dollars to help with the expenses. Keith kept challenging him, and they debated this issue a lot. Buck ended up going back to God to ask him if there was a better way to do it. After a long process, Buck felt the Lord did show him another way.

Keith felt the Lord wanted him to encourage the FCCM and the whole Christian music industry to accept offerings instead of selling tickets. He thought Buck should tell everyone what the Lord had shown him too. So at the next FCCM meeting, Keith presented a clear challenge to everyone present and told them he felt it was wrong to sell tickets.

"The ticket prices for concerts are a nail in Jesus' hand. Unbelievers aren't going to pay to hear about Jesus because deep in their hearts they know they shouldn't have to. The gospel is free!"

Keith knew they could well ask, what's the difference between a Christian plumber charging for his services, and a singer or speaker charging for theirs? Didn't the apostle Paul charge for his tents?

Keith said, "There's a difference between a man's vocation or skill and his ministry gift. If I was just an entertainer, I'd have no problem charging for concerts—but ministry is different. In fact, Paul made tents for a living so he wouldn't have to charge for the gospel. After all, tents are tents and ministry is ministry!"

Then Keith quoted Paul out of First Corinthians 9:18 (NASB): "What then is my reward? That when I preach the gospel, I may offer the gospel without charge, so as not to make full use of my right in the gospel."

Buck stood up at that point and told how the Lord had led him. He said he'd finally made a list of all the reasons to sell tickets at a concert, and a list of all the reasons to do offerings. He told the group, which was pretty somber by now, "All the reasons to do ticketed concerts were logistical. There wasn't one spiritual reason there. But all the reasons to do offering concerts were spiritual. The Lord told me if we would take this step of faith, we'd be able to minister to people in the body in deeper ways because they'd trust us. They'd know ministry was our only motive for being there."

When Buck sat down, the atmosphere heated up immediately. There was quite a bit of open and rather animated discussion. Some people seemed receptive to Keith and Buck. Others were wondering who Keith thought he was to come and challenge them in such an absolute way. A few of the sponsors were worried too. Second Chapter and Keith were doing some of the largest Christian concerts in America at that time.

One sponsor said, "If the high-profile artists start doing concerts for free it will make everybody who sells tickets look bad."

The meeting ended with sharply divided positions. But Keith came away feeling that he'd poured out his heart, and that was all he could do.

Besides the selling of Christian music, Keith was also grieved by all the Christian merchandising. Everyday items like clocks, coasters, drinking mugs, and wallets were selling for twice their usual price just because some enterprising Christian—or non-Christian—stamped a fish or a dove on them. Not that everything with a fish or a dove on it was wrong, but Keith wondered how far it should go. We'd actually seen ads for Christian doggie sweaters and even Christian ashtrays!

One day we saw what we felt was the ultimate slap in the face of Jesus. Browsing in a large Christian bookstore, we came across a handmade ceramic piggy bank. Engraved on the side of this plump little pig were the words "Jesus Saves." We felt sick at heart.

It seemed that selling Christian products was very big business, not only in Christian bookstores, but at festivals as well. I was with Keith the day someone told us that at one Jesus festival they sold more than ninety-eight-thousand-dollars worth of "Jesus junk" in just a few days! Keith nearly fell over from hearing those two words casually linked together.

"Jesus and junk?" he said angrily. "Those must be the two most opposite words in the English language!"

On one hand, Keith saw Christian ashtrays, doggie sweaters, and piggy banks. On the other hand, he saw Jesus—like a pure, white rose—crushed beneath tons of garbage and debris that claimed to be promoting him and his sacrifice. Keith saw Jesus' heart cry sinking from view. He decided to write an article for the *Last Days Newsletter* called "The Selling of Jesus." He described his feelings when he saw that "Jesus Saves" piggy bank, and he quoted the book of Revelation:

> I could hear the echoes of those who "were slain for the word of God, and for the testimony which they held: and they cried with a loud voice, saying, 'How long, O Lord, holy and true, dost thou not judge and avenge our blood on them that dwell on the earth?'"
>
> How do you think the Lord feels, after giving His life for the sins of the world, to be reduced to something that helps sell merchandise? I'm certain He would make a whip and cleanse the Church of such garbage if He were on the earth today, but a more permanent remedy is planned. It's called Judgment Day.

It seemed that Keith had an unending and, for some, an unnerving jealousy for God to be honored. Maybe it was because of all the years he'd spent lost in a spiritual maze that he couldn't bear to see the truth taken for granted or compromised in any way.

As Keith kept studying the Bible, he continually examined every doctrine he came across against the Word of God. He was avidly reading many Christian books on a broad range of topics too, mostly issues that he felt needed to be addressed in the body of Christ. In Keith's zeal, both the Protestant Church and the Catholic Church got caught in his line of fire.

After reading a book about the Catholic Church, he came flying into the kitchen, particularly upset. "Mel, can you imagine this? Most Catholics are really devoted to Jesus, right? They build big churches with beautiful statues and everything. But this book claims some of them don't realize they can really know Jesus, or know for sure that they are going to heaven. Imagine, loving Jesus, but having no assurance of going to heaven."

As Keith read more books with similar themes, he began thinking he should write something about it. He prayed for a long time and got counsel from several Christian leaders. But the counsel was divided. Some felt the Lord was leading Keith to write something, but others counseled Keith not to write anything about Catholic doctrine. They said, "It's not the Lord. What you're reading in those books isn't totally accurate."

Keith was torn. In the end, he believed he was supposed to write something. He prefaced it with, "We know of many loving, committed, and sincere believers among their ranks." He even mentioned a priest in New England who had been corresponding with him regularly. Keith wrote, "If you're reading this now, I love you!"

So while Keith was concerned about the Catholic Church making God too mysterious, distant, and unknowable, he felt the Protestant church had almost the opposite problem. Many Protestants seemed to be too familiar with God—taking him for granted. If it seemed too hard for some Catholics to get saved, it seemed too easy for some Protestants. So Keith took on the Protestant church in a series he called "What's Wrong with the Gospel?"

From what we'd seen while traveling in born-again circles for six years now, many things were coming to a head in Keith's thinking.

Some of the writings of A. W. Tozer were having a strong influence on him, and at one of our Bible studies Keith picked up his book, *The Root of the Righteous*, and read:

> The cross of Roman times knew no compromise. It never made concessions. It won all its arguments by killing its opponent and silencing him for good. It spared not Christ, but slew Him the same as the rest. . . . With perfect knowledge of all this, Christ said, "If any man will come after Me, let him deny himself, take up his cross and follow Me." So the cross not only brought Christ's life to an end, it also ends the first life, the old life of every one of His true followers. . . . This and nothing less is true Christianity. We must do something about the cross, and there's only one of two things we can do—flee it or die upon it!

In his introduction to the two-part series "What's Wrong with the Gospel?" Keith said:

> What's wrong with the gospel? Absolutely nothing! That is, of course, if you're talking about the gospel of the Bible—the very message that Jesus preached.
>
> But what about the stuff that's being preached today? Is it truly gospel preaching?
>
> I believe with all my heart that Jesus would be ashamed of most of the "gospel" messages that are being preached today, mainly because they lack almost every major point he himself preached on. How dare we try to change the gospel! We remove most of its vital parts, and replace them with artificial limbs of our own. Isn't Jesus the master evangelist? Shouldn't we judge our evangelism by his example?

Keith's two-part article ran in the same issue of the *Last Days Newsletter*. The first section was called "The Missing Parts," or the parts that have been "surgically removed in most of today's preaching." The first thing Keith talked about was how Jesus shed his blood so we could have the power to be set free:

> It's a fact that the very word "blood" scares people. It's also a fact that the blood of Christ scares the devil, because it is the only cleansing agent for a sin-sick soul. What we have now is a bloodless gospel!
>
> Remove the blood from the preaching of the gospel, and you remove the power to conquer the devil for the souls of men!

Next Keith talked about removing the cross from the gospel:

> Paul said, "I determined to know nothing among you except Jesus Christ, and him crucified." Nowadays it's "Jesus Christ and what he can do for you!" You cannot have more exact opposites than the Bible's Christ-centered gospel and our modern, cross-less, self-centered "gospel." . . .
>
> Unless people are truly convicted of sin . . . then it is virtually impossible to show them a need for a savior. Why, what would they need to be saved from? Fun? Today the Lord is presented as a sort of "ice-cream man Santa Claus," and the church is the candy store where you can get every goodie your heart desires.

Keith summed up this first section by saying:

> First and foremost, today's "gospel" appeals to the selfish. If people come to Jesus mainly to get a blessing or only to get forgiveness, they will ultimately be disappointed. But if they come to give him their lives in honor and worship, then they will truly have forgiveness and joy—more than they could ever imagine!

In the second section, Keith talked about what he called "the added parts"—the dangers of the traditions of men. Keith listed some of the tools, methods, and concepts that have become so much a part of presenting the modern gospel that they have become almost inseparable from it. Sometimes these practices even distort the gospel—for instance the altar call and the easy assurance of salvation just because someone came forward. He especially examined the idea of the sinner's prayer:

> It is obvious that there is no set sinner's prayer. The words are not important. It's the state of heart of the one saying the prayer. I believe that a true sinner's prayer will gush out of anyone who truly is seeking God, and has been enslaved to sin.

Then Keith took a risky look at the term and concept of Jesus being our "personal Savior." He wrote:

> I find it very disturbing when something unnecessary is added to the gospel. The term "personal savior" isn't very harmful in itself, but it shows a kind of mind-set that is willing to invent terms, then allow these terms to be preached as if they were actually found in the Bible. Would you ever introduce your sister like this, "This is Sheila, my personal sister?" Ridiculous! Nevertheless people solemnly speak of Christ as their personal savior, as if when he returns he will not have two, but three titles written across his thigh: "King of kings! Lord of lords! Personal savior!"

One of the things that really bothered Keith was seeing bumper stickers with what he called "cheap clichés and 'Christian' slogans." He wrote:

> Many think it's wise to get the word out this way, but I believe we're really just inoculating the world with bits and pieces of truth . . . making it hard for people to catch the real thing!

He wanted to call attention to what some of these slogans were really projecting, so he explained:

"Please be patient, God isn't finished with me yet." This can really be a horrible replacement for "I'm sorry!"

It puts the blame on the wrong person. "The reason I'm such a creep is because God isn't finished with me yet!"

Then there is that other fabulous excuse that absolutely ends all quests or expectations for holiness: "Christians aren't perfect . . . just forgiven!" What we're saying by this fabulous piece of prose is, "You cannot trust your teenage daughter with my Christian son. You'd better keep your eye on him. He's not safe. He's just forgiven!"

In summary, Keith pleaded with Christians to examine what they were doing:

> Don't you see what fools we are! We preach a man-made, plastic "gospel." We get people to "come forward" to the altar by bringing psychological pressures that have nothing to do with God. We "lead them" in a prayer that they are not yet convinced they need to say. Then, to top it all off, we give them "counseling" . . . telling them it is a sin to doubt that they're saved!
>
> Beloved family, the world around us is going to hell. Not because of fanatical dictators, television, drugs, sex, alcohol, or the devil himself. It is because of the church! We are to blame! We alone have the commission, the power, and the truth of God at our constant disposal to deliver sinner after sinner from eternal death. Even though some are willing to go . . . they are taking a watered-down, distorted version of God's message, which God has not promised to anoint. That's why we are failing. And unless we admit that we are failing then I'm afraid there is no hope for us or the world around us. We have the choice between causing eternal tragedy for our whole generation, or bringing our beloved God a whole family full of good and faithful servants.

When Keith wrote these articles, it was with an overwhelming desire to see the church free of compromise and counterfeit conversions.

He knew he said some strong things, but he hoped the body of Christ would be all the stronger for it. Keith had no idea how strong a storm of controversy his writings would cause.

Meanwhile, back at the ranch, we were busier than ever. But no matter how busy Keith was, he never lost sight of the personal lives of those at LDM. Especially when it came to romantic relationships. We didn't think casual dating was a good idea in a small community, but Keith loved seeing people fall in love and get married. He was notorious for asking the singles who they were interested in, then playing Cupid. One night during a walk with Terry DeGraff he kept asking him who he liked. Terry was shy and stayed tight-lipped as long as possible, but he was no match for Keith who finally wrangled a name out of him. Later at about 1:00 AM, Keith slipped quietly into the girls' dorm. Carol's bunk was right by the door. Keith crept over and shook her arm, whispering excitedly, "Carol! Carol, wake up!" She roused groggily from a sound sleep to Keith's grinning face. "Carol, guess who likes you?"

One Cupid's arrow Keith shot off while we still lived in California resulted in the marriage of Kathleen Griffin and Wayne Dillard. They made an amazing couple. Wayne was a Southern boy full of wisdom and measured stability, while Kathleen was an adventurous California girl with a fiery prophetic edge. Keith had no doubt that their union would cause serious damage to the enemy. They got off to a head start with Leonard Ravenhill and Keith praying for them—right after Leonard did the ceremony and Keith led worship. We finished with a huge celebration in the Dillard's honor!

Things were growing at a steady pace, and we kept making room for more people and more ministry. The *Last Days Newsletter* was really taking off, and about forty people had come to serve the Lord with us. One department or another had seized every available space in the house, while Keith and I were still cramped into one bedroom with two children. Josiah had graduated to a little homemade floor bed without legs and his crib was inherited by Bethany. Having the kids in our room had its drawbacks, but it was also nice to have them close to us.

One of my biggest concerns was finding Josiah a safe place to play. Almost two years old now, he was curious and into everything. One day I noticed his little mouth working on something. When I got him to spit it out, my heart almost stopped. He'd been sucking on a push-pin that must have fallen off one of the office bulletin boards! I was afraid to think of what would have happened if he'd swallowed it.

Living in a fishbowl did have its challenges. You have to develop certain techniques within a marriage when you're surrounded with people all the time. When Keith and I had differing opinions, we learned to have soft disagreements, and we would flash each other those "let's go talk in the other room" looks without anyone else noticing.

The cramped quarters were especially taking a toll on me. Things always moved so fast. I'd often help Keith with ministry decisions, but sometimes it seemed like I was the last one to know anything. And I often felt lost in the shuffle. The most difficult times were when I needed to talk to Keith and he was so worn out from counseling or being in a long meeting that he just didn't have enough energy left to give me the time I wanted. Even when he had the best intentions, he could get stopped several times on his way to our room, just crossing from one side of the house to the other.

At those times I'd try to look at the privilege of being in ministry, not the price. And I would count my blessings, which were many. *Keith and I didn't have a normal life,* I'd tell myself, *but then neither one of us ever really wanted one.*

Still it seemed like the grace was starting to lift. We'd begun to feel like we needed our own place. There wasn't much housing available out in the country without building it. There was, however, one small white house directly across the road from our ranch. We'd had our eye on it for some time, but it wasn't for sale. Then one day as we were headed to Dallas to catch a plane, Keith said, "As soon as we get back I'm just going to go knock on their door and make them an offer!"

The night we returned, while cooking dinner in the kitchen of the Ranch House, Carol casually said, "Oh, guess what? I was over looking at that house across the road today. It's for sale."

I couldn't believe my ears. "The white house?"

"Yes. They just put the sign out. There's a Realtor showing it," Carol replied.

Keith said, "Forget the Realtor, let's go now."

I agreed, "Tomorrow could be too late. Someone else might buy it." We dropped everything and nearly ran across the road to ask if we could look at the place. The owners told us the house was more than one hundred years old and needed a lot of work. It had three bedrooms and one bathroom, but not one floor was level. In fact, a can placed at one side of the kitchen linoleum rolled across to the other wall. The rooms were covered in dark trailer-type paneling, the rug was matted, and, well, everything was old. But it was available and fixable—and it looked like a palace to us! Keith bought it on the spot as a parsonage, and we moved in right away.

Within weeks I discovered I was pregnant with our third child. We could have squeezed another baby into our old bedroom, but God in his goodness provided a way of escape! It was perfect timing. We spent that winter building fires in the fireplace of our new little home, and that spring watching the wildflowers start to pop up in our fields.

By summer Josiah was almost three, running around the yard in his shorts grabbing grasshoppers and playing with his dump trucks. He was like a blond lightning flash, while Bethany was like a deep well of serene waters—peaceful, pensive, and starting to take her first steps. Dawn had turned sixteen and was growing into a beautiful young woman with a real servant's heart, helping with the children at home and on the road. For us as a family, things were starting to settle down a little bit.

Summer swiftly turned into fall, when Texas is at its most beautiful. One afternoon I glanced out of the Ranch House window to take in the brilliant reds, oranges, and yellows hanging from the treetops, and I spotted Keith bouncing across the field. It was lunchtime, but I could tell he had more on his mind than food. Once inside the Ranch House, Keith quickly scanned the room, then made a beeline straight for Josiah and me. As he got closer, I noticed a letter crunched tightly in his hand.

He got to our table and said, "Mel, you won't believe it! Look at this letter. We've been invited to Mexico!"

"You're kidding," I said, turning from Josiah to take the scrunched-up letter he was holding out for me.

The letter was from a missionary couple living in a Texas town called Hidalgo right near the border of Mexico. They wanted us to visit them so they could take us into Mexico and show us the needs of the people there. Being raised in Southern California, Keith and I loved the Mexican people already. Besides, we'd been praying for further ways to help people with needs.

"We have to go, Melody! I really think it's the Lord," Keith said excitedly.

Josiah popped in, "Where are you going, Daddy? I want to go too!"

"You can come with us," Keith immediately responded.

When I raised my eyebrows, Keith said, "Mel, he needs to understand."

When Keith grabbed on to something, he didn't waste time. We were soon seat-belted on a plane with Josiah on our way to McAllen, Texas. After landing we headed toward the baggage-claim area, but we were intercepted with huge hugs by an exuberant older couple, Bob and Susan Croft.

"We knew you'd come," said Bob as Susan nodded beside him.

We got our luggage and all piled into their station wagon and drove to Hidalgo, where we grabbed some dinner and checked in to a motel.

"Tomorrow we'll take you into Mexico," they both chirped, nearly in unison, as we said our good nights, knowing morning would come quickly.

Our alarm went off way too early by musician standards, but we were excited to start this adventure with our new friends. We'd only been into Baja, Mexico, just across the California border, and then mostly to go to the beach and have fun. But we'd never been anywhere in this area of Mexico—and never with these purposes.

After crossing the border into Reynosa, we immediately entered another world. As the station wagon bumped along, the poverty was apparent, and so were the gutted pot-holed roads. It wasn't long before the roads turned into dirt. We drove into an area by some railroad tracks that was especially heartbreaking in its obvious poverty. We saw little makeshift sheds all along the tracks.

"We're gonna stop here for a while," announced Bob, as he slowly pulled his wagon over to the side of the shoulderless dirt road.

"Let's get out and walk for a while," Susan suggested, and we all heartily agreed. Jumping out of the car, we began walking down the dusty road.

Now that we could take a closer look, we saw that the "houses" were made from odd bits of scrap materials like tin and railroad ties. Many had cardboard and paper stuck in between the cracks to keep out the wind and rain. There were large rocks, tree limbs, buckets, broomsticks, and even old tires leaning against the "walls" to keep them from falling down.

We saw windows and doors, but they were just big gaping holes. A few had some fabric hanging over the openings, but not many were so blessed.

Josiah was uncommonly quiet as we walked. Then suddenly, he asked, "Mommy, why is everything so dirty and falling over?" He looked up at me with big questioning eyes, and I instinctively knew that my answer was going to be an important one.

"Because these people are poor. They don't have money to build their houses like we do. They don't even have enough money to buy good food, or to buy clean water," I said gently.

"But water's free!" Josiah said brightly, knowing he'd found a solution.

"You're right!" I said. Then I added, "But the free water here is from the river . . . and the river is really muddy and dirty. If they want to have clean water to drink or to take a bath in, they have to buy it. They can't buy it very often, and sometimes the little children get sick from drinking the dirty water."

Josiah got quiet and looked thoughtful for his age.

How could he possibly understand? I thought to myself. But Keith and I knew it was important for our children to see and learn from their earliest years. We wanted Josiah's tender heart to be marked by this experience; the sights and faces imbedded into the core of his being as he grew up in the green fields of East Texas with the "American dream" pushing in on all sides.

Keith and I were well aware that these families most likely viewed us for what we were—curious foreigners. We smiled and looked as friendly as we could in hopes that they'd see that our hearts were filled with mercy and love, not judgment.

Bob and Susan spoke fluent Spanish and called out greetings along the way. They had ministered here before, and some of the families recognized them and began popping their heads out the doorways.

But, as usual, it was the children who broke the ice. When they saw Josiah's blond curly hair and fair skin, they ran out of their homes toward him from all directions. They wanted to get a closer look at their new playmate. From that moment on, Josiah was totally distracted from their living conditions and focused on his new friends.

Soon there were about twenty kids jumping around Josiah wanting to play. Josiah, who was having the time of his life, didn't even notice how much they were reaching out to touch him, especially his bouncy blond curls. He was reaching out and touching back—and all of them were laughing and giggling. I didn't think Josiah even noticed that most of his new friends didn't have shoes or sweaters on this cool, windy day.

Keith caught my eye with a knowing glance reflecting his awareness of the sweetness of this moment.

I thought, *Oh, if only the adults in this world could be as loving and accepting as these little children, the world would be a better place.* The words of Jesus came to mind, "Unless you become little children you cannot enter the kingdom of heaven." Like lightning, the reality of his words pierced my heart. *When was the last time I laughed and played so freely?*

Lost in thought for a moment, I looked up to see that Josiah and his crowd of newfound friends had run off down the road. I flashed a "mom look" at Susan and she said, "Don't worry. It looks like they're taking Josiah down to see the train. We'll head that way."

We picked up our pace a bit when Keith said, "Hey, look, their families are coming out!"

There they were . . . mostly moms and grandmas we assumed, beginning to slowly walk toward us from the safety of their doorways.

"They're very bashful," Bob said.

"Yeah, but look," observed Keith, "they're following the children's example!"

Soon a little crowd gathered in the middle of the road. Bob and Susan already knew many of these families and began greeting them with hugs and laughter while making introductions.

Keith's blue eyes were twinkling, and I had a chance to practice the bits of Spanish I'd learned in Los Angeles, but my simple vocabulary ran out in a few minutes. The timid laughter of the adults grew louder as I tried to learn new words and pronounce their names.

Josiah playing with kids in Reynosa, Mexico

Now that we were closer, I could see these sweet people did not look at all like the Mexican friends I grew up with in California. They had much darker skin and they were smaller, shorter. They looked more like the Incas and Mayans I studied in grade school. One thing for sure, they lived in a poverty that was not reflected in their joyful faces.

Our little group swelled in size as more joined us, and we all wandered down to the abandoned train together. Arriving, I saw Josiah wanting to climb on board like many of the other little children had already done. I thought, *How cool is that—a real train to play on! Josiah will remember this forever!*

Keith walked over to lift Josiah onto the train, right near the engine car with the big cow guard in front. I again noticed the tattered clothing and bare feet of the children on a day that was growing colder as the clouds rolled in, covering the earlier sunshine. A slight shiver went down my spine just thinking about the cold winters here that Bob had told us about.

Walking back to the station wagon later, Bob asked us if we'd like to have a look inside a few of the homes. We didn't want to impose, but Bob thought some families they were already friendly with would be happy to let us take a peek.

Susan said softly, "So many of their friends have no homes at all, so they are very proud to show off the little they do have. And now that they see your warmth, I'm sure a few families will let you in."

I don't know what we expected, but as we peeked inside a few of the squatty lean-to homes, we were struck by their starkness. The homes were just one tiny room with freshly swept dirt floors. There might be a chair here or there. Some had a table. Their beds consisted of a pile of blankets on the floor or, if they were lucky, an old battered mattress. Entire extended families all lived together in these small rooms.

We left the homes and started to walk away, when Keith's boldness kicked in. He asked Bob if he thought a family might let us take a photo of him next to their house. One lady seemed happy to let us take a picture, so we headed back toward her house. Then, to my surprise, Keith quickly climbed jumped over to her little shed-house

In front of house in Reynosa, Mexico

that had old tires holding tarp on to the roof. He gave me a look that said, Melody take a picture fast! I snapped away quickly, grateful no one had been offended. Keith quickly jumped down.

It took about ten minutes to say goodbye to everyone. There were many hugs and kisses, even a few damp eyes as we headed toward Bob's car to drive back to town.

Once we were all piled into in the station wagon we felt dusty and thirsty. I pulled out a jug of water to pass around. Josiah took a few big gulps and then promptly asked, "Daddy, when can I go back and play more?"

"I'm not sure, Josiah," Keith said, "but let's pray we can come back really soon, okay?"

Later that night at our motel, Keith wanted to explain to Josiah more about the living conditions he'd seen that day.

"Josiah did you have fun today?" asked Keith.

"Yes Daddy. I want to go jump by the house like you did."

"Do you know why I did that?"

"You're a silly daddy!" Josiah exclaimed.

"I know I am, but did you see Mommy take a picture? We are going to show that picture to a lot of people because I want them to see how small the house is . . . so small that Daddy is too big to even fit inside."

"But I fit inside—" said Josiah.

"Do you know what is sadder than having a tiny little house?" Keith continued. "Having no house at all. Some of your new friends today don't even have a house to live in, so we need to help them."

Josiah looked at me quietly after Keith spoke, as if to ask if that was really true. How could he comprehend that all little boys and girls don't have cartoon sheets, bright-colored toys, and a cozy house to live in, like he did?

Keith and I were so moved that we wanted to help the poor in Mexico in a very tangible way. We found an old church for sale in Texas within walking distance from the Border Bridge, and we snapped it up as a new mercy ministry base. Bob and Susan agreed to lead our new work. We simply called it the LDM Mexico Outreach. Now the very poorest people in Mexico who had no car could just walk across the border to get food and clothing to take back to their families.

The first thing we did when we got back home was to write an appeal in the *LDM Newsletter*. We raised a cry in hopes of getting some needed supplies to Mexico. We asked all our readers to send various items, and the response was huge. There was a total outpouring of love and generosity! Semitrucks full of blankets, food, toys, and clothing began flooding in.

The magnitude of giving was so great it not only overwhelmed us, but also Bob and Susan, whom we'd left to manage the ministry in Hidalgo. Soon we all realized that although we were blessed beyond measure by such a response, it was much more than we could possibly handle as things were. Our friends in Hidalgo were not cut out for such a large job, but we did not want all the gifts to go to waste.

The Mexico Outreach was up and running, but without anyone to oversee it. Keith prayed like crazy asking God what to do, and soon he bounced in to tell me, "The Lord finally spoke to me!" So Keith made a phone call to an LDM board member, Pastor Joe Fauss, and after dinner we jumped into our car and drove a few miles down the road to see him.

When we arrived, Keith got right to the point. He said, "We started a ministry to the poor in Mexico and have a warehouse full of stuff to feed and clothe them."

We knew Joe had a huge heart for the poor and suffering, so Keith continued, "Joe, I want to turn this ministry over to you and Calvary Commission. I have a vision for a three-story building that would be a center for the whole southern hemisphere. I even will help you raise the money for it."

We held our breath waiting for Joe's reply.

After a moment Joe said, "I'm sorry, Keith, but we're just too small of a ministry to take on this project. And besides, we are called to work with those who are in prison."

We knew Joe and Charlotte were maxed out with a ministry they'd developed to help prisoners when they got out of jail. It was a potent mix of Christian discipleship and new job skills. What they were doing was so important. Still we had hoped.

We drove away from Joe's house very disappointed, because Keith really thought he'd heard from the Lord about Joe. But the very next morning it was Joe who was on *our* doorstep saying, "I woke up at 5:45 AM. While I was still in bed I heard the Lord say, 'Do it!' Keith, I will send a team to Hidalgo immediately."

Joe was true to his word and jumped on an airplane so quickly our heads were spinning. He flew to the interior of Mexico to bring up some of his Calvary Commission staff to start the new base at the church on the border.

Meanwhile, Keith and I flew down to Hidalgo with some LDM staff so we could help too. Once there, we found we needed to rent an additional warehouse because there were so many donations.

I will never forget seeing thousands of people stand in lines five people deep all day. The lines stretched down and around the streets coming from the border. We worked for days, giving grateful people all they could carry, but barely a dent was made in all that was left.

Then Joe said, "I've calculated that at the present method of distribution, it will take six years to give everything away!" So LDM rented eighteen-wheelers, packed them full, and sent them out to ministries around Mexico so all the donations got into the hands of thousands of needy families.

One night while the Mexico outreach was unfolding, I was putting Josiah to bed and knelt down for our usual good-night prayers. But this night was different.

As I knelt by Josiah's bed to tuck him in, he simply blurted out a prayer, "Jesus, please put a house over all the children's beds."

It was the sweetest little-boy prayer I'd ever heard. How could I imagine how powerful it would be? Or how it might come to pass?

By the beginning of 1981, even after we moved into our new little house, the Ranch House continued to stretch at the seams. The garage had become the print shop; the living room became the office and literature distribution department; the laundry room (besides housing the washer and dryer) was our art department crammed with two drafting tables and the DeGraff brothers. The kitchen and dining room were used for album packing and mailing as well as eating. The ministry needed more space—and quickly!

Keith decided we needed a real office building and, just before the slab was poured, made it twice as big as originally intended. Before the building was even completed, we not only knew we could fill it—we knew it would not be our last. We now had real offices, a print shop, and a guys' dorm all in one large, two-story barn-red metal building.

We were excited about some of our new neighbors too. Buck and Annie, Steve and Nelly, and Matt had bought land right next to ours! My mom also moved to Texas. She finally had given her heart to her Redeemer a few years before at a home study of Jewish believers in Hollywood and got baptized in their pool on the same night! Her sisters didn't understand and said she wasn't Jewish anymore. But my mom, who'd always been the most observant of them all, had a clear understanding and told them how it fit together. My mom's mobile home was about one hundred yards or so away from our back door. She could be a hands-on grandma now to our growing family.

May 28, 1981

I feel I will be getting a new commission from God very soon. I am also very excited about the new baby on the way!

After having Josiah, we decided we wanted a big family and didn't want to waste any time getting one. I felt blessed that I was able to get pregnant again so easily.

The one sad note was that Michelle, our longtime friend and assistant, decided to leave the ministry about this time. Tension had been building between Keith and Michelle for several weeks, plus some disagreements on how to do things. Michelle was burned-out from the long hours of endless work and the intensity of everyday life at Last Days—and Keith wasn't always the easiest person to serve either. Besides, Michelle felt her experiences as a Christian were very limited. The only thing she'd known was being with Keith and me. She felt she needed more varied experiences, more room to grow.

Both Keith and I tried to talk Michelle out of leaving several times. She was like blood to us, and we couldn't imagine not having her in our lives. We felt really miserable, and let our feelings get the best of us. Toward the end it got very emotional, and Keith slipped up and said some things that wounded Michelle. When she left, she felt very hurt. As Keith and I stood watching her drive away, we couldn't believe it. We thought we'd be serving the Lord together forever. But Michelle wasn't the last one to leave. Over time probably a dozen people left, feeling like some of our old rules weren't changing quickly enough or that Keith wasn't hearing their viewpoint as well as he should have. For the most part, they were probably right.

Then the summer of 1981 brought some definite rays of sunshine.

July 13, 1981

Yesterday was Melody's due date. She's at the doctor's right now and she can literally come any minute. I have been so nervous and on edge about it. I am so excited!

On the morning of July 17, I went into labor with our third child. Keith drove to the hospital as fast as he could, figuring it was his big chance to use the best excuse in town for speeding. Sure enough, we got pulled over and with great urgency Keith told the policeman, "My wife is having a baby!" The officer took one look at me and gave us a police escort to the hospital.

Later that day, our beautiful Rebekah Joy was born! Keith was elated as he picked up Rebekah and showed her off to the roomful of people who'd just watched her being born—including my mother, Dawn, Martha Ravenhill, Carol, and Kathleen. Keith kept saying, "She's so beautiful . . . look at her sweet little lips . . . her eyes!" I noticed that Rebekah even had perfectly defined eyebrows and skin like fine parchment paper. Francine brought Josiah in for a few moments and he crawled up on the bed with me to hold his little sister. Keith videotaped everything, including some very detailed delivery shots. I made him promise that he wouldn't show those to any of the guys. Later he tried to wiggle out of our deal.

"Mel, how about if I just let the married guys see it? It won't be a big deal to them. Please, honey . . . it has such a pure beauty about it."

I immediately replied, "Keith, you promised! I don't care if they're married! I have to eat dinner with these guys every night!"

Within days of Rebekah's birth, we went to California to the Christian Booksellers Convention, where we proudly pushed Rebekah around in a little stroller. No one could believe we were out and about with her so soon. We stayed with our friends Rich and Pam Boyer, who had helped us launch LDM in the correct legal way.

I took the video to show Pam, who also just had a baby—and a birth video of her own. When Pam and I went shopping, we returned to find

Keith and Rich watching Pam's video! Then we got the scoop. After we had gone out, Keith said, "Rich, you've got to see this video of Rebekah being born. It's the greatest thing. Melody did fantastic!" After my video ended, Rich started Pam's video, which is when we walked in. I was stunned, but I couldn't stay mad at Keith after I saw his obvious excitement about his new daughter and his wife's heroic efforts in labor!

Rebekah is the most calm and joyful baby we've ever had—not to mention adorable! I am so grateful.

Along with the joy of Rebekah's birth, the summer also brought something not so pleasant.

In response to Keith's controversial articles, an avalanche of mail hit Last Days. It came from all quarters—bookstore owners and patrons, recording artists and record companies, Protestants and Catholics, pastors and priests. Some of it was positive and some negative, but in sheer numbers nothing topped the negative response from Protestants to one of his articles called "What's Wrong with the Gospel?" Some of it was really fiery. We always liked to get mail—pro and con—and did our best to answer everyone who had a question. Now there were a lot of questions.

Lost in all the controversy that summer was one seemingly insignificant event that would impact us in a way we had no way of anticipating.

Since Keith was gearing up to spend a lot more time out on the road, he was very interested in some news about the YWAM base down the road possibly building an airstrip. Not too long after we'd moved to our ranch, YWAM had bought the Twin Oaks Ranch from David Wilkerson. Keith jumped on to the airstrip idea and went right over to see YWAM's national director, Leland Paris.

When Keith returned, he said excitedly, "Boy, an airstrip would save a lot of time and hassle. Maybe I can even get a pilot's license!"

To his dismay, that idea wasn't well received by anyone, least of all me.

"I don't think you should even consider becoming a pilot."

"Come on, Mel, you know I could do it."

"Of course you could. I just don't think you should."

Keith talked to Wayne about it, but he, too, had a very strong reaction.

"Keith, I don't feel good about it," Wayne said.

Keith got irritated. "Oh, come on. What's the big deal?"

"I don't want any part of it," said Wayne. "Don't do it."

Everyone who knew Keith seemed to see red flags when the subject came up. We all knew the stress and intense pressures he faced every day. Flying an airplane seemed like the last thing he needed to do.

But while we were on the road at the end of that summer, Keith brought up the subject again with a pastor who had invited us to his church.

"It's too dangerous," the pastor replied immediately. "A pastor friend of mine just died because he took off in bad weather. He said he was going to 'trust God' to get him to his destination safely." Our host made some other strong points, too.

"Keith, do you know why ministers have the highest rate of pilot's insurance?"

"Why?" Keith asked, a bit impatiently.

"Because they take the most risks. They think they're indestructible. They have the most accidents."

I could tell Keith was getting upset. Why wouldn't anyone get excited about his idea to be a pilot? He just stood up and shrugged his shoulders.

"Well, I don't know what everybody's so worried about. I'm not gonna take any risks."

All the girls at the ranch, 1979

Melody and Josiah
in Mexico

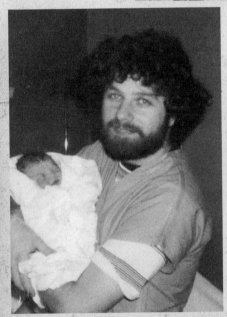

Keith and newborn Bethany

Melody and Bethany

16

"OPEN YOUR EYES"

One day a man named John Dawson accidentally strayed into Keith's line of fire. John had invited Keith to minister at a large concert in the Anaheim Stadium to raise money for "boat people"— refugees fleeing Thailand and Cambodia. A coalition of various groups was working together to pull it off: Episcopalians, charismatics, Catholics, evangelicals, and Pentecostals. John, who was directing the YWAM work in Los Angeles, had seen Keith in concert and believed he would be an important person for the program, so he sent an invitation.

Unknown to John, Keith was very concerned at that time about Christians reducing biblical truth to the lowest common denominator for the sake of unity. So when Keith got the invitation, he shot back a strong but earnest letter turning down John's invitation. Though Keith really wanted to help the boat people, he felt ecumenical gatherings were a compromise, and John was in error for taking part.

Keith was impressed when he received back a thoughtful letter from John, who explained that the Lord had been breaking many hearts over the plight of the refugees. John said, "Brother, the cooperative effort to raise money for six different relief agencies to help the boat people is an expression of concern and compassion—not compromise."

John assured Keith the gathering was not some kind of conspiracy against the truth. He even gave Keith a word of correction. "Keith, in saying some of the things you did, you were entering into the sin of judgment."

John didn't think he'd ever hear back from Keith. He imagined their relationship was probably broken before it even had a chance to begin. But to his surprise, John immediately received what he called "a beautiful letter of repentance."

"I'm in a very dark time in my life right now," Keith wrote. "I'm really struggling and just trying to sort a lot of thoughts and ideas. I'm sorry for coming on so strong. Please forgive me."

John was touched by Keith's humility and thought, *Now here's guy I'm really interested in getting to know.* Keith did not wind up at the Anaheim benefit, but a friendship between Keith and John rooted deeply and grew throughout 1981, giving us another link to YWAM.

The struggle that Keith referred to had grown out of the backlash from that series of articles he wrote and continued misunderstanding about Keith's opposition to merchandising the gospel. Keith didn't feel those ideas were wrong, but his sense of calling left him with many questions that turned like screws in his soul.

It was easy to see how people in the body of Christ had different roles. Some were hands or feet, but Keith always felt like he was an elbow.

"If I had my choice," he lamented to me one day, "I'd much rather be the mercy shower than the prophetic voice. I'd rather be a loving hand that comforts people instead of an elbow in the ribs. It really makes me feel bad sometimes. Everybody tells me I'm a prophet. If I am, what does one look like?"

Keith and his new friend John Dawson, who by now had been to Texas to visit us, had constant discussions about Keith's giftings and calling.

The first time John came to teach, it was an interesting evening. John had planned one of his standard YWAM teachings about the qualities of a mature leader. Then he thought, *I can't teach that tonight. People follow Keith because of his passion and humility, but he's never had any real leadership training.* John felt Keith would think he was using this teaching to purposely lecture him on his shortcomings. So John prayed about what to teach instead. He got an answer he didn't want to hear. The Lord told him to just teach what he'd planned on. John let Keith know his topic just ahead of his speaking time.

Keith introduced John to the whole LDM staff. Then instead of taking a seat, he clomped to the back of the room where he paced back and forth during the entire teaching. I watched the staff stare at John intently as he made a point about being a leader, and then they'd turn to look back at Keith to see what he was thinking.

At the end of the teaching, Keith walked up front and simply said, "Everything he just said is right." Then abruptly disappeared.

The sun was starting to come up when Keith woke me. "Melody, guess what just happened? John just told me who I *am*," he whispered with a kind of wide-eyed wonder.

I replied groggily, "Where've you been?"

Keith explained that he'd taken off to pray after the meeting. Then around 2:00 AM he knocked on John's door and let himself in. He plopped himself down at the end of John's bed and began asking question after question.

Keith said excitedly, "Mel, I think he really gets me. He could see my heart, so I just kept asking questions."

"Why can't I just relax and be the guy who always has something nice to say? Why am I such an intense person?" Keith had asked John.

"God has given you an intense, prophetic personality," John answered. "You see things in black and white. That's a strength—and a weakness. But you have a very definite place on God's leadership team for this generation."

"What kind of place?"

"You're like a John the Baptist. Your role is to prepare the way of the Lord. But like everyone else, prophets have a certain test to pass."

"Another test? Great. What is it?"

"John the Baptist had an intensity about him—his appearance, his tone of voice, his fiery eyes—that enabled him to draw huge crowds. There was a drama in his life that interested people. His message was simple: 'Repent, for the kingdom of God is at hand.' His followers were injected with that message, but there came a time when his younger cousin appeared at the edge of the crowd."

"Yeah, well what's the test?" Keith said.

"The test of all prophets is to take the wide circle of influence that God has given them and, instead of capturing it for themselves, turn it over to one who's greater—so much bigger purposes can be accomplished for God's kingdom."

"Man, that's right," said Keith. "When John the Baptist announced Jesus to the crowd, he knew he was giving his own ministry away!"

"Wow," I said. "John really did speak into your life. So are you gonna give your ministry away?"

"I give it back to God all the time, Mel. It's never really been mine anyway."

Then I said a bit more thoughtfully, "Even the blessings God gives us still belong to him. We need to be willing to let them go if he asks us to."

We were both glad that John was in our lives. Every chance we had with him we'd soak it all up like dry sponges. He'd been raised as a Christian, so he painted in very broad discerning strokes and gave us lots to think about.

John Dawson told us that, just as every individual has a destiny to fulfill, every nation has a destiny to fulfill too. "America is a leader among nations," he said, "but what are we leading people to? America is here to bless the nations, and your message—whatever it is—has got to include a call to turn from sin to *that.*"

John was about Keith's age, and originally from New Zealand. He talked to us about being a teenager six thousand miles away from the States but still being heavily influenced by what was going on in our youth culture. Our blue jeans and music had made it all the way to Red Square, but when God made America such a strong world influence, he must have had more in mind than blue jeans and music. "We're already discipling nations, in a very broad sense—but what are we discipling them to?"

Keith started to expand his scope of thinking as John's challenge stuck a chord. "America is here to bless the nations, Keith. It's one thing to call people to turn from sin, but I think your message needs to somehow include a call for Christians to get involved in being part of that blessing."

Keith was moved and at the same time perplexed. He was already doing more thinking on his message about holiness. *What did holiness mean?*

He'd been encouraging people to hear from the Lord and be obedient to what they were called to do. Now, with John's voice echoing in his ears, he wondered if there was an even bigger picture. Was God painting on a larger canvas than we'd even imagined?

Keith was totally impressed with YWAM and the way its thousands of volunteers served in mission bases all over the world. He was also intrigued by the things YWAM had learned from cooperating with people from different cultures to get the gospel out to the lost—to some who had never heard the name of Jesus! Keith now understood that different churches and ministries were going to need to work together in order to complete the Great Commission.

The fire in Keith's heart for reaching the lost in the world, not just the lost in the church, was being rekindled.

> I have no thirsts for bigger and better things for me or the ministry, so I believe I'm ready to get a thirst for souls. Please Lord, put that thirst and burden for souls and disciples in my bosom.

Something else was being reignited too. One day Keith said, "Mel, start looking through all of our songs and see what we have for a new album."

I said, "Sure, what should I look for?"

"Songs for the lost. I think God is finally releasing me to do my heart's desire—to make an album for seekers in the world, not for the church. I want to take the message of Jesus to those who don't know him—through contemporary music."

This dream of having an important message to share had been in Keith's heart since he was a teenager—only he didn't know God then. But now Keith really had something to say to the world. He wrote about these stirrings in his journal that summer:

June 26, 1981

> *Wow, the Lord has been doing a work in our hearts. We are being led into evangelism. It's amazing. The freedom and peace of my heart is what's so surprising. I have a leading from the Lord to do an evangelistic album. This is the most excited I have been about a project in years, and I fully need the wisdom and anointing from God. Please, holy Lord, give me the secret of winning souls. I want to put it to music . . . O Lord, I wanna transfer so bad to the front lines! I want to see the lost found!*

During the next several months, Keith took another sabbatical from doing concerts, focused on writing for the *Last Days Newsletter*, and drew closer to the Lord. He kept asking God about using his music for evangelism. One day Keith told me, "The Lord showed me that culture is not sin. I didn't get sanitized from my culture when I met Jesus. I feel really free to just be who I am and use the styles and rhythms of my culture to reach others."

Then in October, the Lord released Keith to do a family night concert at YWAM's Twin Oaks Ranch. On the drive over, Josiah sat on my lap and Keith held his chubby little hand, reflecting on how fast time was flying by for him.

That night at the concert Keith talked with a strange sense of urgency. He especially focused on heaven and hell.

"I want to use my music to draw the lost and then preach to them," he told the YWAM audience. "I want to preach from the housetops and then have a life to back it up. That's one of the things I want to do until God takes me home. Life is short. The Bible calls it a vapor. William Booth, from the Salvation Army, wished that every graduate from his training school could be suspended by a rope over hell for twenty-four hours! Then they could see what they were saving men from. I want to have a vision of heaven in my mind and the stench of hell in my nostrils as I go to preach the gospel!"

Some of the things he said that night startled even me. There were huge changes going on inside this dear, loving, intense man I'd been married to for almost eight years.

"As far as I know," Keith said, "I'm not a prophet, and I don't want to be. Since I've been a Christian, I've had hundreds of people tell me I'm a prophet, except I've never had God tell me I'm a prophet—and I figure he's the one that ought to know. So I decided I want to be just a plain old Christian. If I could just stand before the Lord and hear him say, 'Well done. You were a good and faithful Christian,' I'd be really happy."

Toward that end, on January 17, 1982, in Keith's first journal entry of the year, he did the usual taking stock of his life, family, and spiritual state. Along with a growing sense of wanting a deeper walk with God, he wrote:

> I, Keith Green, have three natural-born children—Josiah David, Bethany Grace, and Rebekah Joy—and one adopted (not legally) daughter Dawn. My wife Melody and I love and serve Jesus, and we need to accept ourselves and quit being condemned. I am very far from the way I know I should be, but I also know that God loves me and has been so patient with me.
>
> I am so "religioned" out. I am so weary of the struggle. If I were judged now, I would be judged a failure in my eyes. Yes, I have found much approval in men's eyes, but what about God's eyes? It seems he accepts me and loves me! I know he is not impressed with my works any more than he was with Solomon's. But I think he likes my heart. And if I will be judged on the motive and intent of my heart, then

*I'm OK. For out of a good heart, must come good fruit. Oh,
Lord, help me accept myself as I am. Or help me change.*

A few days later Leonard Ravenhill had a stroke. Keith and I were
stunned. Keith would often joke with him and say, "Hey, Pops! When
you go to be with the Lord, we'll throw a big funeral party for you!"
Then they'd both laugh. Now it wasn't so funny. Leonard loved eagles,
and when we visited him in the hospital, we took him a small ceramic
eagle. Len could barely talk, but he looked at all the flowers in his
room and whispered to us, "When those flowers are all dead and
gone, I will still have this eagle. Thank you." Keith was sobered and
very challenged by seeing his dear friend so close to death.

January 29, 1982

> *God has been so kind and patient with me, and now it's
> time to get serious about the call to serve Him. The Lord
> rebuked me yesterday for just occupying—just looking to do
> the next newsletter, the next album and tour, etc. He showed
> me that my vision was far too small and that I had lost my
> pioneer spirit. I had hidden my talent of potential for revival
> and soul-winning in the ground. I had become a Corporate
> President instead of an apostle—making new territories
> available to God's Spirit to glorify Him. Thank You for rebuking
> me in such love and kindness. I love you. Abba, and Jesus.*

Keith seemed to have a new energy in pursuing his call and working on the album for the lost. I'd found several songs that would work,
and we were writing new ones. Keith was talking about putting
together a "super-band" with some very well-known musician friends.
It all seemed to be coming together, until one afternoon Keith burst
into our shared office with a surprising announcement.

"Mel, you won't believe it, but I was just praying and God told
me not to do an album for the lost right now!"

"Are you serious?" I asked.

"Yeah. I need to put the whole thing on the back burner for a while—and record an album of worship songs first!"

We were both amazed at God's direction—especially since contemporary Christian musicians weren't doing entire albums of worship songs. But even more amazing to me was how quickly Keith set aside his dream album to obey the Lord and record yet another album for Christians. I sorted all of our songs again, this time looking for ones to inspire people to worship.

We were both really excited about the worship album, but I could tell Keith was thoughtful. And that other-worldly tone kept cropping up—just a thread or hint of it—even in our conversation.

One day early in the year, when Keith and I were discussing the songs, I was surprised to hear him say out of the blue, "Melody, for the first time in my life, I feel like I'm ready to go and be with the Lord."

"What do you mean?" I said lightly. "Has the Lord told you something I need to know?"

"No. I just mean that I have a real peace in my heart. I've finally come to a place of rest. I have a total assurance that if the Lord took me home I would go to heaven to be with him."

I'd never heard Keith say something like that before, and he sounded so confident and peaceful. I was so blessed to know that Keith had finally come to that place of inner rest.

There was other evidence of Keith's new feeling of settledness, and it had to do with me. Keith had commissioned me in the past to write some articles in the newsletter. A few—like the one about abortion—"Children, Things We Throw Away?"—had been reprinted as tracts with several million in circulation. But even though Keith and I had worked side by side to lay the foundation of Last Days, I'd always kept a low profile—especially in the recording studio.

On this new worship album, however, Keith wanted to record a song I'd written from Psalm 95. Amazingly, he wanted me to sing the lead on it while he sang harmony. I was thrilled! I had totally let go of the idea of ever singing with Keith. That question had been settled long ago except for a few background parts I'd done. Now Keith even told me I could start taking voice lessons if I wanted. Even though the song would end up getting cut in the final selection, I felt so encouraged. I could have burst!

As the time drew near for us to record, Keith was a bit apprehensive. He wrote:

February 11, 1982

I'm starting to really feel the pressure of leaving for two weeks. I must admit, I'm extremely nervous about this album. I'm always so insecure about the studio.

Keith decided to name this worship album *Songs for the Shepherd*, and we arrived in Los Angeles to record it with all three children in tow. Once again we would be working with Bill Maxwell.

One song I'd written five years earlier did make it on the album— "There Is a Redeemer." I found the lyrics on the original scrap of paper where I'd first written them. The amazing thing was that as soon as I saw the lyrics I remembered the exact melody, something that never happened if I neglected to record the song on a tape recorder. Miraculously, the words instantly triggered the melody I hadn't thought of in five years. When I sang it for Keith in Texas, he fell in love with it and picked it for his album.

There is a Redeemer,
Jesus God's own Son!
Precious Lamb of God,
Messiah, Oh, Holy One!

Thank you, O my Father,
For giving us your Son
And leaving your Spirit
'Til the work on earth is done

Just before we drove off to the recording session, Keith wanted to add a few more words to make the song a bit longer. I was amazed at the way he could seemingly pull them out of the air. In a few minutes of work, he sang:

When I stand in glory
I will see his face.
There, I'll serve my king forever
In that holy place . . .

I liked it, but the added lyrics seemed slightly out of place with the rest of the song. It even seemed a little odd that Keith took the song in that direction, going from thanking God to meeting him face-to-face.

The song was clearly much stronger with Keith's new part. And when he sang it in the studio, the presence of the Lord literally bathed Keith. He sang with a passionate cry in his voice—a voice broken and filled with the awe and wonder of God. Goose bumps raced up my arms. During certain parts Keith wept so much it was hard for him to sing at all. This was no performance. It was some kind of very real experience, just between him and the Lord.

We decided to record three songs that the Lord gave us during the time of revival in 1979. On two of them—"Draw Me" and "The Promise Song"—Keith wrote the music and we wrote the lyrics together. "Draw Me" is a song of desperation—of knowing that it takes God's grace for us to even be drawn into his presence:

Draw me, oh draw me, please draw me my Jesus
Into your presence where I cannot lie
My soul is so thirsty, I cannot endure it
And if I can't get closer, I surely will die
Take me, oh take me, please take me my Jesus
Quickly before I forget that I'm lost
For so many times, my mind has deceived me
That I really don't have to carry the cross

> Help me, oh help me, please help me my Jesus
> Save me from sins that I thought were all gone
> Kill me with kindness and break through my blindness
> I know 'til I'm dead, I can never live on

"The Promise Song" was very happy and upbeat, talking about the many promises the Lord has said he'll keep if we obey him. The mood of the song doesn't reflect its serious message. God gives his *love* unconditionally, but his *promises* are conditional: only for those who live the way he calls us to live.

"Until That Final Day" was another song Keith wrote during the revival. Once again there was a sense of finality in these words—not so much of the end of earthly life, but of finally breaking through to overcome the crises and difficulties in our lives.

> My flesh is tired of seeking God
> But on my knees I'll stay.
> I want to be a pleasing child
> Until that final day . . .
> One sleepless night of anguished prayer,
> I triumphed over sin.
> One battle in the Holy War
> God's promised me to win!

There were also a few songs where we took the words right out of Psalms, and God just dropped melodies into our hearts.

When I wrote the melody to "The Lord Is My Shepherd" from Psalm 23, it took just a few minutes. I was waiting in the car reading Psalm 23 while Keith went to grab us lunch at a fast-food stand. By the time Keith returned with our hamburgers, I had my Bible open like it was a hymnbook. I sang him Psalm 23 with the whole melody the Lord put into my heart as I'd been reading.

Then one morning Keith read Psalm 8 and later told me, "The melody jumped right off the pages and into my ears." Since the psalms are all actually songs, Keith wondered if his melody to "How Majestic Is Thy Name" was close to the original. He said, "I can't wait to meet King David and ask him to sing me his original tune to this psalm!"

During our time in Los Angeles, we did the photo session in Hollywood for the cover. It was the most fun we'd ever had doing a photo session because an animal handler came to the studio with several lambs. We tried the shot various ways, with Keith holding two and three lambs and, finally, just one draped around his shoulders.

As usual Keith did not like having his picture taken. It was hard for him to relax. I needed to stand behind the photographer and talk to Keith continually. The best way to get him looking natural was to tell him a funny story or a joke. I tried to remember every humorous thing I'd heard in the last year while Keith smiled and kept saying through his teeth, "Come on, Mel, think of something really funny!"

Sometime during the session we got the idea for Keith to hold all of the children in his arms. After all, they were his little lambs! It was quite a feat to get Josiah on Keith's shoulders and Rebekah and Bethany in his arms. Then they all needed to look good at the same time the picture was snapped. I was cooing, shaking baby rattles, and trying to get Keith *and* the kids to laugh.

In the midst of the shoot, I had such a great sense of satisfaction rush into my heart. God was so good to us. It was obvious that Keith felt the same way. His face just lit up as soon as the children were placed in his arms. He was such a proud and happy daddy. What a beautiful family we had!

At the end of the session, we all gathered together to take one big family portrait with Dawn. The makeup artist did a fantastic number on Dawn. With her long, straight hair and high cheekbones, she looked like a model, all grown up and beautiful at seventeen. With Keith's determination to avoid cameras, even at home, it was hard to get him even in a casual shot. Getting this family portrait done was a blessing—in more ways than I knew just then.

The dedication Keith wrote for the album overwhelmed my heart:

> This album is dedicated to the Great Shepherd, Jesus Christ, who has given me redemption and hope. It is also dedicated to my beloved wife Melody, with whom I have enjoyed much rewarding work and fellowship, such as went into the making of this album. And lastly, to my precious little lambs who never cease to bring tears to my eyes in both prayer and play.
>
> Oh, how did a wretch like me get such a family as this!
>
> Oh, thank You, my Lord Jesus!

Immediately after the album was finished, Keith had some spring concert crusades planned. We'd be flying to them from our own backyard this time because the much-talked-about airstrip had become a reality. Since we had a longer stretch of straight flat land than YWAM did, Keith offered to build the iron-ore airstrip on our property for everyone's use. We were all excited about this new, time-saving way to travel.

These concert crusades were planned to be different from any other ones Keith had ever done. Keith's new twist was inspired by Charles Finney, who would preach, then have separate "Inquirers' Meetings" where those under conviction could come to find out more about becoming a Christian. Keith decided he would also have these "Inquirers' Meetings" like Finney did the day after each concert for those who wanted to make serious commitments to the Lord. Keith wanted to take some quality time with these new believers to carefully instruct them in the ways of the Lord, and there wasn't much time in a concert setting to do that. Winkie Pratney and John Dawson were scheduled to teach at the Inquirers' Meetings in two different rounds of concerts.

On the first set of concerts, however, not many people were interested in returning the next day for another meeting. The big halls and movie theaters we'd rented weren't needed for the number of people who showed up. Keith was frustrated.

April 5, 1982

I've been mostly disappointed by the so-called crusades. Mainly because I feel like I have no anointing. The worst part is that the audience doesn't even seem to notice. There's nothing more sickening than to turn around and have to use the same methods you've despised for years. The silly altar call is all that seems to separate "the sheep from the audience." The Inquirers' Meeting is a total failure. Maybe I'm being too hard on myself, but that's how I feel in my heart. I feel like a complete idiot and a failure!

At the next concert city, Keith learned the hard way that his heart was crusted over from the too-busy-to-seek-God-enough months in Los Angeles while we were making the album. Afterward he wrote:

April 12, 1982

Things went horrible . . . but God saved the day. On stage I felt the Lord desert me because of my lack of consecration and true devotion. I had not felt so terribly bad on stage since the last night at ORU three years ago. I finally cried out to God for help on stage . . . asked for anointing and help—and He gave it. People gave their lives to Jesus, and I knew that I needed to do something so I wouldn't keep blowing it like that again.

Next day, about an hour before the concert started, I went back to my hotel and cried my guts out before the Lord. After a long time of prayer the day of the concert, things changed. One thing I asked God for in that prayer time was His heart. That's the only thing I needed from Him. . . . That night's concert was one of the best I've ever had. The Word of God flowed out of my mouth in the smoothest way ever. I worshipped God and it didn't matter that there were even people there—it was God that I wanted to impress and bless, and that's all!

He wrote, two days later:

I sure hope the Lord saves me from the fate of another concert without an anointing. I'll just die if I have to go out in front of a crowd again without His love and presence.

During these crusades it was as if the Lord was calling Keith to a deeper level of understanding and a higher vision of what it would take, in the Spirit, to accomplish God's next major move in the world.

The next glimpse came during the second round of crusades when John Dawson came with us. This time Keith had decided to do more extensive after-concert Inquirers' Meetings instead of next-day meetings. He figured he'd get people while he had them—while they were standing up front and in the aisles for the altar call.

Then Keith would say, "Before you go back to your seats, I want you to get some teaching from John on beginning your walk with God." He'd chuckle and say, "Don't worry, no one will steal the stuff you left at your seat. And your ride home will wait for you. This is important!" Often thousands streamed off to a side room.

We always took the offering after the altar call. There were fewer people to give, but Keith knew it would be a distraction from what he came to do. It would interrupt the wooing of the Holy Spirit. Keith wanted to see people give their hearts to Jesus—not make a lot of money. The whole offering went to LDM to pay for the event—and further ministry if there was money left over. Keith didn't get a salary because we supported ourselves with our music royalties.

When the evening was over, Keith and I joined John to meet the new believers and share a few things with them.

On the road the key discussions between Keith and John centered on spiritual warfare. Keith was fascinated by the idea John presented, based on Ephesians 6 and other Scriptures, that every city has a specific ruling principality assigned to it by Satan. If entire cities were going to be stirred by the Lord, the strongman in each city needed to be bound by entering into spiritual warfare.

At dinner the night of the Houston concert, Keith said to John, "Let's do all the stuff you've been talking about for tonight's concert!" So we left the restaurant to pray spiritual warfare prayers over Houston. When we got to the house where we were staying, Keith had another concern.

"I feel really weak and nervous tonight," he said.

"Do you always feel this way?" John asked.

"Yeah. I don't have this great big confidence, but somehow God comes through. We really need to pray."

As Keith and John bowed to pray, the Spirit of God seemed to come in a very strong way—not for the city of Houston, but for Keith, who was kneeling down, head on his knees like a little boy.

John laid his hand on Keith's back and began to pray. But when John spoke, it was like God the Father speaking to his child, telling of his unconditional and accepting love. John spoke of Keith's destiny—that he was going to be used to pull down strongholds—and said that when Keith spoke he was to speak as the mouthpiece of God. Keith's words would be sharp and two-edged with authority. Then the power of the enemy would be broken.

Keith and John then began to pray together. They felt they were shown a certain principality over the city of Houston. The Lord gave them a complete strategy of how to bind this strongman and plunder the goods.

Keith had a powerful night of ministry that night, which God blessed in every way. There were two hundred inquirers and the ten thousand dollars of expenses were met, even though the arena was only one-quarter full!

There were other highlights of our spring tours. For instance in St. Louis, Missouri, the Market Square Arena was packed with ten thousand people loudly chanting "Jesus! Jesus!" an hour before the concert. Many more people had come to hear Keith that night than to see the

Russian ballet dancer Rudolf Nureyev, who was appearing in the smaller arena behind us. About 650 came to the Inquirers' Meeting after the concert!

That night there was an embarrassing moment backstage before the concert. Keith was jovial and started loudly singing "Rudolph the Red-Nosed Reindeer" on the stairs connecting both arenas. A moment later Rudolf Nureyev appeared at a turn in the stairway. We stifled our gasps as we let him squeeze past us in his ballet tights on his way to perform. At our usual post-concert coffee shop breakfast, we laughed until we cried telling everyone what had happened.

Then, in Indianapolis, Keith sang and preached to his largest crowd ever—twelve thousand people. Things were suddenly starting to mushroom. Keith and I had just met with a radio consultant, and we were planning to begin a syndicated program together in the fall.

Perhaps the greatest expansion was the broadening of our spiritual perspective.

> *There's an incredible amount of growth and building going on at the ministry, but it's all so unexciting to me. I know that there's really only one thing that excites my soul and that's being close to Jesus.*

We weren't just caught up in personal struggles, or even in challenges to Keith's ministry. We simply needed more intimacy with God and greater wisdom for our next steps. We were starting to see that we were caught up in frontline spiritual warfare that could affect a generation.

We had leased an airplane for this tour and, just after returning to the ranch, Keith wrote:

> *We flew home in about three hours to our own strip. I flew up in the cockpit for a while and got even more of a desire to learn how to fly. Please, Jesus, do not let me*

even start pilot lessons unless you want me to. I realize that my own fleshly nature is not conducive to being a pilot, and that the devil would like to kill me if he could. . . .

After the album was mixed and mastered, we had our own little listening party. It seemed the Holy Spirit had helped Bill capture the passion and presence of God that we all felt during the recording sessions.

I listened to the new album and I wept and wept, as I heard what the Lord did on it. The songs' anointing was so powerful and they ministered to me in a way that none of my other albums ever could. It's so amazing to me how the Lord stopped me dead in my tracks on doing the rock album and led me to do the worship one. Thank you my precious Savior!

After the spring crusades, Keith and I were exhausted. We'd never really taken a vacation before, so when the idea came up now it sounded wonderful. Keith still joked about delivering pizzas on our honeymoon, and he wanted to bless me with a trip to Europe. We decided to go for two weeks and leave the kids at home. It would be our very first, bona fide vacation ever.

Or so I thought.

The week before we planned to leave for Europe, God brought a chance meeting Keith's way. Keith had dropped in to see Leland Paris at YWAM, and Don Stephens, YWAM's director for Europe, was sitting there. Don immediately set up an itinerary so that Keith and I could see the YWAM bases in Europe and even teach in one or two of their schools.

When we left at the end of May, our first visit was to the base called Holmstead Manor, in southern England. On our drive there I realized why so many of the early masters of art loved to paint the English countryside. It was absolutely beautiful—blue skies, billowy white clouds, and rolling hills of various shades of green. There was a different kind of light in the atmosphere. I just sat back enjoying the peaceful ride. When we arrived at the base, Keith and I were both stunned. It was a huge castle—a real one sitting on a gentle knoll and looking like a picture postcard!

Operating a missions base out of a castle, including a training school and ministry outreaches throughout England, looked like fun. But it was obviously a sacrificial lifestyle. Everyone volunteered their time, and castles don't come with many modern conveniences.

There was a large, dark lobby entrance, with a funky upright piano pushed against the wall. Keith immediately plopped down and hammered out a loud tune. It drew the attention of one little boy who listened in fascination, but not many others. It was a sweet moment for us. Later Keith gave a concert for the whole base and spoke many words of encouragement to them.

We'd seen a big swimming pool on the grounds, but it was cracked, empty, and growing moss. Even if this YWAM base had extra money, which it didn't, we knew fixing the pool would be considered a luxury. But it was really hot, and Keith wanted to bless the people who were there pouring out their lives for the Lord. We'd learned so much about grace, and Keith felt the Lord wanted to give a gift of grace to the group at Holmstead Manor—a blessing they wouldn't give themselves. We slipped out early the next day, and Keith left a large gift designated specifically to fix the pool. We wished we could have been there to see everyone's faces.

Already our vacation was becoming a lot of fun. We were seeing neat places and meeting wonderful people.

Then in Amsterdam we realized there might be a different purpose for this trip. Amsterdam was light-years away from the quiet English countryside. The narrow streets bustled with bicycles and wandering young people from all over the world. We wound our way through the city, which is considered the drug capital of Europe, to YWAM headquarters.

It would be hard to miss the YWAM base, a massive, five-story building across from the train station near the center of town. Across the top, in lights, were the words "Jesus Loves You" in both English and Dutch. But the building serves as a beacon in other ways too. Sitting right on the corner of the world-famous Red Light District, YWAM has an amazing outreach to the people in the city—including the prostitutes, drug addicts, and runaways who gravitate there because of the district's wild reputation.

Floyd McClung, the leader of this center, was like a gentle giant, standing six-foot-seven. His wife, Sally, was a pretty blonde who was very involved in the ministry and raising their two children, Matthew and Misha. I was very impressed at Floyd and Sally's trust in God, taking their children to live in a neighborhood where few people would even choose to walk. The McClungs' commitment impressed me too. They were building for the long haul and praying for the people of Amsterdam with an intensity that moved me.

Floyd took Keith and me on a walking tour after dark, and something gave me the impression of two worlds existing side by side. Even in this modern European city lit by streetlights I felt very uncomfortable. It was not the same city we had seen by daylight.

Earlier in the day, there had been bright blue skies and sunlight sparkling on the famous canals. Now the dark canals only reflected the streetlamps and glare of neon signs from the Red Light District. Row after row of nightclubs and bars advertised naked women, live sex acts, or some other type of perversion. The doors were open and blaring music spilled out into the streets. As we passed, hustlers called out, wanting us to come inside. Everybody was hustling somebody. The streets were full of strange men wearing dark glasses, and women—lots of women.

"Prostitution is legally licensed in Amsterdam," Floyd told us. "It's a way of life for many women. Some of them are even married."

"You mean their husbands don't care?" I asked in shock.

"Nope. Some women just work eight-hour shifts like a regular job—especially the ones who sit in the windows."

The windows. That was probably the thing that separated this

Red Light District from those in the States. Here many women would display themselves in the windows of regular houses, while men—from pimply faced boys to grandfathers—went shopping. It was sick and it was heartbreaking.

"You need to pray for a special grace from the Lord to minister here," Floyd said. "You really need the Father's heart, especially for the prostitutes. But we've reached many of them and seen miraculous transformations."

Just when I thought we'd seen the worst of it, I glanced down a dark, narrow little side street. Standing right out in the street were several women—almost totally naked. Even from a distance, one woman in particular caught my eye. There was something about her. Maybe it was the slouch of her shoulders as she stood there waiting for her next customer. She seemed so lost and dejected. I wondered what incredible wounding had taken place in her life to get her to this point. Any minute someone might walk up and pay money for her and take her off to do God knows what. I knew all of her human dignity and self-esteem must be destroyed for her to sell herself on the street like a piece of meat.

Later that night I was haunted by her image. I could lie there in a nice warm bed with my husband who loved me and was committed to me. But who knew where that woman was right now or how she was being treated. I knew prostitutes were often brutalized and even murdered. I would soon return to America, to my happy children and a nice ministry filled with nice people. But what was the future for this woman? My heart ached over the memory.

"Keith, are you asleep?"

"No, I'm not."

"Do you think it's the jet lag?"

"No." What we had seen had shaken him too. "All this stuff has blown me away. I want to help, but I don't know how."

The next day, Floyd and Sally took us shopping so I could buy a few things—chocolates and toys for the kids, and a few dresses for me. Keith and I were planning our fourth child, so I looked for something pretty but with room to grow. In the daylight, I could see again the

Amsterdam of the postcards—the flowers, canals, streetcars, and skinny buildings with graceful gable tops. But the darker world of the night was somehow still present, like the shadow of a double-exposure on a picture. I couldn't shake that sense. Once you've seen the darkness, how can you pretend it's not there?

We wound up buying ice-cream cones and strolling for a while. I caught myself thinking, *Wow, I'm eating ice cream with missionaries.* Then I felt foolish. *What did I think missionaries were like, anyway?* I guess I wasn't prepared to meet such incredible people. To me, the word *missionary* sometimes conjured the image of a person who couldn't make it in the real world so they retreated to the mission field. But I looked at Floyd—who Keith was pumping with questions just now—and Sally. I thought, *These people could land on the top of the heap in whatever they chose to do.* I wondered if it was the Greens who had somehow forgotten what the real world was really like.

Keith asked Floyd, "What are your greatest needs?"

"We've got so many—"

"If you could pick one, what would it be?" Keith had blessed one YWAM base with money to fix their pool, and I thought maybe Keith wanted to bless Floyd and Sally too. I was sure Floyd was going to say they needed money, but he surprised me.

"People," Floyd said. "More people who have a heart to reach the lost for Jesus."

By now we'd reached the Cleft, a quaint little pancake house YWAM had opened right in the middle of the Red Light District and two doors down from an official satanic church. Talk about facing spiritual warfare!

We sat at a table in the Cleft, and Floyd and Sally told us the strategy the Lord had given them for winning this warfare, one soul at a time.

One of their many stories gripped me the most—the story of Magriet, who had been a prostitute and heroin addict for twenty-one years. Magriet was a street prostitute, which the locals considered to be a step down from working the windows. The YWAMers visited

Magriet regularly on the streets and kept asking her to come to the base for a meal. Touched by their persistence and obvious love, she finally gave in. Magriet stayed for an evangelistic meeting and gave her heart to the Lord. Eventually she left Amsterdam to attend a church in another city, where she was still growing in the Lord.

So there was real light in the midst of this real darkness—bright light!

As we left and headed south, Keith and I talked for a long time. The people who had dedicated their lives to serve had moved us, but we were also overwhelmed by seeing so many lost people with so few to help them. It wasn't like America where there was a church on every corner—and in most cities at least a few of them were really vibrant and alive in the Spirit.

As we traveled through Germany, Austria, and Italy, it was the same. We kept asking the same questions—how could there ever be a big enough movement to meet all the needs we were seeing? What were the systems for getting the people who did go onto the front lines and into the action? You can't just tell people to "go" without helping them get there. At the Lausanne, Switzerland, YWAM base we met up with Don Stephens again, and he had something on his mind.

"I want you to pray about flying to Greece with me tomorrow," he told us. "I want you to see the ship."

Don was launching the YWAM Mercy Ship Ministry, and the chosen vessel of honor was docked in Greece for renovation and to be made seaworthy. It had been a passenger liner, but Don wanted to sail it around the world under the banner of Jesus. He'd named the ship the M/V *Anastasis*, which means "resurrection" in Greek.

Don told us the first time he heard Keith's recording of the "Easter Song" he got choked up with both joy and tears. The Lord used that song to encourage Don not to give up in launching the ship ministry.

Later that night, Keith and I felt a go-ahead from the Lord to go to Greece. Once on board the M/V *Anastasis* we were shocked. This was more than a ship—it was a floating city for the Lord! Staffed with

120 people from 30 nations, the ship was two football fields long, eight stories high, seventy feet wide. It featured huge cargo holds to take donated food, medicine, and clothing to people with little or nothing—evangelizing at every port. Everybody on board was a volunteer, raising their own support—including Don and his wife, Deyon, and Captain Ben Applegate, who had worked for thirty years at a shipping company.

Don said there would be a hospital on board so the medical team could perform surgery right at the docks, and they'd have a training school—only this one would be a traveling one!

The impact from this part of the trip, though, didn't come so much from seeing a first-class ship or the scope of its mission. It came from being touched by the lives of Don and Deyon Stephens.

On the outside the Stephens family looked typical for Southern California natives—good-looking enough to have their pictures in an ad! Don was tall and dark-haired, and Deyon and their three children were all blond. With Don's gift, he could have been a corporate president somewhere, bringing home a hefty paycheck. Instead, he and his family lived in a small ship's cabin that made our old bedroom in the Ranch House look like a palace! It was decorated nicely, but it was tiny.

Being a mom, I focused in on their children—Heidi, Luke, and John Paul. Their youngest, John Paul, was handicapped. At six years old, he couldn't speak, feed himself, or walk without assistance. But he was a beautiful child and obviously had received much love being surrounded by a big, loving family, including the staff family on board. I remembered the times I'd thought (with great relief) that God wouldn't ask me to go to the mission field because I had children—as if that automatically disqualified me. Well, my thinking was getting turned around. By this time I'd seen many children on the mission field with their parents, and they were some of the greatest kids I'd ever met.

The circumstances were hard on the ship. There wasn't enough money to fix everything or put fuel in the tanks, let alone pay for the planned voyage to the States. But everyone had such a joyful spirit. We didn't hear any grumbling or complaining anywhere. It was an obvious sacrifice, but everyone had transcended that. They were on a mission for God. We instantly loved them and loved what they were doing.

Keith wanted to bless them and he asked Don, "Could we pay for you and your family, and two or three other couples that you choose, to go to the beach and enjoy yourselves for a few days?"

So the next day, we wound up at Kinetta Beach, halfway between Athens and Corinth. This particular beach had real significance for our YWAM guests because it was where their "fish miracle" happened.

Just a few months earlier the whole crew was in the middle of a rotating commitment to forty days of fasting and prayer. They wanted to launch the public ministry of the ship and, at that time, the government wouldn't allow the crew to live on board. So some of them had to rent these little concrete beach bungalows at Kinetta. One day, while a crew member was walking on the shore, 12 fish literally jumped out of the water and onto the beach near her feet. A few days later, 210 fish did the same thing while another crew member was sitting on the sand. A few days after that, on the thirty-eighth day of the fast, in the middle of a time of intercession, the fish started jumping again. In all, a total of 8,301 fish jumped onto the beach in those few days in full view of many local residents, who had never seen anything like it!

Don said, "As soon as we began to see what was happening, we took a very accurate account, and the total is not exaggerated by even one fish."

For Don, it was a modern-day parable, a sign from the Lord that he was hearing their prayers and would provide the necessary finances, bring in a harvest of souls, and release a fresh wave of people into world missions. After the fish were counted and cleaned, the crew ate them for months. In fact, we even had a taste.

I sat on the white sand with Deyon one afternoon at the edge of the blue Aegean Sea. She was holding John Paul and letting him splash in the water. We were talking about the Lord and his goodness. She told me one of the ways the Lord revealed himself to her was through this child. She had gone to the Lord in tears of disappointment one day over the lack of relationship she was experiencing with her young son.

"Lord, he doesn't even know me. If I didn't feed him, love him, and clothe him, he would die. Yet he doesn't even acknowledge my presence."

She asked the Lord it if would be possible for John Paul to respond even a little to the tremendous love she felt for him. Just a glimmer of recognition. A turning of the head. A smile.

"In that moment, instead, I had a revelation of how God longs for relationship with his children. John Paul *could* not respond. Men often *will* not respond to God."

Deyon loved her son deeply—you couldn't miss that. She wouldn't have chosen the hardships of his handicap, but she understood in a deep measure how "God works all things together for good to those that love him."

She told me, "Our family has learned lessons of acceptance, service, compassion, and patience that apply far beyond John Paul. We've learned that God loves us for who we are and not solely for what we can do."

"Grace," I responded quickly.

"Yes. Grace."

Meanwhile Keith was excited about the ship's practical expression of Christianity to the needy—feeding, clothing, and giving medical aid from the ship hospital, all of which went hand-in-hand with proclaiming the gospel.

Keith told Don, "You'll need other ships in the future. We'll help get the word out for staff and filling the cargo bay. That's one of the reasons for our friendship!"

By the time we left Greece, we were overwhelmed by all we'd seen on the ship, in Amsterdam, and across Europe. The needs were tremendous, but so were the vision, commitment, and sacrifice we saw in all the leaders we'd just met. Now we knew why Loren Cunningham had given almost twenty years of his life so far to build YWAM and lay a foundation to reach the world.

I could already see what was going on in Keith's mind. John Dawson's counsel was coming back: "What are you telling people to repent *to?*" and "America has a destiny." Keith could see there were organizations like YWAM in place that provided both training and mission trips to reach the lost, and there were Christians who were called to go. He wanted to bridge the gap between the two.

By this time, 230,000 people were receiving our newsletter, and Keith was already planning ways to reach all of them—everyone who came to his concerts too.

I thought of the lady I'd seen down that little side street in Amsterdam. One lost person on her way toward eternal separation from God. The world was full of people like her.

We wanted to go home and sound a trumpet while the message was hot and burning in our hearts—to call together an army of people to rescue those who were perishing. An army marching against the enemy in the power of God!

On a final stopover in London, words and messages were already forming in my head.

Over dinner in a British steakhouse I felt the urgency to get this new message into a song for Keith. Maybe it was the pained reflection in his eyes. Here were fields of souls ripe for harvest, but there were so few workers. We usually wrote songs about our personal experiences, but this time I sensed I needed to capture our feelings right away. I grabbed a paper napkin and started writing:

Jesus commands us to go!
It should be an exception if we stay . . .

Shortly after returning from Europe, Keith moved into action! He planned three large Benefit Concerts to help the M/V *Anastasis* and a fall concert tour to bring a missions challenge to the Christians in America. Keith also had a few previous commitments in California—Jesus West Coast, North and South. Both were still overseen by our friend Bob Maddux, and both still had free admission! They'd be perfect for Keith to try out his new message. As it turned out, Keith would be ministering with Loren Cunningham!

Keith wanted to talk to him about everything the Lord had shown us in Europe.

The first festival, JWC South, was at Devonshire Downs, and there was room for several thousand people in the bleachers and on the field. Keith sang in the afternoon under a blazing sun, but at his evening concert his message came across most powerfully.

There was a new kind of excitement in Keith when he walked onto the stage that night in June. He sat down purposely at the piano and took a moment to talk about our international God. "God is not an American or even a Republican as some of us like to think! He loves everybody the same, and his heart goes out to the masses whether they're known or forgotten."

Then he picked up his Bible. "There's a little command found in the Bible that says, 'Go ye into all the world, and preach the gospel to every creature,' and make disciples of men. We like to think that was for the disciples or for old ladies who can't find husbands and need to bury their troubles on the mission field. That it's for humanitarians. Or that it's for real Christians who are so spiritual they can't stay in society so they gotta go overseas or bury themselves in some tribe somewhere down in the Amazon!"

Keith was really starting to warm up now, and he had everyone's attention.

"I'll tell you what, folks, the world isn't being won today because we're not doing it! It's our fault! This generation of Christians is responsible for this generation of souls on the earth. Nowhere in the world is the gospel so plentiful as in the United States. Nowhere! And I don't want to see us stand before God on that day and say, 'But, God, I didn't hear you call me!' Here's something for all of you to chew on—you don't need to hear a call. You're already called!"

Besides our recent trip, Keith was being fueled by shocking statistics we'd heard. They were hard to believe, but true. There were only 85,000 people on the mission field in the whole world! And only a small percentage were trying to reach the 2.7 billion people who had never even heard the gospel once—that's about one for every 450,000.

Meanwhile in America there were more than one million full-time Christian workers, which is one worker for every 230 people! To top it off, 94 percent of all ordained preachers worldwide ministered to only 9 percent of the world's population—those who spoke English.

"It's either God's will that the world's going to hell or it's the church's fault because we're not being obedient to what the Bible says about going into all nations and preaching the gospel," Keith said. "If you stay home from going into all the nations, you'd better be able to say to God, 'You called me to stay home. I know that as a fact!'"

Like all outdoor events there's always a little shuffling around the fringes, but the crowd was riveted by Keith's direct message. He asked everybody who knew they had a definite call from God to stay home to raise their hands. Then he counted!

"One . . . two. Two. Might be three or four that I missed. Well, the rest of you are called unless God tells you otherwise. Now don't go out and sell everything and leave tomorrow! Get some training.

"There's a rule in the armed forces—always obey the last order you got, until you get new orders from command headquarters. The last order I got in my Bible was 'Go!'"

Then Keith played two of our new songs. Together we'd finished "Jesus Commands Us to Go," and I'd just written another song that was so new Keith had to pull a lyric sheet out of his Bible to read as he sang. Even from the side of the stage, I could see his eyes fill with compassion as he sang "Open Your Eyes."

Open your eyes to the world all around you,
Open your eyes . . . open your eyes.
This world is much more
Than the things that surround you.
You must arise and open your eyes.
Sometimes we're too busy to share.
But Jesus wants us to care.
Open your arms to the naked and shiverin.'
Open your arms . . . open your arms.

We need a little less taking,
A whole lot more giving.
We're so safe and warm, we can open our arms
And love a little bit stronger
And pray a little bit longer!

Jesus says
When we love someone in his name
We're loving him.
And Jesus says
When we touch someone in his name
We're touching him.

And we need to show them the light,
We've got to pour out our lives!

Open your hearts to the ones who are desperate.
Open your hearts . . . open your hearts.

They may never repay you,
But their souls are worth it!
New life you impart, when you open your heart.
Jesus loves all men the same
So we've got to go out in his name . . .

Unknown to any of us, Sparrow had hired a cameraman to record their artists that night. Keith was no longer with Sparrow, but when he sat down at the piano, this fellow had a sense that he was supposed to record him anyway. So he turned on the camera.

Keith would have objected had he known. He didn't like having cameras rolling during his ministry. This would be one of the only fully recorded concerts of Keith.

After the concert we had a late-night meal at a coffee shop with John Dawson, who was also at the festival. Keith figured John would be excited about his strong missions message.

"Keith," John said, "God is getting ready to use you in a big way to challenge a multitude of young people into missions. But if you keep overstating the point, you'll disqualify the whole message."

"Well, that's how strong I feel it! God's heart is broken because his people refuse to go when the need is so great!"

"That's true! But it's up to God to tell each person where to go. Keith, I know your heart is right, but you can't say 99.99 percent are called to leave America and everybody else is in sin."

Keith realized that in his urgency he had overstated the point.

"Well, how would you say it then?" he asked John.

They had quite a lengthy discussion about presenting the truth of missions in a way that wouldn't put guilt on those genuinely called to serve the Lord in America.

Keith saw John's point and realized he could still present a strong challenge, but in a slightly different way. As we got up to leave the coffee shop, Keith said, "Next time, I'll say it differently."

We had asked Loren and his wife, Darlene, to join us at a beach house we'd rented for a week in Oxnard. On the first evening, we sat up talking a long time—sharing visions and dreams in the Lord. The next morning, some new ideas crystallized.

Keith and Loren had ministered together a few times now, and Keith thought they made a great team.

"Loren, let's keep doing this!" he said. "Let's go across the nation together and get the word out about missions and challenge people to go! I'll have big concerts and you can come and share the vision."

"That sounds wonderful," Loren agreed, "and let's have a faith goal of seeing one hundred thousand people raised up for world missions."

One hundred thousand! That number jumped out at me. While in Greece, Keith and I had sat on the beach under the stars with Don and Deyon Stephens and prayed for the lost. Keith looked up into the clear sky of countless, twinkling lights and asked God for one hundred thousand short-term missionaries. We all agreed in prayer. Now, on another continent, at another beach, Loren had come out with the same number to pray for.

A beautiful sense of God's presence filled the room. We all felt it was a special moment, and knew we needed to pray together and seal everything in the Spirit. Like old friends, we moved almost effortlessly into deep levels of prayer.

Loren prayed about the vision.

"Lord, you see the whole world and all the needs in it. Show us how to get more laborers to the field. We're asking for one hundred thousand, Lord."

Keith was lying on the floor, face down before the Lord.

"O God," Keith said, choked with emotion, "help me be a vessel to carry this message to your people. I want to do my part. Give people open hearts—to hear."

"And God," said Darlene, "we ask that you would especially speak to the Christian youth. Show us how to stir them with a vision to reach the lost."

I'd felt a prayer building up in my heart as well, and I jumped in after Darlene: "Lord, please let your people see that being a missionary is not 'weird,' but that it's the most exciting way to live on the face of the earth!"

By the time we were done praying, our hearts were bonded together. We knew the Lord had knit us for ministry purposes as well as the joy of friendship. For Keith, it was even deeper than that. In a way, his heart had found a home. Loren was so full of grace, and he wasn't rattled by Keith's high intensity. Loren loved and accepted Keith, and Keith knew it. As they embraced to say good-bye, there was a very tender spirit between them. There were tears in Keith's eyes.

"You're a father to me," Keith whispered.

It was an awareness in both of their hearts—a rare and special relationship. A gift from the Lord.

As we watched the Cunninghams drive off, we had such a rush of excitement in our hearts. Keith was going to travel all across America with Loren, stirring people toward missions!

How could any of us have known it was not to be?

Top: Keith with the kids, fall 1981

Bottom: A beautiful picture of Keith with the kids, spring 1982

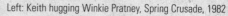
Left: Keith hugging Winkie Pratney, Spring Crusade, 1982

Below: Keith and Loren Cunningham in Oxnard, California, just a few weeks before Keith died

Keith marrying Terry and Carol DeGraff, June 13, 1982

Don Stephens with daughter Heidi and wife Deyon; Melody and Keith on M/V *Anastasis*, Greece, 1982

Left: Keith and Josiah.

Below: Keith and Rebekah

Above: The photo of the fishing story Melody writes about—Colorado, Keith and Melody's last photo taken together. Right: Last Days Ministries staff on the water wheel at the ranch.

17

"UNLESS A GRAIN OF WHEAT . . ."

A string of strange events happening around the same time left us with an unsettled feeling after we returned to Texas. First, our dog started acting strange. We got her in California just before Libre died, and we had named her Cy because she was part coyote. Keith took her to the vet, and he discovered she had cancer. Cy was headed toward a slow, painful death, and we had two options: we could put her to sleep, or Keith could bring her home and shoot her. The vet said shooting her would be quicker and more humane.

"Shoot her? I don't even own a gun," Keith objected.

When he got home and told me the news, he was visibly upset.

Nevertheless he borrowed a gun and walked out into the fields, Cy walking painfully at his side—totally unsuspecting. I choked up as I watched them go.

When Keith came back, he told me he took Cy to the edge of the grave he'd dug and told her to sit. She was wagging her tail and looking at him with her big liquid-brown eyes. Keith closed his eyes and pulled the trigger. He returned home spattered with her blood and very upset by the whole thing.

Next, a freak fire started in the storage closet of the new family room we'd built on our home. We were up after midnight having a meeting with some of the ministry leaders when we smelled smoke. At first we couldn't figure out where the smell was coming from, but we sniffed our way over to the closet. Somehow a feather comforter stored on the top shelf had gotten too close to a bare lightbulb that might have been left on for days. When we opened the door, it was smoldering and smoking, ready to ignite. Only the fact that we'd been awake and in that part of the house had saved us from a more disastrous fire quickly consuming our one-hundred-year-old wooden farmhouse.

Then Keith and I were talking in the family room one day when we heard a loud crash! We jumped at the impact and rushed into the kitchen. Part of the ceiling had fallen down—a huge, six-by-four-foot chunk of drywall was lying on the floor right in front of the sink. It was soaking wet and felt like it weighed a ton. There must have been a slow leak in the roof. My first instinct was to be sure one of the kids wasn't trapped underneath. They were in another room, Josiah playing with his little men and Bethany with her "babies." I sent up a prayer of gratitude, knowing that if either one of them had been playing on the floor there, the weight of the ceiling could have caused severe injury—or worse.

Then there was this other, more vague feeling. Keith was the one who voiced it. "I just don't know what it is. Things are going too good. I feel it's the calm before the storm, like something bad's going to happen."

Just hearing him gave me an uneasy feeling too.

The truth of the matter was things really were going good—very good. Even Keith's journal entries reflected the mood:

> We have so much to be grateful for. The only thing we need is a closer walk with God. We have everything else a Christian couple could ever want, and for this I'm eternally grateful, Jesus.

Earlier in the year, we had started a ten-week, Intensive Christian Training School for believers interested in learning more about the character of God and about Christian service. We were also just raising the beams on our new, half-million dollar cafeteria and worship center with classrooms, bookstore, guest rooms, and plenty of space to fellowship.

At one of those early ICT classes still being held in the Ranch House, Keith said, "I've been going back through our tracts and rewriting them a little bit. Taking out some of the rough edges and barbs. Keeping what's from Jesus and taking out a lot of what's from Keith. There are even a couple of them I'm just going to take out of print. Our message, as you will see, will be to strengthen, encourage, and build up believers—not so much to shoot at things that are wrong but to build up the areas that are right. I'm not saying that what I wrote or preached in the past was wrong. It's just that some of it could have been said a little differently—and with a lot more grace."

Grace. That was the operative word in Keith's life these days. Keith had already decided to quit distributing "The Selling of Jesus," and he was making changes in his "What's Wrong with the Gospel?" message to Protestants and in his message to Catholics too. He believed he'd been too harsh in places and realized how wounding pure doctrine could be without considering the state of someone's heart toward the Lord.

He told me, "There's just too much of me in them."

Keith had even come to a place of believing that God could direct some Christian artists to do ticketed concerts. In his heart, I think he hoped these artists would make a way for those who could not afford the price of a ticket to still attend—but Keith was no longer willing to say someone who sold tickets was automatically in sin. He knew the Lord had led him in a totally different way, but he also knew God might tell someone else to do things differently.

I was seeing a new kind of thoughtful maturity coming into Keith's life. In part, I could attribute it to some of the relationships Keith had developed with people like Winkie, Leonard, John, Leland, and now with Loren. The grace, wisdom, and patience of these men were starting to rub off on Keith. Hungering for more contentment in his own life, Keith soaked it up.

One day Leland saw Keith walking down our road as he was driving in. He pulled over and rolled down his window. Keith had made some strong statements again, and Leland took a fatherly moment with him. As Keith poked his head into his car, Leland spoke kindly but firmly. "God is preparing you to become a strong voice," he told Keith. "I have no doubt about it. But as a friend I want to tell you that if you strike out at everyone and turn them off, you might lose your ability to speak into their lives. When God is ready for you to speak to leaders, the doors might not be open."

Keith looked at him for a moment and simply said, "Thank you. I need that. I need people speaking into my life."

Keith was coming into a lot of new light, and at each glimpse of higher ground he took action. Several months before, he'd begun to realize that his own humanity had crept into his leadership style at Last Days, and he wrote a very sincere and heartfelt letter to those who might have been offended. He acknowledged that we had erred with some of our rules and policies in the past, and he let people know how things had changed. To those who had been hurt, Keith said, "I am totally, completely, and utterly sorry."

Keith was also in the midst of writing letters of apology and making phone calls to different individuals whenever the Lord showed him there was something he needed to make right. It was a beautiful thing to watch, because Keith was so excited about seeing relationships restored that had been strained. He went at it with urgency. He wrote a letter to a huge listing of Christian bookstore owners across America, saying that when he decided to pull his recordings from the bookstores, he'd said some things too strongly, offending a lot of good people who really did love the Lord. Keith said he was only trying to be obedient to what God wanted him to do, but that bookstores were also a God-ordained way of distribution.

"My desire to not exclude anyone has not decreased at all," he wrote. "I hope you can understand that I am a man of principle, and yet, like a pendulum, I have a tendency to go too far to make a point. I fear that in the past I have done just that."

Keith wanted the bookstores to go ahead and sell his albums, but he wanted to have a sticker on each one that said, "If you cannot afford the retail price of this album, write to Last Days Ministries and we'll send you information on how you can get it for whatever you can afford."

Keith felt he might have been too absolute in some areas. There could have been another way to say the same things—that would not compromise his beliefs, but at the same time would make it easier for others to hear the spirit of what he was saying.

Keith also knew there were many others out there with strong personalities who might be trapped in their giftings, as he had been. Using himself as an example, he wrote an article in the newsletter called "For Prophets Only" (see KeithGreen.com; the article is retitled as "Man Behind the Message). Keith knew there was a prophetic gifting from the Lord, but this article was a balancing word for those who liked to think of themselves as "prophets." He wrote:

> This is something I think is a very common problem in the church today—young people (usually men) who believe that God has raised them up to tell people what is wrong with their ministry or their lives, or both. A common problem in the church today, these people are usually hurt, independent, talkative, stubborn, unteachable, and unyielding. I know because I have been one of them!
>
> They don't beat around the bush, but say exactly what's on their mind . . . aren't very popular, but don't care because they believe they're being persecuted for righteousness' sake. They find fault with almost everything and . . . say to be "kind" would be phony for them. They know that the fruit of the Holy Spirit includes kindness, gentleness, self-control, and long-suffering, but say most people misinterpret those Scriptures. Besides, there's a lot more in the Bible about zeal, judgment, and the wrath of God. Deep inside most of them really do want to please God, but they're so insulated from criticism (because they think they're a rejected prophet) that no one can reach them. Unless God intervenes in their lives they cannot truly be used in any long-term way because of their unteachable, uncorrectable spirit.

So many people told me I was a prophet over the years I believed they must be right.

It's not that I no longer believe I'm called to do that. It's just that now I see that every believer is called to do that.

I'm not called to be a prophet. I'm called to be a *Christian,* a servant of the living God! That is the highest calling that anyone can realize.

When I first saw all these changes Keith was going through, I found myself thinking, *I hope Keith doesn't lose his edge.*

No chance. As remarkable as his changes were, Keith was still unmistakably Keith—intense in his faith, outspoken in his opinions, and very strong in his convictions. Only now he wasn't quite as driven. He still got impatient and edgy sometimes, but he had more peace than ever before. As Keith received the grace God had given, he could extend more grace to others. And much of Keith's new hope seemed to be connected with his newest friend, John Dawson.

John Dawson invited us up to the YWAM base in Cimmaron, Colorado, where he was teaching for several days. Keith was ecstatic. He was hungry to spend more time with John—just talking, learning, and praying. I was all for it. Every time they hung out together Keith came away with a greater capacity to embrace God's love. And it was rubbing off on me too! I packed for all of us while Keith planned the travel. To my surprise instead of flying commercially, Keith worked it out with the YWAM Twin Oaks pilot to fly us up in our Cessna. It seemed to me like a long flight in a small plane, but Keith said it would cost less and be a whole lot more fun.

Our little family drove across the road to the airstrip. Josiah had his yellow bunny tucked up tightly under his arm, and Bethany was dangling her baby doll by one leg. The sky was crystal clear, and we were all ready for our adventure. It was so convenient not needing to drive to Dallas to catch a plane.

As we approached the Rocky Mountain foothills, the view was spectacular. It was perfect, except for the intense turbulence we encountered. The shaking and dropping of the Cessna 414 kept me praying under my breath while keeping my calm for Josiah and Bethany. Then seemingly out of nowhere I thought, *We must be crazy! What are we doing way up in the sky in this flimsy piece of tin—and with the children, no less!*

My thoughts were out of character. I'd flown in worse weather and never been afraid. I shook my head as if to clear my mind. But unwanted thoughts tumbled in anyway . . . *I don't think I want do this anymore . . . I don't want to fly in this little plane for fun . . . only if we're going somewhere that we "really need to be" like a concert or something.*

We soon found a smoother flying altitude, and the snow-capped mountains could be fully enjoyed from our birds-eye view. All was peaceful and serene as Montrose came on to the horizon. I forgot the turbulence and my troubling thoughts. I had no way of knowing how deeply they imbedded in my heart during that twenty minutes of turbulence—or that they would soon have a huge impact on my life.

We landed in Montrose and then drove up two hours of winding roads to get to Cimmaron. It sat at seven thousand feet in the last friendly valley before the Black Canyon—a canyon so deep the sun only hit the bottom at high noon. It was dark and foreboding the rest of the time. The first Ute Indians believed if you entered the murky chasm you'd never come out alive. That Black Canyon was just beyond our destination. The Cimmaron YWAM base by contrast was vibrant with life and jumping. It sat on bright green hills filled with colorful wildflowers and a few hundred excited young people following Jesus. But no one was more excited than Keith.

We went to John's teachings every day. Then Keith would monopolize the rest of his waking hours to talk about the Lord, church history, times and seasons, and being fishers of men—and of fish. John knew of a high mountain lake created by beaver dams, and we had one long memorable day there. Keith and Josiah were reeling in trout one after another.

Keith couldn't resist goading John. "Hey, my bucket's almost full. Might need to toss a few into your empty one, bro."

"Wait a minute," John replied with mock superiority. "I'm the Kiwi with honed outdoorsman skills; there's no way a Jewish musician from L.A. is going to out-fish me!"

And so it went all afternoon. I even caught a few. By the end of the day, between us all we had about 120 fish! On the drive back to YWAM Keith was so pumped he tried to figure out ways to get the fish back to Texas to feed all the LDM staff a fresh fish dinner.

"Mel, it would bless everyone so much," Keith said.

He sounded like a proud papa wanting to bring a surprise home for his kids. It took John and the pilot awhile to convince us otherwise. Instead, we had a huge fish feast for the whole YWAM base. It was wonderful.

In fact a lot was wonderful. I couldn't remember the last time we'd had such "normal" days. As I watched Josiah and Bethany jumping on the trampoline, picking flowers, and just playing together, I found myself counting my blessings. What a great time we had—fishing, late-night campfires, good friends—no concerts or writing deadlines breathing down our necks. But here on earth all good things do come to an end.

John came to say good-bye to us as we all loaded into the car for the ride back down to Montrose. There were many hugs and promises to see each other soon. Later, John told me that as our car pulled away he was suddenly gripped by the strangest feeling.

"I travel the world and say good-bye to friends all the time, but I've never felt like this," John said. "It was like an overwhelming sense of loss or grief hit me as Keith drove off. Like I wanted to pull Keith back and not let him go until I told him how I felt. It was so intense I began to chase your car as it headed down the road."

John's eyes filled as he continued, "As I ran after your car, my lungs filled with dust from your tires. I had just had to deliver my heart even if only God and some gawking YWAM students heard me. So I ran like a kid, choking as I cried out, 'Keith! Keith, I love you! I love you! I love you—'"

With the windows rolled up and the air-conditioning roaring, we never heard John. We just chugged down the mountain with big smiles on our faces. Colorado had been great, but we'd missed Rebekah. We were excited to get home and give her big hugs and kisses. On July 17, we celebrated Rebekah's first birthday. My mom and a few of Bekah's little friends came over for a small afternoon party. Later Josiah and Bethany had a sweet birthday moment with her on our back porch. Keith so loved her sparkling personality. She matched her middle name, "Joy" and always bubbling over with lots of chatter and laughs.

We had a lingering bounce in our steps after being in Colorado. Keith went mainly to spend more time with John, but it ended up being the restful vacation we'd envisioned for Europe. Keith was at rest in a new way and loving life. He wrote:

July 22, 1982

> *We went to Colorado and had a great time. The family and I caught about 120 trout. We had some good family fellowship and I can definitely say that I had my vacation. We have found out that Melody is pregnant! Thank you, Father, I truly pray this child is healthy!! Please, Father, I need your help. I am in great need of wisdom beyond my years and ability. Today I went to work on my missions article. Please help me redeem my time!*

I was so excited to be pregnant again! Four children seemed perfect to us. Keith called Doctor Paul in California to explore how he could do something so I wouldn't get pregnant again. I could hear Keith cracking all kinds of jokes with him. But I felt uncertain. After a few days of thought, I had a different idea.

"Keith," I ventured, "you're a few years younger than I am. If I die first, I want you to get married again. You might marry someone who still wants children, and if you couldn't it would be a shame." Keith was listening, wondering where I was going. "But if something happens to you and I remarry, I don't want to get pregnant again. I'm the one who should get something done, not you," I concluded.

Keith was surprised, but we both agreed. It seemed like the right thing to do.

We were making some big decisions, but nothing was as big as the inner changes happening in Keith. Others noticed the changes as well. Soon after I found out I was pregnant, all of Second Chapter came over to the Ranch House for dinner. They were leaving for New York the next day to do some concerts on the inner city streets with David Wilkerson. After dinner, Keith took Josiah outside with Annie and Nelly. There was a storm blowing up in the distance, and the thunderous, black sky was dramatic. They all stood at the top of a sloping field, and Josiah, his blond curls popping out from under his cowboy hat, was jumping up and down in excitement as they watched the colors change and the clouds roll by.

"Wow, Daddy, look!" Josiah shouted.

Annie sensed such a big difference in Keith. For him, everything usually needed a purpose, but now he wasn't saying, "This meadow would be prettier if there was an orphanage for the Lord in it." He was enjoying the simple beauty of God's creation.

Watching Keith hold Josiah in this relaxed moment, it occurred to Annie how different Keith was this summer of 1982 from the way he'd been just a year before.

She recalled a night in 1981 when we went out to dinner with Buck and her. On the drive home, she'd said, "I'm so grateful that God loves me. That's the first thing I knew about God, and it's gotten me through every bit of misery and every bit of joy."

Keith had replied, "Sometimes I'm not sure if God loves me. I know he's right. I know he's God. But as far as really *feeling* his love for me—well, I don't know his love like you do."

Annie's heart had hurt when Keith said that. But tonight, for many reasons, she was sure he'd discovered that love. She'd seen it in him. One afternoon Keith caught her eye in a chance moment and simply said, "I love you." He said it in such a free, yet forever kind of way—just like the love of the Father.

Now he was so relaxed, simply a happy daddy sharing the colors of the deepening sky with his little boy. Annie recalled they were all wondering if we'd get hit with any rain this time. Typical of the weather in Texas—your neighbor can get rained on and you won't. Sometimes storms just blow up out of nowhere.

On July 28, I stepped out onto our back porch and a blast of furnace-hot humid air hit me in the face. It was so stifling I could hardly breathe. It had to be the most oppressive day we'd had that year.

I hoped the air-conditioning would be working in the Ranch House, where I was headed for our regular prayer meeting. The entire ministry fasted one day a week, from after dinner Tuesday until dinner on Wednesday. Today, Wednesday, we'd all stopped as usual on a fast day to gather for worship and prayer.

Keith sat cross-legged with his guitar on the living room floor of the Ranch House and led us in worship. He seemed particularly peaceful as he lovingly gazed around the room at everyone. He was also visibly excited about our missions vision—and about me.

Keith surprised me totally when he announced, "God is going to raise up my wife! She is going to speak out against abortion—but that's not all."

Where was this coming from? Why now, just when I was pregnant again?

"The Lord is going to use Melody in a mighty way," Keith was saying, "and she's going to speak about many different things, in many different places!"

It was news to me. But I was willing, if that's what the Lord wanted.

Once the meeting broke, I eventually ended up in the office. Keith had already been there and had typed in his journal, which he now was keeping on computer. I caught Michelle's name on what looked like a very long entry, and I figured Keith must have been talking about her expected visit the next day. Not too long ago they had a chance to talk, and just last week they'd both written each other to try to sort out things. The letters literally crossed in the mail. My heart felt comforted and relieved that the Lord was healing our friendship. Like Keith, I really felt the loss.

I started to save Keith's entry so I could use the terminal to work on an article I was trying to finish. In the middle of the normal process, I lost confidence. What if I erased Keith's entry by accident? I went and found Keith, and he came in to finish the process. As usual, however, he was moving fast. He hit the wrong button and blipped out his own entry. Keith knew it was his fault, but he was upset with me for even messing with the computer while he was using it. I felt terrible. Luckily, he only lost that one entry.

One of the highlights of this blistering hot day was that John and DeDe Smalley were coming for a quick visit. We'd met them years ago, when we first started going to the Vineyard. They had six children and were on their way to Connecticut to start a home fellowship and eventually a church. They arrived shortly before dinner, and Keith took them on a quick tour of the offices. We sat talking at the dinner table in the Ranch House living room as we broke our fast.

DeDe and I were comparing notes on motherhood, while Keith and John talked excitedly about the new work in Connecticut. John was enthusiastic about the move and the new opportunities for ministry. Keith wanted him to lead one of our New Believers' Meetings after our fall tour on the East Coast. We already had some large arenas booked for it.

Josiah and Bethany came in just then. They were dressed in matching light-blue overall shorts, looking adorable. They had just returned from their swimming lessons, and their hair hung in damp ringlets around their sun-kissed faces. They both looked like little angels. I was proud, to say the least, of these two sweet little children.

After dinner Keith lost no time because it was getting late. Even though we were all tired, they wanted to see the rest of the ranch, including a quick sightseeing flight in our leased Cessna 414. Apparently John and DeDe had promised their children a plane ride, and Keith was excited to give them a bird's-eye view of the area. Our pilot, Don Burmeister, who'd flown in the military, would take them up.

I took our kids home to play while Keith took the Smally family on a tour in our station wagon to see more of the ranch.

Just a little while later, Keith rushed into the house. I was standing at the sink, and Keith wanted me to come with them on the flight. I didn't want to go, which was unusual. I rarely said no to Keith, let alone turn down an offer from him to go have fun.

Maybe that's why he stood there saying, "Please, Mel, I want you to come with us. Pleassse . . . it's gonna get dark soon, so we need to hurry. He glanced at his watch. The sun was going down soon. "Come on—" he said in one final attempt. Every second was inching toward sunset, and Keith could tell I wasn't budging. So he turned and dashed back out the door just as suddenly as he had arrived. I was immediately struck by the sudden silence. The living room was empty. Were our kids going too? No, Rebekah was still playing in her bedroom.

I ran to the front door. Keith was standing on the far side of the station wagon. He was just about to get in, and John and DeDe were inside already with all their kids. Josiah was inside too. I couldn't even see him amidst all the other heads. All I could see was Bethany. She was standing by the gate, and in her sweet, little girl voice, on the verge of tears, she called out, "Daddy, I want to go too!"

Keith said, "Let her in the car."

The door swung open, and Bethany took a few steps toward the car. I stood on the porch and thought, *No! Not her too. I at least want to keep Bethany!* It seemed like a crazy thought, and Bethany was lifted into the car. It was all happening so fast. I didn't expect all the kids to go.

Something didn't seem right. I wanted to run out and call my children back, but I didn't want to be a spoilsport. I knew they'd cry if I tried to separate them from the other kids, and chances were Keith would tell me he wanted to take them anyway. I couldn't understand where these awful feelings were coming from. I felt stupid for being a worried mother, and I told myself they'd be back in a few minutes, all safe and sound. Besides, with only Rebekah at home I could easily use the time to work on that article I kept trying to finish.

Just as Bethany was lifted into the car, Keith hesitated. He called across the yard to me in an offhanded way.

"If I don't come back, raise Rebekah to be a woman of God."

With Keith traveling so much, we'd talked about the possibility of death before, but this seemed like an odd time to bring up the subject. Of course, he was kidding.

"What about this one?" I said with a slight laugh, patting my just-pregnant tummy.

"If it's a boy, name him Daniel!"

"You mean you don't want me to name him after you?"

I said it playfully, but suddenly I really felt like I needed to know what Keith wanted. The conversation was starting to take on serious tones.

"Okay. If it's a boy, you can name him after me," Keith said with a grin.

Keith jumped into the car, and they drove off. As I walked back into the house, it felt so empty. So quiet. I really didn't like Keith taking the kids on the airplane any more than necessary. I felt so uneasy, but I figured I would grab the opportunity to work on my article. So I sat down at the computer and started to write. I knew I was going to feel silly about my fears when they all got back in just a few minutes.

But in a few minutes the phone rang.

It was one of the girls from the office. "Our plane just went down! I'm going to call an ambulance, but I wanted to tell Keith first. Will you tell him?"

It was like getting kicked in the stomach.

"Sure," I said numbly. I didn't want to take even a moment to explain that Keith already knew.

I grabbed the car keys and ran out the door, leaving Rebekah with one of the girls who was staying with us to help me with the kids.

It took me less than a minute to get to the mile-long runway, but try as I might to find our plane at the far end, I couldn't see anything. I drove down the airstrip, and there were people running. I saw Carol and asked her to jump in with me along with one of the guys. At the far end of the runway there was a large field owned by someone else. And beyond that there were woods. From the end of the airstrip I could now see a thin column of smoke rising out of the woods in the distance.

I remembered the phone message, "Our plane just went down." What did that mean? I'd thought maybe it just went down at the end of the airstrip—malfunctioned or skidded on its side after an aborted takeoff. But it had obviously meant the plane was in the air and "went down" from there.

Every breath I drew became a prayer, *Jesus . . . Jesus . . . Jesus . . . this can't be happening.*

I couldn't drive through our neighbor's field to the woods because it was fenced off. People were jumping the fence and going on foot, but it was a big field and I thought I'd get there quicker by driving. One of the guys I'd picked up said he knew how to get there on another road, but from the highway that bordered the south end of our property there was a locked gate across the road we needed to go through.

I waited in the car, while he ran to the nearest house to see if they could let us through. I was getting angry now. Did anyone know where we were going? I kept thinking I should have been there already. A numb feeling was covering me—only my stomach was turning. *Please God, let them be alive.*

The property owner came running out, and we all jumped in his pickup truck. Unlocking the gate, he drove us across the field and onto a road that wound through the woods. "Thank you," I said to him. "My husband and children are in the plane." Just saying it out loud gave voice to my mounting panic. I felt like I was going to be sick. I kept praying quietly. All I could utter was, "Jesus, Jesus, please, O God . . ." Finally it looked like we were close. It had taken so long that an ambulance was already parked at the edge of the woods by a barbed-wire fence.

I jumped out of the pickup and someone lifted me over the fence. Then I took off through the thick, uncleared woods—my thin gauze skirt catching on the sharp branches and underbrush—not really knowing what direction I should go. Other people were running through the woods, too, and I was very frustrated because they all seemed to be passing me.

I stopped a few times totally out of breath, feeling like I might pass out, but I had to keep going. My husband and children needed me.

I kept running, listening for their screams or cries. It was totally quiet, except for my heavy breathing and the sound of people running through the woods. Since I didn't hear anyone crying out in pain, I told myself that everyone was probably fine. Maybe a little shook up, but fine. I thought, *Keith might even be amused when he sees how distraught I am. I'll never hear the end of it.*

After what seemed like an eternity, I broke into a clearing.

Instantly I was overwhelmed by the awesome silence that just hung in the air. Everyone there was standing still. No one said a word. I felt something warm beneath my feet. The ground I was standing on was black and smoldering. Hopefully, I peered through the smoky haze, but I didn't see Keith or the children, or anyone else who was on the airplane. I didn't even see the plane.

One girl I knew walked toward me. Tears were slipping down her face. She looked at me as if to say something, then quietly passed by. I didn't understand. Walking forward into the silence, I headed toward what seemed to be the center of the charred area. Some trees were broken off halfway up, and the ground was littered with downed limbs, like there had been a big explosion. Everything was totally calm—and hushed.

I finally came in sight of a blackened, smoking metal shell. *Where were my babies? Where was Keith?* One of the men walked up and hugged me—wrapped his arms around my shoulders and almost hung on me, sobbing out loud. I started crying too, but I wasn't sure why. I thought, *Maybe this isn't even our plane! Maybe another plane crashed and we only thought it was ours.* I asked someone, but it was our Cessna. *Maybe someone had been thrown from the plane.* They had already searched and found no one.

I got as close as I could to what was left of the airplane. I looked right inside because the top was completely gone. Everything was charred. I couldn't see anyone. I tried to focus on shapes . . . Is that Keith there . . . or my babies? I suddenly stopped myself and thought, *What are you looking for, Melody? What do you want to see? Do you want to see your husband and children burnt to a crisp? Is that the way you want to remember them?*

I quickly turned and walked away and didn't look again. In a few minutes, Janet, our pilot's wife, arrived. She was stunned, but calm as we spoke.

"Where's Keith?" she asked.

"Keith was in the plane with Josiah and Bethany and the Smalleys."

"Oh, no!" she exclaimed.

Then, because there was another pilot who sometimes flew besides her husband, Don, Janet asked, "Do you know for sure who was flying the plane?"

"As far as I know, Keith said Don was the one taking them up," I replied. I realized my answer would crush her world, too. Some rescue workers arrived. They were asking how many people were in the plane, and I was the only person who knew exactly who was on board.

The wreckage of the Cessna 414

I started counting. "There were the Smalleys with their six kids—that's eight. And Keith and our kids, and Don. Twelve."

The rescue workers just looked at me when I told them. Then it hit me too. *Why on earth did twelve people go up in that plane?*

Now I felt so weak I wanted to lie down, but there wasn't any place there in the woods. I suddenly felt so very vulnerable. There was no point in staying around, so I turned and started back out of the woods. Janet and Carol came too.

When we were almost out of the woods, we passed a fireman on his way in. He must have thought I was a survivor because I'm sure I looked a mess.

He smiled. "Everybody okay?"

I simply said, "There are no survivors." What that meant to him, and what that meant to me, were two different things.

As Janet, Carol, and I, and a few others were driving back through the field, the strangest thing started happening. It had been a totally clear day, but dark clouds suddenly seemed to gather out of nowhere. Large lightning bolts shot from the clouds over our property all the way to the ground, and it suddenly started to rain. The drops were huge, like fifty-cent pieces, as they spattered against the hot windshield.

We turned onto the highway and drove along our property line. It was easy to see that the clouds and lightning hits were only over our land! The raindrops looked like huge, heavenly tears. We felt the distinct presence of the Lord in those moments. He wanted us to know he was there. What happened was not apart from his knowing or caring. Most definitely what we were seeing was a demonstration of his power—and his presence.

When I got home, I headed straight for the phone and called Leonard before doing anything else.

"Leonard, this is Melody," I said, still numb. "Keith and Josiah and Bethany have gone to be with the Lord."

"What? I'll be right over!"

Then I fell on my knees beside my bed and started sobbing.

Later I was hit with every emotion imaginable. I felt like my insides had been ripped out, but by some mistake I didn't die. Waves of numbness and intense sorrow washed over me again and again. Sometimes I cried my heart out to the Lord. Other times I could talk about the crash as if I were talking about something that had happened to someone else.

My last conversation with Keith kept returning to my mind. *What prompted him to talk about not coming back? Why didn't I say something about my concerns? Why didn't I grab Bethany when I had the chance?* I felt so guilty, and so selfish for wanting to get some writing done instead of thinking about my children's safety. Maybe the plane wouldn't have crashed if there had been one or two fewer children in it. Maybe it was all my fault.

One of the most difficult things was not having Keith to talk to, especially about the children. Keith was the only other human being who could possibly understand my anguish over losing Josiah and Bethany, the only one who loved them as much as I did. I'd begin to say things to him like, Keith, you won't believe what happened, or, Keith, our babies are dead. But before I could get the words out, reality came crashing in. Keith couldn't answer me. He was dead too. He couldn't hold me while I cried. He couldn't tell me we would make it, and that he understood. I was on my own with God for the first time. I really wondered if I could make it.

Besides my personal loss, I thought of the others on the plane— they were gone as well. They were such wonderful people who were totally committed to helping others and serving God with all their hearts. And all the beautiful children!

None of it made any sense.

I also grieved over losing Keith's ministry to the world. What a terrible loss. We so desperately need people like Keith, people who love us enough to tell us the truth. With all that the Lord had been showing Keith recently, I knew his ministry would have been more powerful than ever.

I knew God was ultimately in control. He didn't intervene when the plane started to go down. He could have, but he didn't. That must mean the crash was his will. Or was it? Maybe it was a strategy of the enemy to get rid of Keith. Even if God allowed it, I had a million questions. But even knowing why wouldn't change anything.

The only thing that kept me going was a sense of the presence of God. I was blanketed in his grace. I felt his presence like I'd never felt it before. Buffering the blows. Holding me. Comforting me. It didn't erase the pain. But I felt God's tender heart for me. The pain was real and it was constant. When I wanted to lie down and not get up, he helped me to my feet. When I didn't want to eat, he reminded me of the new life inside me that he'd given me to take care of. And my precious little Rebekah needed me too.

Some things I had to just put on hold. For now the loss of my husband, two children, and nine others was enough to deal with. The reality of the situation demanded my immediate attention.

Word about the crash traveled quickly through our quiet little community of Garden Valley, and my home was filled with activity, especially the coming and going of friends. Leonard and Martha Ravenhill, Leland Paris, Jimmy and Carol Owens, who had moved here from Hawaii. Many others came too. I was comforted by so many people who loved me and showed it by their caring presence. They brought me food, cried with me, and dropped their lives to help me pick up and go on with mine.

On the night of the crash, John Dawson phoned. His first words to me were, "What we need right now is just to hear from Jesus. Get a pencil."

I grabbed one immediately and wrote swiftly as John spoke the heart of the Lord to me:

> They are with me.
> My glory is revealed to them.
> They are in my arms, in my presence,
> Not far from you, for I am with you also.
> Nothing has been in vain.
> I will build on this foundation.

In gentleness I will lead you
And a multitude will enter my presence.
But a little while, my daughter,
And you, too, shall enter my presence—
For life in the body is as a passing shadow.
In that day I will wipe away every tear,
For you will all sit at my table.

Then John said, "Melody, your own healing comes from entering into their joy." That really spoke to me. I knew it was right.

But it was easier said than done. I did rejoice that Keith and the kids were with the Lord. I knew I would see them again in heaven, which made heaven all the sweeter to me. It was deeply comforting to know that my loved ones were in the presence of the Lord. I knew they were fine, but I was miserable. I missed them. I not only missed them now, but I was missing the years of relationship I expected to have with them. My faith in Jesus was strong, but still I was devastated. My whole world was blown apart. Life as I knew it would never be the same.

On the morning following the crash, I opened my eyes and for a split second it felt like any other morning. That was the only relief of the day as reality hit like a ton of bricks. I had a scheduled doctor's appointment that day to go in and have my pregnancy officially confirmed. I decided to keep it. I had to spend my time doing something. My mom went with me.

My pregnancy was confirmed, but being in town was terrible. The plane crash was headline news, complete with pictures. I saw newspapers in the drugstore and outside the restaurant where I stopped to eat. I wanted to stop and scream out loud to everyone—"That's my family! My husband! My children! How can you act like everything is normal? How can you be smiling today?"

I felt a sudden flash of anger when I saw older people too. I knew it was irrational, but still I wondered, *How come they get to live so long when my precious family died so young?*

For a few days, my friends Chris and Carole Beatty slept in the family room by the front door to provide a sense of security for the household. It was a good thing because as news of the crash broke, the media came out in full force. It got crazy. News helicopters circled overhead, and we were swamped with reporters and camera crews wanting statements. A blockade was finally set up at the Last Days driveway to maintain some sense of privacy. So the news teams camped out there, just a few hundred yards from my door. Reporters knocked on my door too, but Chris was there to talk to them.

In the next few days, I ended up having a lot to do. I had to find X-rays of Keith and the children so the coroner could identify bodies. I needed to buy a coffin, pick out burial clothing, find a cemetery, and plan a public memorial service and private burial. Keeping busy was a helpful diversion from my mounting nightmare.

As word got out, friends began arriving for the memorial service scheduled for Saturday, July 31 at the Agape Force ranch. Among them were Bill Maxwell, Don Stephens, Billy Ray Hearn, Todd Fishkind, Rich and Pam Boyer, and many others from around the nation.

Michelle came too. It wasn't the reunion we'd expected, but just being together sealed the healing that had already begun.

Word also started to fan out all over the nation and literally around the world. Loren Cunningham was in Okinawa, Japan, when the news came over the U.S. Armed Forces radio station. Don Stephens was in Finland when he heard. Keith's parents were tracked down in the middle of the night at a campground. Keith's grandmother, also in Southern California, unfortunately found out when she saw Keith's picture flash across her TV screen on the early morning news.

Phone calls, letters, flowers, and telegrams poured in from people of all walks of life who had been touched by Keith and his music. I even got a message that Bob Dylan had phoned. It touched me that he cared, and I was sad that his call wasn't sent over to me. But the majority of messages came from Christians out on the front lines somewhere, who had been encouraged to serve Jesus in a deeper way because of Keith's ministry.

One of the important details I wanted to take care of was to write a letter to everyone who received our newsletter. On Friday, July 30, I sat at a computer to tell what happened to those who hadn't heard over the news—to let everyone know that I was all right and that God was faithful. With all my heart I believed God was sovereign, and I held fast to that truth. I wanted everyone else to hang on to it too.

As I sat there thinking, praying, and crying, a phrase came into my mind out of nowhere—*a grain of wheat.*

I thought, *Isn't there something in the Bible about a grain of wheat?* I looked it up. It was John 12:24 (NASB): "Unless a grain of wheat falls into the earth and dies, it remains by itself alone; but if it dies, it bears much fruit."

I caught my breath as I read this. It was the first time I'd ever received a scripture in that way, and it was so specific. Was this the Lord speaking his heart to me regarding Keith's death? One of the things I was troubled about was the loss of Keith's ministry to the world. *Was this God giving me a promise? Could he redeem even this disaster? The verse seemed to be a promise, but how on earth could it be fulfilled?*

On Saturday we had a memorial service for Keith, Josiah, Bethany, and our pilot Don. Several people were going to speak, and I decided I wanted to say something if I could get through it. The memorial service was open to whoever wanted to come, but I was shocked to see all the cars lining the highway as we approached. Thousands of people had come from all over. Inside, it was standing room only.

Wayne Dillard, in his opening prayer, brought a very personal and sweet remembrance. "Lord, I see today that we're not the ones to have suffered the greatest loss—but also those who never knew Don and Keith and the Smalleys and the kids, those who were never touched by their lives or drawn closer to you because of their love and their commitment to you."

Bill Maxwell reflected on meeting Keith, and on those who had been impacted by his life. He said, "I met Keith before he did his first album. Billy Ray Hearn said, 'I have an artist who would like to talk to you about producing his album.' My first question was, 'Does he love Jesus?' Billy Ray said, 'You're gonna be in for a shock!' Keith was the kind of person that pricked you! He would arouse something in you. Sometimes it wasn't pleasant, but it all worked for good. Keith said we were like two rough edges working together, but something smooth came out of it."

John Dawson brought a word of comfort, encouraging us not to look at the situation from our own perspective. "Our friends who are departed from us are in a greater place of joy and contentment and fulfillment than they have ever known—or we could ever understand. And this, which we regard as a tragedy, prematurely put them in a position of receiving their hearts' desire."

I was planning to speak after John, but my heart was pounding so hard, I thought I'd pass out. I decided to try, and when I did, I felt the grace of the Lord bathe me.

"I know that Keith is where he wanted to be most," I said. "His heart was so with the Lord—he just had such a desire and burning to be close to Jesus, and he really didn't care about this life! The children were unexpected. I was not prepared for Jesus to take Josiah and Bethany. But I think maybe they needed to be with their dad, and God knew that. He took them on an airplane ride—and they just kept going. I don't understand, but I trust the Lord and I know that he has my best, and everyone's best, in mind.

"For those of you who don't already know, I'm pregnant and I'm due in March. I am so grateful. I think this pregnancy is God's mercy to me. I am not empty. Jesus gave Keith two babies, and he's given me two. We're gonna share them. I'm really rejoicing in that."

Next Tracey Hansen shared about Don. Tracey had worked closely with Don at Last Days. "I really loved Don," he said. "Don has two strong sons who know the Lord and Savior, Jesus Christ, and they desire to serve him with their whole heart. That's the mark of a successful father. The desire of Don's life was to serve the Lord God with all that he had."

One of the keynotes from Leonard Ravenhill's message was that this tragedy was making people all over the world respond to a sermon that none of us could have preached more powerfully. Somehow the Holy Spirit was saying to people all over, "Are you living too much for time, and not enough for eternity?"

"Hundreds of phone calls came to me," Leonard said. "Nobody said they loved Keith's preaching. Everybody said, 'We loved Keith.' David Wilkerson called from New York. He recently went into a town after Keith had been there and he said, 'That boy's got a message! Some of the churches were shaken in that town and the pastors ran home to do a bit of adjusting!'"

"The Salvation Army never spoke about dying—they always talked about being promoted," Leonard continued. "The embarrassment is if you get to heaven without any blood on you—without any notches on your sword. You'll have to go back to the junior class, I'm sure.

"Supposing Keith had just relaxed and said 'Let somebody else do it.' No, we're not going to be saved by works, but we're going to be rewarded for them! Someone once said, 'Any road will do if you're going nowhere.' I thought, *Wait a minute! There are only two roads.* Either you're marching to Zion on the narrow way that leads to life eternal, or you're in the jazz band going to a lost eternity!

"There are three kinds of people in the world this afternoon—those who are afraid, those who don't know enough to be afraid, and those who know their Bibles. The only people entering are those whose names are written in the Lamb's Book of Life. Isn't that wonderful? Is your name written there? . . . Nobody has ever cheated their way into eternity, into the presence of God. We preachers have the most serious job in the world. It's not to be popular, not to be nice. It's to get people to step out of darkness into the light. Life is short. Eternity is long."

Leonard spoke again at the funeral on Sunday. We had the burial, open only to personal friends, and I buried the children in the same coffin with Keith—in the arms of their daddy.

The only consolation I had in the terrible way everyone died was to hear that it was almost certain that they were all knocked unconscious from the impact of the crash and that they didn't suffer in the fire.

When it was over, in Jewish tradition, I picked up the first handful of dirt and threw it into the grave. My mother followed suit, and so did several others as the small crowd dispersed.

Just ten days after Keith and the children went to be with the Lord, the M/V *Anastasis* was due to dock in Southern California after its voyage from Greece. Keith loved the vision of the mercy ship so much that he'd sent twenty-eight thousand dollars to pay for its Panama Canal crossing and to provide food for the six-week voyage.

Keith planned to greet the ship, but I went instead. Leland Paris just happened to be on the same flight so we sat together. We talked about the future of the ministry that Keith and I had begun, and Leland was deeply encouraging about my role in seeing it continue. He said, "I was on a national radio program just before catching this flight, and they asked me about the ministry." Leland continued, "I told them don't worry, it will continue with Melody at the helm." I thought, *He must know something I don't know.*

At the docking ceremony, I spoke for about ten minutes along with several others. As the *Anastasis* pulled into the docks, Keith's recording of "Holy Holy Holy" was playing loudly over the sound system. It was a very moving moment for everyone.

In the coming days and weeks, talk centered around the impact of Keith's ministry and what it might continue to be. But when the visitors slowed down, in my quiet moments, many questions remained. I knew the Lord could tell me anything he wanted me to know. I didn't know if he would. I wasn't going to demand anything from him, but I did ask for any understanding he could give me. Trust was made for the darkness. I resolved to trust God's character, whether I got any insights or not. Still, I knew people were wondering why?

That was one of the biggest questions people asked over and over: "Why did the plane crash?"

Months after a long investigation, the FAA would conclude that the crash was caused by human error, rather than some type of equipment failure. Thinking back it had been a very hot and hectic day, and our pilot had been fasting too. He had just landed another plane that handled differently than the Cessna. And Keith could have been hurrying everyone along to beat the darkness. Really, only God knows exactly what happened. For me, the question wasn't so much why? I knew I'd never have a complete answer to that this side of heaven. For me, the questions were: How was I going to make it without Keith? What would Rebekah and my new baby do without a father? What would God do with Keith's ministry now? Would the Lord fulfill the promise of the Scripture he had given me?

The thought about the grain of wheat turned out to be very significant. At the same time I'd received that Scripture at my desk in Texas, God was speaking to someone else on the other side of the world. In Japan, when Loren Cunningham heard the news about Keith, a Scripture immediately leapt into his mind, "Unless a grain of wheat falls into the earth and dies . . ."

This was far more than a poetic note of comfort. In the months following Keith's death, remarkable reports came from across the country and around the world. Almost at once I was beginning to see how the falling of this one grain of wheat was indeed going to bear fruit for the kingdom of God.

The Lord touched millions of lives through Keith, and he would be missed. When he died, a deep grieving swept through the body of Christ. There was a sobering too. God took one of his choice servants home at the age of twenty-eight, and it spoke reality to all of us. We have no time guarantees. I wondered if I would have been ready to stand in front of God with no advance warning. A lot of people asked themselves the same question.

Winkie spoke at several summer festivals that year. And every night after he spoke, it was the same. Crowds of young people gathered around him and opened their hearts. Most of them were weeping as they told Winkie, "I've gotten serious with God since Keith died!" "God told me he wanted me to shine his light in the darkness!"

Winkie missed Keith so much that sometimes these moments were difficult. But he was overjoyed to see firsthand how so many lives were being turned around everywhere.

And of course, many told me their reactions when they heard about the crash. One guy I'd never met before told me he was driving in his car when he heard the news on the radio. Stunned, he pulled off to the side of the road and wept. Another fellow I hadn't known told me he took three days off work and grieved as if someone in his family had died.

Both said they'd cried out to God, saying, "Lord, who's going to speak to our generation now?"

Both got the same answer: "You are."

God was using the pain people felt over losing Keith to call them forth. Not to replace Keith, because no one can ever be replaced. Keith's unique expression of Jesus was gone. But the void was used to point believers to Jesus. Many realized they'd been cheering Keith on, but the things he was doing or saying could never replace what God wanted them to do.

Who was going to speak out now? The answer was in Keith's "For Prophets Only" article where he said, "Every Christian is called to speak to their generation."

One day, while I was sitting in a Dallas coffee shop with our good friend John Dawson, John brought up the conversation he'd had with Keith about the prophet's test of taking his or her wide circle of influence and using it for God's bigger purposes.

"John, do you think Keith passed the test?" I asked.

It was quiet for a moment as John studied his hands. Then his face brightened.

"Oh yeah! Of course, he did."

"How?"

"Keith was really well-known, and many people were willing to follow him. But he wasn't going to amass all that power and influence for himself or even for Last Days! He wanted to raise up one hundred thousand people for short-term missions, and millions of dollars for missions service—and not just for YWAM, but for missions groups everywhere."

"Wow, Keith really did pass the test! He really did yield his life and his ministry to God's larger purposes for reaching the world!"

"Keith simply wasn't into just building his own kingdom," John concluded. "He wanted to work with others to build God's kingdom."

"That's true," I said. "I'm so incredibly proud of him!"

"I am too," said John. "I am too."

Over the years, I kept hearing wonderful things about Keith from people who knew and loved him. One of them, perhaps the experience I remember most clearly because it was so precious, came almost by accident.

I was on the East Coast to make a guest appearance on a Christian television program. Right next to my waterfront hotel was a little mall with lots of specialty shops. In a few stray moments, I decided to wander over and look around. I ended up in a little import store.

There was a young girl working there who patiently helped me look at some imported jewelry. She was very thin and delicate looking, which might be why the cross around her neck looked so huge. I wondered if she was a Christian. Then I noticed her faded blue-jean purse and jacket behind the counter, with several slogan buttons pinned on them. One of them read "I Love Jesus."

"I'm looking at that cross around your neck," I said. "Are you a Christian?"

Her eyes lit up. "Yes, I am. Are you?"

"Yes. I'm part of a ministry out in Texas."

"Really? What one?"

"Have you ever heard of Last Days Ministries?"

"Last Days? It sounds kind of familiar, but I can't really place it."

"Well, have you ever heard of Keith Green?"

"Keith Green? Oh yes! I love his music. I listen to it all the time."

"Well, I'm Melody. I was married to Keith."

She looked at me in surprise. Then her eyes immediately brimmed with tears.

"You're Melody Green? What are you doing out here?"

I told her, and then asked her how long she'd known the Lord.

"I've been a Christian for a year and a half. Keith's music is just about the only music I listen to. I love his music. It's changed my life and drawn me closer to the Lord. I sit down my friends who don't know the Lord and say, 'You have to hear this song!' I give Keith's music away all the time and keep having to buy more."

As we talked I could tell she'd been through some rough times. I could also tell that she was sold out to Jesus. She was new in her faith, but she'd already helped many friends and strangers come into a relationship with the Lord. She had a fire burning in her soul for God—and apparently Keith played, and continued to play, a big part in lighting the flame. As I saw the way her life had been touched by Keith's life, I saw how his ministry continued. Not before thousands, but in one life.

One precious life.

Wasn't that what it was all about?

This girl thought I was someone special, but she had no way of knowing how special she was to me. Before I left, we held hands and prayed while a few customers browsed. As I walked back out into the sunshine, and later caught my airplane home, my heart was filled to overflowing with thoughts of the goodness and mercy of God. He had just given me another glimpse of what loving him was all about.

Top left: Melody with Rebekah and Rachel

Top right: Melody with President Reagan in the Cabinet room

Left: Rebekah and Rachel singing on tour

Above: LDM Team in Moscow

Right: Keith Green Memorial Concert Tour

"WHEN TRIALS TURN TO GOLD"

There are no words to express the extreme mercies and blessings God has continually poured into my life. I have walked through some difficult times, but the wonder of it all is that I've never walked alone.

I am convinced that God looks at death differently than we do— especially the death of the righteous. The Lord sees it from the other side of the veil. Those who get left on earth have one experience. But for those who enter into the presence of the Lord, it's a new beginning.

A long time ago Keith told me I could do something with his journals if anything ever happened to him. "Edited of course," he said with a smile. And some editing was needed for length, clarity, or privacy. No meanings or intents were altered, however.

I know Keith would have been comfortable with what is printed since he shared his testimony freely. Keith's family asked to remain unnamed for privacy's sake. And to protect the privacy of others, I changed some names or a few revealing details when their stories crossed paths with ours.

When this book was completed the first time, it was seven years to the day when Keith, Josiah, and Bethany had gone to be with Jesus. It was a signpost to me that God was with me in the timing. I did try to write it sooner, but maybe I needed time to heal before I could intentionally reopen the wounds.

This new updated and expanded version of the book was finished just a week after the twenty-sixth anniversary of the plane crash, which again I found interesting. I've taken on the work of this new larger edition only because the Lord keeps using it in such powerful ways. I receive letters or hear stories almost daily to attest to that fact. I am amazed by how this book has gone around the world. It has been translated into several languages and more are in the works.

Keith was extremely serious about his relationship with God. He wanted to cooperate with the Lord so that his own life would be increasingly transformed. He also did all he could to convince others that God could change their lives too. I'm certain he hoped his ministry would make a difference. But I don't think he ever imagined that God would also use the story of his own short life as a tool.

One of the important messages of this book is that what God did in Keith's life, he can do in yours! Keith had only known Jesus for seven years when he went home. Because of his high profile as a new believer, he did a lot of his growing in the public eye. He didn't have the luxury of years of obscure service so that he could emerge in a more tidy way. Keith hit like a bombshell, and then left just as suddenly.

I believe the Lord has something he wants to impart through Keith's story. I hope you will be encouraged personally to find the call God has on your own life. I also think there's something precious to glean from closely observing the strengths and weaknesses of a fellow struggler in the faith. Maybe it's the simple fact that we all have areas of weakness, but God is faithful to use us to the fullest when we totally give ourselves to him. God accepts us right where we are and keeps working with us!

The Lord has given all of us gifts and talents to use for his glory. Your gifts may be different from Keith's, but they're just as important. Whether you're most comfortable "up front" or "behind the scenes" doesn't matter. God wants to display his glory through you right where you are! For this to happen, you first need to be sure you are plugged into the giver of all gifts and all life—Jesus Christ.

If you don't already have a relationship with Jesus, I encourage you to open your heart to him. Jesus is knowable. Jesus is real. Jesus is waiting for you. God will be faithful to reveal himself to you if you sincerely ask him.

God knows what you've been through, what you've done, and how you feel—yet he has never, ever stopped loving you. There's not a life that can't be transformed, a heart that can't be mended, a wound that can't be healed. I know this from personal experience. When we give our lives to Jesus, he is faithful in all things! He may not spare us from every pain and sorrow, but he certainly carries us through those storms when our hearts belong to him.

The Grieving Season

There was no way around it, my time of grieving was very long and extremely painful. There were different waves, measures, and seasons.

The first year I was a mess. I couldn't get through worship without crying. I was always the needy one in the room. Always the one who received special prayers. I needed them desperately, but I felt bad sometimes, knowing others had needs too.

But I had decided I would walk through my valley in a genuine way. Not saying things like, "Oh, praise God! I'm so happy they are all in heaven now." Of course it was great to know where they were, but it didn't take away the pain of not having them with me. I didn't agree with some teachings that said mourning was selfish and self-centered. Granted, it's not healthy to get stuck grieving forever. But to think we shouldn't mourn the loss of someone we love is foolish.

When people asked me, "How are you doing?" I usually said, "Just keep praying for me." That was real. Still sometimes I lied and said, "I'm fine, thanks," to avoid saying something that might make me cry.

I came to dread that question. But I did realize it usually came from a heart of concern when someone didn't know what to say but wanted to say something. I had to protect myself sometimes by avoiding certain situations that made me feel too vulnerable. And I had many close friends to comfort me and to provide safe shoulders to cry on.

The most amazing thing was that within two months LDM launched the Keith Green Memorial Concert tour. I was suddenly traveling across America with Rebekah and a big team of people—and I was speaking in public for the first time. I had never done any speaking when Keith was alive and now I was in stadiums.

It was new to me. I spoke at every event along with the showing of a recording of Keith preaching, and with different YWAM leaders. These Memorial Concerts played a big role in helping me during my early stages of grief.

The leaders with me, and their wives, ministered to me deeply in wisdom and maturity. I was also part of taking a message about missions to the nation. It was a message I really had a burden for, and I knew it mattered to God. It was all much bigger than I was, so it helped take my eyes off of my own shattered life for bits and pieces of each day.

I was still a big mess, but backstage each night before going out to speak I said to the Lord, "Okay, God. Help me go out and share tonight. And please don't let me cry after I get my mascara on." Getting my eye makeup on became the moment of having to pull it together, and it worked more often than not.

As I spoke each night, God was faithful to me and I was blanketed in his grace. We traveled just into my eighth month of pregnancy. A wonderful side effect turned out to be that I was both trained and launched into public ministry during this painful yet rewarding season.

On the one-year anniversary of the crash I did two things. I took off my wedding ring, and in Jewish tradition I had a small graveside ceremony to put up the headstone. I wasn't actually trying to keep that tradition, but I had driven to the stonecutters several times and started sobbing in my car when I thought of going in and telling a stranger, "I need a headstone with three names on it, please."

It was too much. And too many.

Of course others were willing to do this for me, but I wanted to do it all myself. One day I made it out of my car, gave the stonecutter my design, and picked out the size and type of stone. The headstone was finished just before the first anniversary. It was set and unveiled at the one-year ceremony. So I kept Jewish tradition after all.

It easily took another few years to feel like I had made it past the worst of it. There were many milestones along the way. It was the grace of God that carried me through. I read in a book that gratitude would help keep bitterness from my heart.

And I *was* grateful. The time I had with Keith and the children was indeed a precious gift from God. I was also grateful to know the Lord. I can't imagine walking through such a valley without him. I do understand how easy it would be for someone to go off the deep end without help from God and understanding friends.

Like Keith and my children in heaven, God had a new beginning for me too. It just took awhile to realize it.

A Precious New Life

In March 1983, my beautiful daughter Rachel Hope was born. My hospital room was filled with family and friends—and a video camera. Keith would have loved it! Rachel had the sweetest little face and the biggest eyes looking up at me as I wrapped her closely to take her home with me.

But I wondered what kind of home was I bringing Rachel into? And what about little Rebekah? She wasn't even two yet. How would she react to a new member of the family? She'd already had her world rocked when the plane crashed.

How could such a young child grasp it when her whole world was turned upside down? At least I understood why we suddenly went from a loud energetic family of five to—something else.

When we were home, I was in shock and utterly dazed. I became a barely-making-it pregnant mom, with a very confused little one-year-old. The house was quiet, still, and lonely.

One of my daily duties before had been to keep Josiah and Bethany from hurting their little sister as they piled on top of her to play. Rebekah began walking around the house wondering where everyone had gone. Looking. Searching.

It was beyond heartbreaking for me to watch. Especially when she starting picking up Keith's first album cover, which had a big photo of his face on it. She would walk around the house kissing his face while saying, "Da Da. Da Da."

I tried to stay cheerful around Rebekah. Enough of her little world had fallen apart and then changed again when I began taking her around the country with me on the Memorial Concerts tour. I wondered if that would end up being a good thing for her—or not? But I certainly wasn't going to leave her behind.

I had so many big questions with no way to know the answers. Now with baby Rachel in the house I felt more like we had a little family again. And my mom was still next door as well.

Prayers, Songs, and Journals

I kept a journal and wrote a lot of songs the first few years after Keith and the kids died. What could I do to change things? Absolutely nothing. So I sat at the piano a lot and poured out my heart to God in prayers and songs. One song in particular rang in my spirit for a long time. It's a song I wrote for Rebekah and Rachel from my mother's heart, knowing they would never know the amazing father who absolutely adored them.

The following lyrics came from a very broken place. Only one or two people have ever heard the song. I've never shown the lyrics to Rebekah or Rachel, but I will before this book comes out. I'm sure many can relate to the feelings behind some of the words. It's called "Daddy Isn't Coming Home No More."

I know it's hard to understand
When you're so young
Bright eyed and bushy tailed
And on the run

And there's oh so many questions
I don't have the answers for

But daddy isn't coming home no more
Sometimes it hurts to know
You're going to miss his love
The other part of you
That you know nothing of

In my mind, sometimes I see you
Just wrestling on the floor
But daddy isn't coming home no more

But there is a Father in heaven
Who watches each move that you make
He tenderly holds out his arms
Applauding each step that you take

Yes there is a Father in heaven
Who catches you each time you fall
Compassionately kissing each bruise
Until the day of your own final call

Looking to the Future

In the first years after the plane crash, having a family to raise and becoming the leader of a large, busy ministry was a huge change. But having children made me want to live and take care of myself. And having the ministry gave me a purpose bigger than myself.

Both helped me look to the future. When I focused on what could have been, I stalled. But the Lord kept telling me he still had a call on my life even though Keith was gone.

Following my call to missions, when Rachel was about a year old, I took a trip all through Asia with a few YWAM leaders. The living conditions I would encounter caused me to go without my children. I went to several countries and ministered in refugee camps, a leper colony, mission bases, and various other places.

Mostly it was to observe and determine how LDM might be able to help. But in my heart I was asking God a big question: Did he want me to take my girls and move to Asia to be a missionary? I was willing, but the Lord told me clearly that part of my job was to call forth more missionaries, not become one full-time. But that trip was life changing, especially India, Thailand, and Indonesia.

East Texas: Loving God and Others

Meanwhile we had a comfortable life in East Texas. But I wanted my girls to experience the poverty and needs of the world firsthand. I wanted them to develop hearts of empathy and mercy so they would become women with generous spirits toward the needs of others.

I also wanted them to care about people of all kinds and colors. East Texas was not the Southern California melting pot of ethnic diversity I had enjoyed growing up in. Sadly there was some overt racial bias in a few areas around us. I wanted my daughters to understand prejudice and injustice from God's perspective, no matter what they might notice a few others saying or doing.

Starting when they were very young I created or seized situations and opportunities that would hopefully imprint their hearts. We went to the orphanage in Mexico several times. One time I helped the girls wrap a bunch of their own toys to give away to children who had no toys. We went to Mexico with a big box of presents, and the girls handed them out to the orphans and other children living in abject poverty.

In Texas we often saw people on the highway or in town holding a "hungry" sign. We'd stop to give some money or any food we had in the car. A few times we went to buy a bag of burgers to take back. Object lessons, I guess. Loving God and loving others was at the top of my list.

On the Road—Globally

In the coming years I still traveled, so my children did a lot of their growing up "on the road." Rachel had her first birthday in Canada during a concert tour. Rebekah lost her first tooth in New Jersey during a missions conference. After that we literally traveled around the globe together on several ministry trips. When they were about five and seven years old, we went with the LDM leadership team to places including Europe, the Netherlands, Poland, the Soviet Union, and Estonia.

In Estonia we were taken to the town square in Tallinn. Ulo was the Estonian believer housing us. He found a spot, looked at me, and said, "This is a good place. Preach here."

A crowd began to gather as I spoke loudly. My message was translated into Estonian first, then into Russian. Later that day I spoke in a large church.

Ulo traveled with us all the way to Moscow to translate for us. He could have been arrested. Estonia was separating from the Soviet Union and Estonians were not welcome. In Moscow we smuggled Ulo right past the hotel police guards every night, in very creative ways. And we visited two underground churches where we could only enter homes in twos. It was illegal to have foreigners in their homes.

We did get to go to Odessa, where secret police followed us after I tried to use American dollars to buy from a street vendor. We had to ditch them before we went to the church. I stood in the pulpit in Odessa and started with, "My grandparents were born here."

We had tiny soaps to give out at the end of the services, and people wept to receive them. That's unimaginable when you live in America.

It was quite an adventure for all of us, especially Rebekah and Rachel. And we discovered that the ice cream in that part of the world was the best we'd ever tasted!

"Mama, Why Is There a Baby in the Soup?"

Rachel and Rebekah also traveled with me during the mideighties when Americans Against Abortion began. We did a two-year campaign to share life principles across America and show the truth about abortion.

I remember Rebekah coming to my side while I was looking at a photo. She saw it before I could turn it over. It was a little baby who had been aborted and left in a bucket of liquid. She wasn't confused about what she saw. She simply asked, "Mama, why is there a baby in the soup?"

AAA was asking the same question across America. How can we do this to little babies? We partnered with two pastors we had just met, Norman Stone and Jerry Horn, from Wisconsin. They had a plan to walk shore to shore to share life principles, and that's what we were talking about too. So we supported their efforts and just called it "AAA Walk America for Life."

AAA also launched a petition drive, and gathered three million signatures appealing to Congress to change the abortion law. We met up with the pastors who were walking across America in strategic places and did countless events together for two years.

During the AAA campaign I had another divine appointment. We were on tour in Chicago and met Ed and Cathi Basler, who became dear friends and first introduced me to Israel. It took about ten years before Cathi and I made our first trip there together. But it wasn't our last trip.

Going to Israel set an important piece into place for my life and I'll have exciting news to report soon! We raised our children together and became partners in ministry too. It's amazing how God links you with certain people in a forever kind of way when you least expect it.

The Single-Mom Challenge

Being a mom has been my greatest joy. But being a single mom was my greatest challenge. It was especially difficult because I worked full-time just like most single moms. Because I was leading LDM, however, it was not a nine-to-five job. When ministry deadlines or crisis hit, I might work into the wee hours and on weekends.

I often felt torn, as all working moms do. When I was working, I felt bad I wasn't with my kids, and while I was with them, my mind was often preoccupied with work and deadlines. I felt guilty so much of the time. *How could I do it all? How could I be a mom* and *a dad?*

Father's Day and father-daughter events of every kind always accentuated the void. And some of the areas Keith would have been strong in, like being the disciplinarian, were areas of weakness for me.

Living in community, however, was a huge blessing. If my car or washing machine broke down, I only had to phone the office across the street. Someone from the right LDM department would come do what was needed. Unlike most widows and single moms, I didn't have to worry about strange workmen coming into my home.

I had plenty of help with my housework too. And until my girls were in junior high I always had help caring for them. The kind of help I received is certainly not usual for any mom, let alone a single one. I was in an extremely blessed situation, which helped take off some of the normal stress a newly widowed woman would face.

The last girl helping us was Debbie Schneider, who lived in our house for six years. Debbie married Chuck Farrington, one of the leaders at LDM, and is still one of my dearest friends and remains a true auntie to Rebekah and Rachel.

I've always said, "I suffered one of the worst of tragedies, but I was in the very best of all places when it happened"—a community of people who loved God and loved me.

It wasn't a church or a church community. It was a community of people living on the same land together. Like a village. I couldn't have made it without everyone's constant help and prayers. I owe them all a great debt of gratitude.

I share this because I'd never want another widow or single mom to measure their experience by mine. I was not a superwoman. I was simply surrounded by super people.

God has been amazingly faithful to Rebekah and Rachel and therefore to me. Early on I decided I would fully trust him to add into their lives the things that I just didn't have to give them. And to minimize the mistakes I made. I prayed in faith that God would be faithful to them, and I have watched him do it.

As teenagers Rachel and Rebekah went on numerous trips to do volunteer service in places like Africa, Mexico, Peru, India, and Israel. God made provision for my daughters to be able to go on such amazing travels. It gave them a peek at the world while being educated and tutored through personal experience. I am so grateful.

Mother-Daughter Trip

Rebekah turned seventeen during a pre-graduation mother-daughter trip we took overseas. We went to some really beautiful places. But I added a stop to the beginning of our trip. It was a place from our family history—Auschwitz-Birkenau. I had my own reasons for wanting to go, but I felt there was also a purpose for Rebekah to have the experience as well, although I'm not really sure why.

We traveled to Poland. This time we rode the rails from Germany to Krakow. We were there on Rebekah's birthday and celebrated with a dessert in the town square. We took a taxi to find the factory owned by Oskar Schindler, who is credited for saving almost twelve hundred Jews from the Holocaust. We jumped out, and I took a picture of Rebekah in front of the iron gates made famous in the movie *Schlindler's List*.

Next, we did what we came for. We got on a bus and went to see the Auschwitz-Birkenau trilogy of Nazi death camps. These camps were the most likely ones where my mom's family would have been sent, had they not escaped Odessa when they did.

The Jewish population of that vast "Jewish City" was decimated. I'm certain many of our relatives spent their final days in Auschwitz-Birkenau. Someday I'll share in more detail, but it was a day I will never forget.

Gifts from Melody and Keith

I decided to give something to the girls from their father and me when they were in their late teens. Something meaningful. I gave my wedding ring with the little engraved cross to Rebekah. She wears it all the time. I gave Keith's wedding ring to Rachel, which she has on a chain.

Our rings meant so much to us that after Keith's was stolen at the beach we went back to the jeweler's. I gave him my ring to cut in half, and he made us two new rings. Each one had half of the original ring we were married with. Now the girls have them.

Update: Rebekah Joy and Rachel Hope

People always ask how Rebekah and Rachel are and what they're doing today. Many of you around the world have told me how much you prayed for the girls and me over the years. So I want to tell you your prayers were certainly heard! Thank you. Thank you. A million times thank you! It was prayer and the grace of God that got us all through.

Today Rebekah and Rachel are lovely grown women. They are great singers and gifted songwriters, too—which should be no surprise! Both chose wisely and married wonderful men who I love dearly.

Rebekah Joy

Rebekah met George LeBeau in Kansas City and they were married in 2002. I had the honor of walking Rebekah down the aisle to Keith singing "Oh Lord, You're Beautiful." After Rebekah and George both graduated from Wheaton University in Chicago, they moved to Los Angeles, where they've been furthering their education and careers.

A few years ago they put their lives on hold for about eight months, when I was sick and needed someone with me. I will never forget their amazing generosity. They've also traveled to India a few times together doing volunteer work.

They love living in California and have a great family of friends there, many of whom Rebekah has known since her childhood. Even though we live far apart, we remain close in heart, seeing each other often either here in Kansas City or in my old stomping grounds of Los Angeles.

Rachel Hope

Rachel met Bobby Taylor through Roddy MacIvor, a mutual friend who used to live at LDM with us. Afterward they had a chance to travel together for seven months with a ministry touring the States.

They were married in 2004 at the Little Brown Church where Keith and I eloped. They had a small private wedding and arranged for the son of the pastor who performed my wedding ceremony with Keith to marry them. George, like a big brother, proudly walked Rachel down the aisle while Keith sang "Rushing Wind."

Bobby is a graduate of Belmont University in Nashville and is now a worship pastor in Kansas City. Rachel and Bobby write songs together, and she joins him in leading worship as often as a busy mom can. They have two gorgeous little boys—so far. I just love being a grandma, and having them live so close to me is an added blessing.

Welcome to the Family!

I wanted to give George and Bobby something meaningful to welcome them into the small but mighty Green family. Keith had two rings besides his wedding ring. I gave Keith's high school ring to George because it had a big *G* on it. I hoped Rachel's husband, whenever he arrived, would like the remaining ring. It has a fish-shaped top with the letters "JESUS" inside. It suits Bobby perfectly! George and Bobby wear their rings all the time. They are truly sons to me.

A Mother's Thankful Heart

I am very proud of my daughters, and I know their father would be too. I wish they could have known their dad. I see so many of his qualities and personality in them. They would have had so much fun together and Keith would be going nuts over his grandkids.

But life is rarely perfect, and each of us has situations we would change if we had that ability. That's why knowing and trusting Jesus is the only way to live. Only God knows every detail, and only he is faithful to give grace and provide in ways that are humanly impossible.

My daughters are exactly who they are today because of the circumstances of their lives—the happy and the sad—and I absolutely love who they have become.

Pearls in the Wasteland

In the big picture I believe each person has a measure of painful circumstance in his or her life at some point. Pain and sorrow give us a challenge. We can decide if we will let ourselves remain in an angry or bitter place.

With God's help we can eventually come out on the other side of the storm. Then we can become vessels of grace and understanding to others who are in their season of crisis and pain.

Some cuts are deep enough to mark us forever. But after seasons and times of healing and restoration by God, we don't have to be controlled by our wounds. Even with healing we may always be marked by them to the greater good of our souls. Our injuries can be our biggest windows into aspects of God's character we might not have known any other way.

I know my losses deposited something deep into my spirit. Yes, I would have rather read a book to receive what God gave to me in those darkest of times—but some pearls are only discovered when the field looks like an impossible wasteland.

He is the God of the impossible. The God who tells us where to dig for the treasure. The God of great and tender mercies. And I love him with all of my heart.

Full Circle

I spoke at the Creation Festival in Pennsylvania last month. It was so huge I couldn't see the end of the crowd. They were expecting about ninety thousand people. I thought about being there with Keith, at their very first Jesus Festival, thirty years earlier. It was one of those crazy deja vu moments in time. I felt as if I had been there yesterday watching Keith minister from the wings.

Now I was the one standing on the platform speaking. And I wasn't even nervous. Just excited to be able to speak to so many people. As I was talking about having passion for God my mind was thinking, *How in the world did I get here? I never planned on doing this. Not in a million years.* And I smiled. Talk about coming full circle! God is good.

Over the years the ministry that Keith and I began has changed in size and shape several different times. The God of the impossible has kept his hand on us through each season of sunshine and storm.

It's an amazing thing to let go of something fully, only to have God return it to you later in a slightly different but better way. That is what God has done with LDM more than once.

The season we are in right now is really exciting. And I want to tell you about it so we can stay connected and so you can be blessed and challenged by all the pearls we've been able to gather together over the years. They are all in a cluster on our Web site.

We keep finding new treasures all the time, so visit us often. And please, drop me a note if through these pages the Lord has ministered to you in some way. I would love to hear about it—and, yes, I do read my mail.

Thank you for taking your time to read this book. May God bless you as you continue on your journey with him.

With love,

Melody Green

August 4, 2008

George and Rebekah LeBeau

Bobby and Rachel Taylor

Top left: Dan and Jamie Collins, Melody, Julie and John Dawson, July 4, 2001

Top right: Melody with boys from Josiah & Bethany Children's Home, Reynosa, Mexico, December 2007

Bottom left: AAA Walk America for Life Team—Jerry Horn, Melody, and Norm Stone

Bottom right: Melody and Cathi Basler—first time to Israel

THE KEITH GREEN LEGACY

It could have all ended in 1982 when the plane crashed. It could have all ended after Sparrow worked with Bill Maxwell and me to make a few albums of Keith's unreleased songs. It could have ended a lot of times. But it didn't.

So just how do you calculate someone's legacy? Seems you need to consider the fruit that remains. But how is that possible? It may remain today and be gone tomorrow. Only God can know.

And how can someone who always said, "I just want to be remembered as a *Christian*," end up with a legacy? Maybe that's why Keith actually has one.

Keith has certainly left an indelible mark on my generation—those who've walked with the Lord a few decades or more. His life and ministry also keeps impacting the twenty- and thirty-somethings of today. But the more I observe, I can see it's not stopping there.

Those just entering their teens today are listening to Keith's music, watching his concert DVDs, and reading his writings, as well as this book. And now they, too, have given their hearts to the Lord and been inspired to be radical for Jesus. Just like Keith, but in their own ways. Perhaps they will make sure their children and their children's children are introduced to Keith's ministry someday. Who knows?

I have always been reluctant to affirm Keith as being more than he was while he was alive. Keith himself would cringe, if he were here. But he isn't. So I think it's okay at this point to honestly assess the lasting impact he has made—and is still making.

If from his perspective, now being with the Lord, Keith could see how his short ministry keeps changing lives, he might say something like, "Wow, God, it's so cool that you can do that! I only knew you a few years!"

Some things are knowable regarding Keith's legacy, at least in broad strokes. The more distance we have from his death, the clearer it becomes. Let me share some things about Keith's legacy, starting with the most obvious.

Keith's Musical Legacy

If Keith's music were all we had left, it would be enough. It's constantly touching hearts around the world. Friends in Africa have heard it in remote villages. Friends in India report the same. I've heard it from all corners.

His songs are often described to me as "pure discipleship" or "pure worship." I know when people say those things they are trying to express what set Keith's music apart for them. It's very hard to express in words.

It's something you can feel in your spirit. Something that makes a listener's heart leap and say, "Yes! I want to love God like that" or "I want to help people like that." It almost demands a response. It draws you into worship or repentance or off to serve others and reach the lost. It takes you somewhere beyond the places you can usually get to.

In a teenage pre-Jesus song, Keith was candid about the songs he wrote—especially the songs with spiritual ideals. Keith knew even then that he often tapped into something bigger and better than himself when he wrote those songs. The lyrics said:

No one is as pure as the music they write
Because music is pure love
And you will see me crying when I'm alone
But you will join me shining when we go home

Keith carried that understanding into his years of following Jesus. He was never confused on this point. He made it clear he wasn't after the praise of men. He was giving his best effort to walk in humility at the very same time his albums were topping the charts. In a concert he said,

> I only want to build God's Kingdom and see it increase, not my own. If someone writes a great poem no one praises the pencil they used, they praise the one who created the poem. Well, I'm just a pencil in the hands of the Lord. Don't praise me, praise Him!

Assuming you've finished this book, I think you know I'm not interested in putting Keith on a pedestal. It would take too long, however, to qualify some of my following comments, so consider them all qualified now.

I've had a long time to think about Keith's music and to see the results. So why is his music so loved? Why is some of it so anointed and life changing? I have a few thoughts. First of all, Keith put God in charge of his life and talents and God liked that a lot. Then Keith decided he wasn't going to sing about anything he wasn't doing, or trying to do.

Keith also knew his time on stage was only a very tiny slice of the pie called his life. He knew God wasn't impressed with great songs and big altar calls. Keith knew he was like every other Christian. He'd say, "A plumber uses a wrench. I use music."

He knew he was called to live a life reflecting the Sermon on the Mount, 1 Corinthians 13, and the parable of the sheep and the goats. Obviously he understood that having a big ministry didn't exempt him from needing a big dose of the character and nature of God. God appreciated Keith's attitude.

Further, Keith also had a very unique mixture of elements in his life. He was sincere and passionate and people felt it. He had a massive God-given musical and performing talent. He believed music was his tool to share an important message, even before he knew what the message was. He had the energy and charisma of a rock star, but wanted Jesus to be the only star. He wasn't full of himself.

He believed in divine appointments, so he was happy sharing the Lord with a hitchhiker as well as with a large crowd. He remained accessible and touchable in spite of his celebrity. He was led by the Holy Spirit and not managed by an agency. And he had a healthy fear of the Lord, believing he was ultimately accountable to God, even if no one else ever busted him on anything.

In a concert Keith said clearly:

> I repent of ever having recorded one single song and ever having performed one concert if my music, and more importantly—my life—has not provoked you into godly jealousy or to sell out more completely to Jesus!

Keith was a man on a mission. Music was his tool. God loved it and sent him some amazing songs and gave him a lot of favor—in a short amount of time. Keith's music marked people with God, because he himself was marked for God.

All of the above made for some very compelling and memorable songs, recordings, and concerts that God decided he would use.

In 2002, Keith was inducted into the Gospel Hall of Fame on the same night as Elvis. Keith would have gotten a kick out of that. In 2006, ASCAP created the Crescendo Award to honor the increased volume and intensity of the response to Keith's music. I was there to receive both. It was an honor.

I believe Keith's music awards can be translated into changed lives and saved souls. How could they not be? That's what Keith's music was all about. People often tell me, "I gave my heart to the Lord listening to Keith's music." And I always think, *Now that would be music to Keith's ears!*

Keith's music has indeed become a legacy for us to keep listening to as a reminder of our journey to know God better and to love him more deeply.

Here's Keith's take on it all:

> The only music minister to whom the Lord will say, "Well done, thou good and faithful servant," is the one whose life proves what their lyrics are saying . . . And to whom music is the least important part of their life. Glorifying the only Worthy One has to be a minister's most important goal!

Keith's Missions Legacy

Keith and I didn't really know many missionaries until a few months before his death. God just slipped it into our life, and Keith immediately started making big plans. We saw the needs and met people who were giving their whole lives to meet those needs. "The harvest is white, the laborers are few" became totally relevant to us in a new way. Keith wanted to do his part and I did too. Keith began reserving stadiums, and I began writing some missions songs.

But it all hinged on Keith. I was his helper as he prepared to go out to battle. Keith would do the singing and preaching, and I would be by his side. I was content with the way we learned we could serve God together.

The message was firmly rooted in our hearts, and Keith set the stage to take it across America. Keith knew he could draw big crowds. He also knew the Youth With A Mission (YWAM) leaders had the experience and anointing to pull in the net and help people get to their next steps. Keith began inviting YWAM leaders to share the evening with him. Keith wanted to call forth a new generation of missionaries. It did happen, but not exactly the way we planned.

If Keith had not been a man of such decisive action, his message would have died with him—probably to some degree even the message in my own heart, too. I might have written something about it, but Keith had already written "Why You Should Go to the Mission Field" (see KeithGreen.com). He began working on it as soon as we returned from having our eyes opened. I put a few finishing touches on it right after he died so we could print his final message in the *LDM Magazine*.

But what about Keith's fall tour when he planned to take his missions challenge across America? LDM and YWAM came up with an idea. The way it happened would take too long to explain (see KeithGreen.com), but we realized God could use that final recording of Keith at Devonshire Downs preaching his missions message. We believed God could still fulfill Keith's last desire to call one hundred thousand into missions, because it was God who put that desire in his heart.

LDM set up a tour called the Keith Green Memorial Concerts. It was a series of one-night events across America from September 1982 to February 1983. We tackled the Memorial Concerts full force. And people came in full force too. There were often long lines just to get in. More than 300,000 people in 110 cities came to find some closure and to say good-bye to Keith—someone who had touched their lives. They also got to hear his last message.

Although Keith was gone, in a strange way he wasn't. He was still the one to preach his final message and in a way only he could do it. There he was each night preaching his missions challenge as it was being projected onto a seventeen-foot-tall screen for everyone to watch. He sang our two new mission songs.

Keith had so much unction and passion as he cried out about God's heart for the lost all over the world. The altar calls were massive as people committed to get trained and go on at least one mission trip. Even several key LDM staffers got the call to go!

We invited several mission groups to tour with us so they could give out information on the spot about training and outreach opportunities. I'm not aware of another situation in which an award-winning Christian musician decided to pay for his own fall tour, and then gave half of the evening to a missions leader to pull in a harvest of harvesters. That was a first, I believe.

The YWAM leaders who traveled with us included Loren Cunningham, John Dawson, and Floyd McClung. Most had to clear their schedules to come, and God used them powerfully as they painted a picture of God's heart for the lost and told inspiring true stories.

Another YWAM leader, Dave Gustaveson, came to each event to support me as well as the whole effort. He then launched Night of Missions and raised up teams to travel all over with it. It was so incredible. And extremely fruitful in the Spirit.

The kind of unity it took to do those events required humility and a desire to build only God's kingdom. It was Keith's idea, and we got to do it even though he was home with the Lord. Look what can happen when believers with different gifts decide to build something together. Each one of those evenings was a powerful punch in the Spirit for God's glory!

Loren Cunningham said, "I don't know of a time in history when more youth were presented such a missionary challenge."

Afterward, Operation Mobilization (OM) and Youth With A Mission said their training schools around the world were jammed with students. Wycliffe Bible Translators and Gospel for Asia also gave similar reports.

Don Stephens of Mercy Ships told me about a girl who heard Keith's challenge when she was only thirteen. She took a copy of Keith's missions article that we handed out at the Memorial Concerts and put it in her drawer. When she was twenty, she began serving on the M/V *Anastasis*. I currently meet people all the time, everywhere, who tell me they are serving in missions because of Keith's message.

Only eternity will show the fruit that is still being reaped for the kingdom. We're all pretty sure Keith's prayer with Loren and Don for one hundred thousand missionaries has been fulfilled by now.

Who knows how many we'll never hear about who are reaching the lost in some remote and obscure place? And all because of hearing Keith's message in one way or another—from his article, in songs he sang, in person at his Memorial Concert, or by watching the Keith Green Memorial Concert on a DVD (KeithGreen.com).

Our friend, revivalist Leonard Ravenhill, often said of Keith, "He being dead yet speaks" (Heb. 11:4).

When we obey God in faith, we have no way of knowing what he will do with our efforts. We should never underestimate the power of one passionate heart in the hands of the all-powerful God.

Keith has left an amazing missions legacy of soul winners. And the numbers increase even today as young people hear Keith's passionate message for the first time—and discover their destinies in the harvest fields among the lost and suffering.

Keith's Ministry Legacy
Last Days Ministries

When we officially launched LDM, we had no idea how the Lord would let it unfold. Who could have guessed the twists and turns? We started as a rehab house ministry with scruffy new believers and became a voice speaking to the nations. One thing is for certain: without Keith there would not be a Last Days Ministries.

Keith was the driving force—the engine pulling the LDM locomotive up the hills and across the valleys. He had a belly full of fiery coals, and there was no end of track in sight. The rest of us came along to serve God and each other with Keith. We believed in what he stood for—a radical relationship with God, without the trappings of religious systems or dead institutions. We wanted to help Keith get his message out, so we grabbed shovels and jumped on board.

Keith not only laid the foundation for LDM, he also framed it out, closed it in, and filled it with people. Office buildings and dormitories popped up on East Texas farmland, and we were running with the wind. Until the wind shifted.

After Keith died, the eyes of the world lingered on LDM because they were grieving his loss, wondering what was going to happen to the ministry—and praying for our children and me. I'd been a meaningful but mostly silent partner while Keith was alive, as far as anything public went. My name was on some magazine articles or on a song Keith sang in concert, but that was it.

When the wind shifted it blew like a tornado. It picked up everything we'd known at LDM, scattering it to irretrievable places. But unknown to me at that time, a stray breeze somehow landed on the dimly burning wick inside my heart. Eventually it ignited and everything changed again.

For many years I've had the privilege of standing on the platform Keith built. I've hammered in a few boards and nails myself over the years. We've been able to do crusades and take on issues with a lot of freedom and favor. There were a few times we nearly lost it all, but the Lord protected us from the enemy. Perhaps, for such a time as this?

The stunning reality that LDM still has a voice heard around the world is a huge part of Keith's ongoing legacy. I'm grateful and quite certain that part of what we've accomplished without Keith—past and future—will be attributed back to him on the day it really matters.

Keith's Pro-Life Legacy

I bet you didn't know Keith had a pro-life legacy. Well, he does. It was all Keith's idea for me to get involved in pro-life, way back in 1979 when it wasn't cool and preachers were silent about it. One day out of the blue Keith said, "Mel, you should write an article on abortion."

I wondered where that random thought came from. It sounded like a dreary subject, and I didn't know much about it.

Keith prodded, "You should go do some research."

I went to the library, but all the info was antiquated. There wasn't a pro-life movement then—except for a few Catholic groups who got it right. One let me use their photos and research materials.

So I wrote "Children, Things We Throw Away?" The response was huge. Letters flooded in. Families were desperate to adopt, and girls wanted to find good homes for their babies.

Keith said, "Hey, Mel, you should put some people together!"

So I made some introductions. A friend's family adopted the first baby, and two other families also adopted.

For Keith it wasn't enough and he kept bugging me. "Melody, I think you should go out and preach about biblical life principles."

Why couldn't he just drop it? Or just go do it himself? He was the preacher, not me.

Then at a prayer meeting, Keith told everyone that God was going to use me in a big way in pro-life. That was just a few hours before the plane crashed.

At first it didn't look promising. I received a written invitation for a cup of coffee—from the federal government. I was in trouble, and I couldn't introduce people for adoption purposes anymore. However, I was getting more stirred up about abortion.

It took three years after Keith died before I believed God wanted me to put pro-life onto LDM's front burner and launch Americans Against Abortion. Pastors still weren't talking about abortion. But everyone at LDM put their full efforts into AAA's two-year national campaign.

I spoke on radio and TV shows. I preached in arenas in most U.S. capital cities and preached on their capitol steps too. I led thousands in peaceful pickets of abortion clinics in their cities and connected them with local pro-life groups so they could keep going. I also wore a bulletproof vest during that time because of threats.

Then in 1987, I received another written invitation. This time it was from the White House. I met with President Reagan, and he endorsed our work. He also phoned our big Los Angeles rally to greet the crowd.

The AAA Petition for Life was the largest non-wartime petition in American history. A chunk of the petition sits in the Library of Congress. And that article Keith asked me to write? As of ten years ago, when we quit counting, more than twenty million had been distributed world-wide—not counting the unknown numbers of foreign translations.

Obviously Keith had a gnawing in his spirit that was from God. He heard long before most of us even thought of listening. He pushed and poked and frankly annoyed me. He believed I was the one to do something about abortion and wouldn't let it go. In spite of my being such a reluctant recruit, AAA accomplished a lot.

We fasted and prayed, exhausted ourselves, and felt the fire of the enemy's fury. But with Keith's prophetic prodding and his faith in me, somehow he prepared us to believe we could tackle the stronghold of abortion and make a difference. Countless children are alive today because of it.

Throughout the years many pro-life leaders have told me that God used LDM's efforts to open their eyes and spur them on to action. Now they are running hard to make a difference. And Keith is saying, "Hey, Mel! I told you so."

Keith's and Josiah's Mexico Legacy
Josiah and Bethany Children's Home

When we saw the needs in Mexico, Keith bought a building in Hidalgo, on the Texas side of the border, and began the LDM Mexico Outreach. Josiah had prayed, "Jesus, please put a house over all the children's beds." And all of it came to pass—and more.

LDM put out a call to get the supplies, and at Keith's request Pastor Joe Fauss and Calvary Commission (CC) began to oversee it with excellence. How could any of us know when we started the Mexico Outreach what would happen? Or that Josiah's prayer would bear such lasting fruit?

Pastor Joe Fauss was true to his word as they took on the Mexico Outreach to help the poor in Mexico. He made sure a lot of ministry and prayer took place as people waited in line. He also began going into Reynosa, Mexico, to visit the needy in their homes and to respond to their requests for him to pray for their sick families and friends.

On the Mexico side, the poverty in Reynosa overwhelmed Joe's heart. He noticed so many children alone on the streets all day. Many would still be there at night as he headed back to Hidalgo. So he began to bring them food and give them hugs and fatherly words. He knew that without a place inside of Mexico, they couldn't be helped in a substantial way. They needed a family and a home. Their lives needed to change.

Joe decided to rent a small house in Reynosa. A single girl from CC wanted to live there and take care of the children. The house was clean but threadbare as the children began arriving—mostly infants and toddlers, but some older ones came too. Some were homeless and some had parents who couldn't care for them. Many came from homes filled with drug abuse or prostitution and were in danger themselves.

As Keith and I partnered with Joe Fauss and CC, our love for Joe deepened. We put "Mexico Updates" in almost every issue of the *LDM Magazine* and suggested ways to become involved with the children.

Joe Fauss described things this way: "By 1981, the Children's Home was in Reynosa, a new church was forming in Hidalgo, and we saw Mexico as a mighty, reachable missions field."

Joe was one of the first to arrive when he heard there was a plane crash. "I was crushed—" Joe said, when he heard who was on the plane: "Life did change forever that day, but we knew our vision for reaching Mexico was still on God's heart and it remained strong on ours too."

Memorial Funds were sent to LDM in memory of Josiah and Bethany to help needy children. I gave them all to Joe and CC, and I added my own gift as well. I wanted to remember my children in a tangible way. It was the start of the Josiah and Bethany Children's Home.

Josiah's prayer when he was just two is being realized today. Currently forty children have a home because of it. And it's right near the train tracks where Josiah played with the children in Mexico.

I remember Joe asking me if he could name the home after my children. I was surprised. I told him it would be fine, but he didn't need to—but it blessed me that he did.

Some of the children at the home are orphans and some are abandoned—which I think qualifies them as orphans too. They range from five to nineteen. Some arrived as babies, and most have no family members who visit.

Joe explained, "They look like clean, happy, well-educated children, but they didn't arrive that way. They were dirty, had lice, were very sad, had no education, and were without hope. They had no future. Now they know God has a plan and purpose for their lives. Today they are happy, healthy, and growing."

LDM still helps raise support for the orphanage. And you can still visit and help with the children. But many are being turned away as I write. A new wing is underway so more children can receive care. Two more Josiah and Bethany Homes are in the interior of Mexico, and there's one in India too! (For Outreach info: KeithGreen.com)

Needless to say, the Josiah and Bethany Children's Home means so much to me. God gave it as an avenue to help desperately needy children—in memory of my children's lives. But it wouldn't be there if not for Keith's bold step of buying a building because "somebody" needed to do something. That somebody was Joe Fauss, and yes, it's really his legacy. But the way it came about was because of Keith and Josiah. And so I mention it.

Melody's Closing Thoughts

From my firsthand observations I can assure you that Keith never tried to build a legacy for himself. He only tried to add to the legacy of his King—by building His kingdom. That was Keith's stated goal. And the way he lived his life proved he meant it. He always tried his best to do the most pleasing and generous thing he could, for God and for others.

One of Keith's favorite things was reading the Bible. He had many favorite Scriptures and passages, but there's one I know he really took to heart in Galatians. I believe this Scripture was deeply imbedded in his spirit.

Keith knew something about gardening, planting, and harvesting a little crop. I watched him plant a few vegetable gardens.

There were a lot of vegetables Keith didn't like, so he chose his seeds carefully. After Keith had planted those seeds, he would sit in the garden at night with a flashlight to see what might be sprouting—or later, to pick off worms. If he planted tomatoes and corn, he wasn't expecting spinach and squash to appear out of nowhere. So in a small, but very useful way, Keith understood how sowing and reaping worked. Galatians also talks about it:

Do not be deceived: God cannot be mocked. A man reaps what he sows.

The one who sows to please his sinful nature, from that nature will reap destruction; the one who sows to please the Spirit, from the Spirit will reap eternal life.

Let us not become weary in doing good, for at the proper time we will reap a harvest if we do not give up.

Therefore, as we have opportunity, let us do good to all people, especially to those who belong to the family of believers. (Galatians 6:7–10, NIV)

In the *Old Farmer's Almanac* there's a section for first time gardeners. One point says, "Study those seed catalogs and order early." That's some good advice!

The Creator of the very first garden gave us a list of the fruit he wants in our lives. If we study just a little, we can find out what the fruit of the Spirit is—and know exactly what kind of seeds to plant to get the crop God is looking for.

We don't have a choice about sowing. It's something we do every day in this world living with others. We can even sow without words. Just a glance might be all it takes. Although we have no choice about sowing, we do have a choice about *what we sow*. That's why it's so important to look at our lives honestly and see if we are planting the right seeds.

I see something interesting about Keith's life. He said and did some things that bore great fruit that was kept hidden from him or that he didn't live long enough to see. When we love God and try to show his love to others in word and deed, I think something alive is released in the Spirit.

God can use this small "nugget of life" in mysterious ways. If we walk in the Spirit, even a kind gesture or stray comment can bring life and blessing—or yield a hidden reward. When we're bent toward God, he can put good words in our mouths and good ideas in our minds that surprise even us. I think living in that place, along with planting on purpose, is perhaps the most genuine way to build God's kingdom. Some of Keith's legacy came about that way.

What if you walked past a park one day and noticed it had no trees? Then you found an acorn a few blocks away. So on a kind impulse you took the acorn back to the park, planted it, and returned home smiling because you had just planted an oak tree in an empty field.

Then you ended up moving far way. The acorn was a good seed, so it sprouted and took root. Another passerby noticed the frail baby tree and tied it to a stake. As the tree became stronger and bigger, more people saw it and watched after it. They wanted it to thrive and become a beautiful tree in their park.

If you returned thirty years later, you might notice many strangers enjoying a beautifully matured shade tree. You might not remember planting the acorn—or realize the smaller trees nearby had sprouted from the fruit that fell from the now mighty oak.

———

I was teaching at a YWAM Discipleship Training School in 2007. At the beginning of one session I wanted to steal a little time to think about my topic for an extra few minutes. I had a random on-the-spot idea. I told every student to quietly take ten minutes to write out what kind of legacy they hoped to leave after they died.

I said, "Just write down how you want people to remember you." I collected their unsigned papers and read each one out loud to the whole class.

They wrote things like wanting to be remembered for being kind, generous, helpful, wise, loving, forgiving, joyful, humble, peaceful, a good person, a worshiper, a true lover of God. When I finished reading the notes out loud, everyone sat very quietly.

I said, "Now let's talk about how we need to be living our lives today so we can leave behind the legacy we desire."

I didn't fully realize how much that little exercise would impact them. These young people who put their lives in that light—starting at the end and working back to the present—found it very eye-opening.

I abandoned that night's topic. The moment called for some honest classroom discussion instead.

The students left our session with a lot to think about that night. Their hearts were like fertile soil. Perhaps like that old *Farmer's Almanac* suggested, they went off to "study those seed catalogs and order early." Some might even decide to reevaluate their lives every so often, for many years to come. I'll probably never see any of them again. And I have no idea what may take place in their lives because of that little seed planted last year. But I know it was a good seed.

Keith not only did good things, he also planted good seeds along the way—often without realizing it. And it just takes one good seed landing in fertile ground to make a difference. If our hearts are bent toward pleasing God, we'll all have lots of good seeds to sow, wherever we might be.

It's been said that everyone is going to be surprised when we stand before the Lord. It's usually meant in a negative way. But how would we need to live now for most of those surprises to be *good* ones?

Wouldn't it be amazing to one day find out what happened with some of the stray seeds we sowed while living a life led by the Spirit? There would be so many that we wouldn't even remember sowing.

I bet Keith was very surprised. I hope I will be too. I think it's something we can all look forward to if we firmly set our hearts to plant for the Lord's pleasure . . . and to not grow weary of doing good.

MEMORIES OF KEITH

by Leonard Ravenhill

William Booth, founder of the Salvation Army, and Keith Green had one thing in common. They both saw the gates of hell. Booth saw them from the outside. Keith saw them from the inside. Keith had been to the bottom of the barrel. He'd felt the horror and the misery. He was a prisoner and nobody could break the chains. But God rescued him! "Religion" couldn't do it. Vows couldn't do it. Psychology couldn't do it. But Jesus did it!

Keith had a radical New Birth experience plus a Baptism of Fire and became a spiritual revolutionary. God took him, cleansed him, occupied him, and anointed him.

Keith hungered to know about those heroes who moved their generation for God, and he followed in their steps. He had a holy zeal and a purity I've seen in very few. I don't think Keith was preoccupied with the gospel of Christ as much as he was with the person of Christ. I think that was his consuming passion. He wasn't a preacher. He was a crusader. And he poured out the inner passion of his soul through the vibrant lyrics of his songs.

In that great Final Day, many will rise up and call Keith blessed. He bowed his whole being before the One who said, "To bring fire on earth I come," and by Him he was ignited—his heart an altar and God's love the flame.

I'm in my eighty-third year, but it doesn't necessarily mean I'm wiser or stronger. It doesn't mean I've done more. It's not the stretch of life that matters. It's the depth of life. It's not how long we live. It's how we live. Keith was a man who seemed to live on the edge of eternity. And he was ready to step into it.

It can truly be said of Keith that "He being dead, yet speaketh." And he will speak right on to the generations beyond us. I wish we had ten thousand people like him. I pray that many will catch a vision from his life—and trust and obey.

The words of my favorite hymn paint a portrait of my dear friend Keith. I thank God that Keith ever came my way.

I would the precious time redeem,
And longer live for this alone,
To spend, and to be spent, for them
Who have not yet my Saviour known:
Fully on these my mission prove.
And only breathe, to breathe Thy love.

My talents, gifts, and graces, Lord,
Into Thy blessed hands receive;
And let me live to preach Thy word,
And let me to Thy glory live;
My every sacred moment spend
In publishing the sinners' Friend.

Enlarge, inflame, and fill my heart
With boundless charity divine;
So shall I all my strength exert,
And love them with a zeal like Thine;
And lead them to Thy open side,
The sheep for whom their Shepherd died.

Charles Wesley, 1707–1788

Leonard Ravenhill (1907–1994) was a fiery British preacher and a renowned authority on revival. He wrote books filled with pointed, witty sayings such as, "A sinning man stops praying, a praying man stops sinning." He lived near LDM, where pastors around the globe visited him for prayer and counsel. He was also a close friend of A. W. Tozer. Tozer said of him, "To such men as this, the church owes a debt too heavy to pay. The curious thing is that she seldom tries to pay him while he lives."

RETROSPECTIVE

by John Dawson

Every moment with Keith was interesting. We were either having intense dynamic discussions or we were rolling on the floor laughing. He had a huge sense of humor and knew how to laugh at himself.

Keith did not trust indirectness. It was not present in his own personality. When we met I was a leader in YWAM and had developed skills to lead others. I almost had to become another person to

Keith and John Dawson, Spring Crusade, 1982

love Keith the way he needed to be loved. I had to be totally direct and say, "That was really stupid. Why did you do that dumb thing?" Then he could walk away feeling really loved.

Keith was a model of somebody who earnestly went after God with absolute intensity and hunger. We cannot put on him the weight of being a father in the faith. He was a sincere and honest baby believer.

The people who knew him loved him for his inner life. We saw the vulnerable little boy inside, who was humble, who would overstate things, and then change his mind and ask for forgiveness. He became the leader of a dynamic community of people who also saw his heart.

We were brothers in age, but he always related to me with tremendous humility, brokenness, and respect.

It's ironic that he had a reputation for being arrogant. He was really just a young broken guy. In truth, most of us around him were more proud than he was. Keith created a pathway for those of us who were guarded to be more open with each other—and with God.

Keith had a voracious appetite for the character and nature of God. If he thought you had any virtue or value, he would latch on to you, even if you only had a little bit more than he did. He would cling to your ankle saying, "Give me what you've got or I'll bite your ankle off."

The last thing God wants from us is to be balanced. It's not biblical. We just need to get on with our obedience to God and let God balance out the whole.

Keith had the heart of a child with an Ezekiel 37 assignment: "This is what you need to tell the people. They are not going to listen but you need to tell them anyway."

Keith was a revivalist at heart. He wanted to see the open heavens of God, in a time of the outpouring of the Spirit and of the harvest. We were talking about all that, but it hadn't turned into song lyrics yet. It was being processed in prayer. Keith was getting ready to prophesy to those dry bones.

We were also beginning to talk about his Jewishness and all that it implied. He was just coming into that place of being an enormous encourager and multiplier for God and he didn't get to stay to enjoy the fruit. Not on the earth anyway.

Life is long and messy for most of us. But Keith was like a comet. He came and went and left the rest of us here to mop up and run the marathon. I miss my brother.

—John Dawson
    President of Youth With A Mission
    Founder and President of the International
    Reconciliation Coalition

GRATITUDES

When I sat down to write this book the first time, I had no idea I'd spend over a thousand hours typing at my computer. I also never dreamed I would greatly expand it into a Legacy Edition!! Still, this book was not written alone. Many others played vital roles in making it a reality the first time and this time as well. Without all of you, something important would have been missing or left undone. I want to give thanks for the greatest gift on earth besides having a relationship with God—the joy of serving him with family and friends.

With Deep Gratitude to—

My Messiah—for your goodness and many mercies to me. Without your amazing grace and faithfulness, this book as well as my good life today, would not have been possible.

My mother—once you found your Messiah, you never looked back. Thank you for teaching me to love God as a child. I miss you very much Mom. This one's really for you!

My daughters Rebekah Joy and Rachel Hope—you still bring great joy to my life. You also continue to challenge me to keep pressing into God and inspire me to move forward with him, to be the best person I can be.

Carol and Terry DeGraff—for walking such a long winding road with me. All your generous help on this Legacy Edition and with LDM today continues to amaze me.

My dear friends and cheerleaders—John and Julie Dawson, Dan and Jamie Collins, Wayne and Kathleen Dillard, Winkie and Fae Pratney, Ed and Cathi Basler, Jill Austin, Rich and Pam Boyer, Chuck and Debbie Farrington, Buck and Annie Herring, Gordon and Janet Driver—the treasure of your friendship and support gets more precious every year. And you all have the fun factor, too!

Billy Ray Hearn and Bill Hearn at Sparrow/EMI Music—for having such a strong vision and heart for Keith's music and message. Your friendship, advice, and concern have been blessings for many years.

My YWAM family—Loren and Darlene Cunningham, Floyd and Sally McClung, Leland and Fran Paris, Don and Deyon Stephens— for all your input on this book and for years of steadfast support, prayer and encouragement.

David Hazard—for walking me through my first book. It was a blessing to collaborate with such an experienced writer and editor who knew how to connect the dots.

A big thank you to all my friends not already mentioned, who graciously allowed me to mix tiny parts of your story in with mine and Keith's—Michelle Brandes, Todd Fishkind, Randy Stonehill, Peter and Cag Granet, Kenn Gulliksen, Sandy Tullis, Jay Leon, Janet Stabler, Barry McGuire, Jerry and Cindy Bryant, Patricia Forrester (Podie), and Steve and Nelly Greisen.

Clive Davis—a special thank you for not signing Keith to your Arista label when he auditioned for you in New York City. It was his turning point, and it changed the course of both his destiny and legacy.

Bill Maxwell—your friendship and care in stewarding "the sounds" of Keith's music ministry is still heard around the world today.

Joel Miller, Kristen Parrish, and the staff of Thomas Nelson Publishing—for being easy to work with and having a strong vision for this Legacy Edition of Keith's life story.

Jim Houser, Katie Sulkowski and the staff at Creative Trust—for working so hard with me to make this Legacy Edition become an actual reality.

Thank you to Alyssa DeGraff—for all your photos of Keith's journal pages.

My Last Days Family—though most of you are scattered around the globe now, I will never forget your love, encouragement, and support as you read, made suggestions, and stormed the throne for God's anointing on the First Edition. I especially want to thank Claudia Lovejoy, Lori Andrews, Betty Daffin, Fred Markert, and Francine Weisberg for all your extra efforts.

Keith's parents have passed away but I remain very grateful to them for their love and for sharing so many memories of Keith's early life with my children and me.

My dear friends Leonard and Martha Ravenhill—Though you are with the Lord now, your influence and many prayers for my family and the First Edition of this book are still felt in my heart and reaping fruit that remains.

Also I want to thank all of my prayer warrior family and friends in Kansas City and the many intercessors who have prayed for my children and me over the years. God knows who you are, even if I don't. Your prayers supported me through more difficulties than you could have known, when I needed God's help. I feel humbled, and I am very grateful for the times when the Lord put me on your heart, and you listened. Your prayers have made a difference. I am so grateful for you.

KEITH GREEN DISCOGRAPHY
The Music of Keith Green

If you haven't heard Keith's music, you haven't heard his heart. Go to keithgreen.com to listen to songs that reveal Keith's passion for God and his powerful gift of music.

For Him Who Has Ears to Hear
Produced by Bill Maxwell and Keith Green. Released May 20, 1977. Available on CD and all digital formats. (Sparrow Records/ EMI Christian Music Group)

No Compromise
Produced by Bill Maxwell and Keith Green. Released November 9, 1978. Available on CD and all digital formats. (Sparrow Records/ EMI Christian Music Group)

So You Wanna Go Back to Egypt?
Produced by Bill Maxwell and Keith Green. Released May 7, 1980. Available on CD and all digital formats. (Pretty Good Records, distributed by EMI Christian Music Group)

The Keith Green Collection
Produced by Bill Maxwell. Released August 11, 1981. Available on CD and all digital formats. (Sparrow Records/EMI Christian Music Group)

Songs for the Shepherd

Produced by Bill Maxwell and Keith Green. Released April 12, 1982. Available on CD and all digital formats. (Pretty Good Records, distributed by EMI Christian Music Group)

I Only Want to See You There

Produced by Bill Maxwell. Released March 21, 1983. Out of print. (Sparrow Records)

The Prodigal Son

Produced by Bill Maxwell and Melody Green. Released August 15, 1983. Available on CD and all digital formats. (Pretty Good Records, distributed by EMI Christian Music Group)

Jesus Commands Us to Go

Produced by Bill Maxwell. Released July 20, 1984. Available on CD and all digital formats. (Pretty Good Records, distributed by EMI Christian Music Group)

The Keith Green Memorial Concert

(Keith's Final Concert and Message, with Melody Green.) Produced by Melody Green. Released 1984. Available on DVD. (Last Days Ministries)

The Ministry Years—Vol. I 1977–1979

Produced by Bill Maxwell. Released October 23, 1987. Available on two CDs with commemorative booklet and in all digital formats. (Sparrow Records/EMI Christian Music Group)

The Ministry Years—Vol. II 1980–1982

Produced by Bill Maxwell. Released October 18, 1988. Available on two CDs with commemorative booklet and in all digital formats. (Sparrow Records/EMI Christian Music Group)

The Early Years

Released 1996. Available on CD and all digital formats. (Sparrow Records/EMI Christian Music Group)

Because of You: Songs of Testimony

Released 1999. Available on CD and all digital formats. (Sparrow Records/EMI Christian Music Group)

Here Am I, Send Me: Songs of Evangelism

Released 1999. Available on CD and all digital formats. (Sparrow Records/EMI Christian Music Group)

Make My Life a Prayer to You: Songs of Devotion

Released 1999. Available on CD and all digital formats. (Sparrow Records/EMI Christian Music Group)

Oh Lord, You're Beautiful: Songs of Worship

Released 1999. Available on CD and all digital formats. (Sparrow Records/EMI Christian Music Group)

Your Love Broke Through: The Keith Green Life Story

Produced by Melody Green. One hour DVD documentary. Released January 2002. (EMI Christian Music Group)

The Ultimate Collection

Produced by EMI Christian Music Group. Twenty favorite songs plus DVD *Your Love Broke Through*. Released 2002. Available on CD/DVD combo. (EMI Christian Music Group)

Keith Green: The Live Experience

Produced by Melody Green, John J. Thompson, and Bill Hearn. Released April 2008. Available on CD and all digital formats. (EMI Christian Music Group)

Keith Green: The Live Experience (Special Edition)

Produced by Melody Green, John J. Thompson, and Bill Hearn. Released April 2008. Available on CD/DVD and all digital formats. (EMI Christian Music Group)

Keith Green: The Greatest Hits

Produced by Melody Green, John J. Thompson, and Bill Hearn. Released April 2008. Available on CD and all digital formats. (EMI Christian Music Group)

"Love with Me (Melody's Song)" by Keith Green. "Open Your Eyes" by Melody Green. All songs © 1983 For the Shepherd Music.

"He'll Take Care of the Rest" by Keith Green and Wendell Burton. © 1977 EMI April Music Inc./EMI Blackwood Music Inc.

"Because of You" by Keith Green. "You Put This Love in My Heart" by Keith Green. "Trials Turned to Gold" by Keith Green. "No One Believes in Me Anymore (Satan's Boast)" by Keith Green and Melody Green. All songs © 1977, 1978 EMI April Music Inc.

"When I Hear the Praises Start" by Keith Green and Melody Green. "Run to the End of the Highway" by Keith Green and Melody Green. All songs © 1977 EMI April Music Inc.

"The Prodigal Son Suite" by Keith Green © 1983. "On the Road to Jericho" by Keith Green © 1984. "Manchilde" by Keith Green. All songs I Am Music.

"Your Love Broke Through" by Keith Green, Todd Fishkind, and Randy Stonehill. © 1976, 1977 EMI April Music Inc./King of Hearts Publishing. All Rights Controlled and Administered by EMI April Music Inc.

"Life Goes On (And the World Goes 'Round)" by Keith Green and Randy Stonehill. © 1977 EMI April Music Inc./King of Hearts Publishing. All Rights Controlled and Administered by EMI April Music Inc.

"To Obey Is Better Than Sacrifice" by Keith Green. "Asleep in the Light" by Keith Green. "My Eyes Are Dry" by Keith Green. All songs © 1978 Birdwing Music/BMG Songs Inc/Ears to Hear Music.

"So You Wanna Go Back to Egypt?" by Keith Green and Melody Green. "Pledge My Head to Heaven" by Keith Green. "You Love the World" by Keith Green. "Unless the Lord Builds the House" by Keith Green and Melody Green. "Oh Lord, You're Beautiful" by Keith Green. "Grace by Which I Stand" by Keith Green. All songs © 1980 Birdwing Music/BMG Songs Inc/Ears to Hear Music.

"There Is a Redeemer" by Melody Green. "Until That Final Day" by Keith Green. All songs © 1982 Birdwing Music/BMG Songs Inc/Ears to Hear Music.

"I Want to Be More Like Jesus" by Keith Green, Melody Green, and Kelly Willard. © 1980 Birdwing Music/BMG Songs Inc/Ears to Hear Music/Willing Heart Music.

"Don't You Wish You Had the Answers?" by Melody Green ©1984. "Daddy Isn't Coming Home No More" by Melody Green ©1983. All songs For the Shepherd Music

ABOUT LAST DAYS MINISTRIES

Today LDM is a Web-based interactive ministry. Same message. Different delivery system. No ranch. No printing press. No livestock. We turned in our old wineskin for the new. We now use today's technology to share the message of hope, forgiveness, and obedience to God—worldwide.

Our Mission

- *To Proclaim*—the excellencies of God to all people.
- *To Provoke*—all to love and good works.
- *To Prepare*—each person to stand strong until their end of days.

LDM challenges and inspires believers to love, worship, and serve God fiercely within their calling—regardless of age, gender, or nationality.

It's Easy to Visit Us

LastDaysMinistries.com
KeithGreen.com
MelodyGreen.com

Free Subscription! Set up your own private Login to receive: exclusive downloads, special LDM sales and offers and freebies, new release info, and breaking LDM news. We never loan or sell anyone's name or info. (Login not necessary for browsing.)

Online Library of 150+FREE Discipleship Teachings from respected leaders around the globe to deepen your relationship with God. Read at your leisure. Freely share them with your friends and post your comments.

Subjects include: Living Fiercely for God, Forgiving Yourself and Others, Finding God's Will, Hurt and Bitterness, Singles and Sex, Worship, Prayer and Devotion, Spiritual Warfare, Missions, Music, Protecting Our Children, Relationships, Arts and Media, Creation vs. Evolution, Sexual Abuse, Ethnic Bias, Healing After Abortion, Pro-Life Issues, Humility, Character of God, Jealousy, Binding Broken Hearts, How to Share the Lord, Hearing God's Voice, Israel, Dealing with Failure, Taming the Tongue, How to Find God, Taking Action, Honesty, Gossip, Finding Grace, What to Do When You're Walking in Darkness—and much more. (We're always adding to our library!)

Authors include: Keith Green, Melody Green, John Dawson, Loren Cunningham, Ron Luce, Mike Bickle, Paul Baloche, Jack Deere, Winkie Pratney, Bob Sorge, Jill Austin, and many others. Classic messages by Leonard Ravenhill, A. W. Tozer, John Wesley, and the founder of the Salvation Army, General William Booth.

Stay Connected with Melody Green:
- Read her unique Q & A column.
- Sign up for her blog.
- Read her latest articles.
- Get her schedule and go hear her speak.
- Go with Melody on a mission trip.

Find Out More about Keith Green:
- Listen to his music.
- Read his articles.
- Visit his photo gallery.
- Read and make comments.
- Get info on exciting new Keith projects.

LDM Serves You and the World Through:
- Josiah & Bethany Children's Homes—Mexico and India
- LDM Good Neighbor Relief Fund
- LDM Short-Term Mercy Projects
- Missions and training opportunities
- Pro-Life materials for education and healing
- LDM online store has the most comprehensive Keith Green and Melody Green products available. Also hand-selected books, teachings, and music from other cutting-edge lovers of God.

We hope you'll visit us soon to browse, read, and listen. We'd love to hear from you, so please post comments in our guestbook.

Also be sure and let Melody know how this book has impacted you!

Visit our website:
www.lastdaysministries.com
www.keithgreen.com or www.melodygreen.com